T0137933

Lecture Notes in Computer Science 14728

Founding Editors

Gerhard Goos
Juris Hartmanis

The series Lecture Notes in Computer Science (LNCS), including its subseries Lecture Notes in Artificial Intelligence (LNAI) and Lecture Notes in Bioinformatics (LNBI), has established itself as a medium for the publication of new developments in computer science and information technology research, teaching, and education.

LNCS enjoys close cooperation with the computer science R & D community, the series counts many renowned academics among its volume editors and paper authors, and collaborates with prestigious societies. Its mission is to serve this international community by providing an invaluable service, mainly focused on the publication of conference and workshop proceedings and postproceedings. LNCS commenced publication in 1973.

Abbas Moallem
Editor

HCI for Cybersecurity, Privacy and Trust

6th International Conference, HCI-CPT 2024
Held as Part of the 26th HCI International Conference, HCII 2024
Washington, DC, USA, June 29 – July 4, 2024
Proceedings, Part I

 Springer

Editor
Abbas Moallem
San Jose State University
San Jose, CA, USA

ISSN 0302-9743   ISSN 1611-3349 (electronic)
Lecture Notes in Computer Science
ISBN 978-3-031-61378-4   ISBN 978-3-031-61379-1 (eBook)
https://doi.org/10.1007/978-3-031-61379-1

This Springer imprint is published by the registered company Springer Nature Switzerland AG
The registered company address is: Gewerbestrasse 11, 6330 Cham, Switzerland

If disposing of this product, please recycle the paper.

Foreword

This year we celebrate 40 years since the establishment of the HCI International (HCII) Conference, which has been a hub for presenting groundbreaking research and novel ideas and collaboration for people from all over the world.

The HCII conference was founded in 1984 by Prof. Gavriel Salvendy (Purdue University, USA, Tsinghua University, P.R. China, and University of Central Florida, USA) and the first event of the series, "1st USA-Japan Conference on Human-Computer Interaction", was held in Honolulu, Hawaii, USA, 18–20 August. Since then, HCI International is held jointly with several Thematic Areas and Affiliated Conferences, with each one under the auspices of a distinguished international Program Board and under one management and one registration. Twenty-six HCI International Conferences have been organized so far (every two years until 2013, and annually thereafter).

Over the years, this conference has served as a platform for scholars, researchers, industry experts and students to exchange ideas, connect, and address challenges in the ever-evolving HCI field. Throughout these 40 years, the conference has evolved itself, adapting to new technologies and emerging trends, while staying committed to its core mission of advancing knowledge and driving change.

As we celebrate this milestone anniversary, we reflect on the contributions of its founding members and appreciate the commitment of its current and past Affiliated Conference Program Board Chairs and members. We are also thankful to all past conference attendees who have shaped this community into what it is today.

The 26th International Conference on Human-Computer Interaction, HCI International 2024 (HCII 2024), was held as a 'hybrid' event at the Washington Hilton Hotel, Washington, DC, USA, during 29 June – 4 July 2024. It incorporated the 21 thematic areas and affiliated conferences listed below.

A total of 5108 individuals from academia, research institutes, industry, and government agencies from 85 countries submitted contributions, and 1271 papers and 309 posters were included in the volumes of the proceedings that were published just before the start of the conference, these are listed below. The contributions thoroughly cover the entire field of human-computer interaction, addressing major advances in knowledge and effective use of computers in a variety of application areas. These papers provide academics, researchers, engineers, scientists, practitioners and students with state-of-the-art information on the most recent advances in HCI.

The HCI International (HCII) conference also offers the option of presenting 'Late Breaking Work', and this applies both for papers and posters, with corresponding volumes of proceedings that will be published after the conference. Full papers will be included in the 'HCII 2024 - Late Breaking Papers' volumes of the proceedings to be published in the Springer LNCS series, while 'Poster Extended Abstracts' will be included as short research papers in the 'HCII 2024 - Late Breaking Posters' volumes to be published in the Springer CCIS series.

I would like to thank the Program Board Chairs and the members of the Program Boards of all thematic areas and affiliated conferences for their contribution towards the high scientific quality and overall success of the HCI International 2024 conference. Their manifold support in terms of paper reviewing (single-blind review process, with a minimum of two reviews per submission), session organization and their willingness to act as goodwill ambassadors for the conference is most highly appreciated.

This conference would not have been possible without the continuous and unwavering support and advice of Gavriel Salvendy, founder, General Chair Emeritus, and Scientific Advisor. For his outstanding efforts, I would like to express my sincere appreciation to Abbas Moallem, Communications Chair and Editor of HCI International News.

July 2024   Constantine Stephanidis

HCI International 2024 Thematic Areas
and Affiliated Conferences

- HCI: Human-Computer Interaction Thematic Area
- HIMI: Human Interface and the Management of Information Thematic Area
- EPCE: 21st International Conference on Engineering Psychology and Cognitive Ergonomics
- AC: 18th International Conference on Augmented Cognition
- UAHCI: 18th International Conference on Universal Access in Human-Computer Interaction
- CCD: 16th International Conference on Cross-Cultural Design
- SCSM: 16th International Conference on Social Computing and Social Media
- VAMR: 16th International Conference on Virtual, Augmented and Mixed Reality
- DHM: 15th International Conference on Digital Human Modeling & Applications in Health, Safety, Ergonomics & Risk Management
- DUXU: 13th International Conference on Design, User Experience and Usability
- C&C: 12th International Conference on Culture and Computing
- DAPI: 12th International Conference on Distributed, Ambient and Pervasive Interactions
- HCIBGO: 11th International Conference on HCI in Business, Government and Organizations
- LCT: 11th International Conference on Learning and Collaboration Technologies
- ITAP: 10th International Conference on Human Aspects of IT for the Aged Population
- AIS: 6th International Conference on Adaptive Instructional Systems
- HCI-CPT: 6th International Conference on HCI for Cybersecurity, Privacy and Trust
- HCI-Games: 6th International Conference on HCI in Games
- MobiTAS: 6th International Conference on HCI in Mobility, Transport and Automotive Systems
- AI-HCI: 5th International Conference on Artificial Intelligence in HCI
- MOBILE: 5th International Conference on Human-Centered Design, Operation and Evaluation of Mobile Communications

List of Conference Proceedings Volumes Appearing Before the Conference

1. LNCS 14684, Human-Computer Interaction: Part I, edited by Masaaki Kurosu and Ayako Hashizume
2. LNCS 14685, Human-Computer Interaction: Part II, edited by Masaaki Kurosu and Ayako Hashizume
3. LNCS 14686, Human-Computer Interaction: Part III, edited by Masaaki Kurosu and Ayako Hashizume
4. LNCS 14687, Human-Computer Interaction: Part IV, edited by Masaaki Kurosu and Ayako Hashizume
5. LNCS 14688, Human-Computer Interaction: Part V, edited by Masaaki Kurosu and Ayako Hashizume
6. LNCS 14689, Human Interface and the Management of Information: Part I, edited by Hirohiko Mori and Yumi Asahi
7. LNCS 14690, Human Interface and the Management of Information: Part II, edited by Hirohiko Mori and Yumi Asahi
8. LNCS 14691, Human Interface and the Management of Information: Part III, edited by Hirohiko Mori and Yumi Asahi
9. LNAI 14692, Engineering Psychology and Cognitive Ergonomics: Part I, edited by Don Harris and Wen-Chin Li
10. LNAI 14693, Engineering Psychology and Cognitive Ergonomics: Part II, edited by Don Harris and Wen-Chin Li
11. LNAI 14694, Augmented Cognition, Part I, edited by Dylan D. Schmorrow and Cali M. Fidopiastis
12. LNAI 14695, Augmented Cognition, Part II, edited by Dylan D. Schmorrow and Cali M. Fidopiastis
13. LNCS 14696, Universal Access in Human-Computer Interaction: Part I, edited by Margherita Antona and Constantine Stephanidis
14. LNCS 14697, Universal Access in Human-Computer Interaction: Part II, edited by Margherita Antona and Constantine Stephanidis
15. LNCS 14698, Universal Access in Human-Computer Interaction: Part III, edited by Margherita Antona and Constantine Stephanidis
16. LNCS 14699, Cross-Cultural Design: Part I, edited by Pei-Luen Patrick Rau
17. LNCS 14700, Cross-Cultural Design: Part II, edited by Pei-Luen Patrick Rau
18. LNCS 14701, Cross-Cultural Design: Part III, edited by Pei-Luen Patrick Rau
19. LNCS 14702, Cross-Cultural Design: Part IV, edited by Pei-Luen Patrick Rau
20. LNCS 14703, Social Computing and Social Media: Part I, edited by Adela Coman and Simona Vasilache
21. LNCS 14704, Social Computing and Social Media: Part II, edited by Adela Coman and Simona Vasilache
22. LNCS 14705, Social Computing and Social Media: Part III, edited by Adela Coman and Simona Vasilache

47. LNCS 14730, HCI in Games: Part I, edited by Xiaowen Fang
48. LNCS 14731, HCI in Games: Part II, edited by Xiaowen Fang
49. LNCS 14732, HCI in Mobility, Transport and Automotive Systems: Part I, edited by Heidi Krömker
50. LNCS 14733, HCI in Mobility, Transport and Automotive Systems: Part II, edited by Heidi Krömker
51. LNAI 14734, Artificial Intelligence in HCI: Part I, edited by Helmut Degen and Stavroula Ntoa
52. LNAI 14735, Artificial Intelligence in HCI: Part II, edited by Helmut Degen and Stavroula Ntoa
53. LNAI 14736, Artificial Intelligence in HCI: Part III, edited by Helmut Degen and Stavroula Ntoa
54. LNCS 14737, Design, Operation and Evaluation of Mobile Communications: Part I, edited by June Wei and George Margetis
55. LNCS 14738, Design, Operation and Evaluation of Mobile Communications: Part II, edited by June Wei and George Margetis
56. CCIS 2114, HCI International 2024 Posters - Part I, edited by Constantine Stephanidis, Margherita Antona, Stavroula Ntoa and Gavriel Salvendy
57. CCIS 2115, HCI International 2024 Posters - Part II, edited by Constantine Stephanidis, Margherita Antona, Stavroula Ntoa and Gavriel Salvendy
58. CCIS 2116, HCI International 2024 Posters - Part III, edited by Constantine Stephanidis, Margherita Antona, Stavroula Ntoa and Gavriel Salvendy
59. CCIS 2117, HCI International 2024 Posters - Part IV, edited by Constantine Stephanidis, Margherita Antona, Stavroula Ntoa and Gavriel Salvendy
60. CCIS 2118, HCI International 2024 Posters - Part V, edited by Constantine Stephanidis, Margherita Antona, Stavroula Ntoa and Gavriel Salvendy
61. CCIS 2119, HCI International 2024 Posters - Part VI, edited by Constantine Stephanidis, Margherita Antona, Stavroula Ntoa and Gavriel Salvendy
62. CCIS 2120, HCI International 2024 Posters - Part VII, edited by Constantine Stephanidis, Margherita Antona, Stavroula Ntoa and Gavriel Salvendy

https://2024.hci.international/proceedings

Preface

The cybersecurity field, in all its dimensions, is exponentially growing, evolving and expanding. New security risks emerge continuously with the steady increase of internet interconnections and the development of the Internet of Things. Cyberattacks endanger individuals and companies, as well as vital public services and infrastructures. Confronted with spreading and evolving cyber threats, the system and network defenses of organizations and individuals are falling behind, as they often fail to implement and effectively use basic cybersecurity and privacy practices and technologies.

The 6th International Conference on HCI for Cybersecurity, Privacy and Trust (HCI-CPT 2024), an affiliated conference of the HCI International Conference, intended to help, promote and encourage research in this field by providing a forum for interaction and exchanges among researchers, academics and practitioners in the fields of HCI and cyber security.

While technological solutions and institutional measures are paramount in mitigating cyber threats, users themselves are integral components in the defense against cyberattacks. Recognizing the influence of user behavior and practices, submissions this year have addressed topics relevant to privacy perceptions, disclosure attitudes, user behavior and understanding of cybersecurity features and threats, as well as cyber hygiene training and assessment. In an era defined by digital connectivity and data-driven interactions, the complexities and challenges associated with safeguarding personal information and digital assets have garnered the attention of the research community, with submissions in this area exploring human factors and security across contexts such as smart homes, digital twins, and enterprises. Further, submissions have carried out a comprehensive exploration of innovative strategies, experiential learning methodologies and expert perspectives aimed at fortifying defense, raising awareness, and fostering a culture of cyber resilience. Finally, the role of HCI in the design of enhanced technological approaches for uncovering cybersecurity vulnerabilities, mitigating risks and improving security measures in various domains has been a crucial focus. As the editor of this volume, I am delighted to present these diverse perspectives and scholarly endeavors, which collectively contribute to the ongoing discourse surrounding the role of HCI in cybersecurity and shed light on the intricate challenges entailed and the opportunities that emerge.

Two volumes of the HCII 2024 proceedings are dedicated to this year's edition of the HCI-CPT conference. The first focuses on topics related to Cyber Hygiene, User Behavior and Security Awareness, and User Privacy and Security Acceptance. The second focuses on topics related to Cybersecurity Education and Training, and Threat Assessment and Protection.

The papers of these volumes were accepted for publication after a minimum of two single-blind reviews from the members of the HCI-CPT Program Board or, in some cases, from members of the Program Boards of other affiliated conferences. I would like to thank all of them for their invaluable contribution, support and efforts.

July 2024   Abbas Moallem

6th International Conference on HCI for Cybersecurity, Privacy and Trust (HCI-CPT 2024)

Program Board Chair: **Abbas Moallem,** *San Jose State University, USA*

- Mostafa Al-Emran, *The British University in Dubai, UAE*
- Mohd Anwar, *North Carolina A&T State University, USA*
- Joyram Chakraborty, *Towson University, USA*
- Sabarathinam Chockalingam, *Institute for Energy Technology, Norway*
- Ulku Yaylacicegi Clark, *University of North Carolina Wilmington, USA*
- Francisco Corella, *Pomcor, USA*
- Ana Ferreira, *CINTESIS, Portugal*
- Steven Furnell, *University of Nottingham, UK*
- Akira Kanaoka, *Toho University, Japan*
- Mazaher Kianpour, *Norwegian University of Science and Technology (NTNU), Norway*
- Nathan Lau, *Virginia Tech, USA*
- Wai Sze Leung, *University of Johannesburg, South Africa*
- Luca Mazzola, *HSLU - Hochschule Luzern, Switzerland*
- Heather Molyneaux, *National Research Council Canada, Canada*
- Phillip Morgan, *Cardiff University, UK*
- Calvin Nobles, *University of Maryland Global Campus, USA*
- Jason R. C. Nurse, *University of Kent, UK*
- Henrich C. Pöhls, *University of Passau, Germany*
- David Schuster, *San José State University, USA*
- David Stevens, *University of Hawai'i Kapi'olani Community College, USA*
- Kerry-Lynn Thomson, *Nelson Mandela University, South Africa*
- Daniel Wilusz, *Poznan University of Economics and Business, Poland*
- Adam Wojtowicz, *Poznan University of Economics and Business, Poland*
- Temechu Girma Zewdie, *University of the District of Columbia, USA*

The full list with the Program Board Chairs and the members of the Program Boards of all thematic areas and affiliated conferences of HCII 2024 is available online at:

http://www.hci.international/board-members-2024.php

HCI International 2025 Conference

The 27th International Conference on Human-Computer Interaction, HCI International 2025, will be held jointly with the affiliated conferences at the Swedish Exhibition & Congress Centre and Gothia Towers Hotel, Gothenburg, Sweden, June 22–27, 2025. It will cover a broad spectrum of themes related to Human-Computer Interaction, including theoretical issues, methods, tools, processes, and case studies in HCI design, as well as novel interaction techniques, interfaces, and applications. The proceedings will be published by Springer. More information will become available on the conference website: https://2025.hci.international/.

General Chair
Prof. Constantine Stephanidis
University of Crete and ICS-FORTH
Heraklion, Crete, Greece
Email: general_chair@2025.hci.international

https://2025.hci.international/

Contents – Part I

User Privacy and Security Acceptance

Contents – Part II

Cyber Hygiene, User Behavior and Security Awareness

Privacy Perceptions and Behaviors of Google Personal Account Holders in Saudi Arabia

Eman Alashwali[1,2]($\boxtimes$) and Lorrie Cranor[3]

[1] King Abdulaziz University (KAU), Jeddah, Saudi Arabia
ealashwali@kau.edu.sa
[2] King Abdullah University of Science and Technology (KAUST),
Thuwal, Saudi Arabia
[3] Carnegie Mellon University (CMU), Pittsburgh, USA
lorrie@cmu.edu

Abstract. While privacy perceptions and behaviors have been investigated in Western societies, little is known about these issues in non-Western societies. To bridge this gap, we interviewed 30 Google personal account holders in Saudi Arabia about their privacy perceptions and behaviors regarding the activity data that Google saves about them. Our study focuses on Google's Activity Controls, which enable users to control whether, and how, Google saves their Web & App Activity, Location History, and YouTube History. Our results show that although most participants have some level of awareness about Google's data practices and the Activity Controls, many have only vague awareness, and the majority have not used the available controls. When participants viewed their saved activity data, many were surprised by what had been saved. While many participants find Google's use of their data to improve the services provided to them acceptable, the majority find the use of their data for ad purposes unacceptable. We observe that our Saudi participants exhibit similar trends and patterns in privacy awareness, attitudes, preferences, concerns, and behaviors to what has been found in studies in the US. Our results emphasize the need for: 1) improved techniques to inform users about privacy settings during account sign-up, to remind users about their settings, and to raise awareness about privacy settings; 2) improved privacy setting interfaces to reduce the costs that deter many users from changing the settings; and 3) further research to explore privacy concerns in non-Western cultures.

Keywords: Security · Privacy · Policy · Settings · Data · Google · Web · Applications · Saudi Arabia

1 Introduction

Web and mobile application users share a vast amount of their data with multiple parties, including the service provider, other users, and third parties. Although

Eman Alashwali was a Collaborating Visitor at CMU while working on this paper.

many applications include privacy settings, these settings often have fairly permissive defaults (i.e., sharing users' data by default) [7,26], with controls that are confusing, even for security and privacy experts [16,21]. Users who are unaware of default settings and how to change them may share data accidentally [21,37,38,50], sometimes with consequences such as embarrassment, bullying, identity theft, stalking, and fraud [22]. In some cases, regulators have accused service providers of misleading users with privacy setting interfaces. For example, in 2022 Google agreed to a $392 million settlement in the US for misleading consumers with privacy setting interfaces that failed to clearly inform users about how to turn off location tracking [29]. Previous work has investigated users' perceptions and behaviors with respect to privacy settings in various contexts, such as social media [10,22,24,37,38], smart home devices [35,39,59], and mobile apps [12,47]. However, little published research has investigated privacy settings of web services' accounts such as Google, or privacy settings in non-Western societies.

Our study aims to address both of these gaps by exploring Saudi users' privacy perceptions (awareness, attitudes, preferences, and concerns) and behaviors, regarding the data Google saves about them. We focus on Google's Activity Controls, a section in Google accounts that enables users to control whether, and how, Google saves their Web & App Activity, Location History, and YouTube History. To this end, we interviewed 30 Google personal account holders in Saudi Arabia. Our systematic qualitative analysis allowed us to identify fine-grained themes. Our key findings can be summarized as follows:

- Most participants have some level of awareness about Google's data practices and the Activity Controls, but many have only vague awareness. Only a few participants reported they became aware of Google's Activity Controls when signing up for their Google accounts.
- Most participants have not actually used Google's Activity Controls. The cost of knowledge, attention, time, memory, and the fear of messing things up deterred many users from using them.
- Many participants expressed negative sentiments after they viewed their saved activity data in their Google accounts because they felt watched and were surprised by the extent of the data that had been saved.
- Most participants are opposed to the use of their activity data for showing ads on Google's websites and apps or on Google's partners' websites and apps. On the other hand, most of them find it acceptable for Google to use their data for improving its services.
- Most of the participants who plan to take future steps to protect their privacy said they are going to adjust their Google Activity Controls to more restrictive settings, such as turning on the Auto-delete and reducing the data retention periods.
- We observe that our Saudi participants exhibit similar trends and patterns in privacy awareness, attitudes, preferences, concerns, and behaviors to what has been found in studies in the US. However, our study is not a replication of any of the US studies, and further research is needed to directly compare US and Saudi participants.

Based on our results, we emphasize the need for: 1) improved techniques to inform users about privacy settings during account sign-up, to remind users about their settings, and to raise awareness about privacy settings; 2) improved privacy setting interfaces to reduce the costs that deter many users from changing the settings; and 3) further research to explore privacy concerns in non-Western cultures.

2   Background and Related Work

In Sect. 2.1, we introduce the Google account sign-up process, the Activity Controls, and related work on Google's Activity Controls. In Sect. 2.2, we summarize related research conducted in Western societies (in the US, unless stated otherwise) on users' privacy perceptions and behaviors towards privacy settings and data practices. In Sect. 2.3, we provide a brief background on Saudi Arabia, and related work on privacy issues for Saudi users.

2.1   Google Account Sign-Up and the Activity Controls

Google is one of the largest companies in the world. As of 2018, Google reported 1.5 billion active Gmail users [32]. When a user creates a free Google account (Gmail), Google presents the user with it's Privacy and Terms page. The last section entitled "You're in control" informs the user that "You can control how we collect and use this data by clicking 'More options' below." The page presents a blue colored "I agree" button that is more visible than the links to "Cancel" and "More Options." Interfaces with this design are often described as "dark patterns," or "deceptive patterns," as they manipulate users to choose settings that they may not choose otherwise [5]. In Google's case, only if the user clicks on the "More options" link, the page expands and displays privacy settings and the following explanation: "Customize your activity on Google sites and apps, including searches and associated info like location ...." The page shows the settings for the following: Web & App Activity, Ads Personalization, and YouTube History. The settings are binary, and enabled by default (permissive). For example, the Web & App Activity options are: "Save my Web & app activity in my Google account" and "Don't save my Web & app activity in my Google account," with the first checked by default. At the end of the page, there is a check box for: "Send me occasional reminders about these settings," which is unchecked by default.

We are aware of two studies that examined Google's Activity Controls with US participants, investigating different research questions than ours. Farke et al. conducted a pre-post-study, with some similar aspects to our study, to examine the effect of exposing users to the then-called Google's My Activity on their privacy perceptions and behaviors [11]. In a study very different from ours, Ul Haque et al. investigated how trust toward service providers and usage of Google's Activity Controls vary based on users' technical literacy [25].

2.2 Privacy Perceptions and Behaviors Towards Privacy Settings and Data Practices

Heyman et al. defined two privacy concepts: "privacy as subject," which refers to privacy between users, and "privacy as object," which refers to privacy between a user and a business [27]. For simplicity, we rephrase these as "user-to-user" and "user-to-business" privacy relationships. Our work falls under the second category, where the data flow is between a user and a service provider.

Privacy Awareness and Behaviors. While many web and mobile service providers offer privacy settings, users tend to accept default privacy settings without change. For example, a 2005 paper by Gross and Acquisti analyzed Facebook profiles of over 4000 university students and found that only 0.06% restricted their profile information visibility [22]. While subsequent studies in social media privacy showed increased use of social media privacy settings over time [52], researchers found that use of user-to-business privacy settings remains low. For example, in 2021 Farke et al.'s study on Google's My Activity found that only 35% of the participants used Google's My Activity page [11]. Malkin et al.'s study on Google and Amazon smart speaker users found that only a minority made use of privacy settings [39]. For example, of those who knew about the deletion feature, 67.9% never used it [39]. Similarly, Lau et al.'s study on smart speaker users found that most users did not use the privacy settings of their devices [35].

Several studies found that users lack awareness about privacy settings and the data that service providers collect. Farke et al. found that only 12% indicated they were "extremely aware" of Google's My Activity, while most of them were "moderately aware" (35%) and "somewhat aware" (28%) [11]. Malkin et al. found that fewer than half (48.3%) of smart speaker users knew that their audio recordings were saved permanently in their smart speaker devices, while 41.4% incorrectly believed their recordings were saved temporarily [39]. Moreover, of the 44% of participants who were aware of the review feature, nearly half (45%) were not aware that they can use it to delete recordings in their smart speaker devices [39]. Zheng et al. reported that participants had a blurred distinction between device manufacturers and external parties that collect and save data in IoT devices [59].

Researchers have suggested that users' lack of awareness and use of privacy settings is in part due to discoverability issues. For example, Habib et al. found that many users found difficulties in finding the "Ad Preferences" [24] and the opt-out [23] settings. Chen et al. examined 100,000 applications' privacy settings and classified 36.29% of privacy settings as "hidden," with 82.16% of them permissive by default [7]. In addition, lack of knowledge about privacy settings was mentioned among the reasons for UK users' failures to change the mobile phone manufacturer's default settings [47]. Likewise, users' overtrust in device manufacturers to protect their privacy sometimes leads them to assume that there are no additional steps required from them [59], and losing trust in device manufacturers can lead users to believe that using privacy settings is useless [35]. Finally, Willis provided a theoretical framework of the mechanisms that make default settings "sticky" (i.e., unlikely to be changed by users), which inspired initial a priori themes in our qualitative analysis of the reasons not to change defaults [57].

Privacy Preferences, Attitudes, and Concerns. Several studies investigated users' preferences about data sharing practices, such as which uses of data by device manufacturers users found acceptable. Malkin et al. and Zheng et al. studies on smart home devices showed that users found it acceptable to use their data for improving the service provided to them [39,59]. On the other hand, multiple studies reported that participants found use of their data for ad purposes to be unacceptable [24,35,39], especially if the ads are from a third party [35,39]. Zheng et al. found divided opinions among participants regarding using their data for ads, and suggested that users' acceptance of using their data is benefit-driven [59]. Another aspect of users' preferences that has been investigated in prior work is the data retention period. Malkin et al. found that smart speaker users preferred shorter retention periods over longer ones [39]. Khan et al. found similar preferences among cloud storage users [33].

Several studies reported participants' attitudes when they viewed the service provider's actual behavior with respect to their data. Farke et al. reported that 33% were surprised, and 35% indicated that the amount of data was more than they anticipated. Malkin et al. reported that many participants were surprised that their voice interactions with smart speakers were permanently saved, and that they could review them [39]. Similarly, multiple studies on mobile apps reported that most participants were surprised about the amount [28], frequency and destinations [3], of the data that their mobile apps were collecting.

In terms of concerns, Farke et al. found that exposure to Google's My Activity reduced participants who had privacy concerns from 52% to 47% [11]. However, several other studies on US participants in other contexts such as smart speakers and smart home devices reported fewer privacy concerns. Lau et al., Zheng et al., and Zeng et al. studies on smart home devices reported that participants had few privacy concerns [35,58,59]. Reasons for low concerns include trusting the manufacturer, not feeling targeted, incomplete understanding of the privacy risks associated with the device, and trading privacy for functionality or convenience [35,58,59]. Malkin et al. reported only 28.3% of participants had privacy concerns about their smart speakers [39]. However, Malkin et al. also noted that users raised higher concerns in specific contexts such as when recordings contain children's voices or when audio recordings are used for ads [39], offering contextual integrity as an explanation [39,44].

2.3 Saudi Society and Privacy

Saudi Arabia is a developing country in southwestern Asia that was established in 1932 [56], and has one of the youngest populations in the world. As of 2019, 49% of the population was below 30 years old [13]. It has around 17% of the world's proven oil reserves, and is the second-largest member of the Organization of the Petroleum Exporting Countries (OPEC) [45]. Saudi Arabia's economy and young population resulted in rapid development and technology adoption. The Internet penetration rate in Saudi Arabia reached 89% in 2019 [15]. It is reported that over 80% of the Saudi population are social media users [17,31]. The Personal Data Protection Law (PDPL) in Saudi Arabia came into force in September 2023. However, full enforcement of the law is expected to start on September 2024, as the first year is set as a transition period for data controllers to take the necessary steps to comply with the law [41]. At the time of our study's interviews (August, 2021), Internet users in Saudi Arabia have no legal protections for their personal data.

Despite high Internet usage among Saudis, very little online privacy research has been conducted with this population, and none that we are aware of investigated user-to-business privacy issues. Rashidi et al. surveyed 626 WhatsApp users in Saudi Arabia to understand their privacy behaviors and attitudes [48]. They found that Saudis were aware of WhatsApp privacy settings and used them, especially to limit the visibility of the "last seen" setting that shows when they were last seen active [48]. Another study by Alsagri and Alaboodi analyzed the privacy awareness and attitudes of 455 Snapchat users from Saudi Arabia [2]. They found that over 70% of participants were concerned about "misuse or abuse of their personal information" [2].

3   Methodology

We interviewed 30 Google personal account holders in Saudi Arabia about their awareness, attitudes, preferences, and concerns regarding the activity data that Google saves about them, as well as any steps they take to control Google's collection or use of this data. In this section, we describe our recruitment procedure, interview procedure, analysis methods, and limitations. We obtained formal ethical approval for the study from King Abdulaziz University's research ethics committee. We obtained participants' explicit consent before they took part in the screening survey and interview. Participants were informed that the interview would be recorded and that the results of this study will be published without identifying participants. Moreover, they were informed that they can quit the study at any stage.

3.1   Recruitment

Our targeted sample was those who identified themselves as: living in Saudi Arabia (nationals or residents), aged 18 or older, using a free personal (not a business) Google Gmail account with "@gmail.com" extension regularly for at least a month. The rationale behind limiting the study to free personal @gmail.com accounts is that business accounts may be configured by the organization's Information Technology (IT) department and not by the users themselves. We aim to understand users' privacy decisions, not those of the organization. Moreover, paid accounts may have different default privacy settings than free accounts. In the invitation, we also stated that participants must use a personal computer that contains a web browser and Zoom (an online conference software [60]). We required desktop or laptop computers because the Google account mobile interface may be different from the computer interface. Our study targeted non-security-expert users as we are more interested in understanding the baseline non-security-expert user perception and behavior. Moreover, asking security experts about their awareness and usage of privacy settings in an interview setting can make the results more prone to social desirability bias. We screened for university degree(s) and current job unrelated to cybersecurity by asking for degree and job generally, without mentioning security.

To recruit participants, we sent an invitation for the screening survey written in Arabic to King Abdulaziz University's mailing lists, which included academic and administrative staff and students, who come from diverse backgrounds. King Abdulaziz University is one of the largest public universities in Saudi Arabia [30]. In addition, the first author sent invitations to personal and professional networks, mainly through WhatsApp groups [55], which are widely used in Saudi Arabia, and posted invitations on Twitter [53], Facebook [42], and LinkedIn [36]. We encouraged the recipients to share the invitation with their personal and professional networks, especially networks that encompass diverse demographics. Finally, at the end of each interview, we encouraged participants to invite others to take part. Participation was voluntary. We used a screening survey to check that participants met the inclusion criteria before inviting them to the interview. The study's advertised title was: "Users' Experiences on Cloud Services." We avoided using any words related to "security" and "privacy" in the study's title, invitation letter, screening survey, and during the interview, until the very last sections of the interview, to avoid biased answers that do not reflect users' actual privacy behaviors and decisions [51]. We informed participants that they will be invited to an interview that will include a user experiment on their Google Gmail account, where the interviewer will guide them step by step. We informed them that the experiment does not require any technical background or preparation. We also informed them that we will not request access to their devices, ask them to download any file, request any changes to their email, or request their password or any private data. We received 91 completed screening survey responses, we disqualified 27 that did not meet the study's criteria. From the 64 qualified screening responses, we invited a demographically diverse sample of participants. Upon scheduling the interview, an email containing a Zoom link for the online interview was sent to the participants. Interview invitations were sent in batches. If an invited participant did not schedule an interview within 24–48 h, canceled, or scheduled one but did not show up, we invited a replacement participant. This process was repeated until we reached the desired number of completed interviews (30).

3.2 Interview

The interview was designed in a semi-structured format. We prepared a set of multiple-choice, open-ended, and task-based questions. We based some of our questions off of questions from Malkin et al.'s survey [39]. The interview included a user experiment section in which we asked participants to log in to their Gmail accounts using their computers and web browsers. Then, we asked them questions about their settings, awareness, and usage of Google's Activity Controls. We also asked them about their sentiments after viewing their saved activity data, their attitudes regarding the data they considered most private, their attitudes regarding Google's practices with their data, and finally their privacy concerns. We asked follow-up questions where needed. Interviews were conducted online using Zoom, an online video conference system [60], from August 5 to 28, 2021. The interviewer shared their screen with participants via Zoom and displayed each question on the screen as they asked it (except for follow-up questions). In a few exceptional cases, participants voluntarily shared their screens if they needed help, e.g. to locate the right setting. However, we resumed the interview with the interviewer's shared screen once help was provided. Interviews were voice and screen recorded (the interviewer's screen only, with few exceptions to provide help). They were conducted in Arabic language by the first author, who is a native Arabic speaker and proficient in English. Each interview lasted for 33 min on average (mean: 33, minimum: 22, and maximum: 45 min).

3.3   Data Analysis

After we finished all interviews, recordings were manually transcribed by the first author and two paid undergraduate students. All transcripts were reviewed by the first author. The interview questions and the participants' qualitative answers included in our analysis were manually translated from Arabic to English by the first author. Multiple-choice questions were quantitatively analyzed using descriptive statistics. Open-ended questions included in our analysis were qualitatively analyzed using template analysis, a style of thematic analysis [6,34], by a single trained researcher. The coder met with the co-author over multiple sessions to discuss the results and refine coding and themes. While multiple coders can confirm consistent interpretations, a single coder is deemed acceptable in Human-Computer Interaction (HCI) research [40]. In template analysis, for each open-ended question, we started with "a priori themes" (the template), which were mainly inspired by our prior knowledge of the topic and the literature. We then read the data multiple times, and adjusted (added, updated, or removed) the themes accordingly. Finally, we mapped participants' answers to the suitable themes and sub-themes (coding the template) [34].

3.4   Limitations

First, our interviews were conducted in Arabic to reach a wide range of Saudi Arabian participants and to enable rich expression using the participants' native language. As a result, the direct quotes from our participants in this paper are the closest translations of the original questions and quotes from Arabic to English. We tried to accurately translate the interview questions and the participants' answers, including the answers' imperfections. However, "lost in translation" expressions might have occurred.

Second, our participants' demographics are biased toward those located in the Western region of Saudi Arabia (93%), and slightly towards females (63%). The regional bias is very likely due to the fact that the main author was based in the Western region of Saudi Arabia (Jeddah city) and that one of the main survey distribution channels was a large public university at the Western region (King Abdulaziz University). However, the Western region (a.k.a. Makkah Region) is a very large and diverse region, containing several cities and towns with a population of 9,033,491 according to population estimates of Makkah region in mid 2019 [13]. King Abdulaziz University is the second largest public university in Saudi Arabia, comprising students coming from different backgrounds and regions in Saudi Arabia. As of 2019, it had over 165,490 students, 7527 faculty staff, and 6739 administrative staff [14].

Third, some participants' answers might be prone to recall bias and social desirability. To minimize recall bias, our interview utilized task-based questions, where the participants opened their actual account page and answered based on their accounts' actual settings. To minimize social desirability, we informed the participants at the beginning of the interview that there is no right or wrong answer, we are only interested in their choices and opinions, and we do not have a connection to Google. Moreover, we did not use words related to "security" and "privacy" until the very last sections of the interview, to avoid answers biased towards security and privacy behavior.

Fourth, during our study, Google made some updates (detailed in Sect. 6), which included updating a few terms. They changed the term "Data & Personalization" to "Data & Privacy," and the term "Activity Controls" to "History Settings." These updated terms were reported by four participants during the study, and we proceeded using the new terms (verbally), requiring early mention of the word "privacy" with these participants. Interface updates by service providers during field studies are not uncommon, and were reported by similar studies [1,39,54].

Fifth, while we offer some comparisons between our study and those conducted in the US, this is not a replication of a prior study. Furthermore, this study, and most of the studies we compare it to, are qualitative studies. Thus, we only observe trends that appear similar or different across cultures, but cannot make direct quantitative comparisons.

Finally, while we mark participants who reported having technical background with a superscript star (P#*) to make better sense of the data and quotes, analyzing different perspectives based on technical literacy is beyond our study's scope.

4 Results

In what follows, we summarize our results. Participants are denoted by P, followed by the participant number (P#). Participants with technical backgrounds are denoted by a superscript star (P#*). While qualitative analysis is meant to distill themes and not to quantify, we provide the number of participants whose responses were mapped to a particular theme to provide a better sense of our data. See the diagram in Fig. 1 in Appendix A for an illustration summarizing our qualitative analysis themes.

4.1 Participants and Demographics

After conducting three pilot interviews (not included in our results), we completed and analyzed 30 interviews. All of our participants were living in Saudi Arabia. Participants included 19 (63%) females and 11 (37%) males, ranging in age between 18 and 54 years old. Eight participants (27%) reported having technical backgrounds (i.e. having a university degree or working in Computer Science (CS), Information Systems (IS), Information Technology (IT), or Computer Engineering (CE) areas). None of them reported a degree or work in the cybersecurity field (confirmed via a question at the end of the interview).

4.2 Awareness of Google's Activity Controls

Users' Basic Activity Controls Settings vs. Defaults. Before we asked the participants about their awareness of Google's Activity Controls, we asked them to report their current (at the time of the study) basic Activity Controls settings. We guided them to the Activity Controls area in their Google accounts. Then, we asked them to report their Activity Controls basic settings (either "on" or "paused") regarding saving three types of data: Web & App Activity, Location History, and YouTube History. We observe that for both the Web & App Activity and YouTube History, most participants (28/30) kept the permissive default ("on"). On the other hand, for the Location History, where the default setting is restrictive ("paused"), we observe a smaller majority of participants (20/30) kept the default.

Awareness Level. To identify participants' awareness level about Google's Activity Controls, we first briefly described the Activity Controls to the participants as follows: "allows you to control, such as turn on or pause saving your activities such as (Web & App Activity, Location History, or YouTube History)." In addition, we shared Google's definitions of the following terms with participants [18]: 1) Web & App Activity: "Saves your activity on Google sites and apps, including associated info like location." 2) Location History: "Saves where you go with your devices, even when you aren't using a specific Google service." 3) YouTube History: "Saves the YouTube videos you watch and the things you search for on YouTube." We then asked the participants if they were aware of Google's Activity Controls. The majority of participants stated they had some level of awareness about Google's Activity Controls (24/30). However, of those 24 participants, many had only a vague awareness (i.e. answered "I expected there is such a thing" (9), or "I heard about such a thing" (2)), and only 13 answered "yes."

How Users Became Aware of the Activity Controls? For the 24 participants who expressed some level of prior awareness about Google's Activity Controls, we asked them how they knew about, heard of, or expected, the existence of the Activity Controls. We then qualitatively analyzed their answers. From the 23 participants who provided answers (one participant did not remember), we identify seven themes: experiences with or expectations about applications and systems, exploration and search, observed behavior of applications and systems, chance, social channels, consent prompts, and account sign-up or device setup. In what follows, we elaborate on each theme.

Experiences with or Expectations About Applications and Systems: 7/23 participants referred to their experiences with, or expectations about, applications and systems, when discussing how they became aware of Google's Activity Controls. Our participants mentioned experiences with applications and systems from Google and other service providers. In addition, three participants mentioned their experience with their browsers' history interface. P5 was one of two participants who mentioned that they were aware that they can delete their history from YouTube: "I know the YouTube History, but the Location History, and that there is a window called the Activity Controls that combines them all, I did not know honestly." P25 mentioned his experience "on websites and controlling them." On the other hand, P3 and P6 mentioned mere expectations of Google's Activity Controls, as P3 said: "I was expecting that we can control the activity ... because not everyone likes to have their activities recorded and kept."

Exploration and Search: 5/23 participants mentioned becoming aware of Google's Activity Controls through exploration and search. For example, P8[*] said: "By experimentation ... from time to time I open the settings and I look and read them every now and then ...."

Observed Behavior of Applications and Systems: 3/23 participants observed personalized application behavior that led them to expect that controls would exist. P11 described this experience: "while using the device, I see that the things I save, search about, and so on, get saved somewhere, but where? I do not know." P20 said: "once you open YouTube you always find the videos that you recently watched ... and I do not know how exactly."

Chance: 3/23 participants mentioned coming across Google's Activity Controls by chance (accidentally). For example, P27 said: "I wanted to change my account's password ... and found these topics on the activity and YouTube History ...." P14[*] described a similar situation in addition to his awareness through the account's sign-up, he added: "some of them, when I want to edit the theme, or if for example, I want to add the payment and subscription and these things, I go to Data & Personalization, I wonder what is this ...."

Social Channels: 3/23 participants mentioned becoming aware of Google's Activity Controls through social channels. P7 and P17 mentioned WhatsApp [55]. P17 said: "from the messages I receive on WhatsApp ... They were talking about that Google Map[s] knows your location, where you are, and so on, and how to modify it, how to turn it off ...." P26 mentioned Twitter: "I read on Twitter that there are things we are supposed to change to reduce the annoying ads."

Consent Prompts: 2/23 participants mentioned that consent dialogues made them expect that Google's Activity Controls would exist. For example, P23[*] described browsers' prompts for users' permission to share the user's location with websites: "sometimes when I search on Google it tells me: do you want to turn on the location or not?" P9 mentioned consent prompts but was not specific on the type of application: "They usually write these notes: do you agree? Click on agree and you can change it from settings later."

Account Sign-Up or Device Setup: only 2/23 participants mentioned they knew about Google's Activity Controls during Google's account sign-up or device setup. For example, P14[*] described his experience creating his account: "When I first created it ... one of the things was to make the Activity Controls or to skip them, if I am not mistaken." P15 attributed her awareness to Google's phone (Pixel [20]) setup: "I used to have a Google mobile ... When I first turned on the device, I activated my account. I used to control these things from the mobile."

4.3   Usage of Google's Activity Controls

Usage Level. We asked participants whether they have ever used Google's Activity Controls. Despite the fact that 24 participants had expressed some level of awareness of the controls, only 11/30 said they had used them, and one did not remember.

Reasons for Using the Activity Controls. We asked the 11 participants who said they used Google's Activity Controls, why they used the controls, and what changes they made. We then qualitatively analyzed the answers of both questions together. We identify four types of reasons to use Google's Activity Controls: turning off data saving, turning on data saving, temporarily switching between data saving settings, and reviewing or deleting saved data. In what follows, we elaborate on each theme.

Turning Off Data Saving: 7/11 participants mentioned using Google's Activity Controls to "turn off" ("pause" in Google's Activity Controls terms) data saving for one or more types of activity data. Six of these participants mentioned turning off the Location History, with some mentioning privacy concerns. We noted that the Location History was turned off by default in Google accounts at the time of the study. We don't know whether the Location History was turned on by default at some point in the past and these participants turned it off, or whether those participants were confused because the Activity Controls interface does not indicate which setting is the default. Only one participant mentioned turning off the Web & App Activity or the YouTube History, and three participants mentioned turning off data saving using general terms, such as turning off "tracking" and "history." P10[*] changed her settings to avoid targeted ads and explained how ads can be embarrassing in remote working settings: "Sometimes, or mostly, in our remote work, we share the screen ... if you search about something, it will show immediately ... it shows to the co-workers with you. Sometimes it is something personal, not something you share with people."

Turning on Data Saving: In contrast to turning off data saving, only 2/11 participants mentioned using the Activity Controls to turn on data saving for one or more types of data. P4 mentioned using the Activity Controls to "turn on the YouTube History," mainly to review his YouTube history as he described: "For example, there is something I want to recall, see it again, review it." Similar to what we observed in the previous section, YouTube History was turned on by default in Google accounts at the time of the study. Thus, we don't know whether the participant turned it on (for example, if it was turned off by default at some point in the past), or the participant was confused because the Activity Controls interface does not indicate whether a user has selected a setting other than the default. P33 mentioned "I personalized the ads," and we counted it as turning on data saving, although we note that Google's Ad Personalization settings are not actually part of the Activity Controls.

Temporarily Switching Between Data Saving Settings: 3/11 participants mentioned temporarily switching between data saving settings. P8[*] mentioned switching the Web & App Activity setting between on and off depending on the situation. For example, if she is using multiple devices, she turns the Web & App Activity on, to track the activities on those multiple devices, and turns it off if she is using a single device. P31 mentioned switching settings to reduce performance overhead: "the tracking and these things, in general, all take resources." This is a misconception as Google saves this data in the cloud and the amount of activity data stored does not impact the performance of the user's device or account.

Reviewing or Deleting Saved Data: One participant (P24) mentioned that she used Google's Activity Controls to review and delete data: "there are things that I search about which I prefer to delete, while I keep [other] things to return to them later."

Reasons for Keeping Default Settings. For the 18 participants who said they have not used Google's Activity Controls, we asked them about the reasons for keeping the defaults. We qualitatively analyzed their answers and identify four main themes: high cost of change, perceived convenience, the "I have nothing to hide" attitude, and low benefit of change. In what follows, we elaborate on each theme.

High Cost of Change: 8/18 participants mentioned reasons relating to the high cost of change. We identify five types of costs as follows: 1) Cost of knowledge:

four participants said they did not change the default settings because they did not know about the Activity Controls, such as P28: "I do not know about it honestly." 2) Cost of attention or care: two participants mentioned that they did not pay attention to, or care about, the Activity Controls. For example P3 stated: "I do not pay attention to the settings and these things." 3) Cost of time: refers to the time needed to explore, learn about, or change Google's Activity Controls. Two participants mentioned lack of time as a reason for sticking to the defaults. For example P13[*] explained: "I do not go to the account and its settings unless I faced a problem ... I do not have enough time, to be honest." 4) Cost of cognitive memory: refers to the cognitive memory required to remember to change the Activity Controls. This was mentioned by one pilot participant[1]. While some users may overcome the knowledge, attention or care, and time costs described above, they forget to change the Activity Controls. 5) Fear of "messing things up": this was mentioned by P17 who said: "Leave it as it is as long as the email is working ... The fear is to make something then this messes up the email or something like that."

Perceived Convenience: 7/18 participants mentioned convenience as a reason for sticking to the default Activity Controls settings. Perceived convenience is expressed in several phrases such as "It did not bother me," "I did not face a problem," "I find the History useful to me," and "it is very convenient, I find the things that I frequently search about," as stated by P5, P13[*], P19, and P20, consequently.

The "I Have Nothing to Hide" Attitude: 4/19 participants expressed that they have nothing to hide because they have not done anything wrong or embarrassing that they would need to hide, or because their data is not of "high importance" (P16[*]). P9 stated directly: "I have nothing to hide ...."

Low Benefit of Change: 3/18 participants stated that they didn't think they would get much, if any, privacy or user experience benefits from changing their settings. Two participants expressed resignation because Google might save their information anyway or they might be tracked by other parties. P18 said: "because I know that even if I turn off the settings, there might be tracing and tracking for the websites I visit." Similarly, P9 believes that giant service providers such as Google "if they want to save something legally or illegally, they will know how." P6 believes that using the Activity Controls "will not make an impact or difference on usage."

4.4   Attitudes and Preference Toward Google's Data Practices and Activity Controls

Users' Advanced Activity Controls Settings vs. Defaults. Before we asked the participants about their attitudes toward Google's data saving

---

[1] Although this point was mentioned only by a pilot participant, we believe it is a reason worth surfacing.

practices, we asked them to report their advanced Activity Controls settings (another level of choices after the basic "on" or "paused" basic settings). To avoid interview fatigue, we proceeded to the advanced Activity Controls settings only on one of the Activity Controls that the participant reported had a status of "on" (see Sect. 4.2). If the participant reported the Web & App Activity was "on," we proceeded to the Web & App Activity for the advanced settings (28/30). Otherwise, if the participant reported the Web & App Activity was "paused" and the YouTube History was "on," we proceeded to the YouTube History for the advanced settings (1/30). If the participant reported all of the three Activity Controls were "paused," we did not proceed with that participant to the advanced settings (1/30). We then asked the participants to report their advanced options and Auto-delete settings.

Attitudes Towards Data Saving. Following the protocol described in the previous section to select one Activity Controls data type to proceed to the attitude question on, we guided the 29 participants (28 on the Web & App Activity and 1 on YouTube History) to the "Manage data" link, which allows them to "See and delete past activity." Then, we asked them if they found records of any of their previous searches or so. All 29 participants found saved activity data in their accounts. After they viewed some of their saved data, we asked them to describe their feeling. We qualitatively analyzed their answers and classified their feelings toward the saved data into three themes: negative, neutral, and positive. We elaborate on each theme.

Negative Sentiment: 13/29 participants expressed negative sentiments after they viewed their saved data in Google's Activity Controls. This led several of them to remark that going forward they would change their behavior: 2 said they plan to be more aware of what they do on the Internet, and 4 said they will turn off data saving or delete their data. We identify several motivations behind the negative sentiments: 1) Feeling watched: 7 participants mentioned that they felt watched. For example, P27 said: "I feel tracked" and P26 said: "it is easy to surveil me" in their sentiments. 2) Lack of, or incomplete, knowledge about the service provider's data practices: 6 participants mentioned words that express lack of, or incomplete, knowledge about Google's data practices, such as "surprised," "shock," "scary," "if I knew that," and "did not expect that." Most of those participants have incomplete knowledge about aspects of how the data are being saved, such as the breadth, depth, retention period, and linkability of the saved data. 3) Data breadth: 5 participants mentioned surprise at seeing the amount of data saved. The phrase "everything is recorded" was used by multiple participants (P3, P23[*]). For example, P3 said: "everything is recorded, I mean everything is stored and recorded in the History. So this matter is a bit scary." Also, P23[*] said: "I do not know about this, and that everything is recorded about me." 4) Linkability: 2 participants were not aware that their activity data are linked to their accounts, as opposed to only being saved locally in the browser. For example, P25 said: "I know that in the browser, but in Google [account], this is the first time I know that this information appears." 5) Data depth: which refers to the amount of details, was mentioned by one participant: "even the devices that I ... use, where I am, and the location." (P23[*]). 6) Retention period: one participant (P5) mentioned concern about how long the data was saved: "old things, I mean very old History ... I want to turn off ... I want to delete ...."

Neutral Sentiment: 10/29 participants expressed neutral sentiments after they viewed their saved data in Google's Activity Controls. We identify three motivations behind the neutral sentiments: 1) Awareness or expectations of data saving: 5 participants remarked that, simply viewing their activity data was not very surprising to them because they were already aware that Google saves their data. Multiple participants mentioned the word "normal." For example, P21[*] said: "Normal ... as a technical person because I know that Google stores these things." Similarly, P8[*] expected that her data are saved through "personalized advertising and such things, it is clear that it is using my search." 2) The "I have nothing to hide" attitude: 3 participants expressed the feeling of having nothing to hide. The statements "Nothing is worthy," "my search is very general," and "The search I have is purely for work," were mentioned by P10[*], P16[*], and P17, respectively. 3) Resignation: some participants felt powerless towards Google, and believe there are no privacy settings that can stop giant companies such as Google from collecting and saving their data. This reason motivated 2 participants to express neutral sentiments. P14[*] described the activity data saving by Google as "inevitable devil" and noted "any computer you use, your data will go, even if the company claimed secrecy [i.e., privacy], you cannot ensure that. That's why I did not bother myself by turning it off."

Positive Sentiment: Only 6/29 participants expressed positive sentiments after they viewed their saved activity data in Google's Activity Controls. All of those participants referred to the usefulness of being able to retrieve or review their stored data when needed. It is worth noting that none of those participants who expressed positive sentiments have a technical background. We identify two motivations behind the positive sentiments: 1) Retrieve records: 4 participants mentioned being able to retrieve lost or forgotten records. For example, P31 said: "I am happy that I find it, because sometimes I remember that there is something I searched about, so I go here and find it immediately." 2) Review records: 3 participants mentioned reviewing activity records such as searches or YouTube videos. For example, P4 said: "from time to time I like to see what did I do previously, what did I search about ... and watch it again." This theme captures participants' desire to review content a second time rather than retrieve forgotten records.

Informing Users About Data Saving. We asked the 29 participants who reported one or more basic Activity Controls were "on" (see Sect. 4.2) whether they were aware that Google saves this data about them. We observe a pattern similar to the awareness of the Activity Controls. Here we also find an overall high, but vague, awareness of data saving (i.e., many answered "I expected ..." or

"I heard about ..." that Google saved activity data about them). We find 11/29 answered "yes," 6/29 answered "no," while 8/29 answered "I expected that, but I am not certain," and 4/29 answered "I heard about that, but I am not certain." For the 18 participants who were not fully aware (i.e. their answer was not "yes") that their data are being saved by Google, we asked them what would have informed them about the saving of their activity data. We qualitatively analyzed their answers and identify three main themes: transparency, awareness, and nothing can be done.

Transparency: 10/18 participants mentioned suggestions relating to improving the clarity of communication about Google's data practices and the choices offered to users summarized as follows: 1) Explicit consent: five participants said that an agreement about data saving should be clearly stated during the account sign-up. However, several participants admitted that they might have skipped the agreement as P3 continued: "It might be there but we do not notice ...." However, there are reasons for ignoring the agreement, as P5 said: "because it was not very clear." An additional participant (P16*) advocated for privacy-protective default settings in which data would not be collected or saved unless the user explicitly consents: "similar to what happened recently in the iPhone when it asks you: do you want to share your activities with the app? this should be the right situation, that the default is no sharing, and the exception is for sharing." Google asks for users' consent to collect and use their data. However, their approach appears not to be transparent enough, as several participants did not recall seeing it. 2) Better presentation: three participants suggested better presentations, including less text. P9 suggested using videos that show "how the saving method, usage method ...." P20 suggested using bullet points, while P11 suggested placing the Activity Controls "in an easier place, not in the account ...." The latter suggestion can explain why we observed multiple participants were aware of the YouTube data saving but not the Web & App Activity and Location History. YouTube uses the term "Your data in YouTube" in the account's main menu on YouTube, not buried under multiple menus and using opaque terms such as Data & Personalization and Activity Controls. 3) User engagement: two participants suggested user engagement, such as a mandatory step-by-step inter-active wizard to force users to configure their privacy settings as "it involves the user in this. It makes him do the thing by himself. But when they put text no one would read it ..." (P14*).

Awareness: 9/18 participants mentioned suggestions that relate to awareness, which can be classified into two main categories: 1) Notifications or nudges: eight participants mentioned using notifications or nudges to inform users that their activity data are being saved, remind them to delete their saved data, or notify them if sensitive data are being saved. Two participants mentioned in-browser notifications or nudges, such that "when someone visits a website it says it is going to store [the data]" (P13*). 2) Social media: one participant (P29) suggested that Google could use social media to inform users about privacy-related matters.

Nothing Can Be Done: One participant (P28) believes that nothing can be done and blamed herself: "Nothing else they can do. This is the only known way, that they tell you all the conditions for all the things they do, but our problem is that we do not read it."

Knowledge and Usage of the Review, Delete, and Auto-Delete Features. We asked the 10 participants who answered "yes," they know that Google saves data about them[2], whether they knew that they can review the data that Google saves about them. 5/10 answered "yes" (4 in the Web & App Activity, and 1 in the YouTube History groups), while the remaining participants answered "no." We asked them how often they review the data. 3/5 answered "at least once every 6 months," one answered "less than once a year," and one answered "I never reviewed them." We asked the same 10 participants who said they knew Google saves data about them whether they knew they can manually delete some or all the data that Google saves about them, and whether they knew about the Auto-delete feature. 7/10 said they knew they could manually delete data, and only 3/10 said they knew about Auto-delete. Of the 7 who said they knew about manual deletion, we asked them how often they manually delete their data. We find 4/7 said they "never deleted them," and 2/7 "do not remember."

Preferences Regarding Google's Default Data Retention Periods. We asked all the 29 participants[3] whether they find Google's default retention period for each type of activity data suitable (Web & App Activity: 18 months, YouTube History: 36 months, Location History: 18 months). If they answered "no," we asked them to propose a suitable period from their perspective. Our results suggest that the majority of participants find Google's default retention periods unsuitable for all three types of activity data. As the retention period increases, more participants rank it unsuitable. The majority of participants suggested lower retention periods. For the Web & App activity, the top suggested periods are: 1, 3–6, and 12 months, mentioned by 6, 4, and 6 participants, respectively. For the YouTube History: 1, 6, and 12 months, mentioned by 5, 5, and 5 participants, respectively. Finally, for the Location History: 1 and 6 months, and 1 day, suggested by 7, 4, and 3 participants, respectively. Multiple participants mentioned that they prefer the Location History to never be saved (but we asked them to specify the minimum preferred period, assuming that the data saving is on). We also asked all participants about their attitudes regarding the most private and sensitive data type for them. Participants ranked the Location History as the most sensitive data type with the highest level of privacy where 18/30 ranked its privacy as "high," while 9/30 ranked the Web & App activity privacy "high", and the YouTube History was ranked "high" privacy only by 4 participants.

---

[2] An additional participant said "yes" to this questions, but missed Sect. 4.4's questions due to an error.

[3] This question was added after P1 interview was done. Thus, 29/30 participants were asked this question.

Preferences Regarding Acceptable Use of Activity Data. We presented all participants with three different scenarios of how Google may use their Web & App Activity data, and asked them to rank how acceptable each scenario is for them. We limited these questions to the Web & App Activity data to avoid interview fatigue. The Web & App Activity is "on" by default and contains rich data about users. The results suggest that the majority of participants (22/30) would accept using their Web & App Activity data to improve Google services. On the other hand, the majority (17/30) would not accept using their data for ads displayed on Google services, and (20/30) would not accept using their data for ads in non-Google websites and apps that partner with Google.

4.5 Privacy Concerns

Users' Privacy Concerns. We asked all participants whether they previously had any privacy concerns while using Google services. We find 13/30 participants answered "yes," 15/30 answered "no," and 2/30 were "neutral." We did not ask the participants why did they have or have not any privacy concerns. However, some of them voluntarily elaborated their answers with the reasons. Out of the 9 participants who elaborated on why they did not have privacy concerns, 5 participants' responses map to the "I have nothing to hide" category, because they felt they did not have anything either sensitive, wrong, or important. P11 referred to her trust in Google as they are "an international company and aspire to make their [products] better," while P20 added she did not have concerns because she is not a targeted person. For those who had privacy concerns, we asked them about these concerns. 12/13 provided a comprehensible answer. We qualitatively analyzed their answers and classified participants' privacy concerns into two categories: data abuse and data leak. We note that 3 participants referred to service providers such as Google as adversaries, 2 participants mentioned the words "hackers" and "hacking," and one participant said she is more concerned about someone who knows her than Google.

Data Abuse: of the 13 participants who had privacy concerns, 10/13 participants mentioned concerns that relate to data abuse, noting five types of data abuse: 1) Tracking or spying on users: this is a common concern, mentioned by 7 participants. P22 explained: "I am concerned that Google knows a lot of data about me, knows my interests, knows where I go and where I come, what I search about" and described this situation as "somewhat an unpleasant idea." P19 described her concern as: "someone can access my account and see what I am searching for." The word "spying" was mentioned by one participant only. 2) Using users' data for purposes they are unaware of: two participants were concerned about using their data for purposes they are unaware of. For example, P8[*] was concerned that her data are used "in a way that could harm me, or in a wrong way, or in a way that I do not accept." 3) Sharing users' data with other parties: two participants mentioned concerns about users' data being shared with other parties. P8[*] referred to the other party as "an entity that [the data] should not reach to," while P14[*] was concerned that "these big companies sell your data." 4) User impersonation: P7 was concerned about user impersonation where someone falsely claims to be a particular user. 5) Intellectual property theft: P7 described his concern as someone might take someone else's "ideas, and take what he is thinking about and what he is doing."

Data Leak: 5/13 participants were concerned that their data could be leaked, either accidentally, because of an attack on the service provider, or because of a data privacy breach. P29 was particularly concerned about a "photos" leak. Three participants linked data leaks with attacks on the service provider as P18 described: "we heard that even Google and even Apple were hacked and thousands or even hundreds of thousands of millions of personal data for their users were leaked."

Steps Users Took to Protect Their Privacy. We asked all participants if they have ever taken any steps to protect their privacy on the Internet while using Google services. 18/30 answered "yes," while 12/30 answered "no." For those who answered "yes," we asked them what are these steps. We qualitatively analyzed their answers and identify three main themes: change privacy or security settings or control permissions, change browsing behavior, and use software assisting tools. In what follows, we elaborate on each theme.

Change Privacy or Security Settings or Control Permissions: 11/18 participants mentioned changing privacy or security settings or controlling permissions to protect their privacy. Six participants mentioned turning off the location data sharing in Google accounts and other settings. P13[*] mentioned disallowing location sharing in most mobile apps except for government apps. P23[*] mentioned disallowing location permission to websites when asked by the browser. P8[*] mentioned turning on notifications for logins from new devices. P17 said he changed the password after his "email was hacked." Finally, P29 mentioned enabling two-factor authentication.

Change Browsing Behavior: 7/18 participants mentioned a wide variety of practices to change their Internet browsing behavior. P7 mentioned using a privacy-friendly search engine such as "DuckDuckGo" [9] as the main engine and using the Google search engine only if DuckDuckGo did not return results. P8[*] would not use her account on a "public Wi-Fi." P9 mentioned he "delete[s] the cookies from time to time." P10[*] mentioned deleting the YouTube history from the browser's history manually, P26 mentioned reviewing and deleting the account's YouTube History data for kids. P15 mentioned using a Virtual Private Network (VPN). P18 mentioned private browsing modes, such as Firefox's Private Browsing [43] and Google Chrome's Incognito mode [19]. However, a VPN and private browsing cannot prevent a service provider such as Google from saving activity data inside the account.

Use Software Tools: 2/18 participants mentioned using software tools to protect their privacy online while using Google services. P7 mentioned using the "C Cleaner" software [46] to clean the history, "trackers," and "adware." P7 also mentioned using the "Pocket" [49] to "drop the links" he wants to save, while P9 mentioned using "Internet antivirus."

Future Steps Users Plan to Take to Protect Their Privacy. We asked all participants whether they plan to take future steps to protect their privacy online when using Google services. 17/30 answered "yes," while 13/30 answered "no." For those who answered "yes," we asked them what these steps are. We qualitatively analyzed their answers and identified two main themes: review or change privacy settings, and use privacy-friendly systems or products. In what follows, we elaborate on each theme.

Review or Change Privacy Settings: out of the 17 participants who plan to take future steps to protect their privacy, 16/17 participants mentioned that they intend to review or change their privacy settings, in particular, Google's Activity Controls. Most participants want to change their settings to restrictive settings. For example, P23* "will go to the settings and see how much data I am sharing," P10* will turn off the YouTube History and the Location History data saving in her Google account, and P14* said that "the Web & App Activity, once we finish I will change them." Moreover, 8 participants mentioned they want to turn on the Auto-delete or reduce the data retention period. P12* changed her retention period during the interview: "now while I am talking to you, I reduced it to 3 months for example." This suggests that when users are empowered with knowledge, they care about their privacy and can take action to protect it.

Use Privacy-Friendly Systems or Products: one participant (P7) said, he "maybe moving from Google Chrome" to a more privacy-friendly browser and added: "I am currently using Brave [4] to check if it is better to use." Moreover, he is considering returning to Linux OS as he thinks "Linux is more privacy-protecting than Windows."

5   Discussion and Cross-Cultural Perspective

When it comes to user-to-business privacy, many service providers today adopt deceptive interfaces and permissive default settings. Our results showed that while most of our participants had some level of awareness about Google's Activity Controls, many of them were only vaguely aware, most of them had never used them, and many were shocked by the extent of the data saved about them. Our results also showed that many users care about their privacy and once informed about settings and data being saved, said they intend to take future steps to protect their privacy. However, it is unrealistic to expect users to learn how to identify deceptive interfaces and to assume that users will remember to change permissive default settings. Thus, our key recommendations from this research are mainly directed toward service providers, researchers, and policy makers. It has become clear that improved privacy setting interfaces are needed to inform users about service provider data practices and available choices. Research is needed to examine different techniques for when, how, and what to present in privacy settings to users. Service providers should deploy more usable privacy setting interfaces with privacy-friendly defaults and improved transparency. The challenge is to find the right balance between transparency and usability in privacy settings. Policy makers should call out service providers' deceptive techniques in privacy interfaces that result in many users sharing more than intended. Where such practices are illegal under existing laws, regulators should go after offending service providers.

Comparing our results with previous studies in the US, overall, we observe that our Saudi participants exhibit similar trends in privacy awareness, attitudes, preferences, concerns, and behaviors to what has been found in studies in the US. As detailed in the related work (Sect. 2), in terms of awareness, similar to US participants [1,3,11,12,39,59], Saudi participants showed *vague awareness about data saving practices and privacy settings*. Similar to what has been found in multiple studies in the US [3,11,28,39], when Saudi participants viewed the data Google saves about them, *many were surprised*. Similar to US participants, Saudi participants found it *acceptable* for a service provider to use their data for improving the services provided to them. On the other hand, they found it *unacceptable* for a service provider to use their data for ads purposes [24,35,39], and to allow third parties to use their data [35,39]. Furthermore, similar to US participants [33,39], Saudi participants tend to *prefer shorter data retention periods*. In terms of behavior, similar to US participants [11,24,35,39], Saudi participants showed *low usage of privacy settings*, and almost all "types" of behaviors that Saudi participants reported that they have taken previously, or plan to take in future, are common privacy behaviors reported by US participants [8,11]. In terms of privacy concerns, similar to what was reported by US participants in the Google context [11], many Saudi participants reported they previously had privacy concerns. However, the high contextuality of privacy concerns makes it difficult to compare across contexts, for example with studies done in the context of smart home devices [35,39,58,59]. Since our study is not a replication of any of the US studies, we suggest further research to explore whether, and to what extent, cultural differences, and other underexplored contextual factors, such as the free (e.g. Gmail account) versus paid account or device (e.g. smart home device), the service provider's name and its relevant attributes (age, reputation, popularity), affect users' concerns.

6   Google Steps to Improve Privacy Settings

During and after our study, Google took some steps that are in line with our findings. First, they updated some terms, which support our theme of "transparency" through "better presentation" that would have informed unaware users about the data saving (Section 4.4). Namely, they updated the term Data & Personalization to Data & privacy, and the term Activity Controls to History Settings.

Second, Google appears to have started launching nudges about the Activity Controls, which comes under the suggestion of "awareness" through "notifications or nudges" that would have informed unaware users about data saving. A Web & App Activity nudge was first encountered by the main researcher a while after completing the study on Aug. 2022. However, we could not replicate the nudge even if we turned on the Activity Controls. Third, Google also updated their personalized ad settings with more customization, which accommodates users' attitudes against using their data for Google partners' ads. Having said that, our paper provides other issues that may need Google's attention, such as shorter data retention periods. Moreover, despite Google updates, our results can guide other application providers.

7   Conclusion

We interviewed 30 Google personal account holders in Saudi Arabia to understand their privacy perceptions and behaviors regarding the activity data that Google saves about them. Our study focused on Google's Activity Controls. Our results showed that although the majority of participants have some level of awareness about Google's Activity Controls and data practices, many have vague awareness about them, and the majority have not used the available controls. When the participants viewed their saved data in their accounts, many were surprised as they felt they were being watched, and they lack knowledge about Google's data practices. Many participants would accept Google's use of their data to improve the services provided to them, but would not accept using their data for ad purposes. Finally, we observed that our Saudi participants exhibited similar trends and patterns in privacy awareness, attitudes, preferences, concerns, and behaviors to what has been found in studies in the US. However, our study is not a replication of any of the US studies and further research is needed to directly compare US and Saudi participants. Our results emphasize the need for: 1) improved techniques to inform users about privacy settings during account sign-up, to remind users about their settings, and to raise awareness about privacy settings; 2) improved privacy setting interfaces to reduce the costs that deter many users from changing the settings; and 3) further research to explore privacy concerns in non-Western cultures.

Acknowledgment. Eman Alashwali acknowledges the financial support of the Ibn Rushd Program at King Abdullah University of Science and Technology (KAUST). We thank Reema Bamakhramah and Sara Alashwali for their help in transcribing the interviews. We especially thank the three pilot participants for their valuable feedback. We thank all the participants for their time and valuable insights.

Appendices

A   Summary of Our Qualitative Analysis Themes for Privacy Awareness, Attitudes, Concerns, and Behaviors

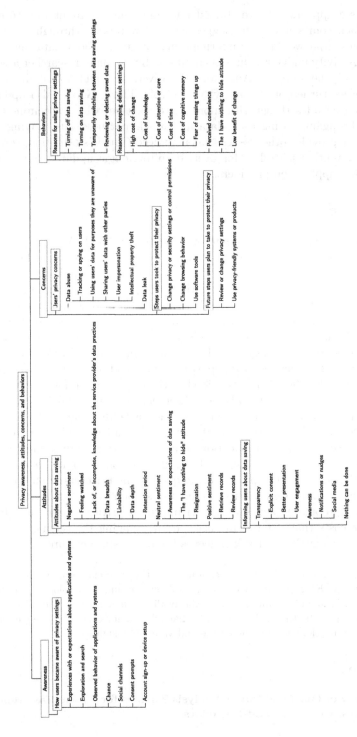

Fig. 1. Summery of themes for privacy awareness, attitudes, concerns, and behaviors distilled from our qualitative data.

References

1. Almuhimedi, H., et al.: Your location has been shared 5,398 times! A field study on mobile app privacy nudging. In: Proceedings of CHI Conference on Human Factors in Computing Systems, pp. 787–796 (2015)
2. AlSagri, H.S., AlAboodi, S.S.: Privacy awareness of online social networking in Saudi Arabia. In: Proceedings of the International Conference on Cyber Situational Awareness, Data Analytics and Assessment (CyberSA), pp. 1–6 (2015)
3. Balebako, R., Jung, J., Lu, W., Cranor, L.F., Nguyen, C.: "Little brothers watching you": raising awareness of data leaks on smartphones. In: Proceedings of Symposium on Usable Privacy and Security (SOUPS), pp. 1–11 (2013)
4. Brave Software, Inc.: Brave Browser (2022). https://brave.com. Accessed 15 Nov 2022
5. Brignull, H.: Deceptive Design (2013). https://www.deceptive.design. Accessed 14 Nov 2022
6. Brooks, J., King, N.: Doing Template Analysis: Evaluating an End of Life Care Service. SAGE Research Methods Cases Part 1 (2014)
7. Chen, Y., et al.: Demystifying hidden privacy settings in mobile apps. In: Proceedings of IEEE Symposium on Security and Privacy (SP), pp. 570–586 (2019)
8. Colnago, J., Cranor, L.F., Acquisti, A.: Is there a reverse privacy paradox? An exploratory analysis of gaps between privacy perspectives and privacy-seeking behaviors. Priv. Enh. Technol. (PoPETS) **3**(1), 455–476 (2023)
9. DuckDuckGo: DuckDuckGo (2022). https://duckduckgo.com. Accessed 25 May 2022
10. Ellison, N.B., Steinfield, C., Lampe, C.: The benefits of facebook "friends:" social capital and college students' use of online social network sites. J. Comput.-Mediat. Commun. **12**, 1143–1168 (2007)
11. Farke, F.M., Balash, D.G., Golla, M., Dürmuth, M., Aviv, A.J.: Are privacy dashboards good for end users? Evaluating user perceptions and reactions to Google's my activity. In: USENIX Security Symposium, pp. 483–500 (2021)
12. Felt, A.P., Ha, E., Egelman, S., Haney, A., Chin, E., Wagner, D.: Android permissions: user attention, comprehension, and behavior. In: Proceedings of Symposium on Usable Privacy and Security (SOUPS), pp. 1–14 (2012)
13. General Authority for Statistics (GAS): Statistical Year Book - Chapter 01 | Population & Demography (2019). https://www.stats.gov.sa/en/1007-0. Accessed 19 Aug 2023
14. General Authority for Statistics (GAS): Statistical Year Book - Chapter 04 | Education and Training (2019). https://www.stats.gov.sa/en/1010-0. Accessed 19 Aug 2023
15. General Authority for Statistics (GAS): Statistical Year Book - Chapter 15 | Technology and Communication (2019). https://www.stats.gov.sa/en/1021. Accessed 22 Aug 2023
16. Germain, T.: Google Settings Still Confusing After $85 Million Lawsuit Over How Confusing They Were (2022). https://gizmodo.com/google-location-history-setting-confusing-settlement-1849619287. Accessed 23 Nov 2022
17. GMI Blogger: Saudi Arabia Social Media Statistics 2022 (2022). https://www.globalmediainsight.com/blog/saudi-arabia-social-media-statistics/. Accessed 3 July 2022
18. Google: Google (2021). https://google.com

19. Google: Browse in Private (2022). https://support.google.com/chrome/answer/95464?hl=en&co=GENIE.Platform=Android. Accessed 25 May 2022
20. Google: The Google Phone (2022). https://pixel.google. Accessed 12 Oct 2022
21. Green, M.: Why I'm Done With Chrome (2018). https://blog.cryptographyengineering.com/2018/09/23/why-im-leaving-chrome. Accessed 15 July 2022
22. Gross, R., Acquisti, A.: Information revelation and privacy in online social networks. In: Proceedings of ACM Workshop on Privacy in the Electronic Society, pp. 71–80 (2005)
23. Habib, H., et al.: "It's a Scavenger Hunt": usability of websites' opt-out and data deletion choices. In: Proceedings of CHI Conference on Human Factors in Computing Systems, pp. 1–12 (2020)
24. Habib, H., Pearman, S., Young, E., Saxena, I., Zhang, R., Cranor, L.F.: Identifying user needs for advertising controls on Facebook. ACM Hum.-Comput. Interact. 6(CSCW1), 1–42 (2022)
25. Haque, E.U., Khan, M.M.H., Fahim, M.A.A.: The nuanced nature of trust and privacy control adoption in the context of Google. In: Proceedings of CHI Conference on Human Factors in Computing Systems (2023)
26. Haselton, T.: How to Find Out What Google Knows About You and Limit the Data it Collects (2017). https://www.cnbc.com/2017/11/20/what-does-google-know-about-me.html. Accessed 22 July 2022
27. Heyman, R., De Wolf, R., Pierson, J.: Evaluating social media privacy settings for personal and advertising purposes. Info 16(4), 18–32 (2014)
28. Jung, J., Han, S., Wetherall, D.: Short paper: enhancing mobile application permissions with runtime feedback and constraints. In: Proceedings of Workshop on Security and Privacy in Smartphones and Mobile Devices, pp. 45–50 (2012)
29. Kang, C.: Google Agrees to $392 Million Privacy Settlement With 40 States (2022). https://www.nytimes.com/2022/11/14/technology/google-privacy-settlement.html. Accessed 23 Nov 2022
30. KAU: King Abdulaziz University (2023). https://kau.edu.sa/Home.aspx
31. Kemp, S.: Digital 2022: Saudi Arabia (2022). https://datareportal.com/reports/digital-2022-saudi-arabia. Accessed 3 July 2022
32. Kerns, T.: Gmail Now has More than 1.5 Billion Active Users (2018). https://www.androidpolice.com/2018/10/26/gmail-now-1-5-billion-active-users. Accessed 19 Oct 2022
33. Khan, M.T., Hyun, M., Kanich, C., Ur, B.: Forgotten but not gone: identifying the need for longitudinal data management in cloud storage. In: Proceedings of CHI Conference on Human Factors in Computing Systems, pp. 1–12 (2018)
34. King, N.: Template Analysis (2022). https://research.hud.ac.uk/research-subjects/human-health/template-analysis/. Accessed 26 June 2022
35. Lau, J., Zimmerman, B., Schaub, F.: Alexa, are you listening? Privacy perceptions, concerns and privacy-seeking behaviors with smart speakers. ACM Hum.-Comput. Interact. 2(CSCW), 1–31 (2018)
36. LinkedIn: LinkedIn (2022). https://www.linkedin.com. Accessed 11 Oct 2022
37. Liu, Y., Gummadi, K.P., Krishnamurthy, B., Mislove, A.: Analyzing Facebook privacy settings: user expectations vs. reality. In: Proceedings of the ACM SIGCOMM Conference on Internet Measurement Conference, pp. 61–70 (2011)
38. Madejski, M., Johnson, M., Bellovin, S.M.: A study of privacy settings errors in an online social network. In: Proceedings of IEEE International Conference on Pervasive Computing and Communications Workshops, pp. 340–345 (2012)

39. Malkin, N., Deatrick, J., Tong, A., Wijesekera, P., Egelman, S., Wagner, D.: Privacy attitudes of smart speaker users. Priv. Enh. Technol. (PoPETS) **4**, 250–271 (2019)
40. McDonald, N., Schoenebeck, S., Forte, A.: Reliability and inter-rater reliability in qualitative research: norms and guidelines for CSCW and HCI practice. Proc. ACM Hum.-Comput. Interact. **3**(CSCW), 1–23 (2019)
41. Meenagh, B., Tucker, L.: Saudi Arabia's Data Protection Law Enters into Force (2023). https://www.lw.com/en/offices/admin/upload/SiteAttachments/Saudi-Arabias-data-protection-law-enters-into-force.pdf
42. Meta: Facebook (2022). https://facebook.com. Accessed 11 Oct 2022
43. Mozilla: Private Browsing (2022). https://support.mozilla.org. Accessed 25 May 2022
44. Nissenbaum, H.: Privacy as contextual integrity. Wash. L. Rev. **79**(1), 119–157 (2004)
45. OPEC: Saudi Arabia Facts and Figures (2021). https://www.opec.org/opec_web/en/about_us/169.htm. Accessed 12 Jan 2021
46. Piriform Software Ltd: CCleaner (2022). https://www.ccleaner.com/. Accessed 25 May 2022
47. Ramokapane, K.M., Mazeli, A.C., Rashid, A.: Skip, skip, skip, accept!!!: A study on the usability of smartphone manufacturer provided default features and user privacy. Priv. Enhanc. Technol. (PoPETS) **2019**(2), 209–227 (2019)
48. Rashidi, Y., Vaniea, K., Camp, L.J.: Understanding Saudis' privacy concerns when using WhatsApp. In: Proceedings of Usable Security and Privacy (USEC) (2016)
49. Read It Later, Inc: Pocket (2021). https://getpocket.com. Accessed 25 May 2022
50. Shih, F., Liccardi, I., Weitzner, D.: Privacy tipping points in smartphones privacy preferences. In: Proceedings of CHI Conference on Human Factors in Computing Systems, pp. 807–816 (2015)
51. Sotirakopoulos, A., Hawkey, K., Beznosov, K.: On the challenges in usable security lab studies: lessons learned from replicating a study on SSL warnings. In: Proceedings of Symposium on Usable Privacy and Security (SOUPS), pp. 1–18 (2011)
52. Stutzman, F., Grossy, R., Acquisti, A.: Silent listeners: the evolution of privacy and disclosure on Facebook. J. Priv. Confidentiality **4**(2), 7–41 (2012)
53. Twitter, Inc.: Twitter (2022). https://twitter.com. Accessed 11 Oct 2022
54. Wang, Y., Leon, P.G., Acquist, A., Cranor, L.F., Forget, A., Sadeh, N.: A field trial of privacy nudges for Facebook. In: Proceedings of CHI Conference on Human Factors in Computing Systems, pp. 2367–2376 (2014)
55. WhatsApp LLC: WhatsApp (2022). https://www.whatsapp.com. Accessed 11 Oct 2022
56. Wikipedia: Saudi Arabia (2021). https://en.wikipedia.org/wiki/Saudi_Arabia. Accessed 11 Mar 2021
57. Willis, L.E.: Why not privacy by default? Berkeley Tech. LJ **29**(4), 1–57 (2014)
58. Zeng, E., Mare, S., Roesner, F.: End user security & privacy concerns with smart homes. In: Proceedings of Symposium on Usable Privacy and Security (SOUPS), pp. 65–80 (2017)
59. Zheng, S., Apthorpe, N., Chetty, M., Feamster, N.: User perceptions of smart home IoT privacy. ACM Hum.-Comput. Interact. **2**(CSCW), 1–20 (2018)
60. Zoom: Zoom (2022). https://zoom.us. Accessed 11 Oct 2022

Seek and Locate? Examining the Accessibility of Cybersecurity Features

Arwa Binsedeeq[✉], Steven Furnell[✉], Xavier Carpent[✉],
and Nicholas Gervassis[✉]

School of Computer Science, University of Nottingham, Nottingham, UK
{Arwa.Binsedeeq,Steven.Furnell,Xavier.Carpent,
Nicholas.Gervassis}@nottingham.ac.uk

Abstract. The ability to use technology has become a necessity for everyone, including users with disabilities, who may encounter additional challenges. Security is one of the significant requirements that many users expect when using digital technology, hence, issues of accessibility and usability are important when considering security. Disabled users need to be provided with the same level of security functionality in an accessible and usable manner. The main aim of this study is to identify the impact of accessibility, usability, and security for users with various types of disability. This study focuses on an in-depth understanding of the nature of disabled users and assessing their interactions with technology in security and non-security contexts. An initial assessment of accessibility features in common operating systems and security features for one of them (Windows) illustrates the current situation for the devices' facilities in practice for disabled users. It then moves on to assess the user experience issues by assessing the accessibility and usability through a series of security seniors. While usability and accessibility features are certainly not new, the specific case of security features appears subpar. This might assist in ensuring that individuals with a disability are secured, and their privacy and personal information are properly protected. Researchers and technology developers need to keep taking accessible security features into consideration for those with disabilities.

Keywords: Accessibility · Cybersecurity · Accessible security · Accessibility features · Disabled Users · Accessibility Challenges · Inclusive Design · User Experience

1 Introduction

Cybersecurity is a significant element that all users should be able to expect when using technology. Achieving such inclusivity can often depend upon the usability and accessibility of the technology concerned. While usability refers to achieving a user experience that is effective, efficient, and satisfying, accessibility seeks to ensure an equivalent user experience for people with disabilities, such that they can contribute equally without barriers [1]. However, despite efforts to improve the user experience in cybersecurity,

A. Moallem (Ed.): HCII 2024, LNCS 14728, pp. 30–42, 2024.
https://doi.org/10.1007/978-3-031-61379-1_2

research on the accessibility and usability of security is lacking [2], especially for users with disabilities [3]. It is estimated that about one billion people worldwide have significant disabilities [5], and they clearly need the opportunity to protect their system and devices in an accessible and usable manner. This paper explores a challenge that may be faced at the most fundamental level, namely getting access to security features in the first instance. In doing so it exposes issues in current design/implementation of security-related user interfaces.

The paper begins by looking at the needs of disabled users and assessing their interactions with technology in security and non-security contexts. It examines the concepts of 'assistive technology' and 'accessible technology' and considers the relationship between them. It then focuses upon examining the current situation in practice for disabled users, by examining the accessibility of a range of standard security features within the most popular desktop operating system, Microsoft Windows. It is relevant to examine how easily security features can be located and used, and to view this from the perspective of the additional challenge that may be posed for those with disabilities.

2 Disability and Technology Support

The World Health Organization [6] included the following definitions in its International Classification of Impairments, Disabilities, and Handicaps to promote the proper usage of these terms:

- **Impairments** are 'concerned with abnormalities of body structure and appearance and with organ or system function resulting from any cause; in principle, impairments represent disturbances at the organ level'.
- **Disabilities** reflect 'the consequences of impairment in terms of functional performance and activity by the individual; disabilities thus represent disturbances at the level of the person'.

Disabled World [7] defines disability as 'a condition or function judged to be significantly impaired relative to the usual standard of an individual or group. The term is used to refer to individual functioning, including physical impairment, sensory impairment, cognitive impairment, intellectual impairment mental illness, and various types of chronic disease'. Disability is a complicated interaction between people and their surroundings, such that people are classified as disabled if they struggle to perform specific daily tasks because of a physical, mental, or emotional condition [8].

Globally, over one billion individuals are estimated to live with some form of disability [4]. This corresponds to approximately 15% of the global population. According to The Council of the European Union and the European Council [9], 87 million Europeans live with some form of disability. Roughly one-in-four European adults report that they have a disability. In the UK, the latest estimation indicated 14.6 million individuals had a disability in the financial year 2020 to 2021[10], representing 22% of the total population [11]. Meanwhile, the number of disabilities in the United States is increasing. According to the Centers for Disease Control and Prevention [12], 61 million adults in the United States live with a disability, and one in four adults (26%) have a disability of some form.

Disability concepts are intricately tied to accessibility, as highlighted by the International Classification of Functioning, Disability and Health (ICF) checklist [13]. Furnell et al. suggest a nuanced approach, proposing ten disability categories based on their interaction with information and communication technologies, such as Intellectual, Attention, Memory, Visual, Hearing, Competence, Life functions, Speech, Dexterity, and Walking [14].

- **Visual** relates to seeing, watching and perceptual functions.
- **Hearing** relates to hearing, listening and perceptual functions.
- **Intellectual** relates to a person's intellectual and higher-level cognitive functions, and the ability to undertake multiple tasks or a single task and to solve problems.
- **Attention** relates to the capability to hold attention and sleep, energy and drive functions, consciousness, orientation, and capability to undertake multiple tasks or a single task.
- **Memory** relates to the capability to remember.
- **Competence** relates to a person's capabilities to learn to read, write and calculate.
- **Dexterity** relates to the capability to undertake tasks involving fine hand use, mobility of joints, muscle power and muscle tone in trunk, head and neck region, shoulder region and in upper extremities, the ability to undertake multiple tasks or a single task, involuntary movements, pain, and vestibular issues.
- **Walking** relates to the capability to walk, mobility of joints, muscle power and muscle tone in trunk, pelvis, and lower extremities, involuntary movements, pain, and vestibular issues.
- **Life function** relates to heart, blood pressure, respiration and skin issues.
- **Speech** relates to a person's abilities to communicate with spoken messages, to speak, to have a conversation, know a language, and have a voice.

Technology offers a means of increasing the independence, productivity and participation of disabled people in various contexts [15]. For these reasons, technology design should grant users ease of access and use with a reasonable amount of effort regardless of their abilities based on universal design. The Disability Act 2005 defines universal design (UD) as 'the design and composition of an environment so that it may be accessed, understood, and used' [16]. There are several levels at which disability can be considered and supported in the technology context, ranging from specific technology products through to related features within wider technologies.

Assistive technology is an umbrella term that covers the systems, devices and services that relate to the delivery of assistive products and services [4]. The Assistive Technology Industry Association (ATIA) defines assistive technology as 'the products or systems that assist individuals with disabilities to perform functions and to maintain or improve functional capabilities that might otherwise be difficult or impossible' [17, 18]. These difficulties could be in speaking, typing, writing, remembering, pointing, seeing, hearing, learning, walking or other areas. Different types of disability require different assistive technologies. For instance, wheelchairs, spectacles, prostheses, hearing aids, communication aids, and memory aids are all considered assistive products. In the context of computers and smart devices, Braille keyboards, screen reader software and speech-to-text software are examples of assistive technologies. A Braille keyboard assists a blind user who can read Braille, screen reader software reads the content out aloud from digital text, and speech-to-text software enables individuals to use their voices to enter text into a word processing document. The aim of assistive technology (AT) is to enable individuals with disabilities to live healthy, independent and productive lives and to participate in education, work and social activities, thereby protecting them from isolation and poverty or from being caught in a cycle of exclusion [19].

Disabilities, Opportunities, Internetworking and Technology (DO.IT) [20] defines accessible electronic and information technology as 'technology that can be used by people with a wide range of abilities and disabilities. It incorporates the principles of universal design allowing each user to interact with the technology in their preferred way [20]. 'Access technology,' 'adaptive technology' and 'advanced technology' are all terms that refer to technologies that individuals can use to interact with their environments, and which meet their unique needs [21]. Accessible technology is the broader concept of designing and developing technology products and services either directly accessible and can be used without assistive technology, or it is compatible with standard assistive technology [20].

Accessibility features generally refer to integrated software or third-party programs that enable persons with disabilities to use common devices. While accessible technology is the overarching approach to creating inclusive technology, accessibility features are the specific functionalities embedded in a product to make it accessible to individuals with disabilities. Operating systems have adopted different approaches to supporting accessibility by including functions and resources that assist everyone in using a computer or a smart device more easily. For instance, a text-to-speech feature can read text aloud for individuals with poor vision, while a speech recognition feature will assist users with mobility impairments to control their devices with their voices. While many accessibility features are built into an operating system, others require assistive technology, either by downloading specific software or by the addition of items of hardware. The latest versions of common operating systems, whether for desktop PCs or for smartphone and tablet devices, support different types of disability through the provision of various features.

3   Exploring Routes to Security Features

This section assesses security features in operating systems focusing on Windows as an example due to it being the most commonly used operating system. Among desktop PCs worldwide, Windows is the most popular desktop OS, with a market share of slightly over 76% in June 2022 [22]. It is interesting to cover an essential point in the availability, usability and accessibility of standard security features area by focusing on how easily accessible security features are in terms of the first-level challenge of being able to locate them and then, to examine using these features when applying accessibility features.

Looking at the Windows interface, users generally have two routes by which to find and reach security features: they can go to them more directly via a search box or they can navigate to them via the menu structure. Search boxes could provide quick access as an alternative option for the multistep process. Users can access security features by searching boxes via keywords. For example, writing or dictating the keyword 'security' in the search box in the Windows menu provided access to the Windows security dashboard as illustrated in Fig. 1, which considers direct access to security features. However, searching for the exact word via a search box in the settings app can yield different results, as shown in Fig. 2, which might reflect a confusing user experience.

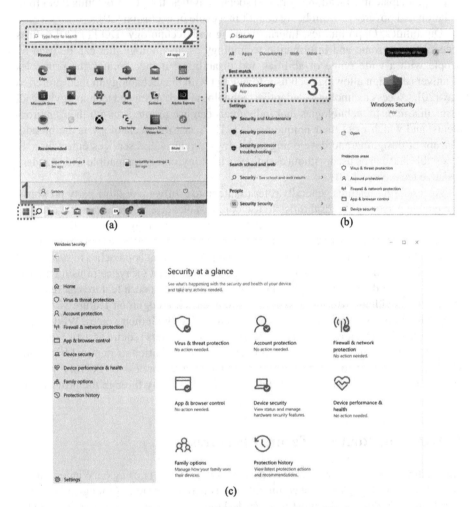

Fig. 1. Searching for the keyword 'Security' via the Windows menu

General users must have knowledge about Windows Security features and notifications to be aware, safe, and protected from cyber threats. Table 1 illustrates the number of steps that users need to manage their devices. The process for setting up Windows Security features on the Home page or exploring its dashboard requires the user to move through 4–5 steps, whereas to set up and manage providers and notifications requires 7 steps. As an illustration of what the steps look like, and the number of interfaces that are encountered on the way, Fig. 3 illustrates the five steps required to reach the Windows Security dashboard (Security at a glance), which is essentially the stage that the user is

Fig. 2. Searching for the keyword 'Security' via the Settings page

required to reach before getting access to any of the further settings. It is important to consider the number of interfaces that people with disabilities require to interact with which might affect their use and management of security features. It is important to consider the number of interfaces that people with disabilities require to interact with which might affect their use and management of security features.

While the Search boxes process can provide quicker access than a multistep navigation process, results may vary depending upon the search term and app used, which may lead to a confusing user experience. In contrast attempting to navigate to the relevant settings can often be an involved process – even if the user knows exactly where the desired feature can be found, it can sometimes take 7–8 navigation steps to get there (see Table 1). This can arguably represent a challenge for all users, but can be especially difficult for those with cognitive, motor and/or visual disabilities to undertake.

Windows Security Features might be ordered based on the importance for the security's users. It might be useful for users to be aware of them, especially the first three features including Virus Threat Protection, Account Protection and Firewall & Network Protection. In terms of Device Security, it has a similar purpose to Virus & Threat Protection features. It might be helpful to include them together. The Windows Security Features dashboard does not include the App & Browser control that might be useful for users to find in the dashboard as well. However, Device Performance & Health features often have not been related to security purposes as the other features.

Table 1. Navigational steps required to reach Windows security features

Security Features	Sub-Option	Steps	Navigational Route
Windows Security Settings	Windows Security Home Page	4 steps	Start > Settings > Privacy & Security > **Windows Security**
	Windows Security dashboard	5 steps	Start > Settings > Privacy & Security > Windows Security > Open Windows Security > **Security at a glance**
	Providers and Notification Settings	7 steps	Start > Settings > Privacy & Security > Windows Security > Open Windows Security > Settings (in the right screen side) > **Manage Notifications/Manage Providers**
Virus Threat Protection	Current threats (Quick Scan/Scan Options)	7 steps	Start > Settings > Privacy & Security > Windows Security > Virus & threat protection > Current threats > **Quick scan/Scan Options**
Account Protection	Mange Signs in Options	8 steps	Start > Settings > Privacy & Security > Windows Security > Account Protection > Windows Hello > Manage Sign-in Options > select **the sign-in methods** (Facial Recognition, Fingerprint Recognition, PIN, Security key and/or Picture Password)
Firewall & Network Protection	Type of Network	7 steps	Start > Settings > Privacy & Security > Windows Security > Firewall & Network Protection > Next, choosing network **Domain, Private and Public networks** to set up its settings
	Troubleshoot	7–8 steps	Start > Settings > Privacy & Security > Windows Security > Firewall & Network Protection > Network & Internet Troubleshoot > **Other trouble-shooters**. Next, choose from the option list and click on "Run the trouble-shooter

(continued)

Table 1. (*continued*)

Security Features	Sub-Option	Steps	Navigational Route
	Restore Defaults Firewall Settings	7 steps	Start > Settings > Privacy & Security > Windows Security > Firewall & Network Protection > **Restore Firewall to defaults**
Apps & browser control	Reputation-based protection setting	6 steps	Start > Settings > Privacy & Security > Windows Security > **Reputation-based protection setting**
Device Security	Memory Integrity	7 steps	Start > Settings > Privacy & Security > Windows Security > Device Security > Core isolation > **Memory Integrity**
	Data encryption	7 steps	Start > Settings > Privacy & Security > Windows Security > Device Security > Core isolation > **Data encryption**
Device Performance & Health	Health Report	5 steps	Start > Settings > Privacy & Security > Windows Security > **Device Performance & Health select** Storage capacity, Apps and software, Battery life and Windows Time service
Family Options	Manage Microsoft family account	6 steps or more	Start > Settings > Privacy & Security > Windows Security > Family Options **> View family settings** to go to the Family website in the user Microsoft family account
Protection History	Protection History	8 steps	Start > Settings > Privacy & Security > Windows Security > Open Windows Security > **Protection History**

It is noted from the above that searching for intended security features in the Windows box that appears after tapping the start button could be the fastest way to get to them. Nevertheless, we cannot guarantee that it is easy for those with disabilities to realize and remember those features. It is also noticed that the Windows Security Features category includes most of the security features. Separating Security from the Privacy & Security app to be just a Security app in the Windows Start menu might be a useful suggestion.

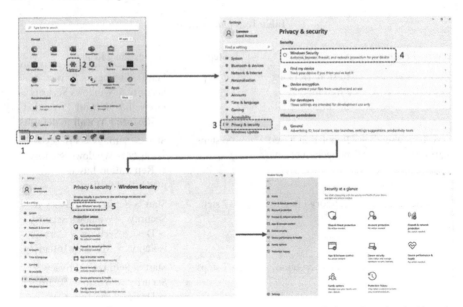

Fig. 3. Illustrating the navigational steps required to reach the Windows Security dashboard

4 Discussion

Customization privacy and security features acts as a crucial tool in ensuring that users maintain the protection of their respective devices and data. While the user interface is the route by which most people will interact with digital technology, it needs to be both accessible and easy to use (usability). Accessible security features are an essential point in terms of the first-level challenge of being able to locate them. We will discuss the potential impact of disabilities on the accessibility of security features.

Accessibility Features aim to improve the user experience by making technology more accessible, easier to use, and more convenient for everyone. Most operating systems provide direct access to accessibility settings. Basic accessibility features are included in the most recent versions of the major operating systems and are grouped by category. The categories may be related to impairment type, such as vision, hearing, and mobility/interaction. Windows follow this type of classification. Users can set these features according to their own needs and preferences. Despite the accessibility features efforts, users with impairments might experience security barriers in their everyday use. These challenges might vary from potential vulnerabilities in cybersecurity safeguards to difficulty in accessing security features that might not be entirely fully aligned with the needs of people with disabilities.

Windows Security provides the latest versions of protection techniques that are downloaded automatically to increase safety, security, and protection from threats. Continuously scanning for malware, viruses, and security threats [23], users can also manually scan, update, and manage Virus and Threat Protection features based on their preferences. This includes running quick or advanced scans, excluding files or apps from Firewall & Network Protection, and adjusting other features, typically requiring seven steps (see

Table 1). Configuring Common steps include configuring Firewall & Network settings, troubleshooting network issues, and restoring firewall settings to defaults, followed by accessing Firewall Notification settings through a similar process.

In terms of authentication mechanisms, Windows offers six different sign-in options including facial and fingerprint recognitions, security key[1], PIN, password and picture password[2]. Users can sign-in to their devices, apps, networks, and online services using preferences sign-in options. This feature assists users who require safe, fast and more secure access to protect their authentication or who might have difficulty in remembering passwords. Signing-in options may be a common task, it can pose significant challenges for users with disabilities who must navigate through a sequence of seven steps to select and manage their sign-in options. This process can be further complicated by the need for configuration, as outlined in Table 1. Users might rely on others to configure security options to expedite the sign-in process. This dependency could potentially introduce security issues for users with disabilities.

Configuring all Windows Security features and their options does not have time limits and do not seem challenging by using these features settings. Typically, it only requires turning them on or off to set up their features, with some more specific processes related to certain features, such as the sign-in options process. However, accessing these feature settings might require extra effort for users with mobility, vision, and cognitive impairment. Ensuring accessibility to these features can pose challenges for individuals with disabilities. While able-bodied users can easily discern hyperlinks and navigate interfaces, users with disabilities may encounter difficulties, requiring more time to navigate efficiently. The resulting time, speed and precision with which users can perform tasks that are operating with a timeout period or require fine movement, in terms of mobility at the level of dexterity, influence their usability, hindering accessibility for users who already face significant barriers.

The navigation paths required to access various Windows security features can be complex and time-consuming. This can pose a challenge for people with different types of impairments as it can be difficult to discover and navigate these paths. For individuals with certain impairments, it can be particularly hard to access these features due to the several steps required. While navigation challenges are common in digital interfaces, it becomes even more critical to consider accessibility in security features, especially for people with disabilities. Navigational difficulties can impact the overall user experience, but when combined with security elements, they may significantly affect the safety and privacy of users, particularly those with disabilities.

Windows Security features have the potential to impact users with impairments, particularly in relation to accessibility features. Computer systems commonly illustrate icons within the security features and notification messages that can be recognized easily

---

[1] A security key is a hardware tool that the user can use instead of a username and password to sign-in. There are various security keys including USB keys that can plug into a computer or Near Field Communication (NFC) keys that can tap on devices with associated readers such as smartphones or access cards.

[2] A picture password is a feature introduced that allows the user to draw three different gestures on any chosen image and then use those gestures as a password. The gesture can be any combination of circles, straight lines, and taps.

to present a level of safety and ensure that users can quickly understand the severity of the situation and take appropriate action. The color and shape of these icons differ depending on the specific needs and security context. Windows security features present a level of safety by status icons as follows: green for good security status with no recommended actions, yellow for a safety recommendation, and red for a warning that requires immediate attention.

Individuals with visual impairments, including those who are blind or color blind, may face difficulties in identifying the security status of a device due to the security icons used. The status icons, such as green, yellow, and red, may not be discernible to them. For instance, blind users rely on Narrator, which is a text-to-speech feature. While it can read instructions related to the status of the device, it cannot identify the level of safety through status icons. Therefore, they have to move the pointer on every option to know the status. Additionally, when verifying a password, only an SMS code is required to be sent, which can be challenging for some individuals with vision impairment. Moreover, Dictation or voice typing is a feature that enables users to input text by speaking instead of typing. However, the user can only use voice typing for dictation purposes once the system has been launched. This can be challenging for some disabilities, including vision and mobility impairments.

It is less likely for hearing impairment to affect security decisions compared to other disabilities such as vision, cognitive, and mobility impairments. However, hearing impairment can still pose some challenges when it comes to security. For instance, warning sounds need to be adjusted in pitch and duration to ensure that even those with mild or moderate hearing impairments can hear them. This is especially important when systems or software use audio signals to alert users about security-related events. Relying solely on audio warnings may not be enough. To address this, accessibility features are available to allow users to customize audio notifications. For example, on Windows, users can choose to use visual cues instead of audio notifications by selecting options such as flashing the title bar of the active window, flashing the active window, or flashing the entire screen. Nonetheless, some audio-only alerts are still necessary, such as when a USB drive is inserted or removed, for desktop mail notifications, low or urgent battery alerts, or when a Windows system error occurs. Hearing problems should not prevent users from receiving notifications. Therefore, setting up visual cues, such as flashing instead of sound, can assist users in staying alert and updated.

5 Conclusions and Recommendations

Individuals with disabilities may encounter challenges while using technology to be secure. It is important to ensure that technologies provide effective tools, functions and features to facilitate accessibility and usability for people with disabilities without conceding their security. Able users may find it easy to access features that involve multiple steps, yet this could be challenging for disabled users. While searching box could be a quick alternative, it might not be the best option in terms of the intended user experience. Although similar accessibility concerns can also be levelled at the provision of non-security features within the OS, the *impact* of encountering difficulties in accessing them is different. In this case, the difficulty in locating and reaching cybersecurity functionality has the potential to mean that it is not accessed as readily, with the user's protection being less suitably configured as a result. In short, it is not that cybersecurity itself is affecting accessibility, but rather that accessibility is potentially affecting the resultant cybersecurity.

Overall, while usability and accessibility features are certainly not new, the specific case of security features appears sub-par. Researchers and technology developers need to keep taking accessible security features into consideration for those with disabilities. It is crucial to consider that security features are easy to find and use for people with different abilities. Simplifying navigation paths and providing alternative ways of interaction can significantly improve the accessibility of security settings for individuals with disabilities. The design of security features interfaces should not only be clear and understandable but also accessible in easier ways, accommodating users with different disabilities, including those with vision, mobility, cognitive, or learning impairments. Inclusive design principles for accessible security features should consider the diverse needs of all users, including those with disabilities. While this paper has offered an examination of common security features in a single operating system, there may be a broader range of security issues in other security contexts. As such, a more comprehensive examination is necessary.

References

1. Henry, S.L., Abou-Zahra, S., White, K.: Accessibility, Usability, and Inclusion. W3C (2016). https://www.w3.org/WAI/fundamentals/accessibility-usability-inclusion/
2. Ronna, N., Scollan, R.I.: Usability of biometric authentication methods for citizens with disabilities (2019)
3. Andrew, S., et al. A review of literature on accessibility and authentication techniques. In: Proceedings of the 22nd International ACM SIGACCESS Conference on Computers and Accessibility (2020)
4. World Health Organisation. Disability and health (2021). https://www.who.int/news-room/fact-sheets/detail/disability-and-health. Accessed 5 Aug 2022
5. World Health Organisation. Disability (2023). https://www.who.int/news-room/fact-sheets/detail/disability-and-health
6. World Health Organization, International classification of impairments, disabilities, and handicaps: a manual of classification relating to the consequences of disease, published in accordance with resolution WHA29. 35 of the Twenty-ninth World Health Assembly, May 1976. World Health Organization (1980)
7. Disabled World Disabilities: Definition, Types and Models of Disability (2022). https://www.disabled-world.com/disability/types/
8. Young, N.A.: Childhood disability in the United States. 2019 (2021)
9. The Council of the European Union and the European Council. Infographic - Disability in the EU: facts and figures (2022). https://www.consilium.europa.eu/en/infographics/disability-eu-facts-figures/
10. GOV.UK. National statistics Family Resources Survey: financial year 2020 to 2021 (2022). https://www.gov.uk/government/statistics/family-resources-survey-financial-year-2020-to-2021
11. UK Parliament. UK disability statistics: Prevalence and life experiences (2022). https://commonslibrary.parliament.uk/research-briefings/cbp-9602/

12. Centers for Disease Control and Prevention. Disability Impacts All of Us (2022). https://www.cdc.gov/ncbddd/disabilityandhealth/infographic-disability-impacts-all.html

13. World Health Organisation, ICF CHECKLIST Version 2.1a, Clinician Form for International Classification of Functioning, Disability and Health. WHO (2003)

14. Furnell, S., Helkala, K., Woods, N.: Disadvantaged by disability: examining the accessibility of cyber security. In: Antona, M., Stephanidis, C. (eds.) HCII 2021. LNCS, vol. 12768, pp. 197–212. Springer, Cham (2021). https://doi.org/10.1007/978-3-030-78092-0_13

15. Burgstahler, S., et al.: Computer and cell phone access for individuals with mobility impairments: an overview and case studies. NeuroRehabilitation **28**, 183–197 (2011)

16. National Disability Authority (NDA). What is Universal Design (2017). https://universaldesign.ie/What-is-Universal-Design/The-7-Principles/#p1

17. Assistive Technology Industry Association (ATiA). What is AT? (n.d.). https://www.atia.org/home/at-resources/what-is-at/

18. GOV.UK, Guidance Assistive technology: definition and safe use (2021)

19. World Health Organisation. Assistive technology (2018). https://www.who.int/news-room/fact-sheets/detail/assistive-technology

20. Organisation Disabilities Opportunities Internetworking and Technology (DO.IT). What is accessible electronic and information technology? (2013). https://www.washington.edu/doit/what-accessible-electronic-and-information-technology?1110=

21. SNOW. Assistive & Accessible Technology (n.d.). https://snow.idrc.ocadu.ca/assistive-technology-2/

22. Statista, Global market share held by operating systems for desktop PCs, from January 2013 to June 2022 (2022)

23. Microsoft. Stay protected with Windows Security (n.d.). https://support.microsoft.com/en-us/windows/stay-protected-with-windows-security-2ae0363d-0ada-c064-8b56-6a39afb6a963

Enhancing Cyber Hygiene and Literacy via Interactive Mini-games

Cameron Gray$^{(\boxtimes)}$ ⓘ and Steven Furnell$^{(\boxtimes)}$ ⓘ

School of Computer Science, University of Nottingham, Nottingham, UK
graycameron@btinternet.com, steven.furnell@nottingham.ac.uk

Abstract. Cyber threats are an increasingly reality for technology users in day-to-day use. As such, it is important to teach people how to protect themselves and follow good cyber security practice. However, while many awareness-raising materials and resources can be found, they run the risk of being read and forgotten rather than providing an engaging context that users will return to. This paper discusses the design, implementation and initial evaluation of a mobile app that seeks to promote cyber hygiene and security principles and practices via a series of mini-games. Each is focused upon an issue of relevance to end-users (e.g. password selection, phishing avoidance, and safe use of networks), and seeks to present learning content via short, interactive experiences. The resulting app is realized in prototype form, with associated practical evaluation suggesting positive findings in terms of user performance and feedback.

Keywords: Cyber Awareness · Cyber Hygiene · Gamification

1 Introduction

Alongside the increasing ubiquity of connected technologies more people are falling victim to cybercrime. Looking at data from Surfshark, tracking the situation in the two decades from 2001 to 2022, the online crime victim count increased by 16 times (from 6 to 91 victims per hour) and related financial losses have grown 570-fold (from around $2K to almost $1.2M losses per hour). In total, it is suggested that cybercrime claimed at over 7.3 million victims and over $36 billion in losses over the 22-year period [1]. Such findings help to suggest why all users of digital devices and services should now have at least a baseline level of cyber security to help protect data and safeguard against online threats. In response to this concern, this paper presents details of a mobile app-based approach to offering small educational tasks which aims to enhance the process of learning around core cyber security topics. The app presents activities in a gamified manner, and enables users to track and monitor their progress across the different topics. The intention is to fill a gap between the currently options of passive engagement with cyber awareness material and practical experiences on their own devices, with the aim of providing an engaging way to learn cyber security that the user will come back to.

© The Author(s), under exclusive license to Springer Nature Switzerland AG 2024
A. Moallem (Ed.): HCII 2024, LNCS 14728, pp. 43–52, 2024.
https://doi.org/10.1007/978-3-031-61379-1_3

2 Background

The need for cyber awareness and good practice amongst users is, of course, already well-recognized. However, while a range of related information sources exist that provide the core advice and recommendations (e.g. the CyberAware guidance from the UK's National Cyber Security Centre [2] and Stay Safe Online guidance in the US [3]), the availability of information does not ensure that people will come into contact or engage with it. A recent study by Bach [4] suggested that most participants had a basic knowledge of cyber security, but not enough to avoid them still being vulnerable to a cyber-attack. All participants agreed that their knowledge is at the level it is because of their own (limited) priority for learning better cyber security. Meanwhile, a study by Oveh and Aziken [5] indicated that even if someone was previously the victim of social engineering it was an insufficient as a learning experience to prevent it happening again. All of this again reinforces the notion that end users can be a weak link when it comes to cyber security, but at the same time relatively little is available to enable users to properly understand or assess their own level of literacy. Users arguably need the ability to educate themselves in a way that is suitable for their own competency level, whilst also being engaged enough to keep learning and eventually develop a good level of cyber security.

Improving user awareness and practices has the potential to offer benefits in different contexts. Most obviously is for them as individual users, as they will be better positioned to protect their own devices, systems and data from potential harms. However, for those users also using IT in a workplace context, the benefits are likely to be shared by their employers (who may find that more cyber-aware users are at less risk of causing unintentional issues or being exploited by attackers). This is particularly relevant in the situations where the organizations themselves may not be doing enough to promote cyber security awareness and good practice locally, and may be relying upon users to already know the basics. Such a lack of related support continues to be evidenced in related surveys. For example, the UK Cyber Security Breaches Survey [6] reports that only 18% of the 2,263 businesses surveyed had provided their general staff with training or awareness raising sessions on cyber security in the last 12 months (a picture that has remained relatively consistent since the survey series first started in 2016).

The above clearly suggests a need for further support, but the key consideration is how the knowledge is delivered to the user. Simply making information available is not sufficient, as many people do not want to learn better cyber security practices. This study considers the use of gamified learning as means to get past this and increase the chances of users wanting to learn. Just as the need for awareness is long recognized, so too is the potential for related gamification. For example, an early and widely cited example is the Anti-Phishing Phil game that sought to help users distinguish between safe and suspect web addresses [7]. Although it is now possible to find a variety of modern cyber security-themed games, including those that exist in the form of mobile apps, they tend to take the form of long form adventure and strategy style games, requiring associated time investment from players (examples being the US Cybersecurity & Infrastructure Security Agency's 'Defend the Crown' game for Android[1], the 'Enter – IT Security

---

[1] See https://www.cisa.gov/cybersecurity-games.

Game' app for iOS[2]) or arcade style games such as the National Cyber Security Centre's 'Cyber Sprinters'[3] (where the experience is cyber security themed but arguably has less educational content). However, looking styles of gamified learning in other domains (e.g. Duolingo, which uses gamification to teach new languages), it is considered that a similar approach could be relevant in cyber security and that principles from one context could be equally valuable in another. For example, a study of the effectiveness of the Duolingo approach has suggested that the streak mechanic "helps users enhance their regular learning activity into serious gaming activity" [8], and that for more advanced users the streak improves motivation once the attractiveness of the badge mechanic depletes. This shows that using gamified learning can increase motivation to learn with the tool and use it regularly, which is exactly what is needed as most people do not prioritize improving their cyber skills. In the UK, the aforementioned Cyber Aware website from the National Cyber Security Centre provides relevant advice and tips for how to stay secure when using technology and the internet [2]. However, this is done in mostly by means of written articles and some videos. There is little in terms of assessment of the users understanding or an engaging way to learn the content. As such, users would arguably benefit from a more fun and interactive experience, particularly if it promoted cyber security awareness to them on a more frequent and regular basis.

3 Prototype Implementation

The above points have motivated the current work to the design, implementation, and evaluation of a prototype mobile app to support cyber security literacy, which in turn aims to encourage and enable users in following good cyber hygiene practices. The specific objectives addressed in pursuit of the aim were:

- To design a series of engaging activities that users could perform in order to build and practice their knowledge of cyber security
- To design a reward/recognition system that enables users to make progress and encourages them to return to the app
- To implement the activity and reward approaches within a practical app

The design of the app began by identifying the cyber security/hygiene topics that needed to be covered. For the purposes of the prototype, the themes selected were password selection, phishing awareness, safe use of Wi-Fi and removable devices. The next step was then to determine what the user was intended to learn for each topic, and how the related lesson can be presented in a gamified activity that is simple enough for the average user to pick it up and understand without prior knowledge of cyber security.

Once the ideas were finalized, storyboard-style diagrams were created for how the activities were anticipated to appear and operate. These were further refined prior to the actual app development. An example of one of the resulting storyboard (in this case relating the mini-game for password selection) is illustrated in Fig. 1. The home screen of the app is shown on the righthand side of the figure, and the storyboard illustrates

---

[2] See https://apps.apple.com/us/app/enter-it-security-game/id1250407023.

[3] See https://www.ncsc.gov.uk/training/ncsc-cyber-security-for-young-people-english-scorm-v2/index.html.

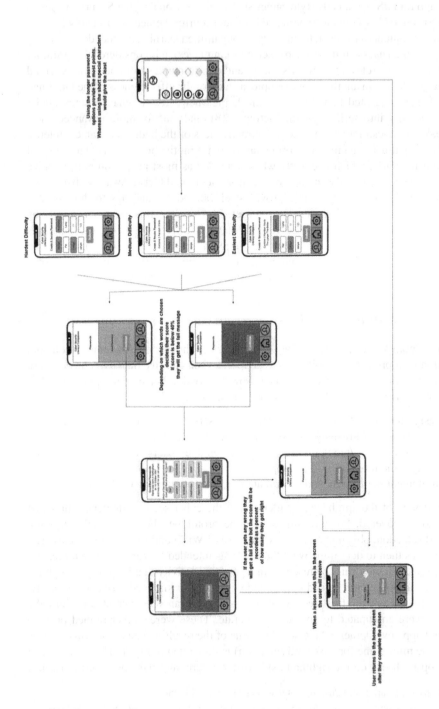

Fig. 1. Storyboard for password exercises

different levels of difficulty available in the game, followed by the forms of feedback that the user would receive based upon the choices they made.

The prototype was implemented as an Android app and intended as a gamified challenge that users can engage with for short periods, and be encouraged to return to on the basis of daily scores and challenges. As illustrated in Fig. 2, which depicts the home screen of the app, the current activities are grouped into several categories relevant to cyber threats and related hygiene practices for end-users – specifically relating to the use of Wi-Fi, Passwords, and Removable Devices, and awareness of Phishing. Users can select one of these themes to learn about a topic of their choice, or if can scroll down and use the shuffle button which will pick a lesson at random. Meanwhile, the top area of the screen shows streak and gold badge counters, enabling users to track progress and achievements.

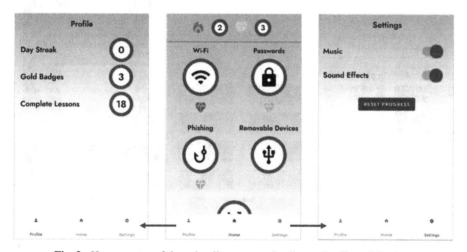

Fig. 2. Home screen of the cyber literacy app, leading to Profile and Settings

A variety of games have been designed and implemented for the prototype. Example screenshots from each of these are presented in Fig. 3, and outlined below (with the numbering of the list items matching the screenshots in the figure):

1. **Password Creator** – In this exercise the user learns how to make a good password. The approach is based upon the UK NCSC's guidance, following the principle of choosing three random words [9]. The user is offered sets of words that they may combine for this purpose. Their challenge is to choose appropriate combinations while avoiding weaker/obvious candidates.

2. **Password Chooser** – Here the user is made aware of the problems of making passwords related to their personal information. They are given a brief scenario about a character, and then a set of potential password options for that character to choose from. They need to mark the options as good or bad, depending upon whether they are linkable to the character concerned (and therefore represent weaker choices as they would be guessable or predictable).

3. **Phishing Hooks** – In this exercise the user learns what to look for in a phishing scam to determine if it is legitimate or not. They are presented with a message and various hotspot sections within it. For each hotspot, they need to judge if it is normal, potentially suspicious, or definitely phishing.
4. **Phishing Spotter** – Following on from the previous exercise, the user can apply what they have learned and attempt to identify phishing scams. They are presented with a series of candidate messages and asked to judge if they appear to be genuine or phishing.
5. **Wi-Fi Etiquette** – In this exercise the user learns about good practice when connecting to and using the internet. It takes the form of a multiple-choice quiz, based on

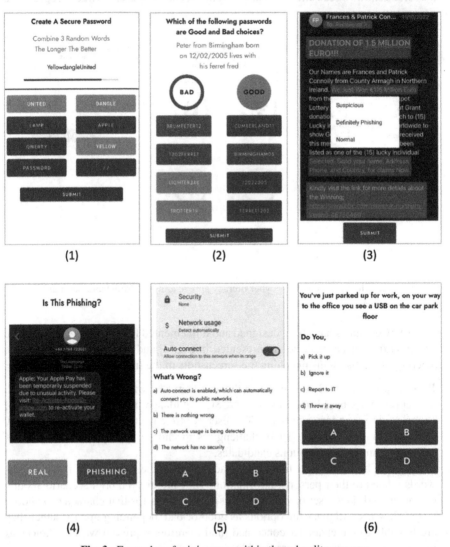

Fig. 3. Examples of mini-games within the cyber literacy app

screenshots related to interfaces and dialogues encountered during everyday Wi-Fi use. The user's task is to identify what – if anything - is wrong in the presented situation. Questions are presented in a random order, and the correct answers are also re-ordered between attempts.

6. **Text Adventure** – The focus of this exercise is around awareness of removable media risks and human curiosity, as well as to determine how the user may responds in difficult situations. The activity uses a scenario-based text adventure. There are 36 screens for different outcomes, as each time the user makes a choice it branches off and results in a different ending. The user starts the game with a description of a situation they are in and must decide which action to take by clicking the corresponding button. At the start of the game the users score is 50, and each choice can affect it (increasing due to a good choice, no change for an okay choice, or down for a bad decision). The user continues their journey until they reach one of the multiple endings. If the user makes bad choices early on, they are faced with later routes that enable them to admit or conceal their mistake, thereby introducing a side lesson the aims to encourage users to seek help and report issues where appropriate.

Each game is accompanied by an optional tutorial feature for new players, and ends with the award of a score that counts toward the user's overall status in the app.

4 Evaluation

The app was exposed to initial evaluation via a small-scale trial involving 12 players. This looked at user performance in the app (e.g. the number of mistakes made, the number of times that they needed to request help, the time taken to complete a set of activities), as well as their engagement with it and feedback about the user experience.

The number of participants was limited to 12 as a consequence of the project time-frame, and also to enable a sample group that could be utilized for two rounds of evaluation (such that findings and feedback from the first round could be used as the basis for changes and enhancements to the app). There was also an explicit intention to involve a mix of genders and backgrounds, in order to get an indication of the app's applicability to different audiences. The resulting 12 participants were comprised as follows:

- 3 males studying computer science or having an IT background.
- 3 males from a non-IT background.
- 3 females studying computer science or having an IT background.
- 3 females from a non-IT background

Participants were asked about their familiarity with cyber security, how much they prioritized it, and the extent to which they considered themselves to be cyber secure. Each aspect was rated on a 5-point scale. Unsurprisingly those from a computing background tended to rate themselves higher (averaging 3/5 compared to 2/5 for the non-IT users). Additionally, the male users in both groups tended to rate themselves a point higher the females.

Two rounds of testing were conducted, with the findings from the initial round being used to inform changes to the app before undertaking the second round. The user experience in each round was evaluated from several perspectives, based upon the metrics listed in Table 1. The performance metrics were recorded by the researcher during each session, while the feedback aspects were collected from each participant after each round (with the factors each rated on a 1–5 scale, where 1 was poor and 5 was excellent). The number of mistakes and the times the users asked for help was tracked in order to give an indication of how intuitive the app design was. Users with a computing background were expected to ask for less help, as they are more experienced in terms of using the technology and potentially more familiar with the issues being presented in the games. Areas in which users made mistakes, needed help, or slowed down provided indications of aspects that could potentially be refined,

Table 1. Evaluation metrics

Performance	User feedback
Mistakes made	Ease of navigation
Requests for help	Ease of understanding
Time taken	Level of engagement
	Level of enjoyment
	Potential to improve cyber skills
	Likelihood to play again

As indicted in Table 2, most of the mistakes were made by users from non-computing backgrounds (all users from non-IT backgrounds made at least one mistake, whereas only half the users from computing backgrounds made one). Following improvements to the app, in round 2, five users made no mistakes at all (compared to 3 in round 1). The male participants were generally quicker, but also seemed more aware of the timer and so wanted to get through the tasks more quickly, potentially rushing. As expected, the users with computing background were quicker overall across both rounds.

Table 2. Average performance metrics from 12 participants

Round	Number of mistakes	Requests for help	Time taken
1	1.9	1.3	7 m 12 s
2	1.3	0.8	6 m 12 s

In terms of the users' opinions and related ratings about the use of the app, the findings across the two rounds are presented in Table 3. As can be seen, all of the results improve from the first to second round, and the final scores are all on the upper side of the scale. The ones that stand out as more challenging are the level of enjoyment and the likelihood of playing again, which are clearly factors in which the app needs to succeed if it is to fulfil the aim of providing a gamified experience. At the same time, in the context of an initial prototype these are still encouraging results (particularly given that the project delivered multiple games and the overall app framework within a relatively short timeframe, without the opportunity to test and trial each game concept individually). As such, it is likely that they could be improved upon via more focused work that looked in more detail at the game dynamics for each of the mini-games, and incorporated support from more specialist expertise in this aspect. At the same time, it can also be observed that the participants from an IT background were already more positively disposed toward these aspects, with both males and females rating the likelihood of playing again in the 3 to 3.5 range. Meanwhile, males from both IT and non-IT backgrounds also tended to find the app more enjoyable than the female participants, with a collective average of 3.5.

Table 3. Average user feedback metrics from 12 participants

Round	Ease of navigation	Ease of understanding	Level of engagement	Level of enjoyment	Potential to improve cyber skills	Likelihood to play again
1	4.0	3.8	2.8	2.7	3.2	2.3
2	4.5	4.4	3.4	3.1	3.7	2.8

The overall results suggested that the app and underlying games were usable and had potential to assist users in developing their cyber security skills. However, there is clearly still potential for further development and refinement. Key themes that emerged from discussion with participants following the 2nd round of testing suggested areas for future enhancement of the app:

- **Additional in-game feedback:** Some of the comments indicated that they would like to have received better, more detailed feedback when they get a question/game wrong, so that they can understand it better and learn for next time.
- **More content/variety:** There were a few comments about having more variety of the games, by increasing the pool of potentially answers/questions featured in the games, as most of the games currently in the app have a level of randomness with either the order questions are asked, or the answers they can pick are selected randomly from a pool of answers. This feedback also referred to just more content generally, so more different games for each of the topics, or even new topics for the user to pick from.
- **Teach before testing:** Teaching the content before the users are tested on it was an initial idea when originally creating the app, but as the app is meant to be used in short bursts it was considered more appropriate for the games to simply be played as the basis from which to learn. Just reading about a cyber security concept is not as engaging as playing a game where you create passwords. However, recognizing that some users requested it, such a feature could be added as an optional part of the app as further reference for those that want it.

It is worth noting that the first two points would in any case be key considerations in taking the app forward from the existing prototype stage.

5 Conclusions

Cyber security literacy and hygiene practices are a key requirement for modern IT users, and yet often represent an area of exposure. Offering a route that enables users to learn and practice concepts through a gamified mobile app represents a further means by which to engage users with a topic that they may not typically consider attractive.

The overall study was considered to be successful in terms of realizing an effective prototype implementation of the cyber literacy app, and receiving the positive feedback from initial use. This provides a relevant foundation for further development.

In conclusion the app had the aim of presenting educational material in a practical and fun way, and from which users can learn better cyber security practices, whilst being able to track and monitor their progress and improvement across different topics. The testing has suggested that even at the prototype level, the app achieves this goal with a subset of users, and all feel that it could help people like them and other members of the public to improve cyber literacy.

References

1. Surfshark. Cybercrime statistics. https://surfshark.com/research/data-breach-impact/statistics. Accessed 27 Jan 2024
2. NCSC. Cyber Aware. National Cyber Security Centre. https://www.ncsc.gov.uk/cyberaware/home. Accessed 27 Jan 2024
3. Online Safety Basics. National Cybersecurity Alliance (2022). https://staysafeonline.org/resources/online-safety-basics/. Accessed 26 May 2022
4. Bach, E.: The impact of digital literacy on the cyber security of digital citizens. In: 83rd International Scientific Conference on Economic and Social Development, Varazdin, 2–3 June 2022, pp. 196–204 (2022)
5. Oveh, R.O., Aziken, G.O.: Mitigating social engineering attack: a focus on the weak human link. In: 5th Information Technology for Education and Development (ITED), Abuja, Nigeria, pp. 1–4 (2022). https://doi.org/10.1109/ITED56637.2022.10051202
6. DSIT: Cyber security breaches survey 2023 - Official Statistics. Department for Science, Innovation & Technology (2023). https://www.gov.uk/government/statistics/cyber-security-breaches-survey-2023/cyber-security-breaches-survey-2023
7. Sheng, S., et al.: Anti-phishing phil: the design and evaluation of a game that teaches people not to fall for phish. In: Proceedings of the 3rd Symposium on Usable Privacy and Security (SOUPS 2007), pp. 88–99. Association for Computing Machinery, New York (2007). https://doi.org/10.1145/1280680.1280692
8. Huynh, D., Zuo, L., Iida, H.: An assessment of game elements in language-learning platform Duolingo. In: 4th International Conference on Computer and Information Sciences (ICCOINS), Kuala Lumpur, Malaysia, pp. 1–4 (2018). https://doi.org/10.1109/ICCOINS.2018.8510568
9. McCormack, I.: Three random words or #thinkrandom, Blog post. National Cyber Security Centre (2016). https://www.ncsc.gov.uk/blog-post/three-random-words-or-thinkrandom-0. Accessed 27 Oct 2016

Hidden in Onboarding: Cyber Hygiene Training and Assessment

Alex Katsarakes[1]([✉]), Thomas Morris[2], and Jeremiah D. Still[1]

[1] Old Dominion University, Norfolk, VA 23529, USA
{ekats002,jstill}@odu.edu
[2] Eastern Kentucky University, Richmond, KY 40475, USA

Abstract. End-users are our first line of defense against cyber-attacks. The U.S. government has endorsed training videos that teach cyber hygiene best practices, aiming to harden our defenses. In this pilot study, we explored the effectiveness of those security training videos under the cover of an employee onboarding scenario and general computer competency questions. Masking the cybersecurity focus of this study was critical to prevent unnatural heightened vigilance. For example, increased awareness of cybersecurity threats can artificially increase sensitivity to phishing emails or identify malicious links. Participants' cyber hygiene knowledge was assessed by pre- and post-tests after receiving the training. In addition, we measured behavioral onboarding task performance based on the training learning objectives. Our findings showed a lack of improvement in quiz knowledge and onboarding security activities after exposure to the training. We echo others in the literature by claiming the need for a paradigm shift in how traditional cybersecurity training is taught and how success is measured.

Keywords: Cybersecurity · Human Factors · Training

1 Introduction

1.1 Current State of Cyber

The prevention of cyberattacks has become a critical concern for organizations worldwide [1]. Cybersecurity attacks have only continued to rise in recent years, with organizations, individuals, and critical infrastructure remaining vulnerable to various threats [2]. The consequences of successful breaches, including loss of productivity, financial destruction, and damage to institutional credibility, underscore the potential severity of the issue [3].

Many cyber incidents are attributed to vulnerabilities associated with human actors, exemplifying the importance of end-user competency in preventing attacks [4, 5]. Users tend to overestimate their cybersecurity expertise and abilities [4], leading to an underestimation of risk. Prior cyber hygiene research has shown that users' self-perception of their expertise in home network cybersecurity is higher than their practical task performance scores [6]. As the Home Computing (HC) environment blends with organizational resources [7], assets become both personal and institutional. Within this new techno-logical ecosystem, lack of cyber hygiene abilities can cost an individual as well as their employer. It is not merely a matter of personal security; it translates into a substantial risk factor for businesses and, by extension, the broader economy. For example, hack-ers demanded a $4.4 million ransom during the 2021 Colonial Pipeline Co. attack [8]. The effects of this attack rippled throughout the US economy, by causing a fuel short-age. Hackers entered Colonial Pipeline Co.'s networks through a compromised Virtual Private Network (VPN) account, which was created to allow employees to access the company's computer network remotely from their home network. A single employee's poor cyber hygiene practices caused significant damage to the company and the U.S. economy. This recent crisis also demonstrates the progression beyond the Bring-Your-Own-Device (BYOD) strategy to a hybrid Bring-Your-Own-Network (BYON) model. The current merge of the HC ecosystem with organizational computing will generate a unique set of human-centered cybersecurity challenges [7].

To address these challenges, cyber defenders are teaching end-users to follow best practices in cyber hygiene [9]. This focus is driven, in part, by the realization that many contemporary cybersecurity threats cannot be entirely mitigated via technological avenues [10, 11]. With most incidents being caused by user error, those interested in avoiding breaches must focus on the human elements of cyber hygiene and information security [4, 11].

The traditional approach taken by cybersecurity training programs is generally referred to as *awareness* [12, 13]. Particularly prevalent in government-led initiatives, these security campaigns target improving cyber hygiene behaviors through compre-hensive education and heightened awareness of potential threats [13]. These programs operate assuming that end users who are aware of cybersecurity risks and provided with information on how to subvert them will change their behavior accordingly [13]. While these campaigns play an important role in cybersecurity training, their effectiveness has been scrutinized. The assumption that providing information alone will induce change has limitations, with many of these programs failing to generate a desirable impact [11, 14]. As Ghazvini and Shukur [15] put it quite concisely, "Even though the number of information security awareness training programs are growing progressively, there is inadequate evidence to verify their effectiveness and impact on daily activities in a work environment" (p. 1). While it is important to ensure that end-users are aware of potential cyber threats, being informed is only an initial step to generating real modifications in behavior [14, 16] Actual change requires more than providing information about risks and prevention; individuals must be able to comprehend the information and be motivated to actively apply the advised practices [17]. Current approaches fall short in multiple aspects, often producing minimal practical outcomes for trainees and organizations [18]. Training users in cyber hygiene competency is essential to preventing cyber-attacks on organizations and institutions, but the field has been unable to determine the optimal approach [9].

1.2 Training Types

In the dynamic landscape of cybersecurity training, an array of methods are employed to reinforce cyber hygiene behaviors and bolster awareness. Some of the most common techniques include game-based, presentation-based, simulation-based, video-based, text-based, and discussion-based [9]. Game-based training involves the gamification of learning, creating interactive scenarios that engage participants in immersive experiences to enhance comprehension [2]. Conventional presentation-based training relies on conveying crucial cybersecurity information through presentations such as slideshows, lectures, or other multimedia formats to deliver key concepts and demonstrate best practices [2]. Simulation-based training replicates real-world cyber threats and scenarios, allowing participants to actively engage with simulated incidents and develop practical skills in response and mitigation [16]. Video-based training employs visual content, such as educational videos or documentaries, to communicate cybersecurity concepts [2]. Text-based training conveys cybersecurity information through written materials, such as documents and manuals designed to educate end-users on security practices and potential threats [9]. Discussion-based training fosters interaction and dialogue among participants, utilizing group discussions, case studies, and collaborative problem-solving sessions to facilitate the exchange of insights [9]. The continual exploration of these diverse training methods and the generation of new ones reflects ongoing efforts to discover effective approaches for developing robust cyber hygiene practices among end-users.

1.3 Assessing Effectiveness

While analyzing training programs' efficiency, there was a notable lack of consistency in how the outcomes of cyber hygiene and security training are measured [16]. According to Prümmer et al.'s [9] literature review, the measurements often deviate from direct assessments of cyber security behaviors and instead focus on attitudinal changes, user perceptions, or simple behavioral intentions instead of real behavioral change. Although these factors can be considered predictors of behavioral change, they fail to assess the application of the training on end-user competency. Their review concludes by encouraging the implementation of objective behavioral measurements to determine training effectiveness.

Beyond the commonly used perceptual and attitudinal aspects, a wide range of performance measures are currently utilized to assess cyber security trainee performance. In their review of cybersecurity training evaluation metrics, Koutsouris et al. [12] named 20 such measures, ranging from the number of successful attacks to the efficiency of reporting cyber incidents. While the sheer number of metrics speaks to the researcher's attempts to uncover the impact of training on practical outcomes, the evident inability to consistently measure training success sabotages the field's capacity to compare various training types. Across the board, there is a notable lack of agreement on methods for evaluating training solutions, which makes it strikingly difficult to assess the efficacy of solutions [2].

1.4 Our Study

We utilized an employee onboarding scenario to test the transference of cyber hygiene knowledge and skills into day-to-day work activities. One of the primary aspirations of awareness training programs is to push employees to actively engage in cyber security behaviors for their everyday employment activities [15]. Given the increasing overlap between organizational and personal security, ensuring that users within a home computing environment are able to apply knowledge is crucial to safeguarding information and resources [7].

As Ghazvini and Shukur [15] pointed out, many training programs fail to measure user behavior before and after implementing an intervention, which prevents an accurate evaluation of practical outcomes. We attempted to remedy this issue within our research by utilizing a pre/post-test methodology for both the knowledge acquisition and user behavior measures. The knowledge tests include two components: 1) answering questions from the training videos and 2) completing the Cyber Hygiene Inventory (CHI). According to Vishwanath et al. [19], CHI is a valid and consistent measure of five distinct dimensions of cyber hygiene. The measure is meant to be predictive of behavior. We plan to use CHI to capture our participants' general cyber hygiene knowledge and examine its ability to predict behavioral onboarding performance.

Notably, this study camouflages its cybersecurity research focus. This was done by masking the cyber security assessment within general computer competence questions, placing demographic questions at the end of the study procedure, and disguising cyber hygiene tasks within an employee onboarding scenario. The primary justification for this approach lies in the well-documented phenomenon known as demand characteristics, which are aspects of a study that convey what behaviors are expected or desirable, which artificially change behavior [20]. This is particularly pertinent in cybersecurity research, where participants' awareness of being assessed on cyber hygiene might lead them to behave more cautiously than they would in a non-evaluative environment.

Masking the cybersecurity intent in this study was critical to prevent heightened vigilance in tasks such as responding to phishing emails or identifying malicious links. Being aware that the research assessed cyber security could inflate their performance on these tasks, skewing the results and undermining the study's ability to accurately evaluate their adherence to best practices [21]. Using an employee onboarding scenario also increased the ecological validity of the study, making the results more indicative of how individuals may act in everyday cyber scenarios within organizations [15, 22].

2   Methods

2.1   Participants

This pilot study had ten undergraduate students from a large public university in the southeastern region of the United States of America. They were recruited through the Psychology department's SONA system. Each participant was compensated with two research credits for their involvement in the study. The average age of the participants was 19.6 years ($SD = 1.32$). The sample had a balanced gender distribution, with an equal split of the biological sexes.

Other relevant demographics were collected, including average technology use time in a day, college major, and prior cybersecurity experience. In terms of digital technology usage, participants reported an average of 11.1 h per day ($SD = 5.39$) spent engaging with various forms of technology, including academic work, social media usage, entertainment, and other personal use. Two participants were majoring in technical fields, which encompassed disciplines related to engineering, computer science, or information technology. Finally, 2 participants had prior training in cybersecurity. This prior exposure to technical and cybersecurity-related content is notable, as it may influence the participants' interaction with and understanding of the technological aspects of the study. Their performance will be considered separately within the results section.

2.2 Materials

The onboarding tasks and cybersecurity training were conducted using a standard desktop computer. The computer had an Intel Core i5 processor with a Windows 10 operating system. The monitor was a 24-inch LED display with a resolution of 1920 × 1080 pixels. This setup provided a consistent and controlled environment for all participants to engage with the training material. The video training consisted of interactive government-sponsored instructional videos designed to enhance participants' knowledge and awareness of cybersecurity principles [23]. These videos training, totaling approximately 30 min, covered various topics, including password security, phishing, malware prevention, and safe information practices. To assess participants' baseline cyber hygiene knowledge, participants completed a custom cyber hygiene quiz to evaluate the effectiveness of the training. The quiz was integrated into a broader set of computer competency questions and hosted on the Qualtrics survey platform. The quiz consisted of multiple-choice questions designed to assess key learning outcomes from the videos and onboarding tasks. Topics covered in the quiz included identifying phishing attempts, best practices for password creation, and utilizing VPN software. In addition, participants' baseline cyber hygiene knowledge was tested via the Cyber Hygiene Inventory [19]. This inventory is a validated assessment tool comprising items that measure various dimensions of cyber hygiene, including personal cybersecurity practices, awareness of common cyber threats, and knowledge of safe online behaviors. The inventory is structured as a self-report questionnaire with 5 point Likert-scale responses ranging from 'strongly disagree' to 'strongly agree'.

2.3 Procedure

Participants' cyber hygiene skills were assessed through a multi-step process, seamlessly integrated into an employee onboarding experience (Fig. 1). After providing informed consent, each participant completed an initial cyber hygiene quiz, masked within general computer competency questions. This was a deliberate effort to obscure the primary focus of the quiz and prevent participants' awareness of the study's intent from corrupting their answers. We aimed to elicit genuine responses reflecting participants' real-world knowledge levels by embedding the cyber hygiene components within a broader assessment. This quiz, therefore, provided a baseline measure of participants' cybersecurity knowledge and abilities.

Once the survey was complete, participants were immersed in the scenario via a verbal script read out by the researcher. They were instructed to assume a character completing an onboarding process for their new job at POD Corp. The researcher asked each participant to complete tasks utilizing the character's information and adhere to all company policies. Much like the quiz, the onboarding simulation was presented in a manner that did not explicitly reveal its true purpose. This technique was employed to mitigate the risk of participants altering their natural behavior or decision-making processes due to preconceived notions about the study's objectives.

Participants received an onboarding sheet containing three explicit tasks and a list of company policies, which contained instructions for cyber hygiene behaviors. The three primary tasks were (1) Generate a corporate email account and password (2) Keep an eye out for any relevant emails and (3) Fill out and securely store company files. Attached to the task document was the list of company policies, which instructed all employees to perform behaviors such as "Make sure to encrypt files containing sensitive information", "Always enable two-factor/multi-factor authentication on any company-related accounts", and "Keep all software on your system up to date". The three primary tasks, and the implicit steps derived from the company policies, constituted the full onboarding process. Researchers observed, took notes, and marked completed tasks off on a behavioral checklist.

After the initial onboarding, participants were asked if they felt they had thoroughly completed everything the company required. If they did not, they were given more time to complete the tasks. If they responded affirmatively, they were notified that they would be completing an interactive cybersecurity training. This video-based DOD training aimed to enhance participants' understanding of cybersecurity practices and underscored the importance of adhering to policies on cyber behavior. Participants completed the training at their own pace and then moved into the next portion of the study.

Following the training, participants were prompted to revisit, redo, or revise their initial onboarding process based on knowledge gained from the cybersecurity training videos. Each was asked to consider the question: "Is there any part of the onboarding process that you would do differently, based on the information you just learned?" After being encouraged to redo or alter any initial onboarding tasks, participants were given the time to make any necessary changes. Researchers took detailed notes and marked off completed tasks on the behavioral checklist. This checklist served as a systematic record of participants' cybersecurity behaviors. Once participants felt they had completed all the tasks, they indicated to the researcher that they intended to make no further changes. They were then asked to complete a post-hoc Qualtrics survey on computer competency, which was an exact replica of the pre-test with the addition of a few demographic questions. Upon completing the survey, participants were dismissed from the study and received SONA research credit.

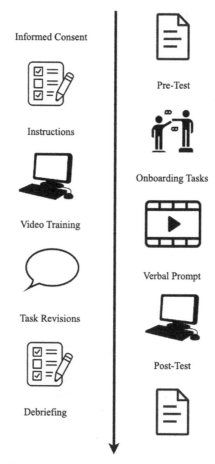

Fig. 1. The figure shows the experimental procedure of the study. The figure is meant to be read from left to right and top to bottom. The center arrow shows the progression of time with the labels and icons on either side of the arrow.

3   Results

3.1   Primary Analyses

The results were assessed for outliers and missing values. Of particular interest were two individuals who self-identified as cybersecurity experts. In terms of potential prior knowledge and skills, they were treated as outliers. We conducted the analyses with and without those participants' data and found that they only performed differently on the behavioral checklist. Therefore, their data were treated separately for the behavioral checklist measure comparisons. No data had to be excluded for any of the other statistical tests. All the measures were converted to percentages for easier interpretation.

A paired samples t-test was conducted to determine the effect of the video training on post-test quiz scores. The findings indicate no significant difference between video training and quiz scores pre ($M = 72\%$, $SD = 18\%$) versus post ($M = 79\%$, $SD = 8\%$), $t(9) = -1.41$, $p = .193$, $d = -.44$. Therefore, we did not observe an effect of training on quiz performance.

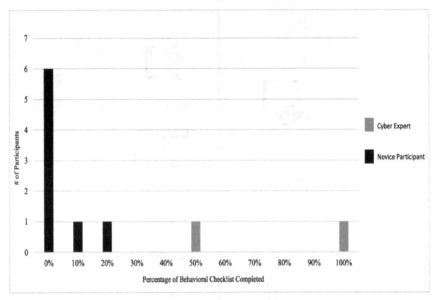

Fig. 2. The figure provides a bar graph showing the distribution of participants by the percentage of onboarding security checklist successfully completed. Cyber experts are represented by grey bars, while the black bars represent those not self-identifying as cyber experts.

Upon analyzing the results of the behavioral checklist, it was evident that participants fell short in their ability to execute cybersecurity behaviors. The checklist was designed to encapsulate both explicitly instructed and implicitly implied cyber hygiene practices as delineated in the company policy document. Initial scores assessment revealed a considerable shortfall in executing practical cyber hygiene behaviors among participants. The pre-intervention data (see Fig. 2), underscores widespread non-compliance with the suggested cybersecurity actions. This initial finding aligns with existing literature that emphasizes the gap between knowledge of cybersecurity best practices and applied behavior [17]. Following the intervention, only two participants demonstrated a tangible improvement in their cyber hygiene practices by completing additional tasks that aligned with the intervention's objectives, one of which was a self-identified cyber security expert. Conversely, a significant portion of the cohort exhibited no change, with completion rates stagnating at 0%. The checklist is also the only measure where the self-identified cyber security experts showed different performance than the novice participants. A stark disparity in checklist completion rates becomes apparent when the two experts are excluded from the analysis. No novice participant scored over 20% on the behavioral checklist, demonstrating a substantial gap in cyber hygiene practices between individuals with specialized knowledge and those without.

Our final analysis compared scores on the Cyber Hygiene Inventory ($M = 61\%$, $SD = 12\%$) with behavioral checklist performance to assess if knowledge translated into the behavioral checklist. Coming into the laboratory, participants performed about average on the Cyber Hygiene Inventory. The CHI and the performance on the behavioral checklist scores were highly correlated, $r(9) = .69$, $p = .03$. However, only when including the self-identified experts. This indicates that for individuals with prior expertise in cyber hygiene, CHI may be predictive of their practical application skills as measured by the behavioral checklist. However, a different picture emerges when we consider the data excluding the experts. Among the non-expert participants, the CHI did not demonstrate predictive validity for performance on the behavioral checklist. The correlation coefficient was only $r(6) = -.22$, $p = .604$; this might be due to the restricted range from our small sample size. This suggests that for individuals without pre-existing expertise, knowledge does not necessarily translate into practical application proficiency.

In summary, the results do not show an improvement in scores from the pretest to the posttest, suggesting that the intervention was ineffective in enhancing the participants' behavior or knowledge.

4 Discussion

This study evaluated the effectiveness of government-endorsed cybersecurity training videos. We considered the impact the training had on enhancing cyber hygiene knowledge and behavioral outcomes during onboarding tasks. Across experts and novices, there was an evident failure to improve post-intervention, which questions the effectiveness of the training videos. This lack of improvement is striking, particularly given the increasing emphasis on the role of end-users in cybersecurity and the resources devoted to training initiatives. However, we do have to recognize this pilot study's limitations. The sample only contained ten participants, and two self-identified as having expertise in cyber security. It seemed participants lacked motivation towards the activities, which may have been due to participants not feeling actual ownership of data or the potential costs associated with not behaving securely. Future research ought to consider ways to address motivation and engagement.

A notable observation was the gap between scores on the CHI and behavioral checklist scores. Despite the expectation that enhanced knowledge would translate into adherence to cyber hygiene best practices, this congruence was not observed in novice users. On the other hand, self-identified cyber security experts showed a distinct proficiency in translating their knowledge into practical application, as observed by their substantially better behavioral checklist scores. This highlights that for those with a higher level of expertise, general cyber hygiene knowledge may be able to predict performance in real-world scenarios. The distinction between experts and novices in their ability to apply information is critical in understanding the efficacy of cyber hygiene training programs and tailoring these programs to different levels of prior knowledge. Future research will have to look closer at the types of knowledge (e.g., declarative, procedural) in training programs to work towards improved real-world outcomes.

Similar to Bada et al. [14] and Van Steen et al. [13], our findings suggest that traditional methods might not be as effective as desired, especially for promoting behavioral change. The contrast may be attributed to differences in intervention design, participant demographics, or evaluation methods.

A key aspect of traditional cybersecurity training that is often overlooked is it application to real-world scenarios [15]. Uniquely, we embedded the cyber hygiene assessments within an employee onboarding scenario. Adding the situational information afforded us a realistic work setting to assess behavioral outcomes. This also enabled us to mitigate potential biases and ensure a more authentic assessment of participants' knowledge and behavior by hiding our research focus on cybersecurity.

Our approach aligns with the call for more objective behavioral measurements in assessing training effectiveness, as well as the need to develop more practical metrics [9]. And, it resonates with the writings of Bada et al. [14] and McCarthy [11], who question the efficacy of information-provision strategies in changing user behavior. Successfully training end-users in cyber hygiene best practices will require updated instructional practices along with more ubiquitous measures of success.

5 Conclusion

Our pilot study explored the effectiveness of government-endorsed training videos under the cover of an employee onboarding scenario. Masking the cybersecurity focus of the study was important to prevent heightened vigilance. The lack of improvement in both knowledge and application among participants after exposure to the training videos signals a need for a paradigm shift in how cybersecurity training is taught, and success is benchmarked. But, our findings must be considered with caution. Future work should address our study's limitations of a small sample size and participant motivation. Our data and real-world technical reports [24] show the current training is ineffective. Hackers are capturing significant amounts of data and society's limited resources. Cybersecurity as a discipline needs a heavier emphasis on human-centered design to address this significant societal issue [25].

Disclosure of Interests. The authors have no competing interests to declare that are relevant to the content of this article.

References

1. Ulsch, N.M. (ed.): Cyber Threat! Wiley (2014). https://doi.org/10.1002/9781118915028
2. Chowdhury, N., Gkioulos, V.: Cyber security training for critical infrastructure protection: a literature review. Comput. Sci. Rev. **40**, 100361 (2021). https://doi.org/10.1016/j.cosrev.2021.100361
3. Abawajy, J.: User preference of cyber security awareness delivery methods. Behav. Inf. Technol. **33**, 237–248 (2014). https://doi.org/10.1080/0144929X.2012.708787
4. Cain, A.A., Edwards, M.E., Still, J.D.: An exploratory study of cyber hygiene behaviors and knowledge. J. Inf. Secur. Appl. **42**, 36–45 (2018). https://doi.org/10.1016/j.jisa.2018.08.002
5. Chowdhury, N., Katsikas, S., Gkioulos, V.: Modeling effective cybersecurity training frameworks: a Delphi method-based study. Comput. Secur. **113**, 102551 (2022). https://doi.org/10.1016/j.cose.2021.102551

6. Vishwanath, A.: Stop telling people to take those cyber hygiene multivitamins. In: Prepared for Evolving Threats, pp. 225–240. World Scientific (2020). https://doi.org/10.1142/978981 1219740_0014
7. Morris, T.W., Still, J.D.: Cybersecurity hygiene: blending home and work computing. In: Patterson, W. (ed.) New Perspectives in Behavioral Cybersecurity. CRC Press, Boca Raton (2023)
8. Bogage, J.: Colonial pipeline CEO says paying $4.4 million ransom was 'the right thing to do for the country' (2021)
9. Prümmer, J., Van Steen, T., Van Den Berg, B.: A systematic review of current cybersecurity training methods. Comput. Secur. **136**, 103585 (2024). https://doi.org/10.1016/j.cose.2023. 103585
10. Craigen, D., Diakun-Thibault, N., Purse, R.: Defining cybersecurity. Technol. Innov. Manag. Rev. **4**, 13–21 (2014). https://doi.org/10.22215/timreview/835
11. McCarthy, K.: Cybersecurity awareness training methods and user behavior. ProQuest Dissertations and Theses (2021)
12. Koutsouris, N., Vassilakis, C., Kolokotronis, N.: Cyber-security training evaluation metrics. In: 2021 IEEE International Conference on Cyber Security and Resilience (CSR), pp. 192–197. IEEE, Rhodes (2021). https://doi.org/10.1109/CSR51186.2021.9527946
13. Van Steen, T., Norris, E., Atha, K., Joinson, A.: What (if any) behaviour change techniques do government-led cybersecurity awareness campaigns use? J. Cybersecur. **6**, tyaa019 (2020). https://doi.org/10.1093/cybsec/tyaa019
14. Bada, M., Sasse, A.M., Nurse, J.R.C.: Cyber security awareness campaigns: why do they fail to change behaviour? (2019). https://doi.org/10.48550/ARXIV.1901.02672
15. Ghazvini, A., Shukur, Z.: Awareness training transfer and information security content development for healthcare industry. IJACSA **7** (2016). https://doi.org/10.14569/IJACSA.2016. 070549
16. Kävrestad, J., Nohlberg, M.: Evaluation strategies for cybersecurity training methods: a literature review. In: Furnell, S., Clarke, N. (eds.) HAISA 2021. IFIP Advances in Information and Communication Technology, vol. 613, pp. 102–112. Springer, Cham (2021). https://doi. org/10.1007/978-3-030-81111-2_9
17. Deakin University Melbourne, Australia, Alruwaili, A.: A review of the impact of training on cybersecurity awareness. IJARCS **10**, 1–3 (2019). https://doi.org/10.26483/ijarcs.v10i5.6476
18. Proctor, W.R.: Investigating the efficacy of cybersecurity awareness training programs. ProQuest Dissertations & Theses Global; SciTech Premium Collection (2016)
19. Vishwanath, A., et al.: Cyber hygiene: The concept, its measure, and its initial tests. Decis. Support. Syst. **128**, 113160 (2020). https://doi.org/10.1016/j.dss.2019.113160
20. Nichols, A.L., Maner, J.K.: The good-subject effect: investigating participant demand characteristics. J. Gener. Psychol. **135**, 151–166 (2008). https://doi.org/10.3200/GENP.135.2. 151-166
21. Sharma, K., Zhan, X., Nah, F.F.-H., Siau, K., Cheng, M.X.: Impact of digital nudging on information security behavior: an experimental study on framing and priming in cybersecurity. OCJ **1**, 69–91 (2021). https://doi.org/10.1108/OCJ-03-2021-0009
22. Fahl, S., Harbach, M., Acar, Y., Smith, M.: On the ecological validity of a password study. In: Proceedings of the Ninth Symposium on Usable Privacy and Security, pp. 1–13. ACM, Newcastle (2013). https://doi.org/10.1145/2501604.2501617
23. Cybersecurity Awareness. Security Awareness Hub: Select eLearning Awareness Courses for DOD and Industry (2014)
24. Basset, G., Hylender, C., Langlois, P., Pinto, A., Widup, S.: Data breach 2020 investigations report - verizon business (2020). https://www.verizon.com/business/en-gb/resources/reports/ 2020-data-breach-investigations-report.pdf. Accessed 10 Apr 2022
25. Still, J.D.: Cybersecurity needs you! ACM Interact. (May + June: Feature) **23**, 54–58 (2016)

"I'm not planning on dying anytime soon!": A Survey of Digital Legacy Planning

Paola Marmorato[1]([✉]), Clarissa Fernandes[1], Lydia Kraus[2],
and Elizabeth Stobert[1]

[1] Carleton University, Ottawa, Canada
{paolachavesmarmorato,clarissadaylefernandes}@cmail.carleton.ca,
elizabeth.stobert@carleton.ca
[2] Masaryk University, Brno, Czech Republic
lydia.kraus@mail.muni.cz

Abstract. Increasing technology integration into daily life has broadened the concept of legacy to include the digital footprint individuals leave behind. However, the lack of social norms, design, and legal frameworks to prepare a digital legacy may challenge users and data inheritors. We conducted a survey to understand the experiences of users who have either prepared for their own digital legacy or inherited someone else's digital legacy. We found that most participants did not make any preparations due to a lack of motivator triggers, discomfort in dealing with the topic of death, and the burden of handling an overwhelming task. Users who did prepare did not consider the entirety of their digital footprint and digital identity elements. They prioritized passing accounts with financial significance and typically created physical lists of their passwords to be found by the inheritor. Inheritors reported navigating uncertainty in handling the leaver's data due to the lack of clear instructions or social norms. We suggest further research to develop tools that can assist users in creating and managing their digital legacies effectively, as well as integrating awareness of this subject into software design to prompt users to make decisions and take action on the matter.

Keywords: Digital legacy · Passwords · Authentication

1 Introduction

In the past, planning a will was primarily associated with passing on tangible assets, such as property, finances, and personal possessions. However, the increasing integration of technology into users' daily lives has added the need to consider the digital footprint they leave behind. Between social media profiles, cloud storage of pictures and memories, emails, text messages, and online banking accounts (among others), users must consider that everything added to the digital world has the potential to outlive them. Digital legacy is therefore

© The Author(s), under exclusive license to Springer Nature Switzerland AG 2024
A. Moallem (Ed.): HCII 2024, LNCS 14728, pp. 64–76, 2024.
https://doi.org/10.1007/978-3-031-61379-1_5

emerging as an important aspect of users' digital footprint, which may result in new challenges and opportunities for individuals and society.

Many users avoid planning for their digital legacies. While they believe others should prepare for their data to be handled after death, they do not always prepare themselves [7]. Besides the discomfort of considering death, they find it a burden to have to constantly update their digital will compared to their traditional will [7].

The task of planning a digital legacy can feel complicated and overwhelming to users. Users who are motivated to think about digital legacy and understand the importance of leaving memories and information for their descendants are not always equipped to prepare their digital inheritance [5,13]. They feel uncertain about their ability to make preparations, fearing that their boundaries and wishes for privacy will not be respected [13].

The preparation of a digital legacy necessarily involves privacy considerations. Users expect their pre-mortem privacy to be respected post-mortem, and if they make a set of data private, they believe it should continue to be private after their death [7].

Inheritors of digital legacies face challenges of their own. Without a clear understanding of a person's digital footprint and established social norms on how to handle it, inheritors may struggle to manage and access critical information after a loved one's demise [13]. Password-protected accounts, encrypted files, and online subscriptions can create complications when settling an individual's affairs [1].

Prior work has focused on qualitative research about users' perceptions, attitudes, and practices towards digital legacy. Building on existing literature, we conducted a survey to collect empirical data that can help us understand users' digital legacy planning and the experiences of data inheritors, particularly in relation to how credential sharing is managed in this process. We asked participants about their motivations to plan (or not plan) for their data to be handled after death, how they intend to pass on their passwords, experiences, and challenges during the preparation process or as an inheritor, as well as information about their essential accounts and devices and how they wish them to be inherited post-mortem.

Our survey findings suggest that most users have not prepared for their digital legacy due to a lack of motivator triggers, discomfort in dealing with the topic of death, and the burden of handling an overwhelming task. Users who did prepare did not consider the entirety of their digital footprint and digital identity elements. They prioritized passing accounts with financial significance and typically created physical lists of their passwords to be found by the inheritor. Inheritors reported navigating uncertainty in handling the leaver's data due to the lack of clear instructions or social norms. Lastly, there is an opportunity for future research in HCI and software design to support digital legacy planning.

2 Background

In the following sections, we briefly present background research on the concept of digital legacy in the digital age; identity representation; privacy and security; and management aspects of legacy planning.

2.1 Digital Legacy in the Digital Age

The increase in the availability of digital technologies and the intertwining of technology and people's lives has created an era in which human lives are recorded in unprecedented quantity and with nuanced details [10]. From managing everyday tasks to communication, photography, memory keeping, and other records, vast amounts of personal digital data and assets are generated every day, enhanced by cheap storage solutions and facilitated copying [2,10,13].

Online records can be a representation of a "digital soul" – a person's social identity [10,12] which has the potential to live on forever online. Data generated throughout a user's life can carry values and meaning to be passed down, constituting a digital legacy that encompasses more than heirlooms and possessions [11].

While the internet proposes an opportunity to fulfill the human wish to be remembered and remember others, it also presents new challenges [10]. Users may not wish to pass on all of their data, and inheritors may find difficulties assessing and accessing what is important. What, how, and to whom records will be left after the owners' death must be considered in the design of digital tools [8].

The digital age also creates a tension between users and service providers, who may also have access to and control over the storage of digital legacy [4,10]. This is an important consideration when planning a multi-generational legacy and even maintaining online records [10]. While some people believe in the importance of keeping records alive for future generations [4,10,13], others believe in the need for "graceful forgetting" and have proposed solutions for "aging files" [10].

2.2 Identity Representation

The concept of legacy is directly linked to the user's construction, presentation, and understanding of their own identity [4]. Although they may not directly consider it, users' every online action potentially creates part of their digital legacy [10] Social media accounts, for example, can leave a representation of a user's identity that may persist after their death. Even the choice to be anonymous online is associated with the wish to maintain a positive identity presentation and to avoid social criticism or stigma [4]. While planned digital legacy can represent the individuals' identity in a curated form, there are not always clear ways for users to integrate private accounts that were never meant to be shared [4].

Gulotta et al. [4] found that users often had experience with abandoned accounts and identities, to which they had either lost access or deleted. Users had deleted or abandoned accounts that did not represent how they felt about themselves any longer, or because they were embarrassed about how the contents portrayed an outdated version of themselves (particularly their adolescent selves). However, some accounts were created either to be anonymous (e.g., health matters) or to portray a specific version of self (e.g., trying to connect to a social network when moving to a new town).

Identity and presentation may also matter to the inheritor of digital legacy: Paul-Choudhury [10] tells the story of his deceased wife, who wished people to remember her as she was during life and not be defined by the circumstances leading to her death [10]. As her husband, he found a place on the internet to fulfill her wishes: he created a memorial website to celebrate her life with curated photos and text that represented her. While the decision was unorthodox and perhaps not well received at the time, he reflects on the digital age's shifting circumstances and social norms, including the way people grieve and remember the ones who are gone [10]. Today, it is commonplace to turn Facebook[1] pages into memorials, where friends and family members can come together and remember the individual through their own posts and photos.

2.3 Digital Legacy Security and Privacy

The consideration of privacy for digital legacy is a complex issue. Social norms about privacy are shifting and do not follow a binary categorization of "private information" vs "public information". Nissenbaum's theory of contextual integrity emphasizes that privacy is a matter of an appropriate flow of information. What constitutes an appropriate flow or a privacy violation, are determined by societal norms, roles, and relationships within specific contexts [9].

For digital legacy, the complexity of privacy may also translate to complexity in planning for that legacy. A participant from Holt et al.'s study [7] reported keeping some Facebook photos of her past invisible to the audience. However, after her death, she wanted those photos to be visible to people who knew her during her life, as she would like these moments to be remembered and associated with her identity [7].

As the digital identity aspect of people's life is a novelty in human history, there are no well-established societal norms about how users should plan or inherit a digital legacy. These norms are constantly being built and shifted to encompass the complexities of modern life. While Holt et al.'s participant wanted the same photos to be private at a specific time, she still wanted these photos to be viewed after her death [7]. While Paul-Choudhury's unorthodox memorial for his wife might not have been well perceived when he created it, now this practice is commonplace [10].

The lack of a clear cultural practice for this theme can complicate not only the data owner's planning abilities, but the inheritors' experiences. Without a

---

[1] www.facebook.com.

clear instructions on how to handle the data left to their care, they can experience emotional stress or even find that the situation hinders from their grieving process [1].

Holt et al. [7] found that users who worry about their privacy during life would prefer to keep the same level of privacy post-mortem. However, users are uncertain about how to think about and organize their data while considering its longevity and ensuring that the identity that remains after death is the one they wished to pass on [3].

Holt et al. [7] also found discrepancies between users' attitudes towards privacy and digital legacy, and their actual behaviors towards it. While they believed at first that they wished their privacy during life to be respected after death (for example, if something is private before their death, it should stay private after it), they made contradictions when questioned about multi-generational information sharing. Additionally, when asked what were their practices to keep their security and privacy post-mortem, many participants responded that they did not have any plan or system in place.

2.4   Digital Legacy Management Challenges

Despite the potential benefits of digital legacy, the task of curating a digital legacy can pose a variety of challenges for users.

The quantity of data created can be overwhelming to both data owners and inheritors [7,14]. Information storage and persistence is often the default setting, which minimizes decision-making for the user, but also fails to prompt them to consider what data represents the owner the way they wish to be remembered [10,11], or the data that would be useful to be kept and shared.

The granularity of account sharing may also pose problems to users planning their digital legacies. Sharing an account creates an "all or nothing" approach [7] which opens the possibility of unwanted information being uncovered after the owner's death, which can be potentially harmful to the inheritor and complicate the intended legacy the owner wished to leave behind [4].

There are some tools available for the management of digital legacy, but tools are primarily provided only for a single service, not for consideration of digital legacy as a whole. Methods provided for handling digital legacy vary, but mainly involve naming a legacy contact to handle the account after the owner's passing. Some services provide specific actions apart from account closure, such as Facebook, which allows the creation of "memorial" accounts[2].

Users who are thinking about their digital legacy and valued digital memories may find themselves unsupported and unsure on how to plan their legacy in a safe manner [6,13]. Digital legacy often involves giving access to accounts, and the most obvious way to do this is often to share passwords. Password sharing carries inherent security risks, but other methods of giving post-mortem access (e.g. adding an inheritor as a legacy contact) may be more complicated to set up, or not available for all services. Users may also prioritize strategies that

---

[2] https://www.facebook.com/help/1568013990080948.

fit in with their existing password management strategies: older adults report preferring physical copies of their passwords over using digital means to pass on their important credentials, which may involve security risks [13].

3   Study

To investigate people's experiences handling digital legacies, we conducted an online survey asking questions about people's preparations for their own digital legacies and also about any experiences they may have had in inheriting another person's digital legacy. Our survey was cleared by the Carleton University Research Ethics Board.

We used a pre-screening survey to recruit participants with appropriate experience to our main questionnaire. The screening survey asked interested participants if they had experiences either preparing to pass on their digital legacy, or being the inheritor of someone else's digital legacy (whether or not that person had already passed). Participants who answered "yes" to at least one question were invited to respond to the main questionnaire. Participants who said they had not made preparations for their own digital legacy were asked to list the reasons why they had not made any preparations.

In the main questionnaire, we asked more detailed questions about participants' experiences with digital legacy preparations. For participants who said they had made preparations for their own digital legacy, we asked about how they were planning to pass down their important accounts/devices, what kind of accounts they were most concerned about, and how they were handling the logistics of ensuring access to their inheritors. For participants who said they had experiences as an inheritor, we asked about what kind of accounts they had inherited and the nature of their goals for those accounts. We also asked about the success of their experiences handling someone else's digital legacy.

We recruited participants through Prolific[3] and collected survey data using Qualtrics. Participants were compensated 0.25 CAD for the pre-screener, and 1.75 CAD for completion of the main questionnaire.

4   Results

There were 188 responses to the pre-screener, and of these, 91 people qualified for and completed the main survey questionnaire.

Of the pre-screener respondents, 64% said that they had not made any preparations for their digital legacy. Figure 1 shows people's reasons for not having made preparations: the most frequently cited reasons were that participants had not considered this aspect of inheritance, or because they did not want to think about dying. When asked if they wanted to add further information, one participant wrote, "I don't plan on dying anytime soon."

---

[3] www.prolific.com.

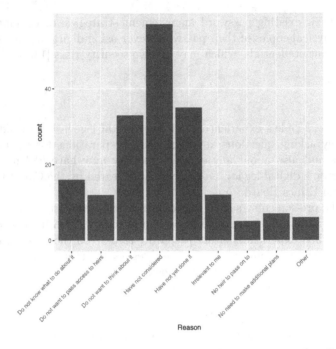

Fig. 1. Barplot showing reasons why participants did not prepare for their passing. Note that participants could choose more than one option.

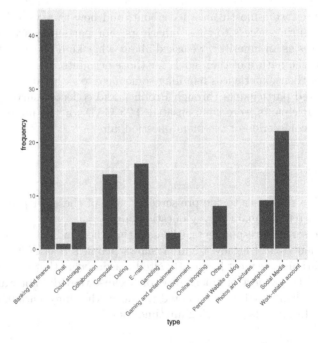

Fig. 2. Histogram depicting the type of accounts participants plan on on passing down.

4.1   Leavers

Forty-two respondents said that they had made preparations for passing on passwords after their death, and of these, 90% people said that they expected another person to assume responsibility for their accounts after their death. Respondents estimated that they were planning to pass on a median of 6 passwords to an inheritor, but estimates ranged between 1 and 200 passwords.

We asked participants about what techniques they were using to communicate their passwords to their intended inheritors. 31% of participants said that they had already shared their passwords with the person/people they expected to inherit the account, and 67% said that they had provided a list of passwords to be found upon their death, but that inheritors did not currently have access to their passwords.

Of the participants who were already sharing passwords with their inheritors, and that their inheritors had current access to accounts, the most frequent way of having shared these passwords was through a physical list (54%) or a digital list (38%). 31% said they had used a password manager, and 23% said that they had relayed their passwords orally. For those participants who had made preparations for their passwords to be shared only after their passing, the most common method of sharing was a physical list (61%), a digital list (57%), or through a password manager (21%). Both groups were generally confident that their inheritors would be able to access their passwords at the appropriate time (Fig. 3).

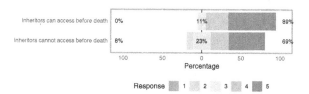

Fig. 3. Likert plot showing participants' level of confidence about the effectiveness of their digital legacy plans. 1 is not at all confident and 5 is very confident.

Respondents who had made plans to share passwords relating to their digital legacy were generally unconcerned about the risks associated with doing so. 62% of participants said they were "not worried at all" or "slightly worried" about the possibility of vulnerability in the process of preparing their digital legacy.

We asked participants to list their three most important accounts that they expect someone to inherit, and to answer a few questions about each of these accounts. Figure 2 shows what type of account these "important" accounts were likely to be: the most common were banking and finance, social media, email, and computer accounts. Respondents said that these accounts were important because they had financial significance (48%), gave access to other accounts (57%), or had emotional significance (30%). Typically, respondents expected their partner to inherit the account (52%), and wanted their inheritor to access information on the account (57%) or to close the account (48%).

4.2   Inheritors

Thirty-eight respondents said that they had previous experiences as an inheritor of someone else's digital legacy (whether or not that person had already passed). Most frequently, respondents were the inheritor for a friend (29%), parent (26%), relative (21%), or partner (11%). Figure 4 shows what type of accounts inheritors had to access. Participants said that these accounts were likely to have been passed down to them because they had emotional significance (68%), financial significance (53%), or because they provided access to other accounts (45%). However, respondents were often uncertain about exactly what to do with the account: only 15% of inheritors had received directions on what to do with the account. The remaining participants were left with no instructions (37%) or only a vague idea of the leaver's intentions (42%).

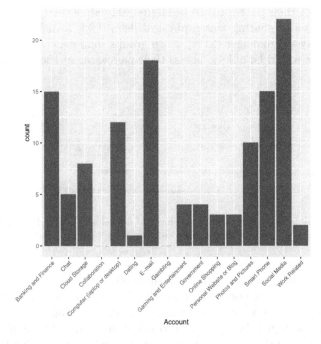

Fig. 4. Histogram depicting the type of account/device inherited.

We asked participants to consider any experiences attempting to access an account left to them. Thirty-two participants (84%) said that they had had an inheritance experience that was "successful" or "partially successful", and only 5% said they had an unsuccessful experience.

The most common sharing strategy was to share information during the leaver's lifetime. For successful inheritance tasks, most participants said that the deceased had shared the account password (53%) or its location (25%) before their death. It appeared that this sharing was mostly happening outside of a written will or legal document (only 15% said that passwords were shared with them through a written will). In the two cases where participants were unable to access accounts after the leaver's death, all participants said it was because the passwords were not left to them.

5 Discussion

Our pre-screening survey found that the majority of respondents had not made any plans for their digital legacy, primarily because they had not considered the need for it. Combined with a desire to avoid thinking about death and the work involved in the task, this suggests that the bar to considering digital legacy needs to be lowered, and the subject needs to be made more obvious to users. This echoes Pfister et al.'s need for a "motivator trigger" for planning a digital legacy [11].

When asked if they wanted to add further information, one participant wrote, "I don't plan on dying anytime soon", suggesting that they saw no reason for users to think about how their data will be handled. Motivators such as health condition, age, having dependents, or exposure to someone's death might be necessary triggers for individuals. Our findings suggest that in the absence of these motivational triggers, users do not consider the longevity of their data online.

Another factor to be considered is the difficulty in creating and maintaining a digital legacy. Crafting a traditional will can be executed with the assistance of a legal professional, guided by cultural norms, and soon forgotten. On the other hand, the process of digital legacy planning demands ongoing attention and updating practices without the guidance of cultural norms or legal professionals. Supporting tools are scarce, and the amount of data created throughout user's life are typically overwhelming. Aligning these factors with the discomfort of thinking about death may result in barriers that hinder users from planning their digital legacy.

In our survey, participants who had made preparations for their digital legacy were generally creating a password list (whether physical or digital) for their inheritors to find upon their death. Some participants were choosing to share the list pre-mortem, a strategy that invites security risks but ensures effective sharing. The majority of participants said they expected to leave a small number of passwords, suggesting they are not considering their whole digital footprint and digital identity in their digital inheritance planning.

While one would expect digital legacy planning to take place in a digital setting, participants still preferred to leave physical lists of these passwords. Storing passwords in a physical list is tangible, but has disadvantages for password inheritance: the list will not be automatically updated with new accounts or passwords, and if the list is stored insecurely or accessed by another person, the owner will not know. However, the inability to share passwords securely imposes yet another barrier to the safe planning of digital legacies. Despite the potential risks of password sharing, our participants were generally unconcerned about the security risks of adopting this method when planning their digital legacy.

Password managers could be a potential tool to alleviate tensions between creating and updating a password list safely. Besides storing passwords in one single place, most password managers have functions to set up an "emergency contact" or give authenticated access to one or more individuals [7]. However, participants in our study rarely chose this option. The reasons could be related to the lack of knowledge or trust in password managers, the scattered data between different services (e.g., password storage on the Google or Apple cloud and a password manager), or even the wish to keep a few accounts unknown from their inheritors. There are opportunities to reconsider the design and functions of password managers to incorporate and support potential needs of users' digital legacy.

Most participants indicated that the accounts they deemed critical to be passed to their inheritors were related to three main categories. Firstly, accounts of financial significance were consistently prioritized. Secondly, accounts that served as gateways to other accounts. Lastly, accounts that held emotional significance. They wished their inheritors to either access information in these accounts or delete them.

This prioritization could be explained by the nature of inheritance planning. When people think about a traditional will, they often consider the financial assets they will leave to their families or inheritors. This is a tangible and socially expected aspect of inheritance, which can make it easier for people to promptly consider and visualize when making plans. The other two categories show the interconnection between different accounts and their emotional value. However, elements of identity did not seem to be central in our participants' planning.

From the inheritor's perspective, accounts to be inherited were mostly from friends, relatives, or partners. Passwords were generally shared during the leaver's lifetime and in an informal manner, outside a written will. These participants also mentioned the entire lack of or the existence of very vague oral instructions on what to do with the inherited accounts. Without specific instructions or guiding cultural or legal norms, they were left uncertain about what to do with and how to fulfill the deceased's wishes regarding their digital legacy. These findings again suggest that people are not making active plans for their digital legacy, and the lack of it can leave inheritors uncertain and unsupported on how to handle someone else's legacy.

5.1   Limitations

There were several limitations to our study. Our sample size was limited, and because we did not include demographic questions, it is difficult to know how our findings generalize. For future work, we suggest that a specific look at demographic differences could potentially yield further insight. For example, older adults might be more likely to value the memories they leave behind for their descendants [13] and consider identity differently than younger people. Parents may be more concerned about preparing both traditional and digital wills to ensure the support of their children.

6 Conclusion

We conducted a survey to collect empirical data about users' digital legacy planning or experiences as inheritors of someone's digital legacy. We found a prevailing lack of attention given to digital legacies and the need for a trigger motivator to prompt individuals to start making plans for their data to be inherited upon their deaths. Even individuals who did make plans did not put much thought into all the aspects of their digital identity and footprint, limiting their preparations to only a few accounts. Accounts with financial significance and accounts with logistical value were prioritized, with secondary attention to accounts with emotional significance. Most participants created a physical list of passwords and gave oral instructions to their inheritors, suggesting a lack of effective tools to support them in passing on their passwords safely. While password managers would be a potential solution, they were used rarely.

Inheritors in our study reported a lack of instructions left by the deceased account owner and only the passing of informal password lists while the owner was alive. They felt uncertain about how to handle the data or what the deceased's wishes were.

These results illustrate a lack of legal or social frameworks for digital legacies, as well as a lack of tools or design considerations in existing software. Users with motivational triggers for planning their digital legacy assimilate the standard assumptions of a traditional will and prioritize planning the inheritance of financial assets over digital symbolic representations of their identity.

References

1. Brubaker, J.R., Dombrowski, L.S., Gilbert, A.M., Kusumakaulika, N., Hayes, G.R.: Stewarding a legacy: responsibilities and relationships in the management of post-mortem data. In: Proceedings of the SIGCHI Conference on Human Factors in Computing Systems, pp. 4157–4166. CHI 2014, Association for Computing Machinery, New York, NY, USA (2014). https://doi.org/10.1145/2556288.2557059

2. Doyle, D.T., Brubaker, J.R.: Digital legacy: a systematic literature review. Proc. ACM Hum. Comput. Interact. 7(CSCW2), 1–26 (2023). https://doi.org/10.1145/3610059

3. Gulotta, R., Gerritsen, D.B., Kelliher, A., Forlizzi, J.: Engaging with death online: an analysis of systems that support legacy-making, bereavement, and remembrance. In: Proceedings of the 2016 ACM Conference on Designing Interactive Systems, pp. 736–748. DIS 2016, Association for Computing Machinery, New York, NY, USA (2016). https://doi.org/10.1145/2901790.2901802

4. Gulotta, R., Odom, W., Faste, H., Forlizzi, J.: Legacy in the age of the internet: reflections on how interactive systems shape how we are remembered. In: Proceedings of the 2014 Conference on Designing Interactive Systems, pp. 975–984. DIS 2014, Association for Computing Machinery, New York, NY, USA (2014). https://doi.org/10.1145/2598510.2598579

5. Gulotta, R., Odom, W., Forlizzi, J., Faste, H.: Digital artifacts as legacy: exploring the lifespan and value of digital data. In: Proceedings of the SIGCHI Conference on Human Factors in Computing Systems, pp. 1813–1822 (2013)

6. Gulotta, R., Odom, W., Forlizzi, J., Faste, H.: Digital artifacts as legacy: exploring the lifespan and value of digital data. In: Proceedings of the SIGCHI Conference on Human Factors in Computing Systems, pp. 1813–1822. CHI 2013, Association for Computing Machinery, New York, NY, USA (2013). https://doi.org/10.1145/2470654.2466240

7. Holt, J., Nicholson, J., Smeddinck, J.D.: From personal data to digital legacy: exploring conflicts in the sharing, security and privacy of post-mortem data. In: Proceedings of the Web Conference 2021, pp. 2745–2756 (2021). https://doi.org/10.1145/3442381.3450030, arXiv:2104.07807 [cs]

8. Massimi, M., Odom, W., Banks, R., Kirk, D.: Matters of life and death: locating the end of life in lifespan-oriented HCI research. In: Proceedings of the SIGCHI Conference on Human Factors in Computing Systems, pp. 987–996. CHI 2011, Association for Computing Machinery, New York, NY, USA (2011). https://doi.org/10.1145/1978942.1979090

9. Nissenbaum, H.: Privacy in Context: Technology, Policy, and the Integrity of Social Life. Stanford Law Books, an imprint of Standford University Press, Stanford, California (2010)

10. Paul-Choudhury, S.: Digital legacy: the fate of your online soul. New Sci. **210**(2809), 41–43 (2011). https://doi.org/10.1016/S0262-4079(11)60930-5, https://www.sciencedirect.com/science/article/pii/S0262407911609305

11. Pfister, J.: "This will cause a lot of work": coping with transferring files and passwords as part of a personal digital legacy. In: Proceedings of the 2017 ACM Conference on Computer Supported Cooperative Work and Social Computing, pp. 1123–1138. CSCW 2017, Association for Computing Machinery, New York, NY, USA (2017). https://doi.org/10.1145/2998181.2998262

12. She, W.J., Siriaraya, P., Ang, C.S., Prigerson, H.G.: Living memory home: understanding continuing bond in the digital age through backstage grieving. In: Proceedings of the 2021 CHI Conference on Human Factors in Computing Systems, pp. 1–14. CHI 2021, Association for Computing Machinery, New York, NY, USA (2021). https://doi.org/10.1145/3411764.3445336

13. Thomas, L., Briggs, P.: An older adult perspective on digital legacy. In: Proceedings of the 8th Nordic Conference on Human-Computer Interaction: Fun, Fast, Foundational, pp. 237–246. NordiCHI 2014, Association for Computing Machinery, New York, NY, USA (2014). https://doi.org/10.1145/2639189.2639485

14. Walter, T., Hourizi, R., Moncur, W., Pitsillides, S.: Does the internet change how we die and mourn? Overview and analysis. OMEGA - J. Death Dying **64**(4), 275–302 (2012). https://doi.org/10.2190/OM.64.4.a, publisher: SAGE Publications Inc

Are UK Parents Empowered to Act on Their Cybersecurity Education Responsibilities?

Suzanne Prior[1](✉)🄳 and Karen Renaud[1,2,3,4]🄳

[1] Abertay University, Dundee DD1 1HG, Scotland
s.prior@abertay.ac.uk
[2] University of Strathclyde, Glasgow G1 1XQ, Scotland
karen.renaud@strath.ac.uk
[3] University of South Africa, Pretoria, South Africa
[4] Rhodes University, Grahamstown, South Africa

Abstract. The UK government responsibilizes its citizens to take care of their own cybersecurity. They provide extensive advice but no other direct support beyond a portal to report cybercrimes. Responsibilization works best when citizens are empowered to act in accordance with their responsibilities. Now, consider that UK parents, as part of their parental role, are probably also responsibilized for educating their children about cybersecurity. The question is whether they are sufficiently empowered to fulfill their cybersecurity education responsibilities. Our studies found that UK parents felt it was right and proper to be assigned the responsibility for educating their children about cybersecurity. However, they generally did not possess up-to-date cybersecurity knowledge nor benefit from UK government-provided cyber-related advice. Hence, they are responsibilized but not empowered to educate their children about cybersecurity.

Keywords: Cyber Hygiene · Education · Children · Responsibilization

1 Introduction

The Internet is used by billions of people globally. The UK, where this study was carried out, has an Internet penetration rate of 92.7% [1], with citizens spending an average of 4 h per day online, as reported in April 2020 [2]. During the COVID-19 pandemic, children, too, spent hours online every day to learn, socialize, and play entertain themselves. By the age of 10–15 years, 89% of UK children reported being online every day in 2020, a figure that is likely to be close to 100% since the pandemic.

Similar to the physical world, criminals operate in the online world to pursue their nefarious purposes. Now, consider that the UK responsibilizes its citizens

© The Author(s), under exclusive license to Springer Nature Switzerland AG 2024
A. Moallem (Ed.): HCII 2024, LNCS 14728, pp. 77–96, 2024.
https://doi.org/10.1007/978-3-031-61379-1_6

to manage risks in the cybersecurity domain [3]. As such, the UK government provides advice to help citizens carry out their cybersecurity risk management activities e.g., [4], but provides no other direct support.

Children's devices and information are equally likely to be targeted by cyber-criminals. Indeed, due to the devices children use to access the Internet, they may be at greater risk [5]. Children need to learn how to keep themselves safe and secure online. So, who teaches children these skills? We cannot expect them to consult government advice. They could get the knowledge from books, from their school teachers or their parents. However, there is evidence that they do not get up-to-date information from children's cybersecurity-related books [6]. We also know that UK schools' coverage of cyber-related topics is rather patchy [7,8]. Hence, it is reasonable to assume that UK parents are also implicitly responsibilized to teach their children how to keep themselves safe and secure online.

Willems [9] argues that when citizens are responsibilized, they ought also to be empowered as two sides of the same coin. Willems explains that it is empowerment that enables duty-bearers (in this case, parents) to fulfill their responsibilities.

It is thus important to determine whether UK parents are indeed empowered to fulfil their cybersecurity education responsibilities. Section 2 reviews related research, and outline the methodologies of the studies we carried out to answer the empowerment question, with the three research questions to be answered. Sections 3 to 5 report on the three studies we carry out. Section 6 returns to the research questions, discusses the results and considers future research and the practical implications of our findings. We also acknowledge the limitations of this investigation. Section 7 concludes.

2   Related Work

2.1   Child Safety and Security Online

Children need to be cyber-safe and secure when online, and these are different concepts. Cybersafety is related to preventing harm resulting from online content (seeing adult content), contact (being contacted by unknown adults), and conduct (misbehaving online) [10]. Cybersecurity can be defined as "the protection of cyber-systems against cyber-threats" [11, p.29]. As such, cyber safety is related to the protection of the child's person and well-being, while cybersecurity is related to the protection of their devices and personal information.

Various cybersecurity educational resources are freely available, e.g., [12]. However, there are issues with many of these, particularly books, which have often been found to contain out-of-date or incorrect guidance [6]. In addition, even when children can engage independently with the many online resources, they still require adult input to explain how to apply the principles. That being so, we cannot expect children to teach themselves the correct principles or secure their own devices.

Technology companies' approaches to cybersecurity risk vary [13], meaning they cannot be relied on to keep children safe and secure online. While teachers will deliver some cybersecurity education in schools, they, too, often struggle with confusing information or lack of training [14].

On the other hand, parents have taught their children how to keep themselves safe for centuries [15] - parents universally accept this responsibility. UK parents are also the primary source of cybersafety information [1] - probably a natural extension of their responsibility for the physical safety of their children. In this paper, we explore the situation concerning children's cybersecurity education.

2.2   Responsibilization

Pellandini-Simányi and Conte [16] explain that responsibilization refers to assigning responsibility to citizens and engendering the sociocultural factors that persuade citizens to embrace those responsibilities.

The aim of responsibilization [17] is to *"transform individuals into self-reflexive, self-produced do-it-yourself projects"* (p. 60). Trnka and Trundle [18] argue that the aim is to produce *"self-reliant citizens who do not make too many demands on government services"* (p. 2). Citizens under this kind of governance are expected to accept responsibility for many aspects of their lives without expecting direct government support or intervention beyond the provision of advice.

2.3   Parental Responsibilization

The term 'parental responsibilization' is well established in other domains. For example, Cooper *et al.* [19] points out parental involvement is critical to children's academic success. Several other publications highlight parents' responsibilization in various areas [20–24].

Renaud *et al.* [3] argue that a responsibilization strategy is likely to fail when the domain within which it is applied is characterized by two dimensions: first, people need non-ubiquitous skills to embrace the responsibility, and second, a citizen's inability to shoulder their responsibilities will not affect other citizens.

Concerning the first requirement, we know cybersecurity skills are not ubiquitous across the general population [25]. Moreover, Quayyam *et al.* [26] reported that parents were challenged with the required knowledge in this domain, and Amankwa [27] reported that parents are unaware of the risks. Ab Hamid *et al.* [28] reports on a cyber parenting model to give Malaysian parents the necessary information to educate their children in this domain.

There is no compelling evidence that UK parents are different from these studied groups in terms of possessing the requisite knowledge and skills to care for their children's cybersecurity needs.

This makes it crucial for cybersecurity responsibilized parents to be empowered - we cannot expect them to shoulder the responsibility without knowing what to do and how to do it.

2.4   Parental Empowerment

Cooper *et al.* [19] argue that parents need to be empowered to help them to fulfill their responsibilities. The Center on the Developing Child at Harvard University published a report titled "Three Principles to Improve Outcomes for Children and Families" [29]. One of these is related to 'Strengthen core life skills' which can arguably apply to cyber skills, very important in our modern era.

The Convention on the Rights of the Child (CRC) was adopted by the General Assembly of the UN in 1989 and suggests several mechanisms for empowering parents, including providing information and guidance and assisting parents materially or financially. We already know that the UK government's responsibilization approach provides advice and guidance, but not material or financial assistance. Hence, we should explore how effectively their advice provision reaches and empowers parents.

If responsibilized parents do not have the required cybersecurity knowledge or are unable to act on their knowledge, it is likely that cybersecurity education responsibilization will fail. As a consequence, their children will be more vulnerable online.

2.5   Testing Whether Parents Are Empowered

The first step is to determine whether parents accept the responsibility to educate their children about cybersecurity. If they do not, empowerment becomes moot because people do not act on things that are not their responsibility. Section 3 reports on a study addressing **RQ1:** *"Do parents believe they should be responsibilized for teaching their children about cybersecurity?"*.

The next step is to determine whether UK government advice empowers parents in reality. Section 4 reports on a study that aimed to answer **RQ2**, *"Is parents' cybersecurity knowledge current?"*. If we find that parents do have the knowledge and can apply it, we can conclude that they are indeed empowered to act in alignment with their accepted responsibilities.

If we find that parents do not have the knowledge to embrace their parental responsibilities, or can not apply the knowledge they do have, we need a final study that answers **RQ3:** *"Where do parents get their knowledge from?"*.

If responsibilized parents do not have the knowledge and are indeed accessing government advice, we can conclude that mere provision of advice is not sufficiently empowering. On the other hand, if they are not consuming government advice, there is a clear need to find better ways to reach parents with government advice.

2.6   Methodology

Rather than attempting to answer all research questions through one large survey, the research questions were addressed using three short surveys. Shorter surveys have been shown to increase completion rates and reliability of answers

[30]. Three small studies were particularly appropriate in this study because they allowed us to explore issues that emerged in previous surveys.

Our studies were conducted online using Prolific to recruit participants. Adulthood is reached in the UK at 18 years old [31] so we recruited UK-based parents of children under 18 years of age. All surveys were piloted with small groups of adults representative of the participants to ensure clarity and to determine how much time was required to complete the surveys to ensure fair reimbursement. We paid people the UK living wage for their participation.

Participants in previous studies were excluded to ensure no cross-contamination. We used attention questions to ensure that participants were answering thoughtfully. All studies were approved by the first author's institutional ethics review board.

Study 1 elicited parents' acceptance of the responsibilization to educate their children about cybersecurity. Participants in the survey were paid £1.60 for participation, which took, on average, 5 min. This study revealed that parents strongly accept responsibilization but felt unsure about their and other parents' capabilities in managing their responsibility.

Study 2 proceeded to test parents' cybersecurity knowledge. Participants in the survey were paid £2 for participation, which took, on average, 6.5 min. This survey revealed a general lack of current cybersecurity knowledge.

Study 3 elicited information about the sources UK parents used to gather cybersecurity knowledge to educate their children. We also assessed the emotions cybersecurity elicited. Participants in the survey were paid £1.50 for participation, which took, on average, 4 min.

3   RQ1: Do Parents Accept Cybersecurity Reponsibilization?

While prior research suggests that UK adults are responsibilized for taking care of their own cybersecurity [3,32], there has been limited examination as to the impact of this strategy on UK parents and their children. Thus, Study 1 aimed to determine whether parents believed they were responsibilized in this regard, and, if so, to determine how they felt about this.

3.1   Demographics

After excluding respondents who failed attention tests, 123 participants participated and were paid the UK living wage for their participation. Respondents had an average of two children (min = 1, max = 4). Respondents' youngest children were, on average, 7.46 years of age and their eldest children were an average of 11.53 years old. The majority of participants were employed either full-time or part-time (n = 106, 86%). The remainder were currently seeking work (n = 3, 2.34%), unemployed but not seeking work (n = 12, 9.7%) or in education (n = 2, 1.6%). This employment rate is higher than the UK rate of 75.5% [33].

Table 1. Perceptions of Cybersecurity *Study 1*

Please indicate the extent to which you agree with the following statements:	M	SD
I think other parents are afraid of making mistakes when dealing with cybersecurity on their devices.	3.86	0.75
I think other parents have no difficulty understanding most cyber security matters.	2.74	1.04
Cyber security expertise is essential - I think other parents embrace learning new skills.	3.65	0.89
I think most parents feel cyber security is kind of strange and frightening.	3.48	1.01
I think most parents think that cyber security terminology sounds like confusing jargon to me	3.39	1.03
I think most parents can deal with a hacking attempt on their devices.	2.37	1.09

3.2 Questions

(1) **Acceptance of Responsibilization:** Participants were asked "*Who do you think is REALLY responsible for teaching children about password best practice?*" and given the multi-select choices of: (1) Teachers, (2) Parents, (3) TV Programs, (4) Books, and (5) Other. There was no limit on the number of choices that could be selected.

(2) **Feelings Towards Cybersecurity:** Participants were asked a series of Likert questions relating to cybersecurity responsibilization. They were asked to select the degree to which they agreed with statements (Strongly Disagree = 1, Strongly Agree = 5) – see Table 1.

(3) **Password 'Best Practice' Knowledge:** In order to gain a snapshot into parents' cybersecurity knowledge application, we investigated their understanding and enforcement of password best practices. Passwords are the one ubiquitous cybersecurity tool, encountered by every online user, and one of the first children will encounter (in the UK, this is guaranteed at age 4 when they start school).

3.3 Findings

Parent Acceptance of Cybersecurity Responsibilization. 'Parents' were the most common choice, with 96.7% (n = 119) choosing this option. Teachers were the second most likely option with 68.3% (n = 84) selecting this choice. Only a minority chose TV Programs (n = 15, 12.2%), books (n = 9, 7.3%) and 'other' (n = 7, 5.7%). Of those who selected 'other,' only two participants provided further information: one suggested social media, and the other felt the technology industry and manufacturers should take responsibility for educating children. This response profile is remarkably similar to the one published by Statista [1].

3.4   Parents Feelings Towards Cybersecurity Responsibilization

Participants tended to slightly agree with the statement that *"Cybersecurity is essential - I think other parents embrace learning new skills"* (M = 3.65, SD = 0.89). However they also slightly agreed that *"I think other parents are afraid of making mistakes when dealing with cybersecurity on their devices"* (M = 3.8, SD = 0.75) and slightly disagreed that *"I think most parents can deal with a hacking attempt on their devices"* (M = 2.36, SD = 1.09).

Parents Enacting of Cybersecurity Responsibilization. Participants were asked to identify nine password "best practice" principles. Despite sterling efforts from the National Cybersecurity Centre to educate UK citizens on the importance of passphrases, only 11.3% of parents mentioned this as an important password principle. Indeed, on average, participants only identified two principles each. Only the latest password guidance was considered valid, such as the use of a passphrase over LUDS (**L**ower case, **U**pper case, **D**igits and **S**ymbols) and not enforcing frequent password changes [34].

Many provided incorrect or out-of-date information (on average, 2.4 incorrect principles per participant), for example *"Mix of capital letters and numbers and punctuation"*.

Participants were asked if they knew all their children's passwords, given that guidance in the UK is that parents should be aware of what accounts and passwords their children have [35]. Only 20.16% (n = 25) reported not knowing any, while 27.42% (n = 34) knew some but not all. A Mann-Whitney U test found that parents with 1 or 2 children were significantly more likely to know all their children's passwords than those with 3 or more children (z = 2.00982, p = .04444). This highlights the challenges in managing accounts for a group of children of different ages. It should be noted that the average age of children whose parents reported knowing all their passwords was also lower (7.58 years) than those who knew some (11.84 years) or none (11.23 years). This indicates the changing role of parents' involvement in their children's cybersecurity as the child matures [36].

3.5   Summary

We discovered that parents believed that they were appropriately responsible for educating their children on cybersecurity. However, they also often felt unsure of their own cybersecurity capabilities to act upon this responsibility. We found they had limited knowledge in one area of cybersecurity, namely passwords. It was therefore then necessary to conduct a second survey to understand better if parents held sufficient knowledge in other areas in order to be able to educate their children in this area.

4   RQ2: Parents' Actual Knowledge

Having found that parents were willing to embrace being responsibilized for their children's cybersecurity education but showed some unease in their opinions of their cybersecurity abilities, we further explored their feelings towards technology in general and measured their cybersecurity and privacy knowledge.

4.1 Demographics

In total, after excluding participants who failed attention tests, the responses from 169 participants who participated in this survey were retained for analysis. All participants lived in the UK and had children aged under 18. Participants had, on average, 1.86 children (min = 1, max = 5). The average age of the participants' children was 8.87 years. The majority of participants were employed (n = 141, 83.4%), the remainder were unemployed and not seeking work (n = 23, 13.6%), unemployed and seeking work (n = 4, 2.7%) and in full-time education (n = 1, 0.5%). This employment rate is higher than the UK rate of 75.5% [33].

4.2 Questions

(1) **Technological Affinity:** To explore emotional responses to technology in general, given that a negative attitude is likely to lead to avoidance of cybersecurity [37], we used the Affinity for Technology Interaction Scale (ATI) [38]. The nine ATI statements were provided to participants who were asked to respond on a Likert scale from 1 (completely disagree) to 6 (completely agree). This scoring was inverted for Questions 3, 6, and 8, which were negatively worded.

(2) **Privacy Knowledge:** The second aspect to explore is actual knowledge of privacy concepts. We used the Online Privacy Literacy Scale (OPLIS) to gauge privacy-related knowledge [39].

(3) **Cybersecurity Knowledge:** Participants were asked a series of questions to assess their own habits in regard to cybersecurity in order to determine how they applied their cybersecurity knowledge. These questions were drawn from NCSC cybersecurity guidance for UK individuals (as opposed to organisations) [4]. Other organisations, such as NIST, agree with this guidance on cybersecurity [40]. The advice provided by the NCSC includes: "Use three random words for your password", "Use a password manager or save passwords in your browser", "Use multi-factor authentication (MFA)", "Back up your data", "Update your software".

4.3 Findings

Technological Affinity: ATI. Participants responded most positively to the statement *I try to make full use of the capabilities of a technical system*. They were most likely to agree with the statement "*It is enough for me to know the basic functions of a technical system*" (See Table 2). The average ATI score showed participants had a mildly positive attitude towards technology. This suggests that participants are less than likely to avoid cybersecurity measures and education.

Table 2. ATI Responses *Study 3*

ATI Statements	Mean	Std Dev
I like to occupy myself in greater detail with technical systems	3.75	1.31
I like testing the functions of new technical systems.	4.38	1.14
I predominantly deal with technical systems because I have to	3.36	0.99
When I have a new technical system in front of me, I try it out intensively	4.09	1.26
I enjoy spending time becoming acquainted with a new technical system	4.21	1.25
It is enough for me that a technical system works; I donŠt care how or why	3.62	1.20
I try to understand how a technical system exactly works.	3.96	1.24
It is enough for me to know the basic functions of a technical system	3.44	1.02
I try to make full use of the capabilities of a technical system	4.44	1.12

Privacy Knowledge: OPLIS. Responses to the 19 questions in the adapted OPLIS were graded with 1 point for a correct answer and 0 for an incorrect answer. On average, participants scored 12 points (63%) with the highest score being 18 (94.7%) which was scored by one participant and the lowest score being 6 (31.6%), which one participant scored.

The question with the correct answers was the completion of the sentence *"The protection of personal data is"*, which was answered correctly by 93.5% (n = 158) of participants. The question with the fewest correct answers was *"Please state whether the statements below are true or false. If you don't know please select 'don't know' "* - In the UK the same standards and conditions apply to all online social networks. Any deviations have to be indicated. Participants were given the option of 'True', 'False' or 'I don't know'. This was answered correctly by 21.3% (n = 36) of participants.

Overall, participants scored higher on questions that asked for definitions of terms rather than questions that asked if an interpretation of the data protection and cybersecurity laws and guidance was correct or faulty. This suggests that they may require further guidance on how to apply the facts that they have learned.

Cybersecurity Knowledge - Government Advice. (a) Passwords: Participants were presented with 10 passwords of varying strengths and memorability (see Fig. 1). These included some well-known poor passwords (123456), passphrases and short passwords featuring LUDS *(Lowercase, Uppercase, Digits, Symbols)*. (LUDS were advised in the past as the best way to create a strong password. However, since 2017 best practice advice points people towards pass phrases rather than LUDS passwords [35].) Bl2ckadd3r is a reference to a widely popular UK cult classic TV series called Blackadder[1].

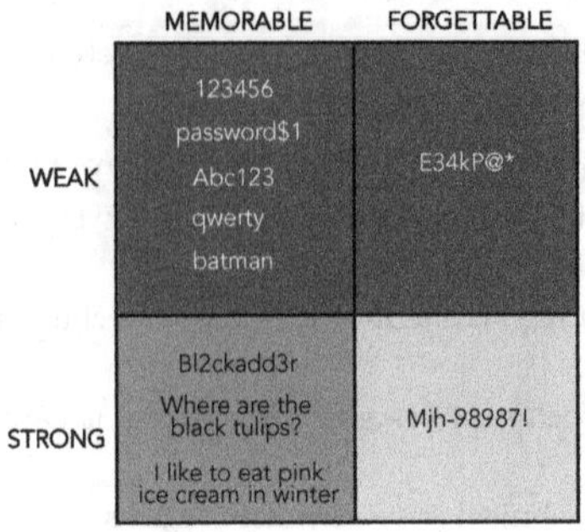

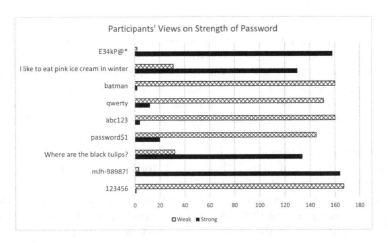

Fig. 1. Password Strength and Memorability (Strength based on Bennish Score: strong score ≥ 4; Memorability based on semantic and function-related properties [41].)

The two passwords rated most strongly by the participants were short LUDS; these, in reality, have a lower strength than the passphrases (see Fig. 2).

Fig. 2. Participants' Views on Password Strength

Participants were also asked to give their own example of a strong password. These passwords were then assessed using the Bennish algorithm [42]. This showed a mean strength of 4.48 (SD = 0.73). Only 9% (n = 13) of participants gave a passphrase as an example. The NCSC website provides guidance on using three-word passphrases, and it is clear that this advice has yet to reach these parents. While many participants could generate strong passwords, the majority were long strings of LUDS, which would be difficult to recall (see Table 3). Interestingly, when their passwords were scored using the Bennish algorithm [42], they scored lower than 9-year-old children completing the same test [43].

---

[1] https://en.wikipedia.org/wiki/Blackadder.

Table 3. Strength & Memorability of Participant-Generated Passwords

	Memorable	Forgettable
Strong	13	116
Weak	6	7

(b) **Password Manager Usage:** Participants were asked how they remembered passwords (to test the advice to use a password manager). The most common response was memorisation (39.8% n = 67). By contrast, only 27.38% (n = 46) used a password manager. The least common response was to store them in a browser (4.17% n = 7) while "*Use the same one all over so its easy*" and "*Write them down*" were both chosen by 16 participants (9.52%).

(c) **MFA:** All participants reported using Multi-Factor Authentication (MFA), 51.75% (n = 74) stated that this was on every account, 48.25% (n = 69) stated that this was when it was offered.

Participants were presented with 6 potential definitions of Multi-Factor Authentication, of which two were correct. Participants could select as many as they wished, 44% (n = 63) of participants chose an incorrect definition.

(d) **Backing Up:** Participants were asked if they regularly backed up data on their own devices, 44.05% (n = 74) said yes with 26.19% (n = 44) saying no. However, a further 29.17% (n = 50) were unsure whether they did or not. Those participants who stated they did backup regularly were then asked how they did this through an open text field. The majority of participants (89%, n = 64) relied on cloud backup or external devices. The remainder either stated they could not give a correct definition, gave incorrect definitions such as 'different email and passwords,' or assumed working directly from the cloud would ensure their data was secure, suggesting a poor understanding of backups.

(e) **Updating Software:** When questioned as to their action after receiving a notification that their operating system needed to be updated, participants were most likely to select "*Install after work when I don't need it so much*" (36.31% n = 61) followed by "*Tell it to try again tonight*" (27.98% n = 47). Immediate installation was the 3rd most popular choice (27.38%, n = 46). Only 3.57% (n = 6) of participants would dismiss it altogether. This indicated that the majority of participants were aware of the need to install updates, although they did not act on this immediately.

4.4 Summary

Having found that parents did not possess adequate cybersecurity knowledge in the areas covered by the UK Government advice, we explore the sources parents consult in gathering cybersecurity knowledge and the sources they would be willing to accept support from.

5   RQ3: Sources of Knowledge

Based on the findings, which showed limited cybersecurity knowledge, we ran a survey to determine where people obtained their cyber knowledge and what confidence this gave them in their own knowledge.

5.1   Demographics

In total, after excluding participants who failed attention tests, the responses from 186 participants who participated in the survey were retained for analysis. All participants lived in the UK and had children aged under 18. Participants had, on average, 1.7 children (min = 1, max = 5). In total, participants had 179 children under the age of eight and 51 aged 14–17 years old. Participants were asked for their employment status, 65.5% were employed (n = 120), 20% were unemployed (n = 38) and the remainder failed to disclose this information (14.5% n = 26).

5.2   Questions

(1) **Cybersecurity Knowledge Sources:** Participants were asked where they obtained advice about online cybersecurity. Participants were given ten multi-select choices with no limit on the number of choices they could select.

(2) **Support from UK Government:** Participants were then asked if they felt they had been given enough support by the UK government in managing their children's online security.

(3) **Acceptable Sources of Help:** Participants were also asked where they would accept help from in managing their child's online security. This was a multi-select question featuring seven options.

(4) **Acceptable Kinds of Help:** As well as determining where parents would accept help from, it was also necessary to understand what help they wanted. Participants were asked to select the areas in which they needed support from a list of eight (Fig. 3).

5.3   Findings

Cybersecurity Knowledge Sources. Perhaps unsurprisingly, Google was the most common advice source (n = 124, 66.7%). After Google, parents were most likely to seek information from their child's school (n = 70, 37.6%). The government's website was the fourth most likely choice and was only chosen by a minority of participants (n = 51, 27.4%), fewer than participants who consulted their friends (61 participants - 32%).

Support from UK Government. Concerning being given enough support, the majority (52.41% n = 98) felt this was not the government's responsibility. A further 31% (n = 58) felt they needed more support, while the remainder (16.58% n = 31) felt they were given enough support. This confirms parents' willingness to take personal responsibility for their child's cybersecurity education, (see Fig. 4).

Acceptable Sources of Knowledge. Again, the UK government ranked low, with only 32% (n = 57) of participants stating they would definitely accept help from the government. This was the lowest-scoring option. Participants were most likely to accept from academics qualified in cybersecurity (79.67% n = 145) (see Fig. 3).

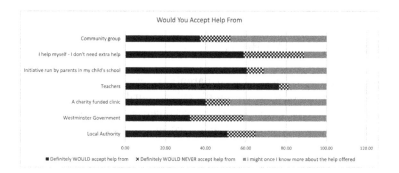

Fig. 3. Participants' Likely Responses to Being Offered Help From Various Sources

Acceptable Kinds of Help. Participants were most keen to have monitoring apps they could use and detailed instructions that they could use at home. They were least likely to want to access groups in person to get cybersecurity guidance.

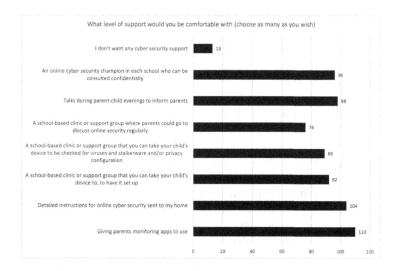

Fig. 4. Forms of Help Participants Are Looking For

5.4   Summary

Having confirmed that parents embraced being responsibilized in regards to their children's cybersecurity education, we also found that they did not possess sufficient cybersecurity knowledge. While the UK government provides excellent advice through the NCSC website, parents do not want to look to them for cybersecurity guidance.

6   Discussion and Reflection

Study 1 answered RQ 1, showing that parents believed they ought to be responsible for the education of their children's cybersecurity education. Study 3 confirmed that parents felt it was not the government's responsibility but demonstrated uncertainty and a lack of confidence in their cybersecurity knowledge and abilities.

Study 2 (RQ2) led us to assess the cybersecurity knowledge people had. We found that participants were mildly positive towards technology and had some theoretical cybersecurity knowledge. However, they reported suboptimal habits and often did not apply the knowledge that they did have. For example, despite correctly identifying that a given passphrase was a strong password (Fig. 2) when asked to create their own password, they defaulted to LUDS (Table 3). If these complex but forgettable passwords are indeed the types of passwords they use, they likely engage in other insecure practices, such as reusing passwords across multiple accounts [44].

Study 3 (RQ3) led us to identify which information sources parents relied on for their cybersecurity information. Participants reported relying primarily on Google for information. Google is not necessarily a good source of the latest in password advice. For example, For example, a Google search on "strong password" returns the suggestion of "m#P52s@apV", which does not align with the latest in best practice from the UK government [4] nor from NIST in the USA [44]. Users are unlikely to look beyond the first few results, thus seeing incorrect information repeated in the first few hits means it is less likely they will access correct guidance [45]. MMoreover, when we searched for "password manager," the first page presented nine different 'best password manager' lists. This is likely to confuse rather than inform and support choice [46].

We can conclude that UK parents (1) accept cybersecurity responsibilization and (2) do their best to find knowledge to meet its demands. Unfortunately, they rely on Google searches instead of the excellent advice provided by the UK government. As such, their knowledge is patchy and often outdated. This means that Renaud's first responsibilization failure requirement is met [3].

UK parents' inability to fulfill their state-assigned responsibility to educate their children about cybersecurity is likely to result in the unwitting dissemination of incorrect and outdated advice. This, in turn, will result in the spread of sub-optimal cyber practices, especially given that study 3 discovered that people asked their friends for cybersecurity information. The issues ensuing from this are likely to spread further than just the child in question, given that almost one-third of parents sought advice from their own friends. Hence, incorrect knowledge is likely to spread throughout the community. This means that Renaud's second responsibilization failure requirement is met [3].

The empowerment of parents needs to be added to the UK government's responsibilization strategy. However, given that parents express a willingness to accept advice from educational authorities and cybersecurity academics, there is a clear opportunity for intervening to (1) ensure that advice is disseminated more effectively to parents and (2) provide more support to UK parents to empower them in applying their knowledge.

6.1 Future Research

Firstly, we do not know what exactly impacts parents' knowledge levels and practices have on their children's knowledge, given all the other influences they are subject to. A two-part study interviewing parents and their children to explore their knowledge and household cybersecurity practices would offer deeper insights. Moreover, we must discover how one child's flawed 'best practice' knowledge will influence other children's knowledge and cybersecurity practices in their social circle. Investigating how children share cybersecurity 'best practice' knowledge requires an ethnographic approach, observing what children tell each other and how they learn principles, both good and bad, from each other.

Secondly, it would be interesting to understand why parents so willingly embrace cybersecurity education responsibilization, given the relative complexity of risk management in this domain.

It is possible that the desire to be responsible for their child's online presence and activities is linked to the desire to be perceived as 'good parents.' The idea of good parenting is linked with, along with warmth and nurture, being appropriately controlling and engaged in their child's life [47], including their online activities [48]. The view of a 'good parent' has changed dramatically over the years, fueled in part by social media [49]. Parental responsibilities may well include the creation of rules around technology to meet societal expectations, but these rules may not be grounded in research or current guidance [50]. More research is required into how the narrative of "good parenting" informs cybersecurity education in the home.

Third, our studies did not examine ethnicity. Work in other areas of responsibilization of education (for example, during the lockdowns of 2020 and 2021) demonstrated that those from ethnic minorities were affected more negatively than others [51]. It also did not closely examine socioeconomic groups, work in other areas of technology has found that enforcement of rules around technology decreases as socioeconomic status decreases [52]. This might also be the case for our participants. Our participants were, on average, better educated and more likely to be employed than the UK average, so more work is needed to reach other communities. This presents an opportunity for more targeted future studies.

6.2   Practical Implications

Parents are embracing cybersecurity responsibilization regarding their children's cybersecurity education. Therefore, rather than suggesting the deresponsibilization of parents, we need to find ways to empower them more effectively in keeping up with the latest cybersecurity guidance and improving their cybersecurity behaviors.

There have been many successful programs that have aimed to improve a parent's theoretical knowledge in a subject and thereby pass this on to the child [53]. However, changing behaviours is a more complicated task, and studies in other areas involving child health and actions have highlighted the difficulty in changing behaviour in the medium to long term [54]. Programs that parents designed have shown more promising results [55].

Participants reported confidence in their cybersecurity knowledge but then displayed poor habits in their cybersecurity practice and gaps in applying this knowledge. Further research is warranted into how to raise awareness of the need for parents to increase their knowledge and change their behavior, along with programs to help them act on this.

This study has indicated that these programs should not come from the government and that they are more likely to be accepted if they come from academics, peers, or a child's school. The challenge will be to design these so that they not only improve knowledge but create positive behavioral changes [13].

6.3   Limitations

Participants in Study 3 were least likely to seek advice from the Westminster Government. However, it should be noted that this survey was launched a week after the UK Prime Minister Boris Johnson resigned after a series of scandals [56]. This may have impacted the trust participants felt they could place in government advice.

We also have yet to determine what parents are doing instead of what they say they are doing. A more ecologically valid study would observe parents interacting with their children in the home environment to explore this.

7   Conclusion

The burden for citizens of managing their cybersecurity practices and protections rests on parents regarding their children's cybersecurity education and devices.

These studies have shown that while parents embrace this responsibility, they are not sufficiently empowered to carry it out independently and correctly. This study has highlighted significant gaps in parents' knowledge and indicated that parents may be unaware of these gaps and have misplaced confidence in their knowledge and ability to educate their children about cybersecurity.

As wonderful parents, UK parents accept the responsibility but are insufficiently empowered, so they cannot do this as well as they would like. As a cybersecurity community, we should try to find better ways to support them.

Acknowledgements. We thank the participants for their time and considered answers. We also thank Natalie Coull for her feedback on an earlier draft of this paper.

References

1. Statista: Internet usage in the United Kingdom (UK) - Statistics & Facts (2022). https://www.statista.com/topics/3246/internet-usage-in-the-uk/. Accessed Aug 2022

2. Ofcom: UK's internet use surges to record levels (2020). https://www.ofcom.org.uk/about-ofcom/latest/media/media-releases/2020/uk-internet-use-surge. Accessed Sept 2022

3. Renaud, K., Flowerday, S., Warkentin, M., Cockshott, P., Orgeron, C.: Is the responsibilization of the cyber security risk reasonable and judicious? Comput. Secur. **78**, 198–211 (2018). https://doi.org/10.1016/j.cose.2018.06.006

4. National Cyber Security Centre: Create your cyber action plan (2022). https://www.ncsc.gov.uk/section/information-for/individuals-families. Accessed Sept 2022

5. Hazlegreaves, S.: Children are becoming more vulnerable to cybercriminals as IoT device use explodes (2019). https://www.openaccessgovernment.org/children-vulnerable-to-cybercriminals/72665/. Accessed Sept 2022. Open Access Government

6. Renaud, K., Prior, S.: Children's password-related books: efficacious, vexatious and incongruous. Early Childhood Educ. J. **49**(3), 387–400 (2021). https://doi.org/10.1007/s10643-020-01067-z

7. Pencheva, D., Hallett, J., Rashid, A.: Bringing cyber to school: integrating cybersecurity into secondary school education. IEEE Secur. Priv. **18**(2), 68–74 (2020). https://doi.org/10.1109/MSEC.2020.2969409

8. Lamond, M., Renaud, K., Wood, L., Prior, S.: SOK: young children's cybersecurity knowledge and skills. In: EuroUSEC, Karlsruhe, Germany, pp. 14–27. ACM (2022). https://doi.org/10.1145/3549015.3554207

9. Willems, J.C.: Children as subjects of rights: three waves of emancipation, from past and present cruelty to future creativity? Maastricht Centre for Human Rights (2018)

10. Byron, T.: Safer children in a digital world: the report of the Byron review: Be safe, be aware, have fun (2008). https://dera.ioe.ac.uk/7332/. Accessed Mar 2023

11. Refsdal, A., Solhaug, B., Stølen, K.: Cyber-risk management. In: Cyber-Risk Management. SCS, pp. 33–47. Springer, Cham (2015). https://doi.org/10.1007/978-3-319-23570-7_5

12. Google, Play interland - be internet awesome (no date). https://beinternetawesome.withgoogle.com/en_us/interland. Accessed Mar 2023

13. de Bruijn, H., Janssen, M.: Building cybersecurity awareness: the need for evidence-based framing strategies. Gov. Inf. Q. **34**(1), 1–7 (2017). https://doi.org/10.1016/j.giq.2017.02.007

14. Kumar, P.C., Chetty, M., Clegg, T.L., Vitak, J.: Privacy and security considerations for digital technology use in elementary schools. In: Proceedings of the 2019 CHI Conference on Human Factors in Computing Systems, CHI 2019, pp. 1–13. Association for Computing Machinery, New York (2019). https://doi.org/10.1145/3290605.3300537

15. Wurtele, S.K., Gillispie, E.I., Currier, L.L., Franklin, C.F.: A comparison of teachers vs. parents as instructors of a personal safety program for preschoolers. Child Abuse Neglect **16**(1), 127–137 (1992). https://doi.org/10.1016/0145-2134(92)90013-H

16. Pellandini-Simányi, L., Conte, L.: Consumer de-responsibilization: changing notions of consumer subjects and market moralities after the 2008–9 financial crisis. Consump. Mark. Cult. **24**(3), 280–305 (2021). https://doi.org/10.1080/10253866.2020.1781099

17. Ekendahl, M., Månsson, J., Karlsson, P.: Risk and responsibilization: resistance and compliance in Swedish treatment for youth cannabis use. Drugs Educ. Prev. Policy **27**(1), 60–68 (2020). https://doi.org/10.1080/09687637.2018.1544224

18. Trnka, S., Trundle, C.: Competing Responsibilities: The Ethics and Politics of Contemporary Life. Duke University Press, Durham (2017)

19. Cooper, C.W., Christie, C.A.: Evaluating parent empowerment: a look at the potential of social justice evaluation in education. Teach. Coll. Rec. **107**(10), 2248–2274 (2005). https://doi.org/10.1111/j.1467-9620.2005.00591.x

20. Ribbens, J.: Mothers and Their Children: A Feminist Sociology of Childrearing. Sage, London (1994)

21. Nesbit, S.: Paying for the gift of education: a critical discourse analysis of the intown academy of Atlanta., Ph.D. thesis, Thesis, Georgia State University (2014). https://doi.org/10.57709/5813869

22. Hartong, S., Manolev, J.: The construction of (good) parents (as professionals) in/through learning platforms. Tertium Comparationis **29**(1), 93–116 (2023). https://doi.org/10.31244/tc.2023.01.05

23. Willems, J.C.: Children as subjects of rights: three waves of emancipation, from past and present cruelty to future creativity? Net J. Soc. Sci. **7**(1), 28–43 (2019)

24. Williams, F.: What matters is who works: why every child matters to new labour. Commentary on the DfES green paper every child matters. Crit. Soc. Policy **24**(3), 406–427 (2004). https://doi.org/10.1177/0261018304044366

25. Dodel, M., Mesch, G.: Inequality in digital skills and the adoption of online safety behaviors. Inf. Commun. Soc. **21**(5), 712–728 (2018). https://doi.org/10.1080/1369118X.2018.1428652

26. Quayyum, F., Bueie, J., Cruzes, D.S., Jaccheri, L., Vidal, J.C.T.: Understanding parents' perceptions of children's cybersecurity awareness in Norway. In: Proceedings of the Conference on Information Technology for Social Good, Rome, Italy, pp. 236–241. ACM (2021). https://doi.org/10.1145/3462203.3475900

27. Amankwa, E.: Relevance of cybersecurity education at pedagogy levels in schools. J. Inf. Secur. **12**(4), 233–249 (2021). https://doi.org/10.4236/jis.2021.124013

28. Ab Hamid, R., Yunos, Z., Ahmad, M.: Cyber parenting module development for parents. In: 12th International Technology, Education and Development Conference (INTED2018), IATED, Valencia, Spain, pp. 9620–9627 (2018). https://doi.org/10.21125/inted.2018.2411

29. Center on the Developing Child at Harvard University: Three principles to improve outcomes for children and families (2021). https://developingchild.harvard.edu/resources/three-early-childhood-development-principles-improve-child-family-outcomes/

30. Kost, R., Correa da Rosa, J.: Impact of survey length and compensation on validity, reliability, and sample characteristics for ultrashort-, short-, and long-research participant perception surveys. J. Clin. Transl. Sci. **2**, 31–37 (2018). https://doi.org/10.1017/cts.2018.18

31. Government Digital Service, Age of criminal responsibility. GOV.UK, October 2014. https://www.gov.uk/age-of-criminal-responsibility. Accessed Jan 2023

32. Renaud, K., Orgeron, C., Warkentin, M., French, P.E.: Cyber security responsibilization: an evaluation of the intervention approaches adopted by the Five Eyes countries and China. Public Adm. Rev. **80**(4), 577–589 (2020). https://doi.org/10.1111/puar.13210

33. Watson, B.: Employment in the UK: November 2022 (2022). https://www.ons.gov.uk/employmentandlabourmarket/peopleinwork/employmentandemployeetypes/bulletins/employmentintheuk/november2022

34. Grassi, P.A., et al.: NIST special publication 800-63B, digital identity guidelines, Technical report, NIST (2017). https://pages.nist.gov/800-63-3/sp800-63b.html. Accessed Aug 2022

35. Prior, S., Renaud, K.: Age-appropriate password "best practice" ontologies for early educators and parents. Int. J. Child-Comput. Interact. **23–24**, 100169 (2020). https://doi.org/10.1016/j.ijcci.2020.100169

36. Muir, K., Joinson, A.N.: An exploratory study into the negotiation of cybersecurity within the family home. Front. Psychol. **11**(424) (2020). https://doi.org/10.3389/fpsyg.2020.00424

37. Renaud, K., Zimmermann, V., Schürmann, T., Böhm, C.: Exploring cybersecurity-related emotions and finding that they are challenging to measure. Hum. Soc. Sci. Commun. **8**(1), 1–17 (2021). https://doi.org/10.1057/s41599-021-00746-5

38. Franke, T., Attig, C., Wessel, D.: A personal resource for technology interaction: development and validation of the affinity for technology interaction (ATI) scale. Int. J. Hum.-Comput. Interact. **35**(6), 456–467 (2019). https://doi.org/10.1080/10447318.2018.1456150

39. Trepte, S., et al.: Do people know about privacy and data protection strategies? Towards the "Online Privacy Literacy Scale" (OPLIS). In: Gutwirth, S., Leenes, R., de Hert, P. (eds.) Reforming European Data Protection Law. LGTS, vol. 20, pp. 333–365. Springer, Dordrecht (2015). https://doi.org/10.1007/978-94-017-9385-8_14

40. NIST: Multi-factor authentication, nIST, March 2022. https://www.nist.gov/itl/smallbusinesscyber/guidance-topic/multi-factor-authentication. Accessed Aug 2022

41. Madan, C.R.: Exploring word memorability: how well do different word properties explain item free-recall probability? Psychon. Bull. Rev. **28**(2), 583–595 (2021). https://doi.org/10.3758/s13423-020-01820-w

42. Kennish, B.: Password Strength Checker (2019). https://www.bennish.net/password-strength-checker/. Accessed Aug 2022

43. Prior, S., Renaud, K.: The impact of financial deprivation on children's cybersecurity knowledge & abilities. Educ. Inf. Technol. **27**, 1–21 (2022). https://doi.org/10.1007/s10639-022-10908-w

44. NIST: Easy ways to build a better p@$5w0rd, nIST, October 2017. https://www.nist.gov/blogs/taking-measure/easy-ways-build-better-p5w0rd. Accessed Jan 2023

45. Advanced Web Ranking, CTR Study: How SERP Features Affect Organic Results [Infographic], advanced Web Ranking Blog (2019). https://www.advancedwebranking.com/google-ctr-study/

46. Greifeneder, R., Scheibehenne, B., Kleber, N.: Less may be more when choosing is difficult: choice complexity and too much choice. Acta Physiol. (Oxf) **133**(1), 45–50 (2010). https://doi.org/10.1016/j.actpsy.2009.08.005

47. Smith, M.: Good parenting: making a difference. Early Human Dev. **86**(11), 689–693 (2010). https://doi.org/10.1016/j.earlhumdev.2010.08.011

48. Czeskis, A., et al.: Parenting from the pocket: value tensions and technical directions for secure and private parent-teen mobile safety. In: Proceedings of the Sixth Symposium on Usable Privacy and Security. Association for Computing Machinery, New York (2010). https://doi.org/10.1145/1837110.1837130. p. Article 15

49. Assarsson, L., Aarsand, P.: 'how to be good': media representations of parenting. Stud. Educ. Adults **43**(1), 78–92 (2011). https://doi.org/10.1080/02660830.2011.11661605

50. Mazmanian, M., Lanette, S.: "Okay, one more episode": an ethnography of parenting in the digital age. In: Proceedings of the ACM Conference on Computer Supported Cooperative Work and Social Computing (CSCW), pp. 2273–2286. Association for Computing Machinery, New York (2017). https://doi.org/10.1145/2998181.2998218

51. Bayrakdar, S., Guveli, A.: Inequalities in home learning and schools' provision of distance teaching during school closure of COVID-19 lockdown in the UK, Technical report. ISER Working Paper Series No. 2020-09, Institute for Social and Economic Research (2020). https://www.econstor.eu/handle/10419/227790

52. Yardi, S., Bruckman, A.: Income, race, and class: exploring socioeconomic differences in family technology use. In: Proceedings of the SIGCHI Conference on Human Factors in Computing Systems, CHI 2012, pp. 3041–3050. Association for Computing Machinery, New York (2012). https://doi.org/10.1145/2207676.2208716

53. Muir, T.: Numeracy at home: involving parents in mathematics education. Int. J. Math. Teach. Learn. **25**, 1–13 (2012). https://eric.ed.gov/?id=EJ970698

54. Zeedyk, M.S., Wallace, L., Carcary, B., Jones, K., Larter, K.: Children and road safety: increasing knowledge does not improve behaviour. Br. J. Educ. Psychol. **71**(4), 573–594 (2001). https://doi.org/10.1348/000709901158686

55. Huebner, C., Milgrom, P.: Evaluation of a parent-designed programme to support tooth brushing of infants and young children. Int. J. Dental Hygiene **13** (2014). https://doi.org/10.1111/idh.12100

56. Meredith, S.: UK Prime Minister Boris Johnson resigns (2022). https://www.cnbc.com/2022/07/07/boris-johnson-resigns-as-uk-prime-minister.html. Accessed Aug 2022

To Bot or Not to Bot?: Analysing Mental Health Data Disclosures

Deborah Taylor[✉][iD], Clare Melvin[iD], Hane Aung[iD], and Rameez Asif[iD]

School of Computing Sciences, University of East Anglia, Norwich NR4 7TJ, UK
{debbie.taylor,c.melvin,min.aung,rameez.asif}@uea.ac.uk
https://www.uea.ac.uk/

Abstract. Disclosure of personal information about wellbeing and mental health is a nuanced situation requiring trust between agents. Current methods for initial mental health assessments are time and resource intensive. With increases in demand for mental health services and decreases in funding and staffing levels, this paper explores whether conversational agents can be sufficiently 'trusted' to collect the sensitive data disclosed in initial mental health assessment, thereby reducing the workload for trained professionals.

An initial study identified the desired characteristics of a conversational agent designed for mental health assessment purposes and produced a MoSCoW design framework of desirable features.

A second study tested the framework by investigating whether a conversational agent, displaying these desirable human-like features, could establish sufficient trust to collect data, comparable to completing forms online which are sent from a mental health service provider, or requested through social media. Participants (n = 236; female = 58%, non-binary = 5%, Prefer not to say = 1%, age 18–80+yrs) were recruited from a UK mental health service provider and through social media.

Of the participants, 50% (n = 126) engaged with the bespoke conversational agent to disclose sensitive personal information in an initial mental health assessment; the remaining participants provided the information by completing the online forms though social media or from a mental health service provider.

Results indicate a conversational agent can be used to collect sensitive mental health data for initial assessment. Whilst such a tool may not be appropriate for all individuals and demographics, the conversational agent shows promise for reducing the administrative workload of those in the mental health profession, thus increasing resources for treatment and therapy.

Keywords: Conversational agents · Trust · Mental health · Personal disclosure · Sensitive disclosure

1 Introduction

Disclosure of personal information about wellbeing and mental health is nuanced and requires trust between agents. Any relationship between a healthcare pro-

© The Author(s), under exclusive license to Springer Nature Switzerland AG 2024
A. Moallem (Ed.): HCII 2024, LNCS 14728, pp. 97–115, 2024.
https://doi.org/10.1007/978-3-031-61379-1_7

fessional and their patient requires a certain level of trust as our bodies and wellbeing are the most private and personal aspects of a person; however, there are recognised differences between perceptions and experiences of physical illness compared to mental illness [1], which means that a 'one-size-fits-all' service model is not appropriate and creates added challenges for use of technologies for initial assessments.

Healthcare strategies equating to mental health with the status of physical health have been proposed for over a decade in the United Kingdom (UK) such as 'no health without mental health' [2], yet such parity of esteem [3] is still to be reflected in funding priorities and service provision [4].

Initial healthcare assessments of patient presentation to establish symptoms and inform treatment plans can pose different challenges in mental health and physical health settings. For example, physical health may draw on more invasive or aversive procedures such as blood tests, endoscopies or scans, in addition to touch (which may cause pain), however verbalising symptoms of physical discomfort or distress can be more straightforward, with test/scan results supplementing the patient's answers to guide the treatment plan, for example, if the patient's problem is: 'I cannot get out of bed', or 'I cannot work', an initial assessment could establish this is because 'my back hurts', and a physical examination and/or scans may result in a recommended treatment course of rest and painkillers, or physiotherapy, surgery, etc.

When the same presentation stems from mental illness, establishing an underlying cause and appropriate treatment can be complicated by the subjective experience of psychological distress (mental illness), and the patient's ability (or willingness) to verbalise something that is often less tangible and more fluid than physical symptoms. Not being able to get out of bed due to low mood, or feeling too scared to go to work, is the same presentation as the patient with the back pain, however, establishing the root cause of such behaviours as depression and anxiety, requires the patient to communicate this to the healthcare profession so they can recognise it as such. Expressing feelings of worthlessness (core to depression) [5] or feelings of vulnerability without the personal resources to cope (core beliefs in anxiety) [5] can require heightened levels of trust compared to when disclosing something hurts.

The requirement of such trust may impact the use of technologies for collecting initial health assessment data. Mental and physical healthcare professionals share some attributes in achieving a good 'bedside manner', including empathy and compassion [6], however, they may or may not be required for the disclosure of some physical symptoms and thus lend themselves to non-human or technology aided initial assessments [7,8]. For mental health settings, however, there are recognised therapist characteristics which promote trust and willingness to disclose sensitive information, including openness, active-listening, non-judgemental and person(patient)-centred approaches [9,10].

Patients seeking mental health support often need to disclose very sensitive and personal information about their innermost thoughts, feelings and belief systems. If not done correctly the patient may be misdiagnosed or experience missed-diagnosis, which could exacerbate symptoms and decrease trust in professionals and future-help seeking behaviours [4,11]. Therefore, utilising 'humanness' to create trust in initial assessments is of vital importance in mental health disclosures.

Following the COVID-19 Global Pandemic healthcare procedures and 'trust' of technology was changed to allow exploration of computer science and artificial intelligence (AI), for health service provision and delivery. Despite an increase in digital online functionality and usability, the utilisation of conversational agents for sensitive personal data collections is still uncommon in the mental health sector, compared to other health sectors and industry. For example, despite a range of wellbeing and therapy support applications [12] Gaggioli et al. [13] highlighted an absence of generic processes for eliciting a patient's sensitive mental health personal data, which results in initial assessments being resource intensive for healthcare processions. An initial mental health assessment provides the necessary information to inform client treatment and support, however, these are still being completed by trained professionals, which reduces time available for them to deliver therapies [14–16].

With over 3 billion smartphones and 4.66 billion internet users worldwide it is reasonable to consider utilising conversational agents for initial mental health sensitive data collections, as a method to reduce the administrative workload for mental health professionals. [17–21].

2   Current Mental Health Conversational Agents

Current use of conversational agents in provision of mental health services varies in services offered and personal data collected. For example, the top two mental health agents are Wysa and Youper which use differing levels of Artificial Intelligence (AI) to identify potential triggers as well as offering tools such as activity monitors, mood trackers and therapeutic processes such as mindfulness and relaxation. Both target mental health issues such as poor sleep, anxiety and depression and collect a range of personal data (age, contact information, financial identifiers and medical information) in addition to identifying triggers and sources of stress [22–25].

2.1   Wysa

Wysa was released by Jo Aggarwal and Ramakant Vempati in 2015, for Android and iOS mobile users, by employing a blend of AI interaction and human communication. It was designed to decrease stress by improving sleep and mindfulness, using empathy, positive reinforcement, mindfulness suggestions and motivational interviews [22,23].

The application enables the AI to access sensitive personal data, such as date of birth, age, contact information, addresses, financial identifiers and minimal medical information. Users can choose the level of data they wish to share, however the more data collected the more accurate the AI is at providing improved user experience [22, 23].

During 2022 Malik et al. [26] completed a study utilising Wysa user feedback, $n = 7929$. They identified that including some low-level human-like interactions enabled the majority of users to feel more engaged, for example one user stated 'The app made me laugh with its silly jokes and play.' [26]. Some users, however, 'did not find it helpful for their specific concerns and suggested further expansion' [26].

Such feedback highlights the positive contributions these technologies can provide, however, also illustrates the complexities in meeting the mental health needs of all users. Malik et al. [26] identified that enhancements in the application, could include an improved understanding of less common mental health illnesses, more human-like interactions, and an increased level of privacy and security, to enable the AI to return more bespoke human-like replies [26].

The study's authors [26], two of whom hold equity in Wysa, acknowledge that the cross-sectional design, with reviews taken from a 'single point in time' and 'lack of knowledge on the duration of app use or the rate of attrition' limit conclusions drawn from the study [26].

Additionally, whilst collecting information from over 7,000 users, data from Apple Store users was unfortunately not accessible. Furthermore, in September 2022, Wysa had over 6.5 million registered users, so the overall participant pool was 0.0012% of total available users [27].

Some of the methodological issues in Malik et al. [26] were considered by Legaspi et al. [28], as part of their 2022 review of Wysa's usefulness during the COVID-19 lock-downs.

Participants were students aged 16–19, and completed a daily form over a one week period. Results were analysed for perception of effectiveness and usability, which related to relevance and appropriateness of Wysa's responses [28].

This study was similarly limited by sample size ($n = 10$) and duration of the data collection window, however, it was an external evaluation and run independently of Wysa.

Findings from Legaspi et al. [28] showed students were dissatisfied with 'the talk feature's repetitiveness and lack of fluidity' [28] and that the 'rigid conversation flow not only causes difficulty in communicating with Wysa but can also make the user feel neglected when the chatbot does not acknowledge the user's input' [28].

These issues can be characterised as being the result of the conversational agent's lack of human-like responsiveness. This may be due to the low-level of personal data collected about the user, meaning the AI could not access sufficient information to create a bespoke simulated human-like conversation, thereby decreasing user engagement.

Such views were not universal across the study as one participant specifically stated they felt more comfortable relating to a conversational agent, verses a human, as they could be more open due to the application being non-judgemental, throughout the entire conversation [28].

Even though this study was also limited by the sample size, their conclusions agreed with some of the findings from Malik et al. [26]. The most essential being that simulating human-like features could be the key to increasing engagement and impact the level of personal data collected. This may be particularly pertinent for certain demographics, such as the younger generation (18–39 years) who grew up using technology.

2.2   Youper

Youper was released by psychiatrist Dr. Jose Hamilton in 2016, for Android and iOS users, as a free and payable application, designed to 'cure the world of anxiety and depression' [29].

The free version currently provides low-level AI personality tests, ongoing mood tracking, suggests goals and encourages journal writing, to enable the user to recognise their personal mental health and wellbeing triggers. The payable version provides enhanced AI conversations and improved wellness techniques [24,25,29,30].

The AI replies and suggestions, for both free and payable versions, are formulated by utilising the personal data collected when a user registers to access Youper's support. This includes email addresses, names, passwords, low-level health information and ongoing monitoring of features used within the application [24,25,29].

In 2021, Mehta et al. [31] completed a longitudinal observational study analysing Youper's effectiveness and acceptability. They examined data from 4,517 users, with primary measures of user ratings gained throughout system use and retention of users, across the study's timeline of four week's from subscription [31].

They concluded that including a minimal range of human-like emotions enhanced the AI replies, and a more detailed set of human-like features could help extract a superior data collection, which the AI could then utilise when replying to users. They stated that further research was needed to identify what constituted the correct level of human-like features and could include a more detailed personal data collection, so the AI could draw on this when creating the human-like conversations and replies [31].

Study limitations again included sample size, alongside issues with the chosen emotion regulation measure in analysis. Youper had approximately 2 million users in 2021, but the percentage participating in the study was just 0.002%. The authors also state that 'our emotion regulation measure was not designed to assess the magnitude of emotion regulation success, meaning that our metric included only success or failure response with each conversation' [31]. This narrowed the scope of the results received and analysis performed.

Findings from these studies, for the two market leaders in online mental health care technology, support the requirement for human-like responses and features when gaining trust by conversational agents, and the potential to increase personal data collections so the AI can utilise more data when replying.

An interesting difference found across the studies, concerned the age of the participants when utilising mental health applications and technologies. Wysa appeals to younger age participants (18–39 years), whereas Youper did not show any differences in trust, data collection, or engagement across age.

2.3 Utilising Conversational Agents for Initial Data Disclosure in Mental Health

Applications such as Wysa and Youper fulfill a purpose by providing a level of mental health support for clients that prefer not to access traditional face to face counselling, or do not exhibit medium to severe symptoms. This technology, however, cannot currently collect enough personal sensitive data disclosure to achieve complete engagement via human-like conversations, or reliably decrease the administrative burden on mental health professionals, when formulating treatment and support plans.

Furthermore, it is unknown whether conversational agents can be used to perform the function of a trained healthcare professional in an initial mental health assessment, particularly in light of the core therapist competencies required for developing a therapeutic rapport and relationships, including active listening, non-judgemental, warmth, person-centred, etc. [9, 10]

Existing research has identified possible improvements to engagement when utilising conversational agents with some human-like features, however, which features and to what extent they facilitate engagement is yet to be explored in detail, or in relation to mental health care.

This paper, therefore, presents the results of two studies identifying the human-like features needed in a conversational agent to elicit the level of trust required by users for sensitive personal data disclosures and testing a conversational agent with such features for initial mental health assessments.

The current project was designed with primary objectives of (i) investigate the, as yet, unexplored scope of a trusted and engaging mental health conversational agent, when collecting the highest possible level of sensitive personal data, and (ii) review whether such a conversational agent can decrease the administrative burden for mental health service providers by collecting the level of sensitive personal data required for an initial mental health assessment.

Such collection may be done by using AI to gather all the sensitive personal data needed for a trained professional to immediately identify the right treatment and support for their client, or a more complex system that can identify individuals who require mental health treatment from a trained professional, and those whose needs can be met by existing online applications such as Wysa or Youper.

A third aim of the current research is to explore feature-preference, notions of 'trust' and disclosure of sensitive and personal data in relation to user demographics, such as age, gender identity or continental nationality.

The first stage of the research was designed to understand and establish what human-like features people believe a mental health conversational agent should exhibit to increase trust.

The second stage tested the human-like features, within a simple bespoke conversational agent, for trust, level of data collected and for which demographics.

Both studies are explored in more detail below.

3   Understanding Human-Like Requirements

To explore the potential of cultivating trust in mental health conversational agents and identify the human-like features required to facilitate personal data disclosures, an initial study was completed.

The study [30] commenced with in-person and online discussions, across twenty industry and health contacts, then expanded to shadowing trained professionals at a local mental health service provider, over a period of four weeks.

This resulted in a set of 25 questions that related to different human-like features that are used in existing conversational agents, alongside extra attributes such as compassion and empathy that trained professionals utilise when completing the initial mental health assessment conversation.

One hundred and seventy-seven participants (Female (F) = 53%, Non-binary (NB) = 2%, Prefer not to say (PNS) = 1%) were recruited from the shadowed mental health service provider and through social media, using Leo Goodman's statistical snowball data sampling [32], to achieve a wide range of global participants.

The study's primary task was for participants to rate the importance of human-like features, from insignificant to essential, when building trust in mental health conversational agents. The higher the percentage rating and participant engagement with each question, the more weight was placed on the feature being essential for cultivating trust. For example one question asked 'How do you expect a human-like chatbot to greet you?', with quantitative answer choices of:

- Friendly: 'Hello, how are you today?'
- Formal standard greeting: 'Hello, what can I do for you today?'
- Depends on the type of chatbot: Different organisations e.g. financial, mental health, security etc.

The participants were asked to rate each answer from 1 to 5, with 1 being insignificant and 5 being essential, then qualitatively explain their answers via an open text field.

Both the quantitative and qualitative replies were collated and a review completed at demographic levels of age range, gender identification and continental nationality. Review of the data identified 12 human-like features that were universal across the participants and a further 7 that diverged based on demographics. The comments in the universal data column of Fig. 1 states the similarities found and the comments in the diverging data column of Fig. 2 state the differences.

Feature	Percentage	Universal Data
Patience	99%	Required partially or fully patient conversation
Decisiveness	98%	Required a high level of decisiveness
Focus and Consistency	98%	Required partial or fully focused and consistent questions and answers
Sentence length	95%	Required either medium or full sentences
Empathy and Compassion	95%	Required some empathy and compassion. Could encompass some language shortcuts, such as emoji's
Humour	90%	Required some humour throughout, as this would improve engagement with the system
Text or Voice	86%	Required text rather than voice-based conversation. Evidenced by UK charity - text only preferred
Formal or informal language	80%	Required a mix of formal and informal language, as this would make the system feel more human
Small talk	76%	Required some small talk, especially at start as this is standard for human conversations
Greeting	76%	Required a friendly greeting. Further 10\% dependent on what the agent relating to, e.g. mental health= friendly, but financial = formal
Biography	71%	Stated a biography not required, as most organisations don't offer this feature
End conversation	60%	Required a friendly end to a conversation

Fig. 1. Study 1: Universal human-like requirements across demographics. Source: [30]

Age and gender identification were established to be the two main factors where trust differs, but there were also some divergences across continental nationality.

The analysis resulted in a software engineering MoSCoW (Must have, Should have, Could have, Won't have) [34] feature framework, see Fig. 3, that was implemented during study 2.

4   Analysing Data Disclosures

Testing the human-like MoSCoW framework was undertaken in the second study, with aims of (i) identify if a bespoke conversational agent could collect more sensitive personal data than standard online Microsoft forms, sent by a mental health service provider or requested via social media, (ii) exploring if the data collection method (conversational agent verses online forms) differed across demographics, such as age and gender identification, and (iii) establish if a simple bespoke conversational agent can demonstrate sufficient trust to potentially

Feature	Percentage	Diverging Data
Static Avatar	99%	Required a static avatar. Divergences for Non-binary and prefer not to say who require zero gender identification. Ages 45-49 and 65-69, and those that prefer not say do not want age or nationality reflected
Language Shortcuts: Phrases	75%	Required phrases such as `I believe'. Divergences for South American and Asian participants. They required zero phrases
Optimism or Pessimism	63%	Required a mix. Divergences for 80+, African and Prefer not to say. These required zero use of either
Language Shortcuts: Colloquialisms	51%	Required some colloquialisms. Divergences for age range 60-69 and African participants. They required zero colloquialisms
Language Shortcuts: Emojis	49%	Required some emojis. Divergences for age range 70+ and African participants. They require zero emoji use
Spelling and grammar	43%	Required zero errors. Divergences for African, Non-binary and Prefer not to say. They required some errors
Language Shortcuts: Pop Culture	43%	equired some pop culture references. Divergences for age ranges 60-64 and African participants. They required zero pop culture references
Language Shortcuts: Abbreviations	37%	Required some abbreviations. Divergences for age range 70+ and South American and African participants. They required zero abbreviations

Fig. 2. Study 1: Diverging human-like requirements across demographics. Source: [30]

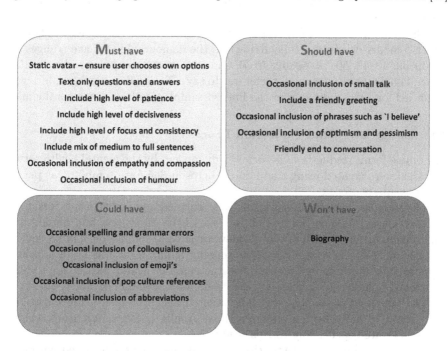

Fig. 3. Study 1: MoSCoW framework for human-like features in conversational agents. Source: [30]

decrease the burden of trained professionals when completing initial mental health assessments.

Due to the novelty of this research, consultation with the same local mental health service provider from study 1 was sought, to ensure the online social media and mental health service provider forms, and the bespoke conversational agent, covered the basic data currently collected and included the more sensitive disclosures asked by a trained professional during an initial assessment. Ethical approval was supplied by the University of East Anglia (UEA) School of Computing Science, with input from the mental health service provider, and non-disclosure agreements were signed by the primary author to enable the sensitive data to be collected.

Questions during the assessment (either by the conversational agent or statistically presented in the online form) ranged from low-sensitivity items such as age, continental nationality, pet ownership, career enjoyment, etc. to high-sensitivity and/or controversial subjects such as gender identification, sexuality, religion, physical health and mental illness, abuse/misuse of drugs or alcohol, family relationships and conflicts, financial debt, etc.

Participants were instructed to only complete questions they felt comfortable answering and to choose the data collection tool they felt was most trustworthy. The data collection tools available to participants were (i) the online Microsoft form requested via social media, (ii) the online Microsoft form sent by the mental health service provider, and (iii) the simple bespoke, secure, conversational agent developed using the human-like framework from study 1.

The same questions were asked across all data collection tools, to allow for direct comparison of data collected across the demographics of age (ranges 18–29, 30–39, 40–49, 50–59, 60–69, 70–79 and 80+ years) and gender identification (male, female, non-binary and prefer not to say). Nationality demographics were discarded for this study, due to the limited sample size from some continents.

4.1   Design and Data Collection Process

The online forms (requested via social media or sent by the mental health service provider) were created using a standard Microsoft 365 form template, as per the current request process [35].

The bespoke conversational agent was designed and coded using React and Node js, [36, 37]. It incorporated all but one of the Must have and Should have requirements from the MoSCoW framework (Fig. 3) for use on mobile devices, laptops and personal computers. The missing requirement was a static avatar, as more data was required to establish the types of avatar participants prefer, for example picture of themselves, their pets, or a cartoon character, etc.

The conversational agent was fully secured and protected using a database that linked to a secure University of East Anglia (UEA) computing sciences server, allocated specifically to this study.

As a proof-of-concept study, the conversational agent was coded without a complex AI, as the application needed to ask the same questions in the same order for analysis. The single manipulation in the data collection tool was that the conversational agent displayed the human-like feature requirements from study 1, and provided a low-level 'friendly' conversation, rather than depicting the questions solely in static, formal text, as was the format of the online forms, see Fig. 4.

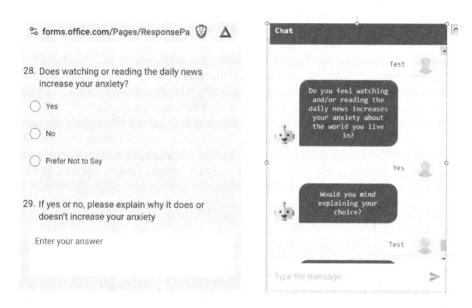

Fig. 4. Differences in language between formal online forms and informal conversational agent

Data collection took place over three months from September 2023, with analysis starting in December.

5 Results

Initial descriptive statistical analysis has been conducted to establish early findings relating to the study's three aims (identified in Sect. 4) with further exploration, including a regression analysis, planned.

Two hundred and fifty three participants (F = 58%, Non-binary (NB) = 5%, Prefer not to say (PNS) = 1%, across age ranges = 18–80+yrs and continental nationalities of Africa, Asia, Europe, North American, Oceania, South American, UK and Prefer not to say) were recruited, over a three month period from September to December 2023.

Early findings established that the demographics of gender identification, age and source of request are essential considerations for technological data collection processes, in initial mental health assessments, however, nationality, which was used in study 1, was discarded for this analysis, due to the limited sample size of several continents.

Participant spread across the data collection tools was: 126 (50%) participants used the conversational agent, 81 participants (32%) used the online form from the mental health service provider, and 46 participants (18%) used the online form from social media.

The percentage of participants completing the collection tools for low-sensitivity questions was 100% (n = 126) for the conversational agent, 94% (n = 76) for the online mental health service provider form and 86% (n = 39) for the online social media form. For the high-sensitivity and/or controversial questions the conversational agent acquired a completion rate of 86% (n = 108), the online mental health service provider form achieved 78% (n = 63) and the online social media form obtained 70% (n = 32). The remainder related to prefer not to say or participants choosing not to answer some questions.

Initial results support the use of conversational agents with these human-like features, as a viable alternative to traditional mental health assessment, performed by a trained professional for certain demographics. The findings for gender identification, especially those identifying as non-binary, age and source of request are explored in more depth below.

5.1 Gender Identification

Gender appeared to be a factor in selection of data collection tool with 49% of those using the bespoke conversational agent identifying as female (n = 62), 10% with non-binary gender identities (n = 13) and 1 participant preferring not to disclose their gender. For the online forms sent via the mental health service provider, 67% (n = 54) identified as female, and for the online forms completed via social media 65% were female (n = 30). Two individuals who completed the online forms (one via social media and one through the mental health service provider) preferred not to disclose their gender.

When shadowing mental health professionals for study 1, it was identified that gender identification is often difficult to obtain from the current form process, as people do not feel comfortable raising it until their initial mental health assessment conversation with a trained professional.

The information collected by this study partially supports this experience, as data collected from both online forms achieved zero non-binary participants. However, the bespoke conversational agent engaged 13 non-binary participants, 10% across conversational agent participant pool and 5% across the overall study, see Fig. 5.

The non-binary participants, using the conversational agent data, provided answers to the low-sensitivity questions, such as pet ownership (92% yes, n = 12 and 8% no, n = 1), having siblings (85% yes, n = 11 and 15% no, n = 2), etc., as well as the higher-sensitivity questions including childhood family conflicts. In some instances, non-binary participants provided more information than male or female participants using the conversational agent. For example, 8 out of 13 (62%) non-binary participants advised they did experience family conflict, whereas this decreased to 45% (n = 28) for female participants and 52% (n = 26)

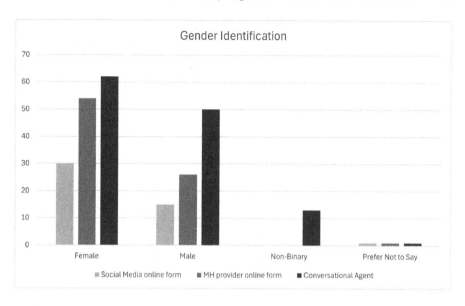

Fig. 5. Gender Identification across collection tools

for male participants, with the remaining male and female participants declining to complete this question.

In comparison to the online form, 37% (n = 20) of female participants and 42% (n = 11) of male participants who completed the form through mental health service provider answered this question on family conflict, and for participants completing the form via social media, 46% of male (n = 7) and female (n = 14) participants answered the question. When reviewing this question via the online forms, the family conflict data from the mental health service provider form collected 37% (n = 20) female and 42% (n = 11) male, and the social media form collected 46% for both female (n = 14) and male (n = 7). As said, there were zero non-binary participants for those completing the online forms.

Despite the low sample size, collecting this non-binary data from the conversational agent was a significant result. As discussed by Jones et al. [38], Reczek et al. [39], A Carlile [40] and Sapien Labs [42], family conflict can be more prevalent when there are members of non-binary gender identities, due to culture, social expectations, parental disapproval, lack of validation, etc. Therefore, mental health support, and access to mental health support, is vital for these individuals who are at increasing risk of poor mental health.

Whilst 13 participants is a small number, the results suggest that non-binary individuals may be willing to engage with a bespoke conversational agent, with human-like features, more so than an online form.

Gender also appeared a factor for questions concerning use/abuse of illegal drugs. This is a high-sensitivity question asked by mental health professionals during an initial assessment, due to the potential impact of some substances on mental health [41] and/or use of such substances as coping/management strategies. For the online forms, the mental health service provider form identified females (n = 10 and M = 4) were more likely to confirm yes, as did the online social media form (n = 5, M = 4), but the conversational agent engaged more men (n = 9, F = 6, NB = 2) to admit they were taking these types of substances, see Fig. 6.

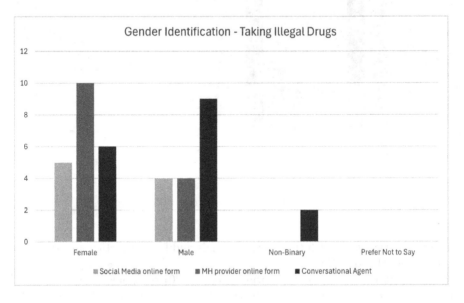

Fig. 6. Illegal drug taking across gender and collection tool

5.2 Age and Source of Request

Initial findings indicate that age and source of request were are key factors in choice of tool selected to collect sensitive mental health data. Eighty-seven percent (n = 110) of participants who chose the conversational agent were aged 18–29 years (n = 83) or 30–39 years (n = 27). For the mental health online form the 18–39 age group accounted for a total of 40% (n = 32) and the social media online form achieved 83% (n = 38), see Fig. 7.

Such findings echo those by Malik et al. [26] and Legaspi et al. [28], whereby younger age groups appear more familiar and 'trusting' of technology, including new technologies such as conversational agents.

Trust of such technology was indicated in the findings via another high-sensitivity question about whether participants easily feel anxious and the impact it has on their mental wellbeing. The UK Mental Health Foundation identified that in 2021 people aged 16–29 were 28% more likely to report some form of anxiety, with this decreasing considerably as participants get older, with only 5% reporting this from age 70+ [45].

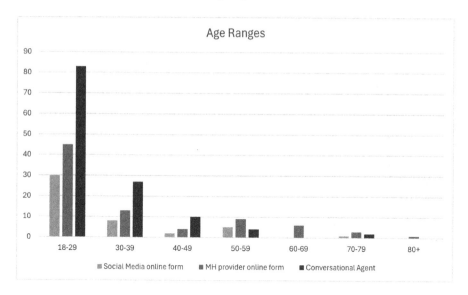

Fig. 7. Age Ranges across collection tools

Findings from the current study 2 show a similar trend with participants in the age ranges of 18–39 years, including those who chose the conversational agent to make their disclosure, were more willing to answer with an affirmative when asked this question than those in the 39+ years age groups, see Fig. 8.

A similar pattern was identified, across multiple high-sensitive questions, where more data was collected from the conversational agent. This, however, was largely due to the 18–39 year age group being considerably more engaged with the conversational agent, than the online forms, see Fig. 7.

Although smaller numbers of participants were recruited from the older age ranges, findings did indicate some trust of technology in that the assessment questions were completed through an online form, however the source of such form, appeared important and more in line with traditional approaches to health-care, such as from a mental health service provider as opposed to social media

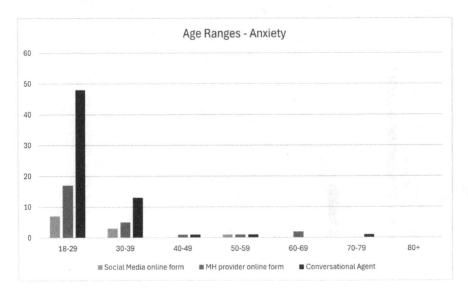

Fig. 8. Age Ranges and anxiety confirmation across collection tools

6   Conclusion

There is currently little research on utilisation of conversational agents, with human-like features, for mental health data disclosures. Initial findings from the two studies within this paper indicate that conversational agents can be used to collect sensitive personal data for initial mental health assessments, for some individuals.

This paper has addressed the three aims of the research and established (i) that a bespoke conversational agent can, in some circumstances, collect more sensitive personal data than existing online forms (ii) that the type and sensitivity of information disclosed differ across demographics such as age and gender, as does the method of data collection selected for an initial mental health assessment, with younger participants and those of non-binary identities more likely to engage with a conversational agent than participants in older age ranges (39+years), and (iii)) that a bespoke conversational agent, with human-like features may be able to establish sufficient trust to potentially decrease the burden on trained professionals.

Whilst such a tool may not be appropriate for all individuals in need of a mental health assessment, the bespoke conversational agent shows promise for, at the very least, enabling trained professionals to develop a treatment plan for an individual without the face-to-face consultation time, as the tool collects the data for them. However, further analysis of the findings from the current studies and data from a final study, will explore the potential of such a bespoke conversational agent to identify who requires mental health support and a suitable care package, for example counselling from a trained professional, group Cognitive Behavioural Therapy (CBT), or for those with a lower level of need, online support mental health applications such as Wysa and Youper.

Acknowledgments. We wish to thank Joseph Agagwuncha for his help and support when coding the bespoke conversational agent

References

1. Kendell, R.E.: The distinction between mental and physical illness. Br. J. Psychiatry **178**(6), 490–493 (2001)
2. No health without mental health. https://shorturl.at/fhCEQ. Accessed 30 Jan 2024
3. Mental health: Achieving 'parity of esteem'. https://shorturl.at/fhwy8. Accessed 30 Jan 2024
4. Baker, C.: Mental Health Statistics for England: Prevalence, Services and Funding. UK Parliament (2020)
5. Beck, A.T.: Cognitive models of depression. Clin. Adv. Cogn. Psychother. Theory Appl. **14**(1), 29–61 (2002)
6. Barker, M.E., Leach, K.T., Levett-Jones, T.: Patient's views of empathic and compassionate healthcare interactions: a scoping review. Nurse Educ. Today, 105957 (2023)
7. Goodman, C.S.: Introduction to Health Technology Assessment. The Lewin Group. Virginia, USA (2004)
8. Facey, K.M.: Health technology assessment. In: Facey, K.M., Hansen, H.P., Single, A.N.V. (eds.) Patient Involvement in Health Technology Assessment, pp. 3–16. Springer, Singapore (2017). https://doi.org/10.1007/978-981-10-4068-9_1
9. Blatt, S.J., Sanislow III, C.A., Zuroff, D.C., Pilkonis, P.A.: Characteristics of effective therapists: further analyses of data from the National Institute of Mental Health Treatment of Depression Collaborative Research Program. J. Consult. Clin. psychol. **64**(6), 1276 (1996)
10. Heinonen, E., Nissen-Lie, H.A.: The professional and personal characteristics of effective psychotherapists: a systematic review. Psychother. Res. **30**(4), 417–432 (2020)
11. Choi, K.W., Jung, J.H., Kim, H.H.S.: Political trust, mental health, and the coronavirus pandemic: a cross-national study. Res. Aging **45**(2), 133–148 (2023)
12. Haque, M.R., Rubya, S.: An overview of chatbot-based mobile mental health apps: insights from app description and user reviews. JMIR mHealth uHealth **11**(1), e44838 (2023)
13. Gaggioli, A., et al.: A mobile data collection platform for mental health research. Pers. Ubiquit. Comput. **17**, 241–251 (2013). Springer
14. Schick, A., Feine, J., Morana, S., Maedche, A., Reininghaus, U.: Validity of chatbot use for mental health assessment: experimental study. JMIR Mhealth Uhealth **10**(10), e28082 (2022)
15. Sharma, V., Goyal, M., Malik, D.: An intelligent behaviour shown by chatbot system. Int. J. New Technol. Res. J. **3**(4) (2017)
16. Shawar, B.A. Atwell, E.: Chatbots: are they really useful? LDV Forum **22**, 137–140 (2020). IEEE
17. Global digital population as of January 2021. https://ico.org.uk/for-organisations/guide-to-data-protection/guide-to-the-general-data-protection-regulation-gdpr/key-definitions/what-is-personal-data/. Accessed 14 Apr 2023

18. Inkster, B.: Early warning signs of a mental health tsunami: a coordinated response to gather initial data insights from multiple digital services providers. Front. Digit. Health **2**, 64 (2021). Frontiers

19. Molodynski, A., McLellan, A., Craig, T., Bhugra, D.: What does COVID mean for UK mental health care Int. J. Soc. Psychiatry **67**(7), 823–825 (2021). SAGE Publications Sage UK: London, England

20. Yarrington, J.S., et al.: Impact of the COVID-19 pandemic on mental health among 157,213 Americans. J. Affect. Disord. **286**, 64–70 (2021). Elsevier

21. Cardno, S., Sahraie, A.: The expanding backlog of mental health patients: time for a major rethink in COVID-19 policy. PsyArXiv (2021)

22. The wisdom of Wysa-Mental health apps, the (AI) friend who is always there. https://blogs.wysa.io/blog/most-read/best-mental-health-apps-for-employees. Accessed 28 Feb 2023

23. How Indian Startup Wysa Built an Empathetic AI Bot to Offer Mental Support to Millions. https://www.news18.com/news/tech/how-indian-startup-wysa-built-an-empathetic-ai-bot-to-offer-mental-support-to-millions-2681669.html. Accessed 27 Feb 2023

24. Youper. https://www.crunchbase.com/organization/youper. Accessed 3 Mar 2023

25. Youper App Review: What's Offered, Cost, and Who It's Right For. https://www.choosingtherapy.com/youper-app-review/. Accessed 3 Mar 2023

26. Malik, T., Ambrose, AJ., Sinha, C.: Evaluating user feedback for an artificial intelligence-enabled, cognitive behavioral therapy–based mental health app (Wysa): qualitative thematic analysis. JMIR Hum. Factors **9**(2), e35668 (2022). JMIR Publications Toronto, Canada

27. Wysa brings mental health digital therapeutic to small to mid-size US employers. https://blogs.wysa.io/blog/b2b-partnerships/wysa-brings-mental-health-digital-therapeutic-to-small-to-mid-size-us-employers. Accessed 19 Jan 2023

28. Legaspi Jr, C.M., Pacana, T.R., Loja, K., Sing, C., Ong, E.: User perception of Wysa as a mental well-being support tool during the COVID-19 pandemic. In: Asian HCI Symposium, vol. 22, pp. 52–57, April 2022

29. The Startup That Wants to Cure Social Anxiety. https://www.theatlantic.com/health/archive/2015/05/the-startup-that-wants-to-end-social-anxiety/392900/. Accessed 10 Mar 2023

30. Taylor, D., Buckley, O., Aung, H.: Understanding user preferences for gaining trust, when utilising conversational agents for mental health data disclosures. In: Stephanidis, C., Antona, M., Ntoa, S., Salvendy, G. (eds.) HCII 2023. CCIS, vol. 1833, pp. 167–174. Springer, Cham (2023). https://doi.org/10.1007/978-3-031-35992-7_24

31. Mehta, A., et al.: Acceptability and effectiveness of artificial intelligence therapy for anxiety and depression (Youper): longitudinal observational study. J. Med. Internet Res. **23**(6), e26771 (2021). JMIR Publications Toronto, Canada

32. Goodman, L.A.: Snowball sampling. Ann. Math. Stat. 148–170 (1961). JSTOR

33. General Data Protection Regulation - GDPR. https://gdpr-info.eu/. Accessed 23 Jan 2024

34. Moran, A.: Managing Agile: Strategy, Implementation, Organisation and People. Springer, Cham (2015). https://doi.org/10.1007/978-3-319-16262-1

35. Microsoft Forms. Accessed 11 Jan 2024

36. React: The library for web and native user interfaces. https://react.dev/. Accessed 11 Aug 2023

37. Node.js® is an open-source, cross-platform JavaScript runtime environment. https://nodejs.org/en. Accessed 11 Aug 2023

38. Jones, B.A., Bouman, W.P., Haycraft, E., Arcelus, J.: Mental health and quality of life in non-binary transgender adults: a case control study. In: Non-binary and Genderqueer Genders, pp. 133–144. Routledge, London (2020)

39. Reczek, R., Bosley-Smith, E.: How LGBTQ adults maintain ties with rejecting parents: theorizing "conflict work" as family work. J. Marriage Family **83**(4), 1134–1153 (2021)

40. Carlile, A.: The experiences of transgender and non-binary children and young people and their parents in healthcare settings in England, UK: interviews with members of a family support group. Int. J. Transgender Health **21**(1), 16–32 (2020)

41. Wilkinson, S.T., Radhakrishnan, R., D'Souza, D.C.: Impact of cannabis use on the development of psychotic disorders. Curr. Addict. Rep. **1**, 115–128 (2014)

42. Newson, J.J., Sukhoi, O., Taylor, J., Topalo, O., Thiagarajan, T.C.: Mental State of the World 2022, Sapien Labs, March 2023

43. Rogers, S.A., Malony, H.N., Coleman, E.M., Tepper, L.: Changes in attitudes toward religion among those with mental illness. J. Religion Health **41**, 167–178 (2002)

44. Johnson-Kwochka, A.V., Stull, L.G., Salyers, M.P.: The impact of diagnosis and religious orientation on mental illness stigma. Psychol. Relig. Spiritual. **14**(4), 462 (2022)

45. Mental health statistics: Anxiety: statistics. https://www.mentalhealth.org.uk/explore-mental-health/statistics/anxiety-statistics. Accessed 25 Jan 2024

Exploring User Understanding of Wireless Connectivity and Security on Smartphones

Ezgi Tugcu(✉) 🆔 and Steven Furnell(✉) 🆔

School of Computer Science, University of Nottingham, Nottingham, UK
tugcuezgi@gmail.com, steven.furnell@nottingham.ac.uk

Abstract. Wireless connectivity is a key feature of smartphones, enabling users to connect to the Internet and communicate directly with other local devices and accessories. However, such channels can also introduce security and privacy risks if not configured and used correctly, which can in turn depend upon the perceptions, capabilities and understanding of the users. This study examines the issue from the potential of iPhone users, a popular platform that is often perceived as being easy to use and offering better default protection. Findings from interview-based data collection involving 16 smartphone users. These revealed that while all users made regular and significant use of their wireless connectivity, there were varying levels of awareness in relation to security and related usage. The findings also revealed notable variations in users' abilities to navigate and interpret related interfaces, with the potential consequence that related features are not located or are misinterpreted.

Keywords: Smartphone · Wi-Fi · Bluetooth · AirDrop · Security

1 Introduction

With an ever-increasing range of features and functionality, smartphones have become an indispensable part of the daily lives of many users. One of the key aspects is, of course, the ability to communicate with other devices and the wider Internet, and the so wireless capabilities are amongst the features that users frequently use. At the time of writing, smartphones offer two alternative wireless routes to connect to the internet – namely via wireless local area networks (i.e. Wireless LAN or Wi-Fi) and via cellular data networks. Additionally, a further standard provision is device-to-device wireless connectivity via Bluetooth. However, with these technologies comes related risk of data leakage and malicious contact, as well as potential need for users to understand which apps and services have the related access. As such, it is relevant to consider whether users recognize the potential risks and are familiar and comfortable with the features that they can use to protect themselves. While the security of cellular networks is under the control of the operators and the security of users' home wireless networks is at their own discretion, they can face a more uncertain situation when using Wi-Fi or Bluetooth in public places, where a variety of unknown (and therefore untrusted) networks and devices will exist. It is therefore relevant for users to know how to understand and use

A. Moallem (Ed.): HCII 2024, LNCS 14728, pp. 116–125, 2024.
https://doi.org/10.1007/978-3-031-61379-1_8

their different connectivity options in these contexts and be aware of any security issues and settings associated with them.

The current study specifically considers iOS users, on the basis that they are typically perceived as being are less aware and concerned about security and data privacy issues [1]. An iOS user may consider their wireless connectivity from the perspective of the underlying technologies involved (Wi-Fi and Bluetooth) and/or the service that enables them to transfer data between devices (which Apple terms AirDrop). This paper examines user awareness and behavior in relation to the use of public Wi-Fi, Bluetooth, and AirDrop, comparing their perceptions in terms of security and whether this affects their usage, as well as their ability to understand and interpret some of the related interfaces and indicators.

2 Background

As background to the research, it is relevant to introduce the main technologies under consideration, and to highlight prior evidence of the extent to which users have security-related awareness and concerns in the smartphone context.

2.1 Wireless Communication on Smartphones

Smartphones are routinely equipped with wireless communication capabilities via Wi-Fi and Bluetooth technologies. Wi-Fi enables communications via an access point in the local area, with potential range of 20–150 m (depending upon whether it is used indoors or outdoors, and the presence of obstacles or other factors that may impede the signal). Depending upon the configuration, the Wi-Fi access point may require users to know the password before connecting to it. Bluetooth is a means of personal area networking, offering the ability to communicate between devices within more immediate range (e.g. around 10 m). Bluetooth devices need to be 'paired' before communicating, implying a trust relationship between them, and in order to be paired they need to be 'discoverable' so that other devices can see them. In addition, on Apple devices, the AirDrop technology provides an ad hoc networking solution that makes it easier to transfer data between devices across Wi-Fi and Bluetooth connections [2]. In this context, the user does not need to know a Wi-Fi password and the devices do not need to be pre-paired. However, similarly to device discoverability with Bluetooth, AirDrop can be set to work for 'Everyone' (i.e. any other Apple device user will see the device when they are within range) or 'Contacts Only' (whereby the device is only visible if the sender and recipient have each other 's' details in their respective contact lists).

While the technologies can be used to achieve convenient and flexible communications in various contexts, they do not come without security risks to be considered. Indeed, prior studies have identified potential security issues relating to each of these them. For example, Al Neyadi et al. [3] tested several possible attacks which on a public Wi-Fi network, including evil twin and Man-in-the-Middle, illustrating ways in which users could be exposed unless they were employing appropriate safeguards. Meanwhile, the Bluetooth channel can similarly be vulnerable to a range of attacks, including data theft (so-called Bluesnarfing) and denial of service (Bluesmacking) [4]. Moving to the file sharing service that can run over these channels, Stute et al. [5] explored potential attacks by discovering vulnerabilities in Airdrop and Apple Wireless Direct Link protocol, with the findings suggesting the potential for issue including device tracking, Denial of Service, and Man-in-the-Middle attacks.

The potential for attacks to affect vulnerable devices suggests that users should have some basic awareness of the technologies they use, and know how to operate them securely at the user level. Being aware of the security of the network they are connected to, recognizing the other party's device while interacting such as file sharing, and considering the threats that may come from the peripheral devices are among the awareness that user could usefully have.

2.2   Security Awareness of Smartphone Users

Ramokapane et al. [1] examined Android and iOS users' security concerns about Manufacturer Provided Default Features (MPDFs). The research has revealed that iOS users are more familiar with the widely used MPDFs (such as Siri), but are generally unaware about data transfer and sharing with the provider. Despite this, users were not very concerned about the security consequences. The investigation revealed that users of both platforms were conscious of location services, as this feature is commonly demanded by various other applications. iOS users tended to place more confidence in their platform compared to Android users, with the belief that the iOS platform was developed with their privacy as a central concern.

Maimon et al. [6] examined situational awareness while using smartphones. Their findings suggested that situational aware people are much more likely to hide their devices when utilizing public Wi-Fi and significantly less likely to browse email and banking websites. They also discovered that users with more computer competency (e.g. programming knowledge) claimed to use public Wi-Fi substantially less (only 50%). People who are tech-competent may be more awareness of the risk and steer clear of public Wi-Fi networks in favor of other options like mobile hotspots.

Earlier findings from Imgraben et al. [7] had found that "most participants lacked awareness regarding the potential dangers associated with keeping their Wi-Fi and Bluetooth enabled constantly". The survey ascertained how users would connect to unidentified Wi-Fi and Bluetooth networks and respond to a request from an unidentified source. Around half of the respondents claimed to always have their Wi-Fi active. As a result, there is a higher chance that they will connect to a malicious network and expose their information to a hacker (e.g. unintentionally connecting to a malicious wireless access point). When it came to Bluetooth usage, only a fifth kept their Bluetooth on at all times. Of these, a quarter admitted to having malware on their devices in the previous year, comparing to only 6% of those that always kept their Bluetooth off. While this only considers those who were aware that malware existed on their devices, it does suggests that constantly discoverable gadgets were more vulnerable to infection.

3 Data Collection

Data was collected via a series of semi-structured interviews, covering the participants background and technology literacy, their familiarity with the three technologies, and their considerations around security and protection. The session also included a practical task, which involved navigating within a mock-up of the iOS settings interface.

Following the ethical approval for the study and a pilot phase for the interview questions, the main the participant selection was conducted amongst the university student community, and so was naturally focused towards younger and educated users. All participants held higher education degrees, including masters and one PhD, and were between the ages of 18 and 35. One of the most important reasons for the selection of users in this age group is that they represent the generation that is likely to have the most knowledge and experience of technology as standard. Their frequent interactions with smartphones and technology and their familiarity with smartphones and technology more generally make them stand out as a demographic group. Additionally, their higher level of education leads to the expectation of having a greater awareness and perception in terms of safeguarding their behaviour. Considering these factors, the findings from such groups could be expected to something of a best-case scenario in terms of their security-and protection-related behaviours.

A total of 16 participants were interviewed (9 female, 7 male), all being current iOS users aged between 22 and 35. Two of the participants were studying computing-related topics, with the others being spread across a range of other disciplines including education, electronics, finance, languages, marketing, media and psychology. Additionally, a range of nationalities were represented including Canada, China, India, Pakistan, Taiwan, Turkey and the United Kingdom. The interviews sessions were conducted over four days via Microsoft Teams, with the resulting transcripts then being downloaded for later analysis. The average interview time was 25 min, and the issues covered as guide points for the discussion are presented in the Appendix (noting that these were used as the prompts to be covered within the discussion rather than a strict list of questions to be posed as if simply surveying the participants).

4 Results

The results are discussed in terms the extent to which participants made use of the three technologies under consideration, followed by the key themes emerging from resulting discussion of them. Attention is then given to the extent to which participants proved able to understand and explain particular aspects from a more practical perspective, including their performance in the interactive task.

4.1 Use of Target Technologies

All participants indicated that they were already aware of the three technologies under consideration, and consciously made use of them in practice. Indeed, as shown in Table 1, most of the users had Wi-Fi and Bluetooth on all the time, with Airdrop being the route

Table 1. Participants' responses about enabling different communications.

Participant	Wi-Fi	Bluetooth	AirDrop
P1	On (and connected)	On (headphones)	On (while sharing)
P2	Always on (unless connection is not reliable)	Always on	Off or Contacts only
P3	Always on	Always on (AirPods or AirDrop)	On (If transferring file)
P4	Mostly on	Generally on (AirPods)	Off (after receiving files)
P5	Always on	Always on	Always on
P6	Always on (in accommodation)	Always on (Apple Watch)	Not always on (after certain events)
P7	On (unless battery low)	On (unless battery low)	On (contacts only)
P8	Always on	Always on	Always on
P9	On	Off (battery saving)	Off (battery saving)
P10	Most of the time on	Off (after usage)	Most of the time on
P11	Always on (unless battery low)	Always on (AirPods, Apple Watch, unless battery is low	On (unless battery low)
P12	Always on	On (while using)	On
P13	On (except flight mode)	On (except flight mode)	On (except flight mode)
P14	Usually off Not reliable network	Usually off	Off (battery saving)
P15	Sometimes on (battery saving)	Sometimes on (battery saving)	Sometimes on (battery saving)
P16	Always on	On (headphones)	On (while receiving)

that was enabled more selectively on. The responses in the table reflect their main response, plus any contextualizing comments in brackets.

When participants were asked if they had any concerns while using the technologies, they generally stated concerns about public Wi-Fi and Airdrop usage. The main reason for the low trust in public Wi-Fi was that it is free and accessible to everyone, while in the case of AirDrop, the possibility of accidentally sharing files with recipients whose identity is not known created concerns. Cases such as password theft, credit card information concerns, or accessing user browser history, which are among the worrying scenarios in Public Wi-Fi, were also mentioned. Although some users were worried, they did not take any precautions, while most of them stated that they avoided the public Wi-Fi connection, and if they needed to connect for something important, they immediately disconnected from the network again after completing their task. Meanwhile, among the precautions taken for AirDrop, users mentioned explicitly sending files to a receiver who is physical present in front of them.

4.2 Thematic Analysis of Comments

One of the dominant themes arising from the interview questions was that users considered themselves to be protected by virtue of using Apple devices:

- "As far as I know … compare with the other company iPhone is the most safe phone"
- "I trust more Apple iOS and that's why I am using Apple devices"
- "I'm an iPhone person so I trust Apple enough to buy it every time"

This aligns with a long-standing perspective amongst iPhone users [8], which could potentially see them paying less overt attention to security aspects than may be required.

A further theme was a clear level of mistrust in public Wi-Fi:

- "I try not to use online banking on public Wi-Fi"
- "I would never use Apple Wallet or those kind of applications"
- "I try to find another way until and unless it's an emergency, I would then. Otherwise I don't connect to public Wi-Fi is just for the sake of using social media"
- "I don't trust them that much. So I just want to do my stuff. If I'm done, I'm just get out of it"

Other themes that emerged were concerns about sharing files with unknown users:

- "I am a little paranoid so I always keep that accept from everyone option off, but it's not like it's always on my mind and I make my decisions very consciously because of that"
- "as a habit I would always keep you know that option that from contacts only and stuff like that"
- "I'm concerned I'll send files to a wrong person and something like that. So that concerns me. If I could verify I'm sending to specifically whom I want to, that would be really great"

Participants identified Bluetooth as the technology they trust the most, highlighting its permission-asking feature as the reason for this:

- "Bluetooth is more safe because anytime if you need to use the Bluetooth, Bluetooth, Bluetooth will ask you the code"
- "I would say it Bluetooth, it ask me for my permission"

Other responses suggested signs of the participants attempting to be careful in their usage and taking related precautions:

- "If there's like sometimes they are in like a cafe, they'll have the Wi-Fi name. Written down. So, I'll check it matches the one there"
- "if the network is named after the restaurant then I would be like yeah it's legit and if it is asking me for password then you know it's legit. Otherwise, yeah, there is the doubt"
- "If I want to send picture for you and then I will make sure: You are beside me. Your phone. Your name is this"
- "protection for AirDrop would be to choose contacts only and not go for everyone"

4.3 Understanding of Practical Examples

In common with other Apple devices, one of the key selling points of iPhone platform is its ease of use (indeed, Apple's 'Switch to iPhone' page makes the point explicitly, along with the tagline that 'Everything just works' [9]). However, in practice this does not necessarily to everything being quite as automated and intuitive as some users may consequently assume or expect. Indeed, when it comes to locating and configuring some of the settings, matters are not necessarily straightforward. This was illustrated within the study where some of the discussion involved showing images of communication-relevant interfaces and asking users for their interpretation of what was being shown. One of these, as illustrated in Fig. 1, which depicts different Bluetooth connection states in the iOS Control Centre. Specifically, these states are (a) enabled, (b) disconnected, and (c) fully off. While options (a) and (c) are self-evident, the disconnected mode is more subtle and there is potential for users to believe that they have turned Bluetooth off when in fact it remains active. Apple's support pages label it as "Disconnect from Bluetooth accessories" and its effect is to terminate any Bluetooth connections other than those involving Apple Watch, Instant Hotspot, Apple Pencil and Continuity features such as Handoff. It then remains in this state until 5am local time, unless the user explicitly re-enables it (or resets the phone) [10]. In practice, the fact that 'disabling' Bluetooth via the Control Centre does not turn off the device's connectivity means that it is left potentially exposed to related attacks [11]. It should be noted that the same form of behavior applies to the Wi-Fi option in the Control Centre (i.e. it will disconnect from any network and not auto-join others, but the Wi-Fi interface itself remains enabled).

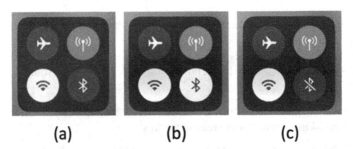

Fig. 1. Alternative Bluetooth status indicators – (a) enabled (b) disabled (c) off

Discussion with the participants revealed that they had varying interpretations of these status indicators. Their responses are summarized in Table 2, and it becomes clear that while they could generally identify the enabled state, they were unclear about the other two, leading to incorrect and speculative answers (particularly in relation to image b). What was observed here is that participants providing these guesses did not pay attention to what the interface was conveying, and furthermore, the essential information was not presented to the user by the interface. To quote from one of the participants: "*I've only learnt through excessive use and trying to figure, trying to learn what it means myself…, it wasn't at all intuitive when you first use it*". This again serves to contradict any assumption of the implicit ease of use.

Table 2. Participants' interpretation of the Bluetooth status indicators.

Participant	Image a (Bluetooth on)	Image b (disabled via Control Center)	Image c (Bluetooth off)
P1	Connected	Not connected to any device	Off
P2	Connected	Its on, tries to connect	Off
P3	On or Connected	Not on	Bluetooth experiencing issues
P4	On and connected	Not on, not paired to any device	Off from settings
P5	Connected	Uncertain, maybe on	Off, not connected
P6	On	Not sure	Do not disturb mode
P7	On	Turns itself on, looking for signals	Fully off
P8	Connected	On and not connected	Off
P9	On	Previous device possible connection	Off
P10	On	Off	Not available, potentially not installed
P11	On	Disabled partially, stays connected to important devices	Off from settings
P12	On	Off from Control Centre	Off from settings
P13	On	Can be active on the backend of app, can be used to connect AirPods	Off
P14	On	Temporarily off, may turn on at 5 AM	Fully off
P15	On	Off	Airplane mode
P16	On	Off	Never seen (new iOS user)

Staying with the Bluetooth theme, the interactive task required participants to explore the mock-up interfaces and determine which applications had access to Bluetooth. The task therefore required users to be able to locate the relevant Bluetooth settings within the menu structure, and then be able to correctly report the apps having access. The mock-up included a number of decoy options (based upon incorrect routes that it was considered might nonetheless be chosen), and participants were able to interact while following a think-aloud protocol, with the researcher observing how quickly the correct navigational path was established and followed. Figure 2 depicts the full range of interfaces within the mock-up, and the dotted boxes represent options that were clickable in order to allow the participants to explore and seek the appropriate route to the Bluetooth app permissions.

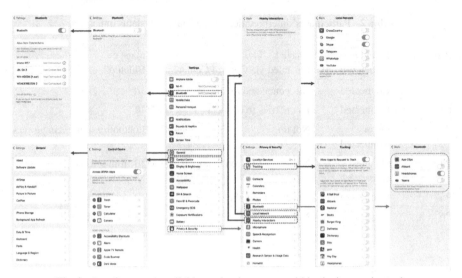

Fig. 2. Interfaces and available navigation routes within the interactive task

The arrows denote the flow from one interface to the next. Routes marked in red are the decoys, and the correct route is indicated in green.

While iOS has a Bluetooth settings option at the top-level (see the upper left route within Fig. 2), this relates to whether Bluetooth itself is enabled and (if so) the devices connected to it. To determining the apps with access instead requires users to scroll to the Privacy & Security settings and then select the Bluetooth option from there (as marked via the green route in Fig. 2). The issues under test within the task were whether the participants were able to determine and find the correct route, and how many mistakes they made in doing so.

When attempting the task most participants initially followed the wrong path and selected the Bluetooth settings, and in some cases still did not realize that they had located the settings for 'Devices' rather than 'Applications'. The task thereby demonstrates that users had limited knowledge of interface navigation and low awareness of the feature they were looking for (e.g. the relationship between Bluetooth access and the Privacy & Security settings).

5   Conclusions

The key findings suggest that while the participants appeared comfortable and felt secure in using their devices, and declared themselves to follow some ostensibly secure practices and behaviors, their actual familiarity with the navigating and interpreting interface-level aspects was limited, with the potential to lead to incorrect conclusions about their level of protection. This in turn suggests that unless their device is naturally delivering the protection they are expecting and assuming, they are unlikely to be well-placed to make clear decisions, or to determine and select appropriate alternative settings. The findings suggest a need to further simplify the process, such that users are more clearly aware of their protection status and are offered more direct routes toward settings that support this.

A clear limitation of the study was the small participant group, itself a factor of a relatively limited timeframe within which to conduct the data collection. Future research may include conducting interviews with a more extensive range of participants and observing the experience of utilising adapted user interfaces. The latter would include approaches that aim towards better notifying users of their device status and enabling them to locate and adjust related settings more easily. Additionally, having examined the situation in the iPhone context, it would also be interesting to investigate how things compare for users on the Android platform, where equivalent features will be offered via a different user environment.

References

1. Ramokapane, K.M., Mazeli, A.C., Rashid, A.: Skip, skip, skip, accept!!!: A study on the usability of smartphone manufacturer provided default features and user privacy. Proc. Priv. Enhanc. Technol. **2019**(2), 209–227 (2019). https://doi.org/10.2478/popets-2019-0027
2. Apple: How to use AirDrop on your iPhone or iPad. Apple Support, 26 September 2023. https://support.apple.com/en-gb/HT204144
3. Al Neyadi, E., Al Shehhi, S., Al Shehhi, A., Al Hashimi, N., Qbea'H, M., Alrabaee, S.: Discovering public Wi-Fi vulnerabilities using raspberry pi and Kali Linux. In: 2020 12th Annual Undergraduate Research Conference on Applied Computing (URC), pp. 1–4 (2020).https://doi.org/10.1109/URC49805.2020.9099187
4. Stouffer, C.: Bluetooth security risks to know (and how to avoid them). Norton, 2 October 2022. https://us.norton.com/blog/mobile/bluetooth-security
5. Stute, M., et al.: A Billion Open Interfaces for Eve and Mallory: MitM, DoS, and Tracking Attacks on iOS and macOS Through Apple Wireless Direct Link (2019). https://www.usenix.org/conference/usenixsecurity19/presentation/stute
6. Maimon, D., Howell, C.J., Jacques, S., Perkins, R.C.: Situational awareness and public Wi-Fi users' self-protective behaviors. Secur. J. **35**(1), 154–174 (2022). https://doi.org/10.1057/s41284-020-00270-2
7. Imgraben, J., Engelbrecht, A., Choo, K.K.R.: Always connected, but are smart mobile users getting more security savvy? A survey of smart mobile device users. Behav. Inf. Technol. **33**(12) (2014). https://doi.org/10.1080/0144929X.2014.934286
8. Winder, D.: Critical Security Warning For iPhone Users. Forbes, 21 June 2019. https://www.forbes.com/sites/daveywinder/2019/06/21/new-critical-security-warning-for-iphone-and-ipad-users/
9. Apple: Switch from Android to iPhone. Apple UK (2024). https://www.apple.com/uk/iphone/switch/. Accessed 25 Jan 24
10. Apple: Use Bluetooth and Wi-Fi in Control Centre. Apple Support, 13 October 2023. https://support.apple.com/en-in/102412
11. Winder, D.: New iPhone iOS 16 Bluetooth Hack Attack—How To Stop It. Forbes, 23 September 2023. https://www.forbes.com/sites/daveywinder/2023/09/06/new-iphone-ios-16-bluetooth-hack-attack-how-to-stop-it/

Why Do Organizations Fail to Practice Cyber Resilience?

Rick van der Kleij[1,2](✉) and Tineke Hof[1]

[1] TNO, The Hague, The Netherlands
Rick.vanderkleij@tno.nl
[2] Avans University of Applied Sciences, Den Bosch, The Netherlands

Abstract. When organizations fall victim to cyber incidents, they are exposed to financial implications, data losses, and potential damage to their reputation. However, the positive news is that many of these incidents can be avoided or have a smaller impact when basic cyber-resilience practices are followed. These practices can include simple actions like regularly updating software or implementing multi-factor authentication. Although these practices might seem simple, organizations are not always taking them despite their best intentions. This may be due to various barriers that hinder practicing cyber resilience. This study investigated why organizations are not practicing cyber resilience. Discussions were held with entrepreneurs in focus groups to understand their reasons for not running a cyber-resilient digital business. We also surveyed a panel of 795 Dutch entrepreneurs about cyber risks and underlying barriers to practicing cyber resilience. A regression model shows that a lack of knowledge, skills, environmental context and resources, and protection motivation intention appear to be the strongest barriers to practicing cyber resilience, closely followed by perceived response efficacy. Implications for government agencies and future research are discussed.

Keywords: Cyber-Resilience Practices · Cyber Security · Protective Measures · Behavioral Change Interventions · Digital Business Practices

1 Introduction

1.1 Minimizing the Imbalance Between Digital Threats and Resilience

Digital security is crucial for the safe and uninterrupted functioning of our society. The digital threat for organizations, however, remains as high as ever and changes continuously. The Cyber Security Assessment Netherlands (CSAN) 2023 issues a stark reminder through the authoritative voice of the National Coordinator for Counterterrorism and Security (NCTV): Organizations must brace themselves for the unforeseen and recalibrate their security accordingly (NCTV 2023). This digital age renders every organization and sector an enticing target for malevolent actors, transcending the traditional boundaries of vulnerability. Even seemingly inconspicuous entities become potential stepping stones for cyber adversaries aiming at more prominent prey. Furthermore, the NCTV continuously warns that cyberattacks compromise the nervous system of society, asserting that cyber resilience in our society is still insufficient, with a notable discrepancy in the level of resilience observed among organizations.

Cyber resilience is a collective term encompassing various means and methods to combat cybercrime and enhance cybersecurity (Hoekstra, De Vries, Berkenpas & Jansen 2021). It is defined as the ability to prepare, absorb, recover, and adapt to adverse effects caused by a cybersecurity incident with the aim of maintaining critical functions continuously (Dupont, Shearing, Bernier, & Leukfeldt 2023; Linkov & Kottt 2019). In practical terms, it means that organizations need four capabilities to deliver cyber resilience: (1) anticipation, (2) monitoring, (3) response, and (4) learning (Van der Kleij & Leukfeldt 2019). This implies that cyber resilience is demonstrated when organizations know (a) what to expect, (b) what to look for, (c) what actions to take, and (d) what occurred in the event of a failure. Within this context, cyber-resilience measures aim to counter both known and unknown digital threats, while also focusing more reactively on swift and effective recovery from a cyber-incident.

Reducing the imbalance between digital threats and resilience remains a significant challenge. The EU aims for a future where this imbalance is minimized, and, at the same time, increases incentives for cyber resilience in digital markets by imposing stricter requirements on digital products and services, organizational risk management, and more. A cause for this imbalance in the Netherlands is the role of the government (Brennenraedts, Den Hertog, Kleter, Ott, Smeitink, Te Velde, & Vankan 2023). Unlike countries where the government heavily invests in cyber resilience, such as Israel and Estonia, the Netherlands prioritizes issues like climate and energy over cyber resilience. And whilst there are many subsidy opportunities in the cybersecurity domain in the Netherlands, they are not always fully utilized.

But there is more. When organizations fall victim to cyber incidents, they are exposed to financial implications, data losses, and potential damage to their reputation. However, the positive news is that many of these incidents can be avoided or have a reduced impact when protective cyber resilience measures are implemented. These measures can include simple actions like regularly updating software or implementing multi-factor authentication. Although these actions might seem simple, organizations are not always taking them despite their best intentions. Consequently, as mentioned above, the NCTV (2023) signals that there is a gap between organizations that have cyber resilience in order and those that do not. Organizations that lag behind need assistance in taking the right measures, such as implementing resilience management processes, enabling them to achieve an optimal level of cyber resilience. An optimal level of cyber resilience in this context refers to a level of cyber resilience appropriate for the risks to business operations and continuity of services, based on a sound risk assessment and balanced with the necessary investments to reach that level.

The challenge in closing the gap between the haves and haves-not is acute and requires a broader understanding of cyber resilience. There is little insight into relevant actors, dependencies, and mechanisms of cyber resilience and how they reverberate across cyber-resilience practices. It is also unclear how laggards can be encouraged to act appropriately to reduce this gap. This research seeks to explain why organizations fail to implement cyber-resilience measures.

1.2 Influencing Entrepreneurs to Run a Secure Digital Business

A crucial determinant of cyber resilience and, consequently, in adopting cyber resilience practices, lies in the behavior of individuals and groups within organizations. Examples of relevant behaviors in the context of this research include the extent to which management takes measures based on threat intelligence, invests in detection tools, and ensures that employees behave securely in the digital workplace. To explain these behaviors, behavioral influence models can be employed. An example is the Behavioral Change Wheel (see Michie, Van Stralen, & West 2011), which posits that behavior is driven by knowledge, opportunity, and motivation. Based on this model, we anticipate that the extent to which individuals and groups within organizations take appropriate measures to enhance cyber resilience depends on their knowledge of risks, ways to protect themselves, the opportunities available, and their motivation to act accordingly. This model also provides recommendations on how to influence cyber-resilience practices, and initial applications of this behavioral model in cyber security are promising (see, for example, Van der Kleij, Van't Hoff - De Goede, Van de Weijer, & Leukfeldt 2021; and Van der Kleij, Wijn, & Hof 2020).

As an initial exploration into the question of why organizations do not take measures to enhance their cyber resilience, and to provide for direction for the research, discussions were held with entrepreneurs in focus groups. In total, two group interviews were organized in 2022, involving 20 entrepreneurs from various sectors and working in companies of varied sizes, including self-employed individuals. The group interviews, conducted via Microsoft Teams, lasted approximately 2 h each. Entrepreneurs were recruited by the researchers through two different panels: the online DTC (Digital Trust Center) community and the entrepreneurial panel Ondernemersdenkenmee.nl, both affiliated with the Ministry of Economic Affairs and Climate. Entrepreneurs received a gift voucher as a token of appreciation for their participation.

Based on the results of the group interviews with entrepreneurs, and in line with behavioral influence models, we have formulated six explanations for why the people responsible for cyber resilience within their organization would practice unsafe digital business. These are:

- They do not see themselves as potential victims: Some entrepreneurs may not recognize the risk of digital threats and do not consider themselves potential targets of cybercriminals.
- They underestimate the consequences of cyber risks: There may be an underestimation of the consequences that may result from unsafe digital business practices.
- They do not know how to conduct cyber resilience practices: Entrepreneurs may be hindered by a lack of knowledge or guidelines on how to engage in safe digital business practices.
- They do not consider cyber resilience important: Some entrepreneurs may not place great importance on cyber resilience practices, perhaps due to other urgent business priorities.
- They do not consider taking cyber resilience measures their responsibility: There may be a perception that cyber resilience is the responsibility of others, such as the government.

- They lack the resources to take appropriate resilience measures: Entrepreneurs may be limited by a lack of social support or financial resources necessary for running a secure digital business.

This research endeavors to enhance our comprehension of the factors influencing the decisions made by individuals responsible for cyber resilience within organizations—specifically, why some take measures to bolster cyber resilience while others do not. To address this inquiry, we have undertaken a quantitative research approach, designed to test the explanations outlined earlier. In the subsequent sections of this paper, we will provide a detailed account of our research methodology, present and analyze the quantitative findings, and finally, engage in a comprehensive discussion on the implications derived from our work and directions for future research.

2 Method

2.1 Participants

A survey study was conducted among an adult sample of the Dutch general population. Participants were recruited, in conjunction with the researchers, by a panel agency. The panel is ISO-certified and consists of more than 70,000 active participants recruited online and offline. It is a good reflection of the Dutch population for characteristics such as education, age, gender, region, household composition, activity, and ethnicity.

The sample was realized as follows. Panel members were selected based on the following selection question: To what extent are you involved in cyber resilience within your company/organization. Respondents who were responsible for cyber resilience were selected for the survey. Based on this selection, we were able to achieve a net sample of n = 795 (co-)responsible/(co-)decision-makers for cyber resilience, spread across different company sizes and sectors. Participation was voluntary.

2.2 Measures

Dependent Variable: Cyber-resilience Practices. *Cyber-resilience practices.* Was considered as a dependent variable in this study. This variable was measured by presenting statements to the respondents related to taking cyber resilience measures in a business environment (11 items, Cronbach's α = .890). The items were organized around the following 5 topics and adapted from the Dutch Digital Trust Center (DTC) Cyber-resilience scan (for more information, see: The five basic principles of running a secure digital business[1]): 1. Identify cyber risks; 2. Choose secure settings; 3. Install updates; 4. Limit access; 5. Prevent viruses and other malware. Answer options for each item were: always, often, sometimes, rarely, or never (5-point Likert-type scale) or not applicable. The highest score is assigned to the safest answer option for each statement.

---

[1] https://business.gov.nl/running-your-business/business-management/cyber-security/the-5-basic-principles-of-running-A-secure-digital-business/.

Independent Variables. For each of the six possible explanations for why the people responsible for cyber resilience within their organization would or would not take the appropriate measures to increase the level of cyber resilience, we searched in the literature for related constructs, validated measuring scales or items. Below we summarize the constructs that were used in this study.

They Do Not See Themselves as Potential Victims. To understand whether respondents see themselves as potential victims of cyber incidents we used *Perceived vulnerability*. This construct refers to the assessment of one's own vulnerability to a threat and was adapted from Van't Hoff-de Goede, Leukfeldt, Van der Kleij, and Van de Weijer (2021). It was measured with the following item: 'How likely do you think it is that your organization will fall victim to a cyber incident in the next 12 months?' This item involved a 7-point Likert scale to indicate a respondent's level of agreement with the statement regarding the likelihood of victimization.

They Underestimate the Consequences. The following 2 constructs were included in our study to assess how respondents interpret the consequences of unsafe digital business practices: *Perceived severity* and *Response efficacy. Perceived severity* was measured with 3 items (Cronbach's $\alpha = .878$) and refers to an individual's beliefs about the seriousness of consequences of an incident or situation (Champion & Skinner 2008, Dodel and Mesch 2017). An example question is: 'I believe that cyber incidents pose a serious problem for my organization.' *Response efficacy* was also measured with 3 items (Cronbach's $\alpha = .860$). This refers to beliefs as to whether the recommended action step will actually avoid the threat (Herath & Rao 2009). An example question is: 'Engaging in safe digital business practices reduces the likelihood of falling victim to a cyber incident.' Each item involved a 7-point Likert scale to indicate a respondent's level of agreement with the statements.

They Do Not Know How to Conduct Safe Digital Business Practices. To access if entrepreneurs may be hindered by a lack of knowledge or guidelines on how to engage in safe digital business practices, we included the constructs *Knowledge* and *Skills* in the questionnaire. Knowledge was measured with 2 items (Cronbach's $\alpha = .898$) based on Cane, O'Connor, and Michie (2012) and Connell, Carey, De Bruin, Rothman, Johnston, Kelly, and Michie (2019) and refers to an awareness of the existence of something. An example question is: 'I know how to do digital business safely.' Skills was measured with 2 items (Cronbach's $\alpha = .744$). This construct refers to an ability or proficiency acquired through practice (Connell, et al. 2019). Items were adapted from Huijg, Gebhardt, Dusseldorp et al. (2014) and Amemori, Michie, Korhonen, Murtomaa, and Kinnunen (2011). An example question is: 'I have the skills to conduct digital business safely.' Each item involved a 7-point Likert scale to indicate a respondent's level of agreement with the statements.

They Do Not Consider Safe Digital Business Practices Important. To understand the role of motivation, we used Protection motivation intention, Normative beliefs, Priority, and Intention to practice cybersecurity. Protection motivation intention is defined as the motivation of people to engage in protective behaviors and is measured with 2 items (Cronbach's $\alpha = .746$) adapted from Van't Hoff-de Goede et al. (2021). An example question is: 'We are willing to do everything to protect the organization against cyber incidents.' Normative beliefs refer to the belief about whether most people approve or disapprove of the behavior. It relates to a person's beliefs about whether peers and people of importance to the person think he or she should engage in the behavior (Ajzen 1991). This construct is measured with 2 items (Cronbach's $\alpha = .771$). An example item is: 'We aspire to be a role model for other organizations in the field of safe digital business practices.' Priority refers to mental representations of outcomes or end states that an individual wants to achieve. Three items were adapted from Huijg et al. (2014) (Cronbach's $\alpha = .883$). An example item is: 'Other topics on the agenda have a higher priority than safe digital business practices.' The Intention to Practice Cyber Security construct was defined by Glanz, Rimer, Orleans, and Viswanath (2015) as a reflective variable consisting of expectations, plans, and desires to perform a particular behavior. To measure people's intentions or willingness to engage in safe digital business practices 2 items (Cronbach's $\alpha = .859$) were adapted from Alanazi, Freeman, and Tootell (2022). An example item is: 'Our organization intends to take measures in the next 12 months to enhance cyber resilience.' A 7-point Likert type scale was used for most variables, except for priority, ranging from 'completely disagree' to 'completely agree', with the highest score always being assigned to the safest answer option. A 5-point Likert type scale was used for Priority.

They Do Not Consider Safe Digital Business Practices Their Responsibility. To understand the role of responsibility, one construct was used in our study. Two *Locus of control* items were adopted from Workman, Bommer, and Straub (2008). These items attempted to gauge individual's belief that he/she is personal responsible for cyber resilience within their organization (internal) or the control of others (external). But due to insufficient internal reliability (Cronbach's $\alpha = .49$) both items could not be combined into a single scale. Consequently, each item was treated as a separate construct. Locus of control was measured with the following sliding-scale item: 'To what extent do you agree that safe digital entrepreneurship is outside the control of your organization (as opposed to within the control of your organization)?' *Perceived responsibility* was measured with the following sliding-scale item: 'Safe digital business practices are the responsibility of my organization (as opposed to others).'

They Lack the Resources to Engage in Safe Digital Business Practices. The construct *Environmental context and resources* was used in the study to investigate whether respondents lack the resources to practice cyber resilience. The construct was measured with 3 items (Cronbach's $\alpha = .739$) and was defined as 'aspects of a person's situation or environment that discourage or encourage the behavior' (Connell et al. 2019). Items were adapted from Van der Kleij et al. (2021). An example item is: 'My organization has sufficient financial resources to conduct safe digital business.' Each item involved a 7-point Likert scale to indicate a respondent's level of agreement with the statements.

Table 1. Scale ranges, means, and standard deviations.

#	Variable	Scale range	Mean	SD
1	Cyber-resilience practices	1–7	5.38	0.93
2	Knowledge	1–7	5.14	1.17
3	Skills	1–7	4.80	1.28
4	Priority	1–5	2.85	0.83
5	Perceived severity	1–7	3.60	1.49
6	Environmental context and resources	1–7	4.85	1.23
7	Protection motivation intention	1–7	5.02	1.20
8	Normative beliefs	1–7	4.52	1.44
9	Intention to practice cyber security	1–7	4.71	1.35
10	Response efficacy	1–7	5.38	1.08
11	Locus of control	1–7	5.21	1.45
12	Perceived responsibility	1–7	2.91	1.74
13	Perceived vulnerability	1–7	3.56	1.47

Control Variables. To explicitly consider the possible effects of being self-employed (41%), outsourcing IT services (including cybersecurity) (53.6%), economic activities[2], victimization in the past 12 months (11.4%), and level of digitalization[3], we controlled for these variables in all analyses.

2.3 Analysis

In this study, two types of analyses were conducted. Firstly, bivariate relationships between all variables were estimated using Pearson correlations. Secondly, multivariate regression analyses were employed to estimate the multivariate relationships, incorporating control variables as mentioned above.

3 Results

3.1 Descriptive Statistics

The scale ranges, means, and standard deviations of the dependent and independent variables are presented in Table 1. Pearson correlation was used to assess the relationship among all study variables. The relationship between the dependent variable and all independent variables was statistically significant. Interestingly, respondents who

---

[2] The list of economic activities was based on the Standard Industrial Classifications (Dutch SBI 2008, NACE and ISIC).

[3] A 5-point Likert type scale was used ranging from 'not digitized' to 'completely digitized'.

perceive cyber resilience as the responsibility of others tend to report a higher level of cyber-resilience practices ($r = .17; p < .01$). Also, the higher the estimated likelihood of becoming a victim, the more likely respondents are to practice cyber resilience ($r = .08; p < .05$). Additionally, companies that have been victims of an incident in the past year report cyber-resilience practices more often than those that have not been victims ($r = .09; p < .01$). Furthermore, there is a noticeable positive relationship between company size and cyber-resilience practices. Sole proprietors are practicing cyber resilience to a lower extent than larger companies ($r = .15; p < .01$).

3.2 Multivariate Regression Analysis

The results of the multivariate regression analysis are presented in Table 2. We tested one model that included all variables, including control variables. All variables together explain 64% of the variance in cyber-resilience practices, which can be considered an impressive result.

The model shows that the control variables for self-employed worker ($B = 0.137; p = 0.015$) and the level of digitization ($B = 0.076; p = 0.004$) are related to our dependent variable. Outsourcing of IT services is negatively related ($B = -0.121; p = 0.020$). This implies that larger organizations, organizations that are more digitalized, and organizations that are not outsourcing IT services are taking more cyber resilience measures. The economic sector in which a company operates is not related to practicing cyber resilience.

Of the assumed barriers of taking cyber resilience measures, lack of knowledge ($B = 0.221; p = 0.000$), skills ($B = 0.139; p = 0.000$), environmental context and resources ($B = 0.131; p = 0.000$), protection motivation intention ($B = 0.149; p = 0.000$), and response efficacy ($B = 0.081; p = 0.006$) are indeed significantly explaining variance of the dependent variable. This means that the people responsible for cyber resilience within their organization who better understand what they need to do, are more capable of practicing cyber resilience, have more resources at their disposal, are more willing to take these measures, and more strongly belief that this helps to mitigate threats, are more often practicing cyber resilience. The coefficients of normative beliefs and perceived vulnerability are marginally significant and strong conclusions cannot be drawn on their basis.

Table 2. Results of multivariate regression analysis for practicing cybersecurity behavior.

	B	SE	t	Sig
(Constant)	0.934	0.263	3.549	0.000
Knowledge	0.221	0.036	6.089	0.000
Skills	0.139	0.035	4.006	0.000
Priority	0.044	0.031	1.394	0.164
Perceived severity	0.036	0.022	1.644	0.101
Environmental context and resources	0.131	0.028	4.646	0.000
Protection motivation intention	0.149	0.033	4.459	0.000
Normative beliefs	0.052	0.027	1.908	0.057
Intention to practice cyber security	0.034	0.024	1.420	0.156
Response efficacy	0.081	0.029	2.783	0.006
Locus of Control	0.003	0.020	0.132	0.895
Responsibility	0.024	0.017	1.394	0.164
Perceived vulnerability	−0.040	0.021	−1.890	0.059
Victimization in the past 12 months (vs NO)	0.071	0.083	0.853	0.394
Self-employed (vs NO)	0.137	0.056	2.440	0.015
Manufacturing & energy (vs Agri & Mining)	−0.021	0.192	−0.110	0.913
Construction (vs Agri & Mining)	−0.164	0.185	−0.890	0.374
Wholesale, retail trade & food serving (vs Agri & Mining)	−0.190	0.163	−1.166	0.244
Publishing & telecommunication (vs Agri & Mining)	−0.110	0.166	−0.662	0.508
Financial & insurance services (vs Agri & Mining)	−0.032	0.169	−0.189	0.851
Real estate activities (vs Agri & Mining)	−0.131	0.197	−0.664	0.507
Professional & support service activities (vs Agri & Mining)	−0.197	0.159	−1.237	0.216
Public administration (vs Agri & Mining)	-0.076	0.215	−0.353	0.724
Education (vs Agri & Mining)	0.036	0.179	0.199	0.842
Health care & social work (vs Agri & Mining)	−0.014	0.169	−0.080	0.936

(continued)

Table 2. (*continued*)

	B	*SE*	t	Sig
Arts, sports & recreation (vs Agri & Mining)	−0.097	0.184	−0.524	0.600
Other service activities (vs Agri & Mining)	−0.130	0.169	−0.768	0.443
Outsourcing IT services (vs YES)	−0.121	0.052	−2.325	0.020
Digitalization	0.076	0.027	2.877	0.004

Notes. $R^2 = 64\%$; $N = 795$; B = unstandardized regression coefficient; SE = standard error.

4 Discussion

When analyzing the reasons why the people responsible for cybersecurity within their organizations fail to take the necessary measures for better protection, this research reveals a diverse range of justifications. Some lack the knowledge and skills required to implement the necessary measures. For instance, they may not know how or where to start, or where to find this knowledge. There may also be contextual factors that discourage practicing cyber resilience, including a shortage of suitable talent, insufficient funds for acquiring cybersecurity tools, or a lack of encouragement from leadership to invest (see also Pawar & Palivela 2022). Moreover, certain ingrained beliefs or myths about cybersecurity can hinder safe digital business practices. For instance, entrepreneurs might be unmotivated to take measures because they underestimate the consequences of neglecting cyber resilience or do not perceive safe digital business practices as crucial. Low motivation can also be attributed to a lack of cybersecurity training and persistent misinformation (O'Donnell 2022).

This research provides a deeper understanding of why lagging companies are not adopting adequate cyber resilience measures. It also highlights the crucial role of psychology in addressing barriers to cyber resilience practices within organizations. Behavioral models offer insights into how individuals responsible for cyber resilience perceive and respond to cyber risks. This understanding is essential for developing behavioral change interventions that effectively address these barriers and resonate with those overseeing cyber resilience. Principles from behavioral economics, such as incentives and nudges, can be employed to motivate entrepreneurs to adopt cyber-resilient practices. Positive reinforcement and rewards can influence compliance with cyber resilience guidelines.

Future research should delve into identifying specific intervention functions that are likely to be effective in promoting the widespread adoption of effective cyber resilience practices within organizational settings. While our current findings shed light on various barriers, a more nuanced exploration is needed to understand the intricacies of these challenges and design targeted solutions. The group interviews conducted as part of this study have unveiled differences in the channels entrepreneurs use to inform themselves about cybersecurity. This emphasizes the necessity of adopting a tailor-made approach in the development of interventions. Recognizing these diverse information sources will be crucial in crafting strategies that are accessible and resonate with a broad spectrum of entrepreneurs. It is imperative to assess the effectiveness of these interventions over time, taking into consideration evolving cyber threats and technological advancements.

In conclusion, future research endeavors should aim for a comprehensive understanding of the intricate dynamics surrounding the adoption of cyber resilience practices within organizations. This involves further exploring intervention strategies, considering the evolving threat landscape, and recognizing the influence of organizational culture and leadership commitment. This nuanced approach will contribute to the development of targeted, effective, and sustainable cyber resilience practices in diverse organizational settings.

Acknowledgements. The authors would like to thank Silke Mergler for her help with the project administration, funding acquisition, and conceptualization of the research. We thank Martin Muller and Bram van der Lelij with their help in collecting and analyzing the data. This work was funded by the Digital Trust Center (DTC) of the Dutch Ministry of Economic Affairs and Climate Policy.

References

1. Ajzen, I.: The theory of planned behavior. Organ. Behav. Hum. Decis. Process. **50**(2), 179–211 (1991)
2. Alanazi, M., Freeman, M., Tootell, H.: Exploring the factors that influence the cybersecurity behaviors of young adults. Comput. Hum. Behav. **136**, 107376 (2022)
3. Amemori, M., Michie, S., Korhonen, T., Murtomaa, H., Kinnunen, T.: Assessing implementation difficulties in tobacco use prevention and cessation counselling among dental providers. Implement Sci. **6**, 50–10 (2011). 1186/1748-5908-6-50
4. Brennenraedts, R., et al.: De economische kansen van de cybersecuritysector. Report 2022.130.2308. Dialogic. The Netherlands, Utrecht (2023)
5. Cane, J., O'Connor, D., Michie, S.: Validation of the theoretical domains framework for use in behaviour change and implementation research. Implement. Sci. **7**, 37 (2012). https://doi.org/10.1186/1748-5908-7-37
6. Champion, V.L., Skinner, C.S.: The health belief model. Health Behav. Health Educ. Theory Res. Pract. **4**, 45–65 (2008)
7. Connell, L.E., et al.: Links between behavior change techniques and mechanisms of action: an expert consensus study. Ann. Behav. Med. **53**(8), 708–720 (2019)
8. Dodel, M., Mesch, G.: Cyber-victimization preventive behavior: a health belief model approach. Comput. Hum. Behav. **68**, 359–367 (2017)
9. Dupont, B., Shearing, C., Bernier, M., Leukfeldt, R.: The tensions of cyber-resilience: from sensemaking to practice. Comput. Secur. **132**, 103372 (2023)
10. Glanz, K., Rimer, B.K., Orleans, C.T., Viswanath, K.: Health Behavior and Health Education Theory, Research, and Practice, 4th edn. Jossey-Bass, USA (2015)
11. Herath, T., Rao, H.R.: Protection motivation and deterrence: a framework for security policy compliance in organisations. Eur. J. Inf. Syst. **18**, 106–125 (2009)
12. Hoekstra, M., De Vries, S., Berkenpas, M., Jansen, J.: De werking van de basisscan cyberweerbaarheid. Thorbecke academie, NHL Stenden (2021)
13. Huijg, J.M., Gebhardt, W.A., Dusseldorp, E., et al.: Measuring determinants of implementation behavior: psychometric properties of a questionnaire based on the theoretical domains framework. Implementat. Sci. **9**, 33 (2014). https://doi.org/10.1186/1748-5908-9-33

14. Linkov, I., Kott, A.: Fundamental concepts of cyber resilience: introduction and overview. In: Kott, A., Linkov, I. (eds.) Cyber Resilience of Systems and Networks, pp. 1–25 (2019)
15. Michie, S., Van Stralen, M.M., West, R.: The behaviour change wheel: a new method for characterising and designing behaviour change interventions. Implement. Sci. **6**(1), 42 (2011)
16. Michie, S., Johnston, M.: Behavior change techniques. In: Gellman, M.D., Turner, J.R. (eds.) Encyclopedia of Behavioral Medicine, pp. 182–187. Springer, New York (2013). https://doi.org/10.1007/978-1-4419-1005-9_1661
17. NCTV: Cyber Security Assessment Netherlands 2023. Expect the unexpected. Ministry of Justice and Security, 9 January 2023. https://english.nctv.nl/documents/publications/2023/07/03/cyber-security-assessment-netherlands-2023
18. O'Donnell, B.: 5 cybersecurity myths and how to address them. Techtarget, 16 March 2022. https://www.techtarget.com/whatis/post/5-cybersecurity-myths-and-how-to-address-them
19. Pawar, S., Palivela, H.: LCCI: a framework for least cybersecurity controls to be implemented for small and medium enterprises (SMEs). Int. J. Inf. Manag. Data Insights **2**(1), 100080 (2022)
20. van der Kleij, R., Leukfeldt, R.: Cyber resilient behavior: integrating human behavioral models and resilience engineering capabilities into cyber security. In: Ahram, T., Karowowski, W. (eds.) AHFE 2019. AISC, vol. 960, pp. 16–27. Springer, Cham (2019). https://doi.org/10.1007/978-3-030-20488-4_2
21. van der Kleij, R., van't Hoff-De Goede, S., van de Weijer, S., Leukfeldt, R.: How safely do we behave online? An explanatory study into the cybersecurity behaviors of dutch citizens. In: Zallio, M., Raymundo Ibañez, C., Hernandez, J.H. (eds.) AHFE 2021. LNNS, vol. 268., pp. Springer, Cham (2021). https://doi.org/10.1007/978-3-030-79997-7_30
22. Van der Kleij, R., Wijn, R., Hof, T.: An application and empirical test of the capability opportunity motivation-behaviour model to data leakage prevention in financial organizations. Comput. Secur. **97**, 101938 (2020). https://doi.org/10.1016/j.cose.2020.101970
23. van't Hoff-de Goede, M.S., Leukfeldt, E.R., van der Kleij, R., van de Weijer, S.G.A.: The online behaviour and victimization study: the development of an experimental research instrument for measuring and explaining online behaviour and cybercrime victimization. In: Weulen Kranenburg, M., Leukfeldt, R. (eds.) Cybercrime in Context. Crime and Justice in Digital Society, vol. I, pp. 21–41 . Springer, Cham (2021). https://doi.org/10.1007/978-3-030-60527-8_3
24. Workman, M., Bommer, W.H., Straub, D.: Security lapses and the omission of information security measures: a threat control model and empirical test. Comput. Hum. Behav. **24**(6), 2799–2816 (2008)

BYOD Security Practices in Australian Hospitals – A Qualitative Study

Tafheem Ahmad Wani[1,2]([✉]) [ID], Antonette Mendoza[1] [ID], and Kathleen Gray[1] [ID]

[1] University of Melbourne, Parkville, VIC 3010, Australia
twani@student.unimelb.edu.au
[2] La Trobe University, Bundoora, VIC 3086, Australia

Abstract. The rapid adoption of Bring-Your-Own-Device (BYOD) in hospitals presents a conundrum, with potential benefits in productivity and mobility counterbalanced by significant data security concerns. This study aims to address the gaps in existing research by offering a comprehensive qualitative exploration of BYOD security practices in hospitals. Seven in-depth semi-structured interviews were conducted among IT personnel overseeing cybersecurity in Australian public hospitals, shedding light on the unique BYOD challenges faced by healthcare institutions. A hybrid thematic analysis was carried out to capture socio-technical factors influencing BYOD security. Results reveal that while BYOD is widely used across several device types, limitations are imposed on device functionalities and services by hospital managements to manage security risks. Furthermore, the over-reliance on staff behavior emerges as a critical challenge, leading to cybersecurity risks such as data leakage, and inadvertent sharing of patient information. Technological solutions like mobile device management (MDM) and virtualisation, though employed to enhance control, face resistance due to concerns about privacy invasion. In terms of policy, enforcement issues contribute to low compliance, emphasising the need for comprehensive, tailored, and updated BYOD policies that align with clinical workflows. The study also identifies awareness challenges, proposing incentivized, broadened, and customised training programs to enhance clinicians' engagement. Establishing a proactive cybersecurity culture, coupled with active stakeholder engagement, is highlighted as pivotal for safe and productive BYOD use. This research contributes valuable insights into the complexities of managing hospital BYOD security, informing future improvements in strategy, policies, and processes.

Keywords: BYOD · Hospital · Healthcare · User behavior · Security

1 Introduction

The use of personal devices for carrying out professional work, also known as 'Bring-your-own-device' has become a common phenomenon in hospitals. The high rate of BYOD use is due to the convenience and ease of use it offers. Modern mobile devices such as smartphones, tablets or laptops are ubiquitous and multifunctional in nature, and therefore improve productivity of hospital staff, allowing better patient care [1].

© The Author(s), under exclusive license to Springer Nature Switzerland AG 2024
A. Moallem (Ed.): HCII 2024, LNCS 14728, pp. 138–158, 2024.
https://doi.org/10.1007/978-3-031-61379-1_10

Moreover, hospitals may also save device procurement costs through BYOD use [2]. Clinicians typically use a variety of services through their personal devices. Productivity applications, patient information systems, diagnostic services, clinical photography, communication and collaboration and drug ordering systems are some of the examples of applications or tasks carried out through BYOD devices [3–6]. Virtual care services such as telehealth and remote monitoring have also seen increased use on BYOD devices, especially after the advent of the COVID-19 pandemic [7].

Though BYOD brings in several benefits for clinicians and hospitals, it is seen as a major challenge for healthcare organisations due to its data security concerns [8]. The concerns primarily arise due to hospitals having minimal control over the security of sensitive patient data residing on staff's personal devices. This means that there is an increased risk of human error and staff misuse, which in itself are among the topmost threat factors causing healthcare data breaches [9, 10]. For example, unauthorised access to patient information by friends or family members or the inadvertent patient data transmission to the wrong recipient by error may occur in a BYOD environment [11]. In comparison, devices provided by hospitals have pre-installed security controls which keep users in check and ensure that hospital's security policies are properly enforced [12]. Lastly, the strict healthcare data privacy laws and compliance requirements is another burden for hospitals, failing which they may have to pay heavy penalties, in addition to reputational damage [13].

Previous research into hospital BYOD security has been fragmented and generally techno-centric in nature [12, 14–16]. Recognising this gap, the authors of this study identified several socio-technical BYOD security issues and relevant mitigation measures in hospitals through a comprehensive review of academic and grey literature [13, 17]. The literature review found that studies in this area were largely expert commentaries and based in the US, meaning that a dearth of real-life empirical studies in hospital settings was found. The literature review was followed up with another study, where a survey was carried out among IT and cybersecurity managers at Australian public hospitals to capture and analyse the hospitals socio-technical BYOD security practices [18, 19]. However, being a quantitative study, this study only provided a limited and objective view of BYOD security practices in Australian hospitals, which may have missed deeper contextual insights into the circumstances in which these controls were employed and the reasons for their success or failure. Qualitative studies in cybersecurity are known to provide deeper insights into socio-technical security practices and therefore provide additional rigour in research [20].

The aim of this study therefore is to explore IT or cybersecurity managers' overall perception of BYOD security management practices and its associated challenges in Australian hospitals through a qualitative interview-based study. This study will extend upon the survey-based study and will therefore provide contextual richness to the survey findings to further improve the theoretical understanding of hospital BYOD, especially with respect to the unique socio-technical factors specific to healthcare BYOD.

2 Methodology

2.1 Ethics

This study was approved by the Human Ethics Advisory Group, Faculty of Engineering and IT, University of Melbourne (ID: 1955486.2).

2.2 Participants and Recruitment

Volunteers were recruited among IT personnel working in public hospitals across Australia, who oversee the security domain within their respective hospitals. These volunteers were expected to have sound knowledge of BYOD security management, including socio-technical BYOD security issues as well as practices used within their hospital to counter such issues. Participant recruitment took place primarily through senior Australian state health department officials. A plain language statement consisting of the study information was shared with them, who then forwarded it to potential participants that met the eligibility criteria within their networks. The study was also advertised through webinars and professional networks such as LinkedIn and the social media groups of Australian Institute of Digital Health (AIDH), and Health Information and Management Systems Society (HIMSS). A total of seven semi-structured interviews were held between May 2020 and March 2021, recognising that COVID-19 hindered the data collection process. To achieve diversity in the types of hospitals as well as participants in the study, purposeful sampling was used [21]. Considering the depth and volume of interview data, subject matter experts as participants as well as using other studies complementing this research, the number of participants can be considered sufficient for thematic analysis, though higher number would have further strengthened this research [22–24]. Participants represented diverse hospital settings such as multisite and large hospital organisations, metropolitan hospitals, suburban hospitals, and regional hospitals. Participant roles within the hospitals also varied (Table 1).

Table 1. Interviewed participants characteristics.

No.	Position	Hospital type/location	Participant background details	Participant pseudonym
1	CISO	Suburban	25 years+ IT, 15 years in IT security	P1
2	CTO	Metropolitan	30 years+ IT, 2 years tech. head	P2
3	CMIO	Suburban	5 years CMIO, health dept. consultant on technology and privacy	P3

(*continued*)

Table 1. (*continued*)

No.	Position	Hospital type/location	Participant background details	Participant pseudonym
4	IT Director	Metropolitan	20 years in IT, 10 years+ as IT Director	P4
5	Program manager	Suburban	20 years+ IT, 10 years+ in IT management roles	P5
6	Cybersecurity lead	Suburban	15 years+ IT, 10 years+ in cybersecurity	P6
7	IT Security head	Suburban	15 years+ IT, 5 years+ in cybersecurity	P7

2.3 Procedure and Tasks

The PPT (People Policy Technology) model and the hospital BYOD security framework was used to develop the interview protocol [13, 25]. The use of these models aided in capturing all relevant social, technical, and managerial factors relevant to BYOD security. Regarding the interview structure, it consisted of three parts. The first part asked for participant and hospital information, the second part asked about BYOD usage in the hospital from an IT management perspective and the third part was for participants opinion or interpretation regarding the PPT (People Policy Technology) aspects of BYOD security within their hospital. This included the relevant procedures, processes, or controls related to each dimension and the context in which they are implemented, their effectiveness or usefulness, as well as the associated challenges with respect to each of the three dimensions. The average interview length was 60 to 90 min. Initial participants of the study also provided feedback which aided in refining the interview questions further.

2.4 Data Collection

Interviews were conducted over phone or via Zoom-based video conferencing. Notes were also taken during the interview. Following interviews, the recorded audios were transcribed and all identifying personal, or hospital information was anonymised and de-identified by using pseudonyms and codes. All interview data was stored on a password-protected and secure cloud data storage platform provided by the university.

2.5 Analysis

A hybrid thematic analysis was carried out using the framework method [26]. The major themes were based on the hospital BYOD security framework and the PPT model, as a deductive analysis was carried out centered around interview themes. Inductive thematic analysis was used to cover underlying themes, which were extracted from the transcribed data through a process of identification, labelling, organisation, and classification of themes. This was done through NVivo, a qualitative data analysis software.

It was followed by an iterative process of triangulation among the study researchers to finalise the codes. The COREQ checklist for qualitative studies was used to maintain best practices during the data collection and analysis process [27].

3 Results

Four themes are covered in this study: Nature of BYOD use, and each of the People, Policy, and Technology aspects of BYOD security management.

3.1 Nature of BYOD Use

This theme describes the type and nature of devices and applications allowed for BYOD purposes, as well as perceived impact of BYOD use within hospitals.

Devices Allowed for BYOD Purposes. As per the interviewed participants, most device types were allowed for BYOD use, though the level of access and support provided to users varied for different device types. The use of smartphones for BYOD received greater backing from IT management, given that they support clinicians' mobility and productivity and therefore have a broader use case within and outside of the hospital. For instance, some hospitals remunerated staff for buying smartphones and/or data plans as they are widely used for clinical care purposes. Laptops on the other hand were allowed so that the clinical staff can carry out complex tasks not possible on a mobile device, as the bigger size of laptops is better suited cognitively to work on complex patient information systems and in certain cases, view patient diagnostic files such as x-rays. Lastly, tablets were generally seen as 'not fit for purpose' in terms of BYOD use, given that they are difficult to carry around and due to very few hospital applications specifically designed for tablets.

Applications/Services Allowed on BYOD Devices. Mostly, access to services through BYOD devices was limited, with email being the main service allowed on personal devices. The primary reason stated by participants in limiting BYOD services was data privacy or security of hospital data. Addressing this question, P1 stated "So they're (staff) only allowed certain applications, the hospital-based applications, that they can use for security reasons. That includes email and a time recording system".

In terms of clinical communication and collaboration, most participants said that there were no authorised platforms for clinical communication on BYOD devices in their hospitals, making use of personal communication applications such as WhatsApp™ common. However, secured platforms such as Microsoft Teams™ or dedicated clinical communication platforms were also being rolled out to support secure communication. For example, P5 said:

From a clinical communication perspective, we don't have a particular tool or set of tools in place. Obviously, what you don't authorise or provide then clinicians will find another way to do what they want to do. So WhatsApp, it's probably one of those ones that is not authorised, it's not approved, but clinicians will use something to get around what they feel they need to do.

P3 and P4 gave examples of sanctioned or dedicated clinical communication platforms such as myBeepr™ used at their hospital. Some hospitals also provide access to other hospital-based services such as patient management portals, electronic medical records or telehealth applications on BYOD devices, but they are generally secured through virtualisation.

BYOD Benefits and Impact. BYOD brings in several benefits to hospital staff. Firstly, the familiarity and convenience of using personal devices can enable better productivity and mobility, especially for clinicians. Describing this benefit, P3 explained:

I think with the handheld smartphone (BYOD), it's about mobile access, I'm walking around, I'm on a ward round. And I think with any work, if you can give the answer straight away, rather than saying, I'll get back to you, then things are more efficient.

3.2 Technology

Participants' opinion was sought on BYOD technical controls used by hospital IT departments and its associated challenges. They were also asked to comment on potential future BYOD technology improvements within their hospitals.

BYOD Security Technical Controls Used in Hospitals. Participants were asked about BYOD security technical controls used at their hospital. The following major controls were identified.

BYOD Identity and Access Management (IAM). Among the IAM technologies, multi-factor authentication (MFA) was found to be common, which according to the interviewed participants has improved the overall security of hospital data by adding an extra layer of protection. The interview data also revealed that MFA is mostly tied with single sign on, where the user needs to prove their identity only once. Explaining the benefits of using multi-factor authentication with single sign on, P2 said:

We've got a good multi-factor authentication tool, and we've got methods to do single sign on. It's probably one of the more streamlined sides of our technology and we try and make it as efficient as possible.

Other identity and access management controls as per the interviewed participants included registration of BYOD devices to get access to hospital services, use of an identity service engine (ISE) to allow or disallow devices into the hospital network, and role-based access control (RBAC) to provide access privileges based on the user role i.e., users can only access information relevant to them. As an example of device registration, P5 mentioned:

Doctors that want hospital email or Wi-Fi connectivity on their phone, they just call and are provided with the URL. They go to the URL and just a couple of steps for the (registration) process where they put in their active directory credentials and once they log in, the profile is pushed to the end device.

Similarly, P5 described how ISE services used at their hospital to only allow those BYOD devices to connect to the network, which meet a certain eligibility criteria, such as those installed anti-virus or registered devices. P2 also explained how RBAC is used to provide application access and privileges to clinicians based on their role.

Mobile Device Management (MDM). Only some participants said that MDM was used at their hospital. It was mostly used for hospital owned devices, and its usage for BYOD devices was limited. The primary reason for limited use of MDM on BYOD devices was that it breaches personal privacy of BYOD users. For instance, P1 stated:

> *We have a mixture of hospital sponsored devices versus personal devices, and MDM's definitely not targeting people's personal devices. So we do not wipe any data on personal devices, because I don't believe the technology offers unlimited data wipe options, because if we trigger a data wipe, it will basically go in and delete even personal photos, and for that reason, we decided we basically don't venture out in that space.*

BYOD Network Security. The predominant network security control was found to be the barring of BYOD devices connecting to the hospital's internal network infrastructure directly by measures such as creation of guest networks, network segmentation, or network access control. For example, P1 said:

> *All BYOD devices, they cannot connect to the internal network. And if they (users) for example, bring their own Mac, they can connect to the wireless network, but it only gives them limited access. All communication to the internet as a user goes through a proxy, which protects from, say, against malicious downloads or viruses.*

One of the common modes through which hospitals allow their corporate applications to be run on BYOD devices is virtualisation. It provides a secure mechanism as data is stored and processed within hospital's own infrastructure, minimising storage of hospital data on BYOD devices. In terms of remote access to hospital services, Virtual Private Network (VPN) and remote virtualisation services were also reported to be used on BYOD devices to access hospital applications remotely.

Storage and Backup Security. Virtualisation is used as an effective tool to minimise storage of hospital data on BYOD devices as per the interviewed participants. Furthermore, in terms of device theft or loss, P5 stated that their hospital has the ability and consent to perform a data lock or data wipe on BYOD devices through MDM.

> *If they call up and say the mobile is stolen, we can push through and initiate an enterprise lock on the device. So the policy in place say if the user loses the device, they have to notify service desk and if you have provisioned any email or what have you, that phone will then initiate deletion of that profile, but not the user data. Regardless, we do have the capability of doing a full enterprise wipe, so if the user says wipe the whole phone, we will do it yeah.*

BYOD Endpoint Security. Endpoint security refers to protection of endpoint user devices to prevent data leakage. In terms of endpoint security, hospitals may take measures such as ensuring that BYOD users have the latest anti-virus/anti-malware or operating systems installed, which are free from security bugs and BYOD devices are encrypted. Device blacklisting is also used as a mechanism to prevent unsecure devices from joining hospital networks.

Technical Challenges Associated with BYOD Use. BYOD security technology related challenges were also inquired as part of the interview. The main challenges identified were:

Limited Control Over BYOD Devices. According to participants, a major area of concern was the limited control they had over the personal devices of the hospital staff. Use of BYOD meant that minimising storage of hospital data on BYOD devices was a challenge. As an example, P4 said:

> *In terms of information they (clinicians) could store potentially on their device, every one of those (patient) photographs can end up in their iCloud or on Google Drive, absolutely! We've got enterprise documents sitting in Dropbox and all sorts of other cloud storage platforms that we have no control over. That's probably our biggest leakage at the moment.*

The reliance on user actions and the inability to control user activities on personal devices was also seen as a major challenge. This was because unlike hospital owned devices, restrictions couldn't be applied on BYOD devices due to personal privacy concern. Explaining this dogma, P6 stated:

> *It's (BYOD) widely used and the issue here is we have doctors taking photos of incidents or episodes of patient care and then chatting it with other doctors on their personal device. (If) a doctor brings in their own personal device that he or she wants to use and if you then apply all those restrictions on their own machine, I don't they're going to like it, so aspects like locking down the machine and having measures in place to prevent any breach, for example anti-virus, anti-malware, locking down the machine as we don't have administrative privileges isn't possible.*

The limited control over BYOD devices can also lead to issues such as inadvertent sending of patient data to the wrong person and introducing malware onto hospital networks when infected BYOD devices are used.

Keeping Up with the Security Requirements. Several BYOD devices and application types are used by hospital staff, therefore making it a burden for hospital IT departments to manage security requirements for all of them. To illustrate, P6 stated:

> *The challenge is to maintain compliance, especially when writing a policy around device models that the user can bring into the organisation because not all devices would be compatible with most of the applications that need to be provisioned onto that device. One day you've got Apple-6, the next day you've got Apple-15. Having to maintain that level of compatibility with the technology as it's changing is challenging in a BYOD environment, especially around developing that policy and the framework around BYOD. And not just the device, but also the version of the operating systems because a major upgrade on an IOS can have a major impact on how you access.*

Another critical issue related to technology described by participants were the large number of in-silos systems or applications, making it difficult for both the management and users to keep up with their individual security or access requirements, due to lack of integration. This means users have to individually login to each application for instance, leading to workflow disruptions. The rapidly evolving cybersecurity threats and the changing technology also becomes a challenge for hospital IT departments. Several participants quoted this during their interview. For instance, P5 said:

> *Technology advances so quickly and cybersecurity issues develop almost daily that you're having to deal and one small weakness can then actually have an impact on your whole network. We're just being very reactive, applying those patches, and then healing to deal with aftermath later. It's a really interesting industry and environment, one that's changing really quickly.*

Loss of Device. Loss or theft of BYOD devices which have patient data residing on them can result in major breaches. The inability of hospital IT departments to take actions such as data wipe or device lock adds to the problem. This is due to the lack of segregation of personal and hospital data, making it difficult for the IT department to selectively apply security policies, such as wiping hospital data only in case of loss, theft, or leaving the hospital organisation. Describing the same, P2 said:

> *So we would not want people downloading patient information and images and things like that to personal devices except for work purposes. Then we wouldn't want it to stay on a device, we would want, if they no longer worked with us, that it was no longer accessible. So as a tool, typically through an MDM, you'd wipe the device when someone left but if it's a personal device you can't wipe the personal stuff. It's just a challenge how you manage that.*

Applying Security Controls to BYOD Devices Used at Multiple Healthcare Organisations. Healthcare professionals and especially doctors may work at multiple health services and may be using the same device for BYOD purposes. This becomes a challenge when technical controls or policies are being applied to that device by multiple organisations. P6 explained:

> *Let's say a doctor brings in their own device, and accesses clinical applications, we have to apply our polices on the device. The same doctor works at multiple other hospitals and you've got the same situation where they want to apply their policies on his personal device. You're pretty much in the situation where a doctor has brought in a device becomes practically unusable with all these different policies being applied by different hospitals. It's a tough one!*

Future Technology Improvements. Table 2 gives a list of technology improvements related to BYOD security management, which the study participants envisaged to be implemented in their respective hospitals in the future.

Table 2. Planned improvements in BYOD 'technology' practices in participants' hospitals.

Technology Improvement	Description
Secure clinical communication	Secure and dedicated clinical communications/collaborations platforms specifically designed for hospitals
Productivity and mobility apps	Applications with enhanced user experience designed usually for mobile devices and integrated with hospital systems and allow clinicians to perform their work productivity and when 'on the go' or mobile
Secure cloud storage	Secure storage platforms which are specifically designed to store organisational data, minimising storage of hospital data on BYOD devices
MDM use for BYOD	MDM use to automate implementation of BYOD security controls on personal devices such as securing devices remotely, whitelisting/blacklisting apps and devices, encrypting hospital data, securing remote connections through VPNs; tracking device location, wiping or locking of device remotely in case of theft/loss/data breach
Dedicated staff Wi-Fi band	Use of a highly secure network dedicated only for staff

3.3 Policy

This theme provides the participant's views on the typical components and characteristics of BYOD policies, their impact, associated challenges, and potential future improvements.

BYOD Policy Components/Role of Policy. Participants described several components in their hospital's BYOD or related policies. These components address various areas related to BYOD. A description of the policy components along with their role is explained in Table 3.

Policy Challenges. The following policy-related challenges were described by the interviewed participants.

Compliance Challenges. Compliance to legislative or regulatory requirements was seen as a major policy challenge as per the interviewed participants. Several reasons were cited for it. For instance, P7 quoted lacking infrastructure and cybersecurity capabilities in hospitals being responsible for low compliance of hospitals. Furthermore, P2 believed that the complex audit process set by state agencies also makes it difficult for hospitals to comply to them. Lack of standardised practices and decentralisation was also believed to be a cause of low compliance levels in hospitals. Explaining this issue, P2 said:

> *I think with mobile device management, the fact that clinicians work across multiple health services and we all do something different is a little bit challenging. We are much more decentralised, and everyone can follow their own what they think is best practice which sometimes makes it harder to manage if you're working across multiple health services or working with other health services. So yeah. I*

Table 3. BYOD policy role and components.

Policy Component	Description
Generic guidelines such as acceptable use	High level generic guidelines which describe aspects such as do's and don'ts within the organisation
Personal device security	Guidelines for staff on how to secure personal devices to reduce the risk of patient data breaches
Restrictions on unsecure devices	Guidelines on what form of devices are not allowed to be used for hospital work
Incident management	Guidelines on procedures to be followed by staff in case of security incidents such as loss/theft or breach of a personal device storing patient/hospital data
PHI security	Guidelines on protecting patient data stored/transmitted via BYOD devices
Device management	Description about how personal and hospital devices would be managed by the hospital IT department and whether they would have any access or control over the devices
Sanctions on non-compliance	Description about sanctions such as warnings or penalties which will be applied on non-compliance with BYOD or related policies

guess some standard practices would help and that government's in a position to influence that.

Complexity in Policy Enforcement. The enforcement of BYOD or associated policies is also a major obstacle, as per several interviewed participants. Due to personal privacy issues, enforcement becomes exceedingly difficult. The lack of control over BYOD devices was also described as a major obstacle to policy enforcement. P6 explained:

I think we're limited to some degree in that we can't actually control what the user does on the individual device. We can provision access and we can authenticate a user accessing a service via the phone, email for example, but we can't stop them from taking a copy of a patient record and typing in details into an email and sending that email, which would be breach of the Privacy Act for example. We can't police what they are doing. We can provide the framework for them to do something, but we can't actually stop them.

P3 described how compliance to policies is greatly dependent upon user intention and commitment, it is therefore important to make the policies user friendly and accommodative rather than being hard to follow.

Low Policy Readership and Engagement. Even though policies for BYOD may exist, low policy readership among clinical user groups are a hurdle in making them successful. Some participants cited low interest among clinicians regarding non-clinical issues as a reason. For example, P5 said:

> *How many of them (clinicians) would have read acceptable use policies and BYOD policies, I would suggest it's probably in single digit percentages. It's not until something goes pear-shaped... I mean it doesn't form part of their mandatory competencies that they have to complete and are reported on every year. So, yes gaining that sort of engagement and agreement and feedback on policy adherence from an IT perspective is an incredibly big challenge.*

P3 and P7 described how low policy readership can also be due to the low priority which hospital's set for BYOD or cybersecurity issues in general.

Future Policy Improvements. In light of the existing BYOD related policies and its challenges, the study participants expected several improvements (Table 4).

Table 4. Planned improvements in BYOD 'policy' practices in participants' hospitals.

Policy Improvement	Description
Improving compliance	Following regulations, laws, and standards by making stronger policies and enforcing security controls
Review of BYOD strategy/policy	Alignment of BYOD strategy and policies according to hospital needs over a period of time
Stricter policy enforcement	Rigorously enforcing security controls and formalising actions on non-compliance
Formalising BYOD policies/strategy	Creating a formal BYOD strategy/policy/program, which stipulates relevant policies, procedures and controls which are then enforced

3.4 People

The People theme explored participant views on the 'human' aspect of BYOD usage. Several areas such as security training and awareness methods and associated challenges, clinical productivity issues and cultural factors such as management support, staff resistance and change management are described.

People Management Practices

BYOD Security Training. The value of training was highlighted by all participants. For example, P2 said:

> *It (training) is actually good because it keeps all the employees informed and up to date and it sets expectations of what is right. I actually think that regular training,*

appropriate to your role, with a refresh and a sign off each year that you've done it and you are up to date actually works.

Several modes of training were provided in the interviewed participants hospitals. These include: 1) generic cybersecurity awareness campaigns to provide basic education to hospital staff on safe user behaviour through posters, bulletins, email reminders, 2) online module based training through e-learning platforms which typically include educational videos or slides followed by a short quiz, 3) targeted training for critical or susceptible staff, and lastly, 4) phishing campaigns to test user compliance through a simulated phishing email sent to staff.

Change Champions as Advocates. Some hospitals utilised technically literate clinicians to advocate and promote cybersecurity initiatives among their peers/within their departments and broadly within the hospital. Following examples illustrate these practices:

P3 mentioned:

We know what works best is the local champion type of thing. So, I'm trying to set up a network of champions for all things, technical, digital, innovative informatics clause, so that there are special interest groups all over the place. So that when you've got any type of thing that you've got to roll out, you can just disperse it down the tree or the roots of the tree, if you like.

Hybrid Roles to Support Change Management. Another practice was to create hybrid roles such as clinical informatics officers to improve engagement between clinicians and technical staff and provide valuable input into policy decisions. For example, P3 said:

I think the whole concept of the position of chief medical informatics officer, chief nursing, or chief clinical informatics officer, is that the clinical person gets involved and provides meaningful input into policy, which would have probably been a bit difficult before. I think in the past, before we developed these hybrid mixed roles, the clinical people just did not understand yet the other side of it. There hasn't been clinical engagement where there should be, as the people that are going to be using it should give their perspective.

People Management Challenges

Lack of Funding for Cybersecurity Initiatives. One of the major challenges associated with BYOD security management at hospitals is the lack of funding which has been a hurdle in improving their cybersecurity posture, P7 explained:

If we did have funding in that area, we would probably enforce more mandatory controls, given that my staff are happy to provide their own devices. Some products have limitations in terms of user experience, so they (staff) would prefer an enhanced user experience, but with our current technology budget, we really can't provide them that. Hence, the reason our BYOD policy hasn't really progressed much in the last five years. In public health, the funding is never what it needs to be.

Maintaining Staff Interest for Training. Most participants stated that low levels of motivation and interest among clinicians is one of the main reasons limiting its effectiveness. For instance, P4 said:

The problem is that hospitals are caught up in mandatory training, and that mandatory training is already being pushed back against. Cybersecurity is just another piece of mandatory training that people don't want to do every year, so it's a challenge. You're basically talking about 10 min of training a year with 10 PowerPoint slides, and you're talking thousands and thousands of staff. People don't have the time to go to formal training, and they don't want to do it.

Gaps in Training Provided. Participants stated several gaps in the training already provided at their hospital. Though the need for a mandatory cybersecurity training was identified, the low interest among clinicians and a lack of funding to support paid training meant that they have to keep it optional. Some participants also believed that the training currently provided is not adequate and hence needs to be broadened. As an example, P4 said:

No, it's (BYOD security training) not good enough. The attack vector is huge. The training is absolutely minimal. It's a risk, absolutely.

P1 believed that regular awareness needs to be maintained through constant user education. P2 also thought that formal cyber education among clinicians can improve overall outcomes.

Clinical Workflow Challenges – Needs Based Practice. Several participants quoted instances of the use of unsecure workarounds by clinicians at their hospital. This was because clinicians highly favoured usability than security of patient data, due to the nature of their work, where patient outcomes are of utmost importance. P7 mentioned:

You can implement as many technical controls, but humans being humans, in any system there's ways to get around the system, and if we don't provide a reliable service in terms of providing an instant messaging platform to meet the needs of the clinicians, then they'll go and do it by other means.

Explaining the use of informal communication tools to support patient care, P4 said:

I think the issue is that it's all right to say, 'Hey, group of clinicians, you can use this communication app inside this hospital,' but it's the fact that they have all their colleagues. Their colleague over in the US or wherever is a specialist. It's actually them that they want to get to, not specifically inside your hospital, because they want to ask a friend the answer to the problem. That's where you end up with leakage. You can't stop that on a personal phone.

Compared to the ease of use of informal applications such as WhatsApp, the hospital sanctioned applications or processes are complex and don't provide an ideal user experience. For instance, P3 stated as to how lack of integration between different systems leads to loss of clinical productivity. Similarly, a poor user experience when using virtualisation was quoted by P4 for low usage of virtual apps on BYOD devices. Thus, managing clinician's expectations is difficult for hospitals, given the time-sensitive nature of their work where patient care takes precedence over patient privacy. P5 described this issue by saying:

The clinician demands that I should be able to do whatever I want on my mobile device and you should deliver it to me for ease of use in whatever way I want. At a very simplistic level that makes perfect sense, but from a technology level, from a security level, and from a patient privacy act level, that just is so full of challenge. The clinician is not interested in that, but rather to actually deliver something that is useful that makes sense at the end of the day.

Low Levels of Engagement with Clinical Stakeholders. Some participants also acknowledged that minimal communication with clinical stakeholders is a major issue as user buy in is important to the success of the BYOD strategy. P7 said:

Where IT comes in and pushes a solution on the organisation and there's no stakeholder engagement, it's never going to be successful. If the clinicians came to us and said, 'This is what we want,' or 'This is the problem we have. What are the options and what's your recommendation?' And there's buy-in from the clinical part of the business' stakeholders, with that clinical sponsorship, then it's more likely to be a success.

Staff Resistance Due to Personal Privacy Issues. Because of the fear of personal privacy intrusion, hospital staff are resistant to allow IT departments to have any form of control over their personal devices through services such as MDM. For example, P5 said:

I think the challenge is if you've got a user who wants to bring a device into the work environment then you have got to make sure that they are willing to provide you with the ability to control that device should it go missing or fall into the wrong hands, which doesn't happen.

The main challenge as per P2 is also the segregation of hospital and personal data.

I think there'd be initial resistance (by staff). They'd say 'how are you going to tell it's (data) hospital related or mine (personal)'?

Lack of Management Support. The importance of management support for BYOD security initiatives was also emphasised by some participants. P3 said:

You've got the clinicians on one side and you've got the IT people on the other. So unless there's somebody who sits above, who says exactly what you've just said and just tells them to make it happen, then it does happen. So it depends on that vision and understanding from overarching management.

Cultural Issues. Security culture is pivotal in determining how cybersecurity issues are handled at a hospital. P5 described how their hospital has a reactive security culture which is a challenge for them:

I think any situations where we've had to deal with potential breaches of patient privacy, they've come as a result of an investigation, as opposed to putting into

*place framework or restrictions ahead or proactively. Could we ever get down to
that level? If we had access to an integrated electronic medical record then if that
person was accessing via a BYOD mobile device then their access to information
would be controlled by their profile on the EMR and they would only have access
to certain things that they could see as a result of the definition of their role and
their permissions.*

Future People Improvements. This study identified several envisioned future improvements at the participant's hospitals, as specified in Table 5.

Table 5. Planned improvements in BYOD 'people' practices in participants' hospitals.

'People' Improvement	Description
Mandating training	Making cybersecurity training mandatory to improve staff awareness
Technology upskilling among clinicians	Providing formal technology and cybersecurity education to clinicians as part of their clinical training and also supporting their upskilling during their career
Periodic training	Providing training periodically to maintain awareness levels
Broadening training coverage	Making training comprehensive and regularly updating training material to ensure staff are aware of major threats, including latest ones
Targeted training	Specific role based training relevant to clinician role to avoid training fatigue

4 Discussion

This study explored the views of IT management professionals such as technology, cybersecurity, and informatics managers to investigate BYOD security socio-technical practices within Australian hospitals. It provided insights about the context in which BYOD security technologies, policies and people management measures are implemented within hospitals, the effectiveness of their implementation, the concerns, or challenges with respect to each of the three PPT (People, Policy, and Technology) dimensions, as well as the future of BYOD management. Being a qualitative study, it provided a comprehensive understanding of BYOD security, which can allow to develop holistic socio-technical solutions, relevant to the Australian hospital context.

Though the extent and nature of BYOD use varied between different hospitals, BYOD was generally seen to be highly beneficial among hospital staff, as it improves their productivity and mobility as per the majority of the interviewed participants. This explains the overall high demand in BYOD use in the hospital sector [28]. In terms of device types or services allowed for BYOD use, due to the limited resources available at hospitals, they restrict the types of devices and services or applications allowed for BYOD purposes, as managing security requirements individually becomes a cumbersome task for the hospital IT department as suggested by previous studies as well [11]. For example, smartphones are supported more than laptops or tablets by certain hospitals due to their broader use-case, as they allow greater mobility and can be used widely for clinical care purposes. Laptops on the other hand are specifically suited for limited applications or services when complex tasks have to be carried out. Tablets were least suited for any type of work as they are difficult to carry, and see less use among clinicians, which is why we see fewer hospital or clinical applications designed for tablets. This aligns with the findings of the survey-based study, where tablets and laptops were allowed in 69.57% of surveyed hospitals for BYOD use and smartphones were allowed in all of the surveyed hospitals [18]. As far as the applications or services are concerned, BYOD use was restricted to basic services such as email, with security again being the main reason for such restrictions. Services such as clinical communication, EMR applications or other applications related to patient care on BYOD devices are either rare or envisaged to be implemented in the future, as per the study findings.

The results further suggest that the main technical challenge with respect to BYOD security management in hospitals is the limited control over staff devices and consequently the reliance on user actions to protect hospital data residing on such devices. This increases the risks of events such as introduction of malware and virus into hospital networks, inadvertently sending patient data to wrong recipients and storage of patient data on public storage solutions such as public clouds, leading to data leakage. Technologies such as MDM, virtualisation, and secure clinical communication solutions may limit storage of hospital data on personal devices and reduce the risk of data leakages. However, such technologies either see limited use in hospitals or may not be fully optimised to protect both patient data privacy and staff's personal data privacy. For example, the use of MDM may compromise personal privacy of staff, and therefore hospitals may abstain its use for BYOD devices. Furthermore, the implementation of virtualisation solutions may not be optimised for all device types, again affecting usability and productivity of clinicians. Also, clinical communication solutions haven't been formally implemented in hospitals, meaning that informal and unauthorised workarounds such as use of WhatsApp™ and SMS finds common place. A positive development though is that several hospitals are already in the process of implementing or considering the use of dedicated, secure, and integrated clinical application solutions, including those for clinical communication which provide an enhanced user experience and are integrated with hospital systems, further improving mobility and productivity of clinicians. In addition, hospitals are also investing in secure storage solutions such as private clouds, which prevents data leakage outside of the organisation as they remove the need of services such as Dropbox™, which may not be secure. Another key technology related challenge is keeping up with rapidly changing security requirements, which causes a management overhead. The use of several device, application and operating system types for BYOD means that hospital IT departments have to individually manage security requirements for each of them, making it an arduous task. In addition, the threats and vulnerabilities keep on evolving, again making it difficult for hospital IT departments to cater to them.

To address this issue, hospitals could potentially invest in advanced technologies such as Unified Endpoint Management (UEM) and Cloud Access Security Broker (CASB), which offer better automation and control over all device types, including BYOD and hospital owned devices, and therefore simplify the work of hospital IT departments in managing BYOD security requirements. It also allows better segregation of hospital and personal data, removing the need for clinicians to provide full access of their personal devices to the hospital [17].

Policy is a pivotal component of BYOD security management, whose importance has been highlighted in previous literature as well as the participants of this study. It provides the necessary direction and guidelines for safe and productive BYOD use [8, 11]. Policy translates into good practice when it is tailored, comprehensive, regularly updated and appropriately enforced. However, most participants conceded that their hospital has generic policies which provide high level guidelines on information security not specific to BYOD. Therefore, they aren't very impactful in terms of improving staff user behaviour. Another key issue related to policy is the complexity and lack of ability to enforce policy in a BYOD environment. Hospital management are greatly dependent on user's goodwill. Furthermore, in a time sensitive and complex environment such as a hospital, productivity requirements are paramount and therefore hospital staff are known to violate policy in favour of usability, which further complicates the issue. Findings from the study indicate the need to develop policies which carefully consider clinical workflow of staff. Moreover, hospitals may also consider providing secure and usable tools to clinicians, as well as streamlining their BYOD related processes, so that they don't have the need to use workarounds and then hospitals can enforce policy more strictly. At the governmental level, the complexities involved in the audit process and the large number of controls which hospitals need to implement is a key challenge as well. This points out the need to restructure, centralise and simplify the audit process so that hospitals can improve their compliance with the set regulatory requirements. Finally, policies need to be well-written and appropriately structured, with a proper dissemination plan to improve policy readership, which has been a major issue for hospitals due to lack of interest among hospital staff.

As with the policy, training also needs to be comprehensive, specific, and periodic for it to be effective. If training initiatives are not prioritised, they may not achieve the desired outcomes. For example, several participants complained of gaps in existing training provided at their hospital such as being optional, generic, and minimal. This reduces clinicians' interest who may prefer not to complete such non-clinical training that is not a part of their work and is generally unpaid. The study also reveals that some hospitals are planning for future improvements in this regard, which include mandating and incentivising training, broadening training coverage, providing targeted training specific to clinical specialty as well as making it periodic which can help a long way in improving the impact of training. Furthermore, an important challenge that was identified was the lack of management support, which may be the difference between the success and failure of cybersecurity initiatives taken by hospitals. The executive management need to be fully committed and show resolve to establish a security culture in their hospitals. This culture transmits from the executive to the staff level, as several participants believed that if the hospital management prioritises cybersecurity in their hospital, it translates into good practices by the clinicians as well. This also means that hospital executives could consider actively investing and funding cybersecurity initiatives so that IT departments can strengthen the related tools and processes which can deal with the latest threats. Lastly, hospital management and IT departments should strategically engage with clinical stakeholders, and also seek their input into the BYOD strategy as well as related policies and processes. This is important especially in a BYOD scenario as clinicians may need to understand how best they can use tools provided on their personal devices in a safe and productive manner, while also providing feedback to hospital IT departments to streamline their processes. They also demand greater transparency into how their personal data on BYOD devices is safeguarded by the hospital. Steps such as use of clinical change champions to promote cybersecurity initiatives among their colleagues and creating hybrid roles such as clinical informatics officers to represent clinicians can help to achieve this goal.

Study Significance. This study provides a deep analysis into BYOD security practices in hospitals from a management perspective. Findings from the study can aid in informing future improvements in the overall BYOD strategy and related policies and processes in hospitals. This is because the study delves deep into the reasoning behind the actions of IT management pertaining to hospital BYOD security, their associated challenges and future actions envisioned by hospitals which can potentially solve those challenges. Findings from this study can also aid government health departments in providing over-arching guidance or recommendations to hospitals.

Limitations. This study may have limited generalisability as only seven participants took part in the study. Appropriate sampling and recruitment practices were conducted to ensure that the participants belonged to diverse demographic characteristics and represented various hospital types. Still, some participant or hospital types may have been under-represented in this study. Also, findings from the study may also be valid for countries with a comparable healthcare ecosystem.

5 Conclusion

This study provides insights into the nature, scope, context, and effectiveness of BYOD security practices in Australian hospitals. Through a deeper understanding of hospital BYOD security, it offers a roadmap for hospitals to navigate the unique socio-technical and human factors associated with BYOD security in healthcare settings. Though this chapter covers the IT management perspective of BYOD security in detail, it is equally important to gain a deep understanding of BYOD security from a clinical user perspective, given its reliance on user actions. Qualitative studies among BYOD clinical users were also conducted therefore by the study authors, as a follow up study.

Acknowledgments. This work was supported by the University of Melbourne and La Trobe University. The authors also want to express their gratitude to the study participants.

Disclosure of Interests. None declared.

References

1. Luk, G.: Mobile Workforce Reports. Strategy Analytics (2018)
2. Williams, J.: Left to their own devices how healthcare organizations are tackling the BYOD trend. Biomed. Instrum. Technol. **48**, 327 (2014)
3. Armstrong, K.A., Semple, J.L., Coyte, P.C.: Replacing ambulatory surgical follow-up visits with mobile app home monitoring: modeling cost-effective scenarios. J. Med. Internet Res. **16**, e213 (2014). https://doi.org/10.2196/jmir.3528
4. Nerminathan, A., Harrison, A., Phelps, M., Scott, K.M., Alexander, S.: Doctors' use of mobile devices in the clinical setting: a mixed methods study (2017)
5. Moreau, M., Paré, G.: Early clinical management of severe burn patients using telemedicine: a pilot study protocol. Pilot Feasibility Stud. **6**, 93 (2020). https://doi.org/10.1186/s40814-020-00637-7
6. Schooley, B., Nicolas-Rocca, T.S., Burkhard, R.: Patient-provider communications in outpatient clinic settings: a clinic-based evaluation of mobile device and multimedia mediated communications for patient education. JMIR Mhealth Uhealth **3**, e2 (2015). https://doi.org/10.2196/mhealth.3732
7. Davis, J.: Must-Have Telehealth, Remote Work Privacy and Security for COVID-19 (2020). https://healthitsecurity.com/news/must-have-telehealth-remote-work-privacy-and-security-for-covid-19
8. Marshall, S.: IT consumerization: a case study of BYOD in a healthcare setting. Technol. Innov. Manag. Rev. **14** (2014)
9. Spannbauer, B.: How can healthcare organizations remedy their cybersecurity ailments? https://www.helpnetsecurity.com/2019/03/11/healthcare-organizations-cybersecurity/. Accessed 09 Oct 2019
10. Verizon: 2023 Data Breach Investigations Report (2023)
11. Sansurooh, K., Williams, P.: BYOD in ehealth: herding cats and stable doors, or a catastrophe waiting to happen? In: Australian eHealth Informatics and Security Conference (2014). https://doi.org/10.4225/75/5798284331b46
12. Moyer, J.E.: Managing mobile devices in hospitals: a literature review of byod policies and usage. J. Hosp. Librariansh. **13**, 197–208 (2013). https://doi.org/10.1080/15323269.2013.798768
13. Wani, T.A., Mendoza, A., Gray, K.: BYOD in hospitals-security issues and mitigation strategies. In: Proceedings of the Australasian Computer Science Week Multiconference on - ACSW 2019, pp. 25:1–25:10. ACM, New York (2019). https://doi.org/10.1145/3290688.3290729
14. Barlette, Y., Jaouen, A., Baillette, P.: Bring your own device (BYOD) as reversed IT adoption: insights into managers' coping strategies. Int. J. Inf. Manag. **56**, 102212 (2021). https://doi.org/10.1016/j.ijinfomgt.2020.102212
15. Soomro, Z.A., Shah, M.H., Ahmed, J.: Information security management needs more holistic approach: a literature review. Int. J. Inf. Manag. **36**, 215–225 (2016). https://doi.org/10.1016/j.ijinfomgt.2015.11.009
16. Zahadat, N., Blessner, P., Blackburn, T., Olson, B.A.: BYOD security engineering: a framework and its analysis. Comput. Secur. **55**, 81–99 (2015). https://doi.org/10.1016/j.cose.2015.06.011
17. Wani, T.A., Mendoza, A., Gray, K.: Hospital bring-your-own-device security challenges and solutions: systematic review of gray literature. JMIR Mhealth Uhealth **8**, e18175 (2020). https://doi.org/10.2196/18175
18. Wani, T.A., Mendoza, A., Gray, K., Smolenaers, F.: Status of bring-your-own-device (BYOD) security practices in Australian hospitals – a national survey. Health Policy Technol., 100627 (2022). https://doi.org/10.1016/j.hlpt.2022.100627

19. Wani, T.A., Mendoza, A., Gray, K.: Bring-your-own-device usage trends in Australian hospitals – a national survey. In: Healthier Lives, Digitally Enabled, pp. 1–6 (2021). https://doi.org/10.3233/SHTI210002

20. Fujs, D., Mihelič, A., Vrhovec, S.L.R.: The power of interpretation: qualitative methods in cybersecurity research. In: Proceedings of the 14th International Conference on Availability, Reliability and Security, pp. 1–10. Association for Computing Machinery, New York (2019). https://doi.org/10.1145/3339252.3341479

21. Palinkas, L.A., Horwitz, S.M., Green, C.A., Wisdom, J.P., Duan, N., Hoagwood, K.: Purposeful sampling for qualitative data collection and analysis in mixed method implementation research. Adm. Policy Ment. Health **42**, 533–544 (2015)

22. Baker, S.E., Edwards, R.: How many qualitative interviews is enough. NCRM (2012)

23. Brinkmann, S., Kvale, S.: InterViews: Learning the Craft of Qualitative Research Interviewing. SAGE Publications, Thousand Oaks (2015)

24. Saunders, B., et al.: Saturation in qualitative research: exploring its conceptualization and operationalization. Qual. Quant. **52**, 1893–1907 (2018). https://doi.org/10.1007/s11135-017-0574-8

25. Schlarman, S.: The people, policy, technology (PPT) model: core elements of the security process. Inf. Syst. Secur. **10**, 1–6 (2006). https://doi.org/10.1201/1086/43315.10.5.20011101/31719.6

26. Gale, N.K., Heath, G., Cameron, E., Rashid, S., Redwood, S.: Using the framework method for the analysis of qualitative data in multi-disciplinary health research. BMC Med. Res. Methodol. **13**, 117 (2013). https://doi.org/10.1186/1471-2288-13-117

27. Tong, A., Sainsbury, P., Craig, J.: Consolidated criteria for reporting qualitative research (COREQ): a 32-item checklist for interviews and focus groups. Int. J. Qual. Health Care **19**, 349–357 (2007). https://doi.org/10.1093/intqhc/mzm042

28. Wani, T.A., Mendoza, A., Gray, K., Smolenaers, F.: BYOD usage and security behaviour of hospital clinical staff: an Australian survey. Int. J. Med. Inform. **165**, 104839 (2022). https://doi.org/10.1016/j.ijmedinf.2022.104839

User Privacy and Security Acceptance

Legal Protection for the Personal Data in Indonesia and Malaysia

Nanik Prasetyoningsih[1(✉)] ⓘ, Nazli Ismail Nawang[2] ⓘ, Windy Virdinia Putri[1] ⓘ, and Muhammad Nur Rifqi Amirullah[1] ⓘ

[1] Universitas Muhammadiyah Yogyakarta, Yogyakarta, Indonesia
`nanikprasetyoningsih@umy.ac.id`
[2] Universiti Sultan Zainal Abidin, Kuala Nerus, Terengganu, Malaysia

Abstract. Rapid globalization in Indonesia has led to the growth of the information technology sector, which has an impact on individuals and global economic growth. However, the country does not have comprehensive laws protecting personal data, resulting in scattered laws and regulations across various sectors. The Personal Data Protection Act (PDPA) is a global law that mandates consent before collecting and processing personal data. Malaysia and Indonesia have similar PDPAs, which adopt principles from the European Union Data Protection Directive, OECD guidelines and the APEC Framework. However, there are differences in implementation. Malaysia's PDPA focuses on commercial transactions and the private sector, while Indonesia's PDPA covers both the public and private sectors. Meanwhile, the Malaysian government is preparing a revision of the Malaysian PDPA to cover both the public and private sectors, which is administered by the Commissioner of the Department of Personal Data Protection and only applies to the private sector. Indonesia and Malaysia have also implemented various laws regulating personal data protection in addition to the PDPA. PDPA Indonesia regulates personal data protection in public and private sectors, but no agency oversees implementation. Institutions must have independence, expertise, transparency, and collaborate with other government agencies. Policies, administrative consequences, and law enforcement collaboration are essential.

Keywords: legal protection · personal data protection · the Indonesian PDPA · the Malaysian PDPA

1 Introduction

The development of information technology in a country depends on its ability to adapt to social dynamics, such as globalization. Indonesia's rapid growth in the information technology industry has influenced lifestyles and experiences, with people of all ages and social strata benefiting from technological advancements [1].

Integrating telecommunications and entertainment computers with the Internet and technology, particularly in the era of Industry 4.0, significantly contributes to the global economy's development and stability. E-commerce platforms, particularly in Indonesia,

A. Moallem (Ed.): HCII 2024, LNCS 14728, pp. 161–169, 2024.
https://doi.org/10.1007/978-3-031-61379-1_11

significantly influence digital-based business growth [2]. Personal data protection is crucial to ensure its intended use and prevent misuse [3]. The digital economy and information technology growth threaten citizens' rights to privacy and personal data [4]. The right to personal data protection has been recognized as a human right in the ASEAN Human Rights Declaration 2012 and the European Charter of Human Rights [3].

Indonesia lacks a comprehensive law protecting personal data, leading to scattered regulations across sectors. The revised principles are context-sensitive, encouraging harm-benefit weighing and mitigation measures. They address government data collection separately and require clear notice when personal data affecting employment, healthcare, financial products, or individual rights is involved [5]. Personal data violations have occurred in various sectors, including telco user data exposure in 2019. Malaysia and Indonesia have faced similar issues, but the Malaysian Personal Data Protection Act 2010 provides a more controlled environment for data protection [4].

Asia has privacy laws except in Malaysia, Hong Kong, and Singapore. Hong Kong's Personal Data Privacy Ordinance (1995) addresses privacy issues. Singapore's Personal Data Protection Act No. 26 (2012) protects data at a sector level [6]. The Singaporean model could minimize ambiguities and inconsistencies [7]. Malaysia also has no specific privacy laws to protect personal privacy, but Malaysian PDPA 2010 was enacted 'to regulate the processing of personal data in commercial transactions'. Indonesia issued the Personal Data Protection Act in 2022 to comprehensively regulate data protection, establish a personal data protection commission, and establish criminal sanctions and civil claims related to data breaches.

This research examines the effectiveness of Indonesia PDPA 2022 and compares it with the Malaysian PDPA 2010. The Malaysian PDPA 2010, which came into force on 15 November 2013, regulates the processing of personal data in commercial transactions and mandates registration in 11 industry sectors. The comparative study aims to understand Malaysia's approach to protecting personal data and enforcing laws against data violations. The research aims to understand how Malaysia protects personal data and enforces laws against data violations.

2 Methods

This research uses normative legal research to explore the implementation of personal data protection strategies in Indonesia and Malaysia. Data was collected through literature studies, including books, journals, and internet media. The research aimed to understand the problems faced in implementing these strategies. The analysis technique used was qualitative descriptive analysis, grouping data according to explanations to form conclusions. The study aimed to understand the relationship between theory and research methods, ensuring a comprehensive understanding of the subject matter.

3   Result and Discussion

3.1   The Role of Personal Data Protection

Personal data is information that can be used to identify or locate an individual, either alone or in combination with other knowledge obtained through electronic or non-electronic methods. It includes data, facts, explanations, assertions, ideas, and signals that carry values, meanings, and messages [5]. The UK Calcutt Committee defines privacy as the individual's right to be protected from intrusion into their personal life or affairs, a fundamental human right recognized in Article 12 of the UN Universal Declaration of Human Rights [8].

The privacy laws in Malaysia remain unclear, though the Federal Court in the land-mark case of Siyarasa Rasiah v Badan Peguam Malaysia & Anor 2010 ruled that the constitutional rights to personal liberty in the Article 5 of the Malaysian Federal Con-stitution includes the right to privacy. Courts have, on certain occasion, recognized the development of personal privacy laws under tort law, which is generally unwritten. Per-sonal privacy laws cover all potential invasions of an individual's privacy, while personal data protection only covers stored information. However, to a certain extent, privacy acts can be reconciled with personal data protection acts, as personal data is a private matter and a matter of privacy [8].

The International Convention prohibits automatic processing of sensitive personal data unless domestic acts provide safeguards. Article 9 outlines conditions for limited guarantee, requiring national legislation and a democratic society's interest in protecting state security, public safety, monetary interests, and data subject rights [9].

Privacy is a personal data protection concept that safeguards one's integrity and dignity [10]. It allows individuals to choose who can access and use their personal information and the terms under which it will be transferred. Privacy rights are connected to data protection and have evolved to create rights to protect personal data [11].

Personal data protection safeguards individual information from loss, alteration, or corruption, allowing individuals to control and manage their data. However, the issue of data privacy violations and abuse has increased in recent years, with reports of mistreat-ment and public concern about central organizations collecting and processing personal information without consent [12]. Data protection is a set of standards that protect pri-vacy and interests related to IT developments. Globalization and digitization increase the availability of personal information, leading to the creation of "Big Data" through data merging [13].

Privacy rights in cyberspace encompass three aspects: recognizing a person's right to enjoy their private life, communicating without supervision, and monitoring and con-trolling personal information [14]. The right to data protection is recognized as a fun-damental, autonomous right by Article 8 of the Charter of Fundamental Rights of the European Union, enacted by the Lisbon Treaty in 2009 and Convention 108 of 1981 for the Protection of Individuals concerning Automatic Processing of Personal Data. The principles underlying the human right to data protection reflect fundamental European legal values, including privacy, transparency, autonomy, and non-discrimination [15].

Digital dossiers, mass data collection using digital technology, were initiated by governments in 1970, primarily in the US and Europe. The private sector now plays a role in digital dossiers, potentially violating an individual's privacy rights [11]. Data protection legislation outlines rules for automatic data processing, including collection, aggregation, storage, dissemination, and erasure. These regulations protect individuals' privacy rights related to their data. The focus is on personal data, and these laws are only applicable when personal data is processed [16].

Regulations for data protection are inadequate to address potential risks and issues related to social investigation paradigm change [17], as privacy and data protection are protected as individual rights [18]. The sixth data protection principle outlines individual rights such as access to personal data, objecting to harmful processing, preventing direct marketing, challenging automated decisions, rectifying inaccurate data under certain conditions, and seeking compensation for damages resulting from a violation. It also allows us to challenge automated decisions to rectify, block, erase, or destroy inaccurate data [18].

Data protection is a fundamental right that protects personal freedom and dignity [17]. It is not acceptable to turn individuals into objects under continuous surveillance [19].

3.2 The Legal Protection for the Personal Data Protection in Indonesia and Malaysia

The Legal Protection for the Personal Data Protection in Indonesia. Data protection is a fundamental right in Indonesia [20], but regulations are inadequate to address potential risks and issues related to this paradigm change in social investigation [18]. The Indonesian PDPA 2022 aims to place Indonesia on an equal footing with developed nations that have implemented personal data protection laws, strengthening the country's reputation as a reliable commercial hub [11].

The Indonesian PDPA 2022 aims to protect personal data across 32 sectors, including finance, health, population, telecommunications, banking, and trade. It includes other laws to ensure standards and references for public service providers. The PDPA aims to protect citizens' rights, raise public awareness, and promote data protection, addressing the impact of breaches on society.

The Indonesian PDPA 2022 provides rights for personal data subjects, including obtaining information about identity clarity, legal interest, purpose of requesting and using data, and accountability. They also have the right to rectify data gaps, request access, stop processing, remove or destroy data, revoke consent, object to automatic processing decisions, file lawsuits, request widely accepted formats, and communicate personal information [21].

The EU GDPR's implementation in May 2018 has significantly impacted the Personal Data Protection Law in ASEAN countries like Thailand and Singapore, requiring adaptation for economic operations [16]. Malaysia is evaluating its PDPA 2010 to align with the EU GDPR, while Indonesia shares similarities with the EU GDPR, including data protection, storage restrictions, controller obligations, security requirements, and penalties for misuse [22].

The Indonesian PDPA requires a controlling agency to implement the law, with the data controller overseeing data processing and ensuring privacy principles are followed.

Officers provide advice, supervise compliance, assess consequences, and act as a contact to prevent violations.

Indonesia's personal data protection authorities must be independent, skilled, and transparent, and should collaborate with other government bodies while adhering to legal provisions and remaining within legal limits. They should also foster international cooperation to protect Indonesian users' and global data [23].

Indonesia's cybercrime management is hindered by the absence of a special institution, such as a regulator or personal data protection commission. The Cyber and Crypto Agency State (Badan Sandi dan Siber Negara) and Directorate of Cybercrime Police of the Republic of Indonesia are responsible for handling cybercrime, but they have not met national average cybersecurity indicators. The need for specialization in cyber handling and mitigation unit specialization indicates weak cyber protection in Indonesia, leading to minimal progress in policy research and encouraging related social and economic sectors. Additionally, these institutions lack the authority to enforce and regulate the Personal Data Protection Law, necessitating the establishment of a personal data protection authority for optimal implementation of Indonesia's PDPA.

The Legal Protection for the Personal Data Protection in Malaysia. The Malaysian Government enacted the Malaysian PDPA to prevent misuse of personal data in non-government transactions [24]. The Act defines "personal data" as information processed by machinery, recorded to process it, or recorded as part of a relevant filing system.

According to the Malaysian PDPA 2010, stated that "personal data" means any information in respect of commercial transactions that relates directly or indirectly to a data subject (i.e., an individual who is the subject of the personal data), who is identifiable from that information or from that and other information in possession of a data user (i.e., an organization that processes any personal data or has control over or authorizes the processing of any personal data), including any sensitive personal data and expression of opinion about the data subject [21]. The Malaysian PDPA protects the personal data and information of natural persons, establishing principles, requirements, and individual rights [25]. Section 6 (1) (a) requires data users to obtain consent before collecting and processing their data, making it one of the earliest and most fundamental data privacy rights globally [26].

Personal data protection principles include Notice and Choice, Disclosure, Security, Retention, Data Integrity, and Access Principles. Organizations must inform individuals about data processing, its purpose, and third parties, and protect it from loss, unauthorized access, alteration, or destruction [12]. Retention ensures data is only kept for processing, while data integrity ensures accuracy and completeness [24].

The PDPA Act, enacted in 2013, regulates the protection of personal data in commercial transactions. It adopts seven principles from the European Data Protection Directive, including collection limitation, data quality, purpose specification, use limitation, security safeguard, openness, individual participation, and accountability. The Act also outlines data owners' rights, data transfer procedures, and storage obligations [25]. Malaysia, a rapidly growing electronic government provider, has implemented legislation to ensure data protection, international recognition, FDI enhancement, and local enterprise protection [27].

The Malaysian PDPA is designed for commercial transactions and protects personal data for e-commerce purposes [28]. The Malaysian PDPA regulates private sector universities, excluding public sector data. Malaysia has implemented various regulations to protect personal data, including the Personal Data Protection Act 2010, Computer Crimes Act 1997, Communication and Multimedia Act 1998, Digital Signature Act 1997, Copyright Act 1987, Electronic Government Activities Act 2007, Electronic Commerce Act 2006, and Credit Reporting Agency Act 2010.

The Malaysian PDPA aims to give individuals control over their data collection, recording, storage, or processing. The Act regulates the use of personal data in commercial transactions and related matters, with Sect. 2 specifically focusing on processing in commercial transactions, not non-commercial or governmental matters [29].

The Malaysian parliament approved the Personal Data Protection Act 2010 in 2011, leading to the establishment of the Personal Data Protection Department (Jabatan Perlindungan Data Peribadi - JPDP) by the Malaysian Government [30]. The JPDP is the main data protection regulator appointed by the minister to carry out the functions and powers granted by the PDPA under conditions deemed appropriate [30]. The department aims to enforce and regulate the Act, promoting data privacy and trust between businesses and consumers. Its primary responsibilities include coordinating and overseeing user forum registration and consumer data registration, thereby advancing national prosperity [31]. As part of its duties, JPDP receives reports of complaints. They will investigate relevant reports and data to determine the actions taken by the alleged violators of the PDPA. If the complainant is dissatisfied with the results of the JPDP's investigation, they may request a review of the JPDP's decision from the High Court of Malaysia [32].

JPDP has its formal process for anyone who reports a violation of personal data owned or against an organization violating the law. These personal data protection laws add another layer of security to the internet. On the other hand, this law broadens the scope of cybercrime and cybersecurity concerns [33]. The Malaysian government is not liable for data leaks or breaches of personal data protection due to the negligence of the data owner [34].

3.3 Legal Protection for Personal Data in Indonesia and Malaysia: A Comparative Study

When comparing the Indonesian PDPA and the Malaysian PDPA, there is a difference in their scope of implementation. The Indonesian PDP applies to all sectors, including the public and private sectors. In contrast to the Malaysian PDPA, its implementation only applies to the private sector, not the public sector.

There are 4 similarities of legal protection for personal data in Indonesia and Malaysia, as follows: (1) data protection principles in Indonesia and Malaysia, (2) state obligations to protect personal data in Indonesia and Malaysia, (3) rights of data subject in personal data protection laws in Indonesia and Malaysia, and (4) norms in personal data protection laws in Indonesia and Malaysia.

The Indonesian and Malaysian PDPAs have distinct principles for processing personal data. The Indonesian PDPA emphasizes limited, specific, lawful, and transparent collection, accurate, complete, and accountable processing, protection from unauthorized access, notifying purposes, and responsible processing. The Malaysian PDPA, on the other hand, includes General Principles, Notice and Choice Principles, Disclosure Principles, Security Principles, Retention Principles, Data Integrity Principles, and Access Principles for data security.

The Indonesian PDPA and the Malaysian PDPA define a data subject as an individual who holds personal data. These rights include access, correction, termination of use, and protection against unfair losses, discrimination, and oppression. The data subject's rights are similar, ensuring they have the right to access, correct, and request protection from data-related issues.

Indonesia and Malaysia have similar jurisdictional norms for personal data protection, with the former adopting an extraterritorial jurisdictional regime. The Indonesian PDPA applies to individuals, public bodies, and international organizations based in Indonesia or outside its jurisdiction, while the Malaysian PDPA applies to individuals established in Malaysia and processing their data or using Malaysian equipment. Both laws apply to citizens physically in Indonesia or Malaysia and those whose data is being processed in another country.

4 Conclusion

The Personal Data Protection Act (PDPA) is a global law requiring consent for data collection and processing. Malaysia and Indonesia have similar PDPAs, but implementation varies. Malaysia focuses on commercial transactions and the private sector, while Indonesia covers both public and private sectors.

Indonesia and Malaysia have implemented data protection regulations to safeguard citizens' personal data rights and basic human rights in the digital era, including the Computer Crimes Act, Communication and Multimedia Act, Digital Signature Act, Copyright Act, Electronic Government Activities Act, Electronic Commerce Act, Credit Reporting Agency Act, Payment System Act, Telemedicine Act, and Communication and Multimedia Content Code.

Acknowledgments. This study was funded by Universitas Muhammadiyah Yogyakarta.

Disclosure of Interests. The authors have no competing interests to declare relevant to this artcle's content. Author Nanik Prasetyoningsih has received research grants from Universitas Muhammadiyah Yogyakarta. Author Nazli Ismail Nawang is the research collaborator. Author Windy Virdinia Putri and Muhammad Nur Rifqi Amirullah are the students that member research.

References

1. Asnawi, A.: Kesiapan Indonesia Membangun Ekonomi Digital di Era Revolusi 4.0. Syntax Lit. J. Ilm. Indones. **7**(1) (2022)
2. Pardomuan, O.A., Wijaya, S.: Pemblokiran Pengusahan Ekonomi Digital atas Cross-Border Transaction Sebagai Upaya Perubahan Skema PPN. J. Penelit. Teor. Terap. Akunt. **1**(7), 92–112 (2022). https://doi.org/10.51289/peta.v7il.502

3. Sholikhah, V.H., Sejati, N.R.F.F., Shabitah, D.: Personal data protection authority: comparative study between Indonesia, United Kingdom and Malaysia. In: Teoksessa Indonesian Scholars Scientific Summit Taiwan Proceeding, pp. 54–63 (2021). https://doi.org/10.52162/3.2021112
4. Nurhasanah, Rahmatullah, I.: Financial technology and the legal protection of personal data: the case of Malaysia and Indonesia. Al-Risalah Forum Leg. Soc. Stud. **20**(2), 97–214 (2020). https://doi.org/10.30631/al-risalah.v20i.602
5. Cullen, P., Mayer-Schonberger, V., Cate, F.H.: Data protection principles for the 21st century. In: Data Protection Principles for the 21st Century, pp. 12–13. Maurer Faculty, Bloomington (2013)
6. Alibeigi, A., Munir, A.B.: Malaysian personal data protection act, a mysterious application. Univ. Bol. Law Rev. **2**(5), 362–374 (2020). https://doi.org/10.6092/ISSN.2531-6133/12441
7. Ayu, A., Anindyajati, T., Goffar, A.: Perlindungan Hak Privasi atas Data Diri di Era Ekonomi Digital, 1st edn. Pusat Penelitian dan Pengkajian Perkara dan Pengelolaan Perpustakaan Kepaniteraan dan Sekretariat Jenderal Mahkamah Konstitusi, Jakarta (2019)
8. Hassan, K.H.: Personal data protection in employment: new legal challenges for Malaysia. Comput. Law Secur. Rev. **28**(6), 697–703 (2012). https://doi.org/10.1016/j.clsr.2012.07.006
9. Chua, H.N.: Compliance to personal data protection principles: a study of how organizations frame privacy policy notices. Telemat. Inform. **34**(4), 157–170 (2017). https://doi.org/10.1016/j.tele.2017.01.008
10. Djafar, W., Komarudin, A.: Perlindungan Hak Atas Privasi di Internet Beberapa Penjelasan Kunci. ELSAM, Jakarta (2014)
11. Nurbaningsih, E.: Naskah Akademik RUU Perlindungan Data Pribadi. Badan Pembinaan Hukum Nasional, Jakarta (2015)
12. Sim, W.L., Chua, H.N., Tahir, M.: Blockchain for identity management: the implications to personal data protection. In: IEEE Conference on Application, Information and Network Security AINS 2019, pp. 30–35 (2019).https://www.proceedings.com/52516.html
13. Enerstvedt, O.M.: Aviation Security, Privacy, Data Protection and Other Human Rights: Technologies and Legal Principles, 1st edn. Springer, Cham (2017). https://doi.org/10.1007/978-3-319-58139-2
14. Bunga, D., Dewi, C.W.D.L., Dewi, K.A.P.: Literasi Digital untuk Menanggulangi Perilaku Oversharing di Media Sosial. Sevanam J. Pengabdi. Masy. **1**(1), 7–8 (2022). https://doi.org/10.25078/sevanam.v1i1.9
15. Politou, E., Alepis, E., Virvou, M., Patsakis, C.: Privacy and Data Protection Challenges in the Distributed Era, 1st edn. Springer, Cham (2022). https://doi.org/10.1007/978-3-030-85443-0
16. Tamò-Larrieux, A.: Designing for Privacy and Its Legal Framework Data Protection by Design and Default for the Internet of Things, 1st edn. Springer, Cham (2018). https://doi.org/10.1007/978-3-030-85443-0
17. Rodotà, S.: Data protection as a fundamental right. In: Gutwirth, S., Poullet, Y., De Hert, P., de Terwangne, C., Nouwt, S. (eds.) Reinventing Data Protection?. Springer, Dordrecht (2009). https://doi.org/10.1007/978-1-4020-9498-9_3
18. Mantelero, A.: Personal data for decisional purposes in the age of analytics: from an individual to a collective dimension of data protection. Comput. Law Secur. Rev. **32**(2), 238 (2016). https://doi.org/10.1016/j.clsr.2016.01.014
19. Goddard, M.: Viewpoint: the EU general data protection regulation (GDPR): European regulation that has a global impact. Int. J. Mark. Res. **59**(6), 6–703 (2017). https://doi.org/10.2501/IJMR-2017-050
20. Mardiana, N., Meilan, A.: Urgensi Perlindungan Data Pribadi Dalam Perspektif Hak Asasi Manusia. J. Rechten Ris. Huk. dan Hak Asasi Mns. **1**(1), 16–23 (2023). https://doi.org/10.52005/rechten.v5i1.108

21. Fauzi, E., Shandy, N.A.R.: Hak Atas Privasi dan Politik Hukum Undang-Undang Nomor 27 Tahun 2022. Lex Renaiss. **7**(3), 445–458 (2022). https://doi.org/10.20885/JLR.vol7.iss3.art1

22. Subekti, N., Handayani, I.G.A.K.R., Hidayat, A.: Konstitusionalisme Digital di Indonesia: Mengartikulasi Hak dan Kekuasaan di Era Digital. Perad. J. Law Soc. **2**(1), 11–17 (2023). https://doi.org/10.59001/pjls.v2i1.74

23. Sutarli, A.F., Kurniawan, S.: Peranan Pemerintah Melalui Undang-Undang Perlindungan Data Pribadi dalam Menanggulangi Phising di Indonesia. Innov. J. Soc. Sci. Res. **3**(2), 10 (2023). https://doi.org/10.31004/innovative.v3i2.760

24. Nasution, S.H.: Meningkatkan Tata Kelola Data dan Perlindungan Data Pribadi melalui ASEAN Digital Masterplan 2025. Center for Indonesian Policy Studies, Jakarta, 46 (2021). https://www.cips-indonesia.org/publications/tata-kelola-data-dan-perlindungan-data-pribadi-melalui-asean-digital-masterplan-2025?lang=id

25. Rizal, M.S.: Perbandingan Perlindungan Data Pribadi Indonesia dan Malaysia. J. Cakrawala Huk. **10**(2), 218–227 (2019). https://doi.org/10.26905/idjch.v10i2.3349

26. Alibeigi, A., Munir, A.B., Asemi, A.: Compliance with Malaysian personal data protection act 2010 by banking and financial institutions, a legal survey on privacy policies. Int. Rev. Law Comput. Technol. **35**(3), 365–394 (2021). https://doi.org/10.1080/13600869.2021.1970936

27. Hamzah, M.A., Ahmad, A.R., Hussin, N., Ibrahim, Z.: Personal data privacy protection: a review on Malaysia's cyber security policies. Int. J. Acad. Res. Bus. Soc. Sci. **8**(12), 1475–1483 (2019). https://doi.org/10.6007/ijarbss/v8-i12/5251

28. Ong, R.: Data protection in Malaysia and Hong Kong: one step forward, two steps back? Comput. Law Secur. Rev. **28**(4), 429–437 (2012). https://doi.org/10.1016/j.clsr.2012.05.002

29. San, T.P.: Predictions from data analytics: does Malaysian data protection law apply? Inf. Commun. Technol. Law **29**(3), 291–307 (2020). https://doi.org/10.1080/13600834.2020.1759276

30. Baskaran, H., Yussof, S., Rahim, F.A., Bakar, A.A.: Blockchain and the personal data protection act 2010 (PDPA) in Malaysia. In: 2020 8th International Conference on Information Technology and Multimedia (ICIMU), pp. 189–193 (2020). https://doi.org/10.1109/ICIMU49871.2020.9243493

31. Hamidon, H., Radzi, S.M., Alias, N.R., Arifin, N., Zukarnain, Z.A.: Personal data abuse: preliminary survey among Malaysian youth netizens. Int. J. Inf. Knowl. Manag. **1**(Spec, Issue), 192–210 2022)

32. Butarbutar, R.: Personal data protection in P2P lending: what Indonesia should learn from Malaysia? Pertanika J. Soc. Sci. Humanit. **28**(3), 2295–2307 (2020). http://www.pertanika.upm.edu.my/pjssh/browse/regular-issue?article=JSSH-5415-2019

33. Walters, R., Trakman, L., Zeller, B.: Data Protection Law a Comparative Analysis of Asia-Pacific and European Approaches. Springer, Singapore (2019). https://doi.org/10.1007/978-981-13-8110-2

34. Phan, T., Damian, D.: Smart Cities in Asia Regulations, Problems, and Development, 1st edn. Springer, Singapore (2022). https://doi.org/10.1007/978-981-19-1701-1

Towards a Harmonised Approach for Security and Privacy Management in Smart Home Contexts

Samiah Alghamdi$^{(\boxtimes)}$, Steven Furnell$^{(\boxtimes)}$, and Steven Bagley$^{(\boxtimes)}$

School of Computer Science, University of Nottingham, Nottingham, UK
{Samiah.Alghamdi,Steven.Furnell,Steven.Bagley}@nottingham.ac.uk

Abstract. Smart homes are based upon Internet-connected versions of household devices that have traditionally operated in a standalone manner. In recent years, the proliferation of Internet-connected devices has increased dramatically, particularly in the context of smart homes. Although services provided by smart home devices can improve our quality of life, they invariably raise concerns regarding the privacy of personal information. It is, therefore, relevant to consider the extent to which users can manage and keep track of security and privacy across an increasing number and varied range of smart devices. A problem at present is that they can be faced with individual devices that perform similar functions in inconsistent ways, thereby complicating (and potentially frustrating) the task of managing security and privacy across a growing range of devices that can be found within their homes. This paper highlights these challenges and proposes the basis of an approach that seeks to improve the user experience by offering a consistent and harmonized approach to monitoring the security and privacy aspects of their devices, thereby enabling them to have better control and awareness.

Keywords: Smart Home · Privacy · Security · Internet of Things

1 Introduction

Smart devices are increasingly important in people's lives due to the significant rise in their numbers in recent years [1]. As a result, many homes now have an array of such devices, making smart homes more prevalent. While smart home devices can improve our lives, they also raise concerns about personal information privacy [2]. Furthermore, the adoption of such technology is accompanied by security and privacy considerations that may not be as immediately apparent to the users as their devices' benefits. At the same time, if users are expected to take on related responsibilities, they need to be aware that there are issues to answer and be able to understand how to use the features concerned.

The main aim of this paper is to examine and address the challenge facing smart home users in understanding and managing the security and privacy status of their various smart devices. A typical smart home can involve a range of devices, each of which can have different security and privacy-related issues and settings. Whether willingly

A. Moallem (Ed.): HCII 2024, LNCS 14728, pp. 170–187, 2024.
https://doi.org/10.1007/978-3-031-61379-1_12

or otherwise, the user essentially finds themselves owning and managing a network of devices, and they are often provided with little guidance on effective use. As such, if they are not aware of the issues of concern and the devices need to be more intuitive to support them, they can find themselves at risk of running devices that are vulnerable or otherwise configured in ways that they do not expect nor desire.

Smart home settings can be configured according to the wishes and needs of the owner, causing wildly various configurations. Smart home devices can interact with each other in different ways, and sometimes, there is no interaction. This, in turn, indicates that devices can be connected to one different device or many devices. The flexibility delivered by smart home devices guarantees that users can execute home automation at their convenience while being beneficial to the consumer by addressing privacy concerns and security issues.

The main problem in smart homes is that devices may share information gathered by smart applications. Collecting and sharing data relating to an individual without their permission is a breach of privacy [3]. One privacy issue is that users cannot express their preferences, manage data sharing, or determine who has access to this data and for what purpose. Moreover, there are rising concerns about privacy because of insecure communication that leaks sensitive information about the home and residents [2], allowing an attacker to gain unauthorised access to IoT devices in the house [4].

This paper focuses on the challenges users face in monitoring the security and privacy aspects of their devices. It proposes an approach to improve the user experience by providing a consistent and harmonized method for monitoring these aspects. This will allow users to have better control and awareness over the security and privacy of their devices.

2 Literature Review

Smart homes have advanced features that allow them to perform tasks automatically, adjust devices to meet user needs and achieve different outcomes. The five fundamental features of smart homes are automation, adaptability, multifunctionality, efficiency, and interaction [5].

Automation lets devices perform tasks automatically or adjust themselves without human intervention. Adaptability allows smart home devices to understand and meet users' needs, while multifunctionality lets them perform various tasks. Efficiency means that smart home devices can perform tasks smoothly and save costs and time. Interaction lets different users control devices and systems using their smartphones or access the home's network.

Contemporary smart homes are equipped with various smart devices that can be managed through a house location network. These intelligent devices include smart TVs, cameras, smart displays, speakers, lighting, smart vacuums, and smart thermostats. Such devices can be linked to phone applications, allowing them to interact with remotely hosted services [6]. For instance, security cameras typically store video data on external servers, enabling users to access the footage anywhere at any time. Additionally, smart assistants like Alexa rely heavily on cloud-based benefits to operate.

Smart home devices are advanced IoT devices that can sense and record data. This data is then transmitted to servers hosted on the cloud, which deliver services to smart home users. For example, when a security camera detects motion, the recording video is saved and transferred to the cloud for further analysis or storage. Most devices also provide smartphone applications that let users interact with and configure these devices easily and conveniently. Regarding security cameras, the smartphone application allows users to configure the camera and connect to cloud servers, making it easy to access and view recorded videos. Researchers classify security issues in smart homes into four categories: application security, device security, network security, and cloud-based security [7, 8].

Information security refers to the measures taken to protect data from unauthorized access. In contrast, privacy concerns involve the user's ability to monitor and regulate the creation and usage of their data [9]. Therefore, privacy is dependent on the security of the system, as the data must be entirely secure before privacy concerns can be addressed. However, privacy is of utmost importance in the context of smart home applications, as multiple users share the same information, and it is important to clarify issues related to data ownership. The domain of suggested solutions for IoT privacy encompasses network, design, and socio-technical efforts. However, understanding users is crucial in creating usable privacy tools [10]. Consequently, it is crucial to assess the accessibility of privacy and security features to users in their search. Therefore, protecting data and ensuring privacy in smart home applications require a comprehensive approach involving technical solutions and user-centred considerations. By understanding users' needs and making privacy and security information readily available to them, we can develop effective tools that meet their requirements.

Researchers in Human-Computer Interaction (HCI) have studied the mental models of individuals who use smart home devices. A study was conducted using semi-structured interviews to gain insight into the privacy concerns and mental models of smart home users [11]. The study found that users of smart homes tend to compromise their privacy in exchange for convenience.

However, researchers investigated smart home security perceptions, determined characteristics that impact security decisions, and studied users' concerns before and after buying the devices [12, 13]. Other researchers investigated access-control procedures for smart home devices [14–16]. For example, Zeng et al. (2019) created a prototype and assessed the usability of an access control application [16]. Colnago et al. (2020) analyzed Personalised Privacy assistants in the IoT to permit users to discover and manage data collection by nearby smart devices [15].

Many user privacy experiments concerning IoT technologies have been performed in temporary or laboratory environments. One such experiment was conducted on five users in one week with a custom IoT device [17]. Moreover, experiments conducted to understand user concerns about privacy with smartwatches [18] and toys connected to the internet have also explained user attitudes and identified more functional designs for IoT privacy [19]. Related work had a few privacy concerns regarding the data itself in nature; with apparent concerns about how businesses would manage the data [20] Participants in this experiment were principally interested in increasing advertising and marketing their data for profit.

3   Inconsistent Provision of Common Features

This section embarks on the representation and evaluation of the diverse security and privacy features that characterize various smart home devices. Furthermore, it explores the consistency of features across devices and the difficulties in comprehending their smart home's overall security and privacy status.

Five distinct categories of smart home devices were considered, namely Smart TVs, Smart Speakers, Thermostats, Robotic Vacuum, and Security Cameras. Within each category, an average of three devices sourced from different manufacturers is subjected to further evaluation.

3.1   Security Challenge

To ensure secure smart devices, it is incumbent upon users to remain aware of these common security issues, and there are various vulnerabilities that they need to be aware of. These include weak passwords, inadequate access controls, and authentication mechanisms. By focusing on these challenges, users can take steps to mitigate risks and improve the security of their smart device ecosystem.

- **Registration:** Registration is essential in creating a unique identity for users to access their smart home devices. Registration involves two incidents: (i) creating an account by providing a valid email address and generating a new password or (ii) linking through social media accounts such as Twitter. Failure to register will result in the inability to access the smart home devices. Therefore, users must complete the registration process promptly to use smart home devices.
- **Authentication**: Accessing smart home devices requires users to complete an authentication process that verifies their identity. This typically involves using a combination of usernames, passwords, and email addresses. However, some users may struggle to keep track of multiple passwords, leading to password fatigue becoming a regular part of their daily routine. Unfortunately, many smart home hubs that connect all the devices on the network have weak passwords, making them vulnerable to hacking. This can allow hackers to easily gain access and tamper with the hub and devices in the smart home. To prevent virtual break-ins, it is crucial always to use complex and unique passwords and to implement two-factor authentication for all devices in the smart home.
- **Authorisation:** Refers to ensuring user's access rights or permissions for specific actions. This involves implementing and testing family-sharing functions across various smart home devices. Establishing a robust system for logging and monitoring user interface activities is crucial for identifying and examining security incidents. Insufficient mechanisms can impede the ability to detect and mitigate potential threats or unauthorised actions. Thus, implementing appropriate measures is essential to safeguard the integrity and security of the system.
- **Security Update**: Smart home devices, including thermostats, cameras, and voice assistants, often run small operating systems vulnerable to their specialised nature and limited resources [21]. To prevent vulnerabilities, it is crucial to keep all smart home devices updated with the latest firmware and security patches. Security patches are

software updates device manufacturers release to address known security faults and vulnerabilities. Firmware updates, on the other hand, provide updates to the device's operating system and other embedded software. Regularly updating the firmware and applying security patches allows users to benefit from the latest security enhancements and bug fixes. These updates often contain patches for identified vulnerabilities that attackers could exploit. Failure to update devices can expose them to potential attacks, as attackers may exploit these vulnerabilities to gain unauthorized access or control over the device.

3.2 Comparative Analysis of the Security Features on Smart Home Devices

This section compares the security features of five types of smart home devices – smart TVs, smart speakers, thermostats, robotic vacuums, and security cameras. These features include registration, authentication, authorization, and security updates. Table 1 shows that the same feature may be controlled differently on various platforms of the same device, and some features may not be available on certain devices. Additionally, the number of steps required to execute features may differ, which may cause inconvenience to the user.

3.3 Privacy Challenges

The increasing integration of smart home devices into our daily routines has brought significant privacy challenges concerning the tracking and intrusiveness of such technologies.

- **Intrusiveness**: This pertains to the perception of excessive monitoring or surveillance, which can be attributed to either the devices themselves or the manufacturers accountable for their design. Nguyen et al. found that individuals who utilise smart home devices equipped with cameras often experience a sense of being surveilled, while those who use voice-activated devices tend to feel like they are being eavesdropped on [22].
- **Tracking:** Certain individuals may express concerns regarding the observation of their actions and movements through smart home devices by manufacturers or service providers. This type of tracking may contain the acquisition of data on the utilization of devices, personal preferences, interactions, or confidential information. One of the primary concerns associated with tracking is the potential infringement on individuals' privacy rights and the need to safeguard collected data. Additionally, there is a risk of misusing collected information, making it essential to handle tracking data carefully. Clear communication, strong security measures, and transparent privacy policies are crucial. Users should control their personal information and make informed decisions about smart home devices to ensure safe and responsible use.

Table 1. Comparing Security Features across multiple smart devices and device categories.

Platforms	Registration	Authentication	Authorization	Security Update
Sony TV	**Name, Email, and Password** • Via product registration site • Needs ~9 choices to complete	• N/A	**Pin Code** • Via Remoter Control • Needs 7 steps to complete	• Can be automatic
Samsung TV	**Name, Email, and Password** • Via Remote Control • Needs 6 choices to complete	• N/A	**Pin Code** • Via Remoter Control • Needs 7 steps to complete	• Via Remote control • Can be automatic while TV watching • Applied on start-up
Roku TV	**Name, Email, and Password** • Via Roku website • Needs 5 choices to complete	• N/A	**Pin Code** • Via Roku website • Needs 6 choices to complete	• Via Remote control • Needs ~7 choices to complete
Amazon Echo Dot	**Username, Email and Password** • Via the Alexa app **Username, and Password** • Via Amazon Product Registration or Alexa app Needs ~7 steps to complete	• Voice • 2FA	**Set Up Voice Recognition** **Payment Authorization** Via Amazon website or Alexa app. with at least 7 steps	• Can be automatic • Requires muting mic and waiting for some time
Amazon Thermostat	**Username, and Password** • Via Amazon Product Registration or Alexa app • Needs ~7 steps to complete	• N/A	• N/A (no option available)	• Can be automatic
iRobot Vacuum	**Username, Email and Password** • To register the user, ensure iRobot is <5 feet from router and phone • Via iRobot HOME app • Needs 4 steps to complete	• N/A	• N/A	• Can be automatic
Ring Security Camera	**Username, Email and Password** • Via Ring app • Needs 9 choices to complete	• 2FA	• N/A	• Via Ring security app • Needs 7 steps to complete

Table 2. Comparing Privacy Features across multiple smart devices and device categories.

Platforms	Microphone Muting	Turning off Location Services	Turning off Camera	Monitoring Using Habits
Sony TV	• Via remote control • Needs 5 choices to complete	• Via remote control • Needs 4 choices to complete	• N/A	**Automatic Content Recognition (ACR)** • Via Remote Control • Needs 6 choices to complete
Samsung TV	• Via Physical Button in the Tv or remote control • Needs 6 choices to complete using remote	• Via remote control • Needs 5 choices to complete	• N/A	**Automatic Content Recognition (ACR)** • Via Remote Control • Needs 7 choices to complete
Roku TV	• Via remoter control • Needs 5 choices to complete	• Via remoter control • Needs 7 choices to complete	• N/A (no camera)	**Automatic Content Recognition (ACR)** • Via Remote Control • Needs ~6 choices to complete
Amazon Echo Dot	• Done via Physical Button in the device	• N/A	• N/A (no camera)	• Do not monitor using habits
Amazon Thermostat	• Via Alexa app • Needs 5 steps to complete	• N/A	• N/A (no camera)	**Temperature Settings** • Via Thermostat or Alexa app • Needs ~5 choices to complete
iRobot Vacuum	• N/A (no microphone)	• N/A	• N/A	• Do not monitor using habits
Ring Security Camera	• Via Ring app • Needs 7 choices to complete	• Via Ring app • Needs 5 choices to complete	• N/A	**Motion Detection** • Via Ring app • Needs 5 steps to complete

3.4   A Comparative Analysis of the Privacy Features of Smart Home Devices

This section, compares the privacy features of five different types of smart home devices, namely smart TVs, smart speakers, thermostats, robotic vacuums, and security cameras. These features include microphone muting, disabling location services, turning off cameras, and monitoring usage habits. We evaluate the availability of these features on each device and platform, as well as the number of steps required to execute each feature. Table 2 highlights that the same feature may be controlled differently on different platforms of the same device, and some features may not be available on certain devices. As with the security features, the number of steps required to execute certain features may vary.

3.5   Comparative Analysis of the Data Management Features on Smart Home Devices

In smart homes, managing data involves ensuring users have complete control over their personal information. It should be easy to access and user-friendly, allowing users to locate and control their data intuitively without confusion. Poorly designed data management can create obstacles for users, preventing them from managing their data effectively.

Managing data is a crucial aspect of utilizing smart home technology, and it involves several key elements, such as deleting specific recordings, removing all recordings, and scheduling deletions. Additionally, keeping track of the usage history of smart home devices is essential to maintaining control over data and ensuring data security. By following these basic data management principles, smart home users can guarantee a secure and controlled environment for their personal information.

This section compares the data management capabilities of smart home devices, including smart speakers, smart TVs, thermostats, robotic vacuums, and security cameras. Our evaluation will consider the availability of features such as scheduling deletions, removing all recordings, deleting specific recordings, and monitoring usage history, as well as the number of steps required to execute each feature. We assess the availability and execution of these features on each device and platform. The results in Table 3 demonstrate that the same feature may differ in how it is controlled on different platforms of the same device. Additionally, some features may not be available on certain devices, and executing certain features may require varying steps, which could cause inconvenience to the user.

Table 3. Comparing Data Management across multiple smart devices and device categories

Platforms	Deleting a Specific Recording	Deleting all Recordings	Scheduling Deletions	Monitoring Usage History
Sony TV	**Recorded Content such as photos or video** • Via remote control • Needs 3 choices to complete	**Recorded Content such as photos or video** • Via remote control • Needs 5 choices to complete	• N/A	• N/A (no information available)
Samsung TV	**Recorded Programme** • Via remote control • Requires six choices to complete	**Recorded Programme** • Via remote control • Needs 5 choices to complete	• N/A	**Recorded Programme** • Via remote control • Needs 3 choices to complete
Roku TV	• N/A (Not enough storage)	• N/A (Not enough storage)	• N/A (Not enough storage)	• N/A (Not enough storage)
Amazon Echo Dot	**Voice Recording** • Done via the Amazon website or Alexa app • User needs to select each specific recording and confirm the deletion (N times to delete N recordings)	**Voice Recording** • Via the Amazon website or Alexa app • Needs at least 9 steps to complete	**Voice Recording** • Done via the Amazon website or Alexa app • Needs at least eight steps to complete	**Voice Recording** • Done via the Amazon website or Alexa app • Needs at least 4 steps to complete
Amazon Thermostat	**Temperature and voice records** • Via Alexa app • Needs 7 steps to complete	**Temperature and voice records** • Via Alexa app • Needs 8 steps to complete	• N/A	**Temperature and voice records** • Via Alexa app • Needs at least 4 steps
iRobot Vacuum	**Location information** • Via iRobot app • Needs 6 choices to complete	• N/A (no option to delete all recording)	• N/A	**Cleaning History** • Via iRobot app • Needs 2 steps to complete
Ring Camera	**Recorded Video** • Via Ring app • Needs 6 choices to complete	**Recorded Video** • Via Ring app • Needs 6 choices to complete	• N/A	• N/A

4 Prototyping a Security and Privacy Dashboard for Smart Homes

The dashboard aims to provide users with an efficient means to ascertain the status of their smart home devices from different perspectives, such as room locations, device types, device users, and data locations. These perspectives serve as the top-level entry points, allowing users to navigate to specific routes that provide views of individual devices and their associated status and settings. The structure of the dashboard and some of the routes to individual devices are illustrated in Fig. 5. It is imperative to note that the dashboard's design is tailored to enhance user experience, providing them with the necessary information in a clear, concise, and intuitive manner.

In our comprehensive analysis of various devices, we have painstakingly categorized the features of interest into three significant categories – Security, Privacy, and Data Management. These categories have been identified based on earlier research into the features, which has revealed that all devices have some form of these aspects, but often within very different presentation formats and menu structures. The Security category encompasses registration, authorization, authentication, and security updates, which are crucial for ensuring the protection of user data. The Privacy category includes a microphone, location services, camera usage, and usage habits - features that are essential for safeguarding the user's privacy. The Data Management category comprises deleting particular or all recordings, scheduled deletions, and usage history – vital features in managing user data effectively.

The prototype currently realized as a tablet-centric design. The primary goal of the dashboard is to provide users with an intuitive and functional means of managing the privacy and security of their smart home devices.

During the design phase of the dashboard interfaces, numerous aspects were considered, to ensure transparency, simplicity, and user-friendliness of the interface. For example, according to Wen (2021), designers must exercise careful consideration in selecting colour schemes, particularly concerning text information, because the text is the foundation of the entire interface and must be easily legible, with a high degree of contrast from its background colour [23]. This is crucial to enable users to promptly discern the unique application characteristics and functions of software upon their initial reading. Moreover, the colours employed must be conducive to guiding the user in operating the software with ease. As part of our design approach, we have deliberately implemented a white background frequently utilized in UI design. This decision ensures that other interface elements are more prominent, creating a clean and minimalist aesthetic.

Furthermore, it is recommended to use a consistent colour scheme for a white background dashboard to ensure a uniform and recognizable look [24]. For this reason, the selection of black, dark grey, and light grey hues was based on their complementary contrast with the white background, which results in clear and legible text. This choice was made to enhance readability and provide ease of use to the user (Fig. 1).

In situations where the design complexity is considerable, it can be challenging to capture the user's attention effectively [23]. As such, during the interface design process, we employ custom images for each button, which effectively enhances the user interface's appeal and ensures it is easy to use.

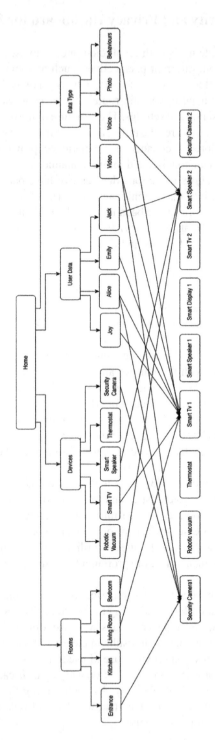

Fig. 1. Dashboard navigational structure

The following subsections analyse the centralised interface in detail, with each subsection being dedicated to a particular aspect of the interface.

4.1   Home Interface

The initial conceptual illustration of the dashboard's interface, depicted in Fig. 2, presents a straightforward design that offers users an efficient means to manage their smart home devices from different perspectives. Therefore, the interface will have four categories, namely rooms, devices, user data, and data types, making it easier for users to browse and display the information they want. These four categories serve as optimal access points due to their direct relevance to users' primary concerns within a smart home environment.

1. **Rooms Button:** This button lets users easily navigate their smart home and find devices in each room. This categorization system simplifies device management based on physical location, providing an intuitive and efficient means of control. This approach aligns with the natural organization of a home, making it easier for users to interact with and manage their smart devices.
2. **Device Button:** This button is created to empower users to control and manage devices based on their category. This button ensures users can tailor their privacy settings to specific devices. This proactive approach enables users to customize security measures.
3. **User Data Button:** The User Data button acknowledges the inevitability of data collection by smart home devices. By dedicating a specific button to user data, the interface aims to provide users with direct access to information related to all household members. This design choice enhances transparency and empowers users to review and manage their data effectively. Including this button demonstrates a commitment to privacy, fostering trust between users and their smart home system.
4. **Data Types Buttons:** Recognizing user data's sensitivity, including Data Type buttons, specifically distinguishing between Tracking Data and Collected Data, offers users granular control and insight. This categorization lets users differentiate between devices that actively track activities through cameras, location tracking, microphones, or TV usage (Tracking Data) and devices that passively collect data (Collected Data). This distinction empowers users to make informed decisions about their privacy preferences, reinforcing the overall security posture of the smart home environment.

The interface comprises six important icons placed on the left-hand side of the screen, each serving distinct functions essential to user navigation and management:

5. **Home:** This icon functions as an entry point, directing users to the main interface, as depicted in Fig. 2.
6. **Information:** Designed to offer guidance, this icon serves as an informational resource, detailing the dashboard's functionality and elucidating the purpose of each category within.
7. **Health Status:** This icon serves a critical role by displaying the security and privacy status of the devices linked to the system. Factors influencing this status may include tracking devices or the duration for which data has been unremoved.

8. **People:** Representing House members, this icon combines pertinent information such as their names, email addresses, and contact numbers for user reference and communication purposes.
9. **Security Notification:** to notify the users about vital updates such as software updates, security patches, and other critical alerts. Its prominence ensures the user remains informed about crucial device security and privacy.
10. **Settings:** This icon grants users access to the general settings, containing language preferences, Wi-Fi settings, and other configurable parameters. Time settings are synchronized with the IP address location derived from the connected Wi-Fi network, ensuring accurate time representation.

Each icon serves a specific and pivotal purpose, contributing to the interface's functionality and user experience and facilitating seamless navigation and control over essential system elements.

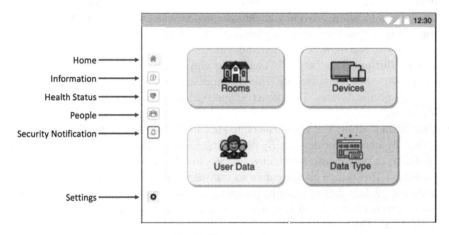

Fig. 2. Home Interface

4.2 Rooms Interfaces

When the user clicks the Rooms button, they will be taken through a series of interfaces, as shown in Fig. 3. The interfaces guide the user from the top level (Fig. 3a) to the Privacy button for a specific smart speaker in the living room (Fig. 3f).

For more clarification, the room button allows the user to access all the rooms in the house, as shown in Fig. 3a. From there, they can add or delete rooms, as shown in Fig. 3b. By clicking on a specific room, such as the living room, the user can view the existing smart devices and add new ones, as shown in Fig. 3b. Clicking on the "Add Room" button takes the user to a panel where they can enter the name of a new room. A suggestion has been made to separate the rooms into different buttons and provide an option for room management [25].

Moreover, clicking on a specific smart device, such as the Smart Speaker in the living room (Fig. 3c). The Data Management category includes features such as deleting

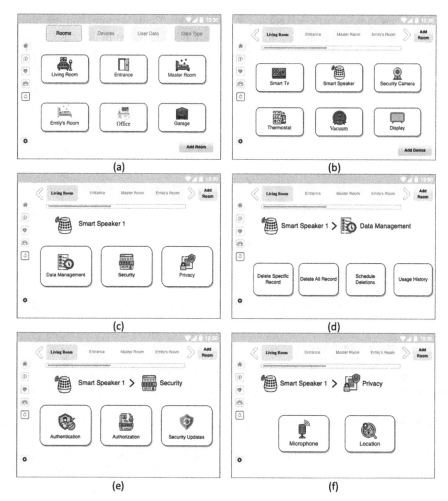

Fig. 3. Rooms Interfaces

specific or all recordings, scheduled deletions, and usage history, which are essential for effectively managing user data (Fig. 3d). The Security category includes registration, authorization, authentication, and security updates, which are crucial for protecting user data (Fig. 3e). The Privacy category includes the microphone, location services, and camera usage. The smart speaker tracks the user via microphone and location (Fig. 3f).

4.3 Devices Interfaces

We have implemented a dedicated button that facilitates browsing and reviewing all devices within a smart home. This button, as shown in Fig. 4a, allows users to select a specific device type, such as a speaker, which will subsequently display all rooms containing such devices. For instance, selecting a speaker device will present the user with all rooms with a speaker device installed. In Fig. 4b, we illustrate an example where the house has three smart speakers in the living room, Emily's room, and the offices. Suppose the user chooses to view the speaker in the living room; in that case, all three main categories, Data Management, Security, and Privacy, will be displayed similarly as presented in Figs. 3c–3f.

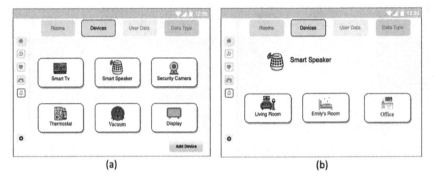

Fig. 4. Devices Interface

4.4   User Data Interfaces

Given the widespread use of smart home devices, it is important to acknowledge that such devices invariably collect and record user data. To facilitate user access to this data, we have designed a dashboard that includes a button display specifically devoted to user data. This interface is designed to display all members of a household (Fig. 5a). Once a user selects a particular household member, for instance, Emily, all her recordings will be displayed. Notably, as illustrated in Fig. 5b, Emily's audio and video recordings will be displayed. Consequently, Emily can easily peruse or delete the data within the smart devices that contain her personal information.

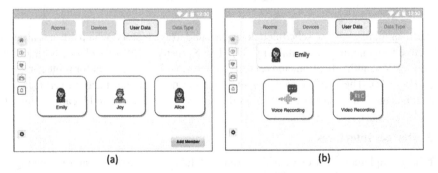

Fig. 5. User Data Interfaces

4.5 Data Type Interfaces

The design of a smart home dashboard must account for the type of data collected by smart devices and how they track users. To facilitate user review of this data and to enable them to determine whether they are being tracked, a categorization of data was employed in the form of tracking data and collected data, as illustrated in Fig. 6a.

Tracking data refers to all devices that track user activity via cameras, location tracking, microphones, or TV usage, as displayed in Fig. 6b. By selecting the camera button from the Tracking Data (Fig. 6c), users can access detailed information about all devices equipped with cameras, enabling them to manage and control such devices effectively. Conversely, the collected data option displays all recorded data categories, such as voice and video recordings and recording content, along with the devices where

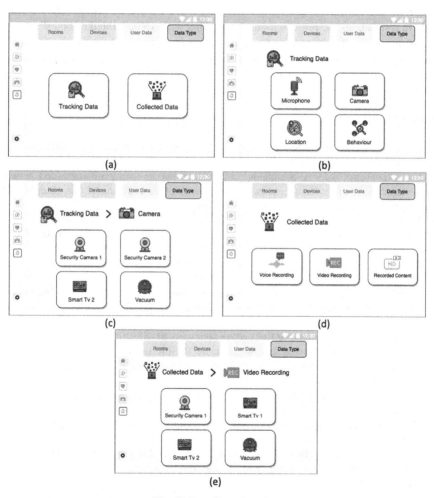

Fig. 6. Data Type Interface

such recordings are contained (Fig. 6d). This allows users to modify or delete these recordings as necessary easily.

5 Conclusions

The research has shown that smart home devices consistently create difficulties for users in managing security and privacy issues. Users are faced with different levels of information and varying ways of managing similar functions across multiple devices, which can be complicated and frustrating. Therefore, improving user experience is required by focusing on HCI aspects. To address this issue, we have designed a smart home dashboard that consolidates status information from various devices in a harmonious manner. This will provide the user with a clear view of the status of all their devices and the smart home as a whole. To confirm the dashboard's effectiveness, we will conduct a proof-of-concept study that simulates the projected outcomes. This will evaluate the dashboard's clarity, ease of use, and effectiveness in facilitating user interaction. The evaluation will also assess the extent to which the dashboard meets the users' requirements and expectations and whether it can facilitate an efficient and streamlined workflow.

References

1. Oberlo: US Smart Home Statistics (2018–2027), June 2023. https://www.oberlo.com/statistics/smart-home-statistics. Accessed 25 Oct 2023
2. Cui, A., Stolfo, S.J.: A quantitative analysis of the insecurity of embedded network devices: results of a wide-area scan. In: Proceedings of the 26th Annual Computer Security Applications Conference - ACSAC 2010 (2010)
3. Keshavarz, M., Anwar, M.: The automatic detection of sensitive data in smart homes. In: Moallem, A. (eds.) HCII 2019. LNCS, vol. 11594, pp. 404–416. Springer, Cham (2019). https://doi.org/10.1007/978-3-030-22351-9_27
4. Denning, T., Kohno, T., Levy, H.M.: Computer security and the modern home. Commun. ACM **56**(1), 94–103 (2013)
5. Madakam, S., Ramaswamy, R.: Smart homes (conceptual views). In: 2nd International Symposium on Computational and Business Intelligence, pp. 63–66 (2014)
6. Mazwa, K., Mazri, T.: A survey on the security of smart homes: issues and solutions. In: ACM International Conference Proceeding Series, pp. 81–87 (2018)
7. Alrawi, O., Lever, C., Antonakakis, M., Monrose, F.: SoK: security evaluation of home-based IoT deployments. In: Proc IEEE Symposium on Security and Privacy, vol. 2019, pp. 1362–1380, May 2019
8. Zhang, B., Zou, Z., Liu, M.: Evaluation on security system of internet of things based on Fuzzy-AHP method. In: 2011 International Conference on E-Business and E-Government, ICEE2011 - Proceedings, pp. 2230–2234 (2011). https://doi.org/10.1109/ICEBEG.2011.5881939
9. Kotz, D., Avancha, S., Baxi, A.: A privacy framework for mobile health and home-care systems. In: Proceedings of the ACM Conference on Computer and Communications Security, pp. 1–12 (2009)
10. Jacobsson, A., Davidsson, P.: Towards a model of privacy and security for smart homes. In: IEEE World Forum on Internet of Things, WF-IoT 2015 - Proceedings, pp. 727–732 (2015)

11. Zheng, S.: User Perceptions of Privacy in Smart Homes. https://dataspace.princeton.edu/han dle/88435/dsp01kd17cw477. Accessed 08 Sept 2022

12. Emami-Naeini, P., Dixon, H., Agarwal, Y., Cranor, L.F.: Exploring how privacy and security factor into IoT device purchase behavior. In: Proceedings of the 2019 CHI Conference on Human Factors in Computing Systems, vol. 12, no. 2019 (2019). https://doi.org/10.1145/329 0605

13. Gorski, L., et al.: Informal support networks: an investigation into home data security practices (2018)

14. He, W., et al.: Rethinking access control and authentication for the home Internet of Things (IoT) (2018)

15. Colnago, J., et al.: Informing the design of a personalized privacy assistant for the Internet of Things. In: Conference on Human Factors in Computing Systems – Proceedings, April 2020

16. Zeng, E., Roesner, F., Allen, P.G.: Understanding and improving security and privacy in multi-user smart homes: a design exploration and in-home user study (2019)

17. Worthy, P., Matthews, B., Viller, S.: Trust me: doubts and concerns living with the Internet of Things. In: DIS 2016 - Proceedings of the 2016 ACM Conference on Designing Interactive Systems: Fuse, pp. 427–434 (2016)

18. Udoh, E.S., Alkharashi, A.: Privacy risk awareness and the behavior of smartwatch users: a case study of Indiana University students. In: FTC 2016 - Proceedings of Future Technologies Conference, pp. 926–931 (2017)

19. Mcreynolds, E., Hubbard, S., Lau, T., Saraf, A., Cakmak, M., Roesner, F.: Toys that listen: a study of parents, children, and internet-connected toys. In: Proceedings of the 2017 CHI Conference on Human Factors in Computing Systems (2017)

20. Rodden, T., Fischer, J., Pantidi, N., Bachour, K., Moran, S.: At home with agents: exploring attitudes towards future smart energy infrastructures. In: Conference on Human Factors in Computing Systems - Proceedings, pp. 1173–1182 (2013)

21. Mcgee, T.M.: Evaluating the cyber security in the Internet of Things: smart home vulnerabilities (2016)

22. Nguyen, D.H., Kobsa, A., Hayes, G.R.: An empirical investigation of concerns of everyday tracking and recording technologies (2008)

23. Wen, G.: Research on color design principles of UI interface of mobile applications based on vision. In: 2021 IEEE International Conference on Advances in Electrical Engineering and Computer Applications, AEECA 2021, pp. 539–542 (2021)

24. Bryson, M.: Principles of color in UI Design. UX Planet. https://uxplanet.org/principles-of-color-in-ui-design-43708d8512d8. Accessed 06 Nov 2023

25. Popov, A.A., Yakimov, S.P., Satsuk, M.M., Artyshko, A.A.: Conference Series PAPER • OPEN ACCESS. J. Phys., 32004 (2021)

Privacy-Conscious Design Requirements to Support Older Adults' Health Information Seeking

Yomna Aly[1] and Cosmin Munteanu[2(✉)]

[1] University of Toronto, Toronto, ON, Canada
yomna.aly@mail.utoronto.ca
[2] University of Waterloo, Waterloo, ON, Canada
cosmin@taglab.ca

Abstract. Older adults (OAs) are active seekers of health information, and increasingly doing so online. Recent research has revealed OAs' motivations, approaches, concerns, and social resources that form their health information seeking practices. However, this has mostly looked at OAs as consumers of information. Comparatively less is known about what is needed from possible tools that support OAs' ability to seek, understand, exchange, and manage health information independently (and privately). We address this gap by first gaining a renewed understanding of OAs' health information seeking behaviours and challenges. This allows us to suggest requirements for designing usable collaborative tools that help overcome health information seeking barriers, and balance older adults' practical support needs with respect for their independence, privacy, and social connectedness. These have been developed through contextual inquiries and participatory workshops with 12 OAs. We validated these design requirements through a usability study of a privacy-conscious collaborative multimedia browser extension.

Keywords: Collaborative · Independence · Social Connectedness · Aging · Caregiving · Health Info Seeking

1 Introduction

Recent years have seen a push to shift the management of care from clinical settings to home-based delivery, especially for older adults (OAs). The rise of e-health has facilitated this transition, yet it can pose challenges for OAs and their circle of care (family or professionals) [27]. The main research approach in the last two decades was to focus on technologies that support older adults to be self-dependent enough to live independently, comfortably and safely in their preferred environment. This can improve the quality of life while delaying the onset of institutionalization [27].

Within this paradigm shift, older adults often face questions and seek information about health care and services revealing two major categories of users [24]. The first category of older adults consists of those who often receive treatments that require daily

© The Author(s), under exclusive license to Springer Nature Switzerland AG 2024
A. Moallem (Ed.): HCII 2024, LNCS 14728, pp. 188–211, 2024.
https://doi.org/10.1007/978-3-031-61379-1_13

intake of several medications and could be suffering from a variety of health conditions. The second category consists of healthy adults who are always keeping pace with the latest health insights [24]. Their motivation to do so is either due to having family history of health complications or to the desire to acquire more knowledge on relevant health matters. Unfortunately, most available technological solutions to support this latter group fall short with respect to several important aspects: enabling privacy control, maintaining older adults' autonomy, facilitating access to and understanding of reliable information sources [1].

While research has been dedicated to studying OAs' health info seeking behaviours (as discussed later), this has been largely conducted from the perspective of information practices. Largely missing is a design lens, for interpreting such perspectives, in order to guide the development of technology that may support OAs in their tasks.

As such, in the research presented here we aim to address issues older adults face with health information acquisition and sharing. Through a 3-phase study, we set to understand challenges OAs face with health information search. We then propose design guidelines to support older adults' information seeking practices that supports their need for privacy, independence, and access to reliable knowledge. We conclude with a validation of the proposed design recommendations by implementing and evaluating a browser extension that supports peer-facilitated health information access while affording OAs full control over their privacy.

2   Related Work

Current research discusses how such technologies can be used to help older adults remain independent, socially engaged and connected to family and friends. The likelihood for adoption of these technologies is influenced by several factors which include benefits of the technology for older adults and the degree of compatibility to their needs and wants. However, several factors, among which usability, digital literacy, health literacy, concerns about privacy of information, and worries of losing control over one's own life discourages older adults from using potentially helpful technologies [22, 30]. In this section, we present the challenges faced on those two aspects as well as some technological solutions offered to address these. We also survey literature on OA's health information seeking behaviours, which provide us with lenses to interpret the technology space. Understanding missing dimensions from previous research will guide our research in successfully proposing design recommendations for health information support, such as privacy-minded online collaboration tools. These design requirements are then validated through the evaluation of a test tool (in the form of a web browser), which was developed by this paper's co-authors in compliance with the proposed requirements.

2.1   Importance of Access to Health Information

Older patients often receive treatments that require daily intake of medications. However, they lack knowledge about them [37]. To promote adherence to treatments and a sense of independence, older adults want to be active members of the decision-making process [37]. This can only be achieved if they are provided with sufficient clear knowledge about treatment plans. A qualitative study [24] revealed that older adults either felt comfortable and satisfied with the information they received about medication, or anxious and insecure. The former was due to OAs' trust in their health professionals and their ability to find sufficient information on their own or from the professionals later. The latter was however due to a lack of physician availability, short appointments, or lacking opportunities for a professional to answer their questions and concerns [24].

Another study [17] described the importance of making health records accessible to patients, needed to strengthen the patient's empowerment to manage their own health [17]. The authors argued for online collaborative tools as a path toward integrated health care, facilitated communication between patients and caregivers, and availability of self-care content, yet acknowledged barriers such as concerns with loss of autonomy, privacy and low digital literacy [17].

Such previous research emphasizes the importance of access to health information in an accessible way for older adults. It also highlights the need to balance the promotion of adherence and compliance to treatment plans with older adults' sense of independence and self-efficacy through involvement in the decision-making process.

2.2 Balancing Privacy and Social Connectedness

Carmien and Fischer [4] have shown that the home environment, unlike long-term care facilities, includes coordination between multiple groups of people with shared, sensitive knowledge about the older adult's life. However, OAs reported decline in levels of control over their lives due to a wide variety of people acquiring information about their daily activities without their permission. Older adults desire to live independently without the help of caregivers.

A study of OAs' willingness to share private health information [27] revealed that sharing behavior is dependent on the type of information shared (e.g. avoiding sharing location info or diet details) and with whom it will be shared (professionals preferred over family members, particularly as they don't want to burden family members). This illustrates how the relationship with the sharing recipient and the perceived benefit of sharing influences how and with whom sharing happens. It also highlights the importance OAs put on maintaining control over their privacy.

Health info is also shared with small social networks where certain individuals assume specific communication roles [26]. Therefore, technology tools should support sharing between small groups, and allow OAs full control over the process.

Another study by Vines et al. [47] presented findings from field trials on a care system named SHel which allowed caregivers to remotely monitor older adults. The aim of this study was to investigate how care activities can have a significant effect on the sense of independence and privacy of older adults' lives. This system has been poorly accepted due to the sense of privacy invasion older adults felt. Older adults reported feeling that their lives are being broadcasted to the public. They had no control over what information is being collected and to whom it is being shared with. Furthermore, older adults emphasized that the remote monitoring reduced the visits and phone calls they received. They believe this is possibly due to caregivers acquiring sufficient information on the older adult's day which previously would have been done through phone calls.

Birnholtz and Jones-Rounds [3] have further emphasized and strengthened the findings from Vines et al. [47] paper. Through semi-structured interviews, Birnholtz and Jones- Rounds were able to better understand how older adults, caregivers and families maintained their social interactions, managed their availabilities and fostered privacy and independence. The authors revealed that the characteristics of the older adults' environment together with routine conversations and activities aid the care-giving process. A set of design guidelines have been proposed to encourage the use of technologies and keep older adults' sense of privacy and independence intact.

Enriching social communication and involvement may appear to be difficult to balance with the desire to maintain privacy. Yet, any technology solutions that facilitate access to health information for older adults must find ways to incorporate both, as both are valued by OAs.

2.3 Technology Solutions and Frameworks

Tixier et al. [40, 41] have proposed a framework to allow for successful adoption of support technologies for older adults. The proposed framework emphasizes that a successful assessment of the older adult's life using ADL (Assessment of Daily living) is required when developing technologies for older adults. Therefore, the likelihood for adoption of a technology and its ability to meet older adults' needs is proportional to the ability of a older adult to perform the basic daily tasks independently [40, 41].

Another study by Consolvo et al. [8] proposed the notion of Computer Supported Coordinated Care (CSCC), which shifts the focus to using technologies to keep up the healthy lifestyle of both older adults and caregivers. In addition to continuous updating and monitoring of older adults' activities, CSCC systems considered both the caregiver and older adult's mental, emotional and overall wellbeing. Among these, two systems introduced four years apart are representative of the tools that addressed those challenges. Care Net [8] and MAPS [4] are systems that attempted to create a socio technical environment supporting customization, personalization and effective collaboration between both older adults and caregivers.

The Care Net Display consists of an interactive picture frame that surrounds the digital photograph of the older adult with relevant information about their daily lives. This digital frame provides caregivers updates throughout the day about the older adult's activities and medication tracking. This technology is accepted by older adults due to its unique focus on them, not only from a health perspective but from an emotional perspective as well. It ensures that the whole caregiver network is updated instantaneously. User studies in [7] presented increased acceptance by older adults of this technology due to the increased level of independence and autonomy older adults enjoyed. However, they reported loss of privacy and control over information shared about them.

The second proposed system known as the Memory Aiding Prompting System (MAPS) [4] created an environment that allows caregivers to create scripts for older adults that enabled them to carry out tasks independently. This would satisfy the independence requirements of older adults and give caregivers full control and awareness of the normal functioning of the elderly life. However, older adults' privacy was invaded and knowing that they are not performing tasks on their own made them feel powerless and, again, led to a loss of independence.

Finally, a system that has been recently developed in and is being slowly introduced to health clinics is Dynacare Plus. It focuses on a much broader spectrum which includes all age groups but not older adults. It helps patients manage their health through understandable and accessible healthcare profiles. Users have access to all their lab results with a simple description of what each test result means. This is a paid system requiring a membership fee and is accessible to all age groups.

2.4 OAs and Health Information Seeking Behaviours

The examples of technological platforms provided in the previous section (along with many other similar technologies) aim to help older adults to remain independent, productive, and socially engaged and connected to family and friends. These technologies are situated within or intersect with the space of health information seeking.

Significant research has been dedicated to understanding users' health information seeking. In particular, age has been shown to be a predictor of the level of activity, with OAs being more active seekers [33]. The same study revealed that other factors such as education and income were not strong predictors, but health literacy and motivation (e.g. to stay healthy) are. These have been confirmed by other studies that show particularly motivation to be a key driver for OAs to engage in health information seeking [28]. Other important factors related to motivation are visits to a medical professional, with OAs engaging more actively in health info seeking (pre and post visit) [18].

This means that it is increasingly important to focus on addressing the barriers toward accessing health information. With the rapid transition to having such information predominantly online, OAs risk becoming marginalized with respect to such technologies [30], as they still encounter more significant barriers to online technologies than other demographics [25]. This has been acknowledged in the health info seeking literature, as studies such as [22] revealed that low digital skills and low health literacy, combined with the usability of tools such as browsers not meeting the needs of OAs affect the ability of this demographic to engage in health info searches. The same study also revealed that OAs have difficulties assessing the quality and trustworthiness of online health info sites (a finding also captured in other research such as [43].

Unsurprisingly then, research such as [28] indicate that caregivers play a significant role in helping OAs overcome the barriers they face when seeking health info. Similar research [23] has shown how OAs seek health information from family members and their social and caregiving circle, especially from relatives who are medical professionals (which we have observed in our own research, as it will be detailed later). While caregiver and family support can overcome barriers to information, other research has looked at digital skills improvement through educational programs as a solution [44] – an acknowledgement of OA's need and desire to manage their health info practices more independently.

The practical solutions and more theoretical research on health info seeking presented in this section illustrate that technology interventions can improve the management of information that is essential to both older adults and caregivers. However, this needs to properly account for OA's skills and abilities, their desire for autonomy and control over the process (e.g. privacy, as we will also see in our research), and their preference for eliciting or cross-checking the information found with trusted sources (e.g. family members, especially if they are health professionals).

3   Research Goals

The dimensions highlighted by our literature survey (Privacy/social connectedness balance; the feasibility of technology solutions as evidenced by research and market products; Barriers, needs, and preferences for health info seeking) have prompted us to consider whether technology can be designed in a way that considers all these dimensions. Namely, we aim to investigate:

What are the design requirements for a technology that assist older adults with health information seeking which: maintains the privacy/social connectedness balance, addresses barriers to health info seeking, and supports older adults in manners that accommodate their needs and preferences.

To answer the above question, we first need to refine our understanding of the barriers, challenges, motivations, and processes related to older adults health information seeking. The literature surveyed earlier provides some insights into this process. However, in order to propose meaningful and informed design requirements (and ultimately build usable and adoptable solutions), it is necessary to approach this step from the methodological perspective of Human-Computer Interaction. We then ground the design requirements in such user-centred approach, followed by the empirical validation (again, through user engagement) of these requirements.

Grounded in the surveyed literature, we identify several threads that can lead our empirical work that aims to answer the overarching research question. First, understanding the dynamic of the relation between older adults and their caregiver circle and how this affects their health information sharing behavior and social interaction. This will help us understand the various roles social connectedness and collaboration plays in OA's health info seeking, and how these roles are fulfilled by peers, family members, etc. Second, understanding the dynamics of the relationship between older adults and health professionals that affect their information acquiring tasks. This may provide insights on whether trust and confidence are leading causes for older adults seeking other sources of information. Third, understanding methods of information collection practiced by older adults and how they are assessed for credibility and reliability. This will help us see how factors such as health literacy, motivation, desire for independence influence the health info seeking and what role they may play when interacting with a potential technology solution that support OAs' health info seeking.

For this, we have conducted a study consisting of three phases. In the first phase of the study, we aim to gain insights and background information to better understand the health information practices of older adults. We assess their level of social interaction and ways of seeking information online and judging the reliability of such sources. In the second phase of the study, we give older adults control of the design process of a collaborative online tool that is easy to use and allows management of health information. The final phase evaluates a prototype built by the researchers as a validation of the design requirements elicited in the first two phases.

4 Methodology

To address our research question, we have designed a mixed method experiment. This experiment followed a traditional approach of conducting qualitative interviews and recording quantitative data. We aimed to empower users in all stages of our work, drawing from methodologies such as Speed Dating [12], Q-Methodology [42], and Co-Design [30]. By incorporating these in our user engagement workshops, we were able to elicit design requirements. Speed Dating [12] is a design methodology that falls between sketching and prototyping. It allows for rapid exploration of concepts and design considerations for an application without implementation of any technology. The outcome would be a thorough analysis and understanding of contextual risk factors and solutions to address them accordingly. Co-design [30] is a methodology that allows designers to develop insights and guidelines and propose new solutions alongside the users who are primarily affected by the new technology. Finally, Q-methodology as proposed in [42] asks users to sort and rank design features and mock-ups based on personal significance eliciting issues that overlap between different users in a user group.

4.1 Development of Design Requirements

Diagram 1 describes the workflow of understanding users and developing early design requirements (Phase 1), refining the requirements (Phase 2), and the using the analysis from the first two phases to finalize the proposed design requirements/recommendations and validate these with a prototype (named MyCare) that implements the design requirements (Phase 3).

Phase	Analysis	Output
1. Contextual inquiry	Thematic analysis of qualitative data from participants exposing their health info seeking practices.	Preliminary design requirements, and design mockups informed by the requirements
2. User engagement and co-design workshop	Round table discussions, participants' brainstorming, and design suggestion activities were analyzed through thematic analysis	A set of design requirements representing a refinement of Phase 1 + additional input from Phase 2
3. Quasi usability testing of prototype implementing Phase 1 & 2 requirements	Thematic analysis of participants' feedback	A complete set of design requirements, build on those from Phases 1 & 2, and refined based on themes emerging from Phase 3.

Diagram 1. Refining the design requirements across phases.

5 Phase 1: In Context Qualitative Interviews

This phase consists of in-context qualitative interviews and administration of a set of validated scales regarding trust and social support. To accurately propose design guidelines for knowledge sharing and acquisition for older adults, it is necessary to get input from the intended users. This builds an accurate understanding of their needs and desires which helps in framing a design tool that better satisfies their needs. Therefore, this phase was designed to explore older adults' levels of trust with the caregiver circle, information seeking habits, and comfort using technology that meets their information seeking needs.

A Contextual Inquiry approach was chosen for this phase as it was judged that the most accurate data on information seeking habits and concerns over health matters would come from observing and prompting that activity in its natural setting [8]. The interviews were held in person at the participants' residences or a place of their choosing and lasted approximately 40–50 min.

Table 1. User Socio-Demographics

ID	Gender	Prior profession	Health status
P1	Male	Engineer	Healthy
P2	Female	Nurse	Multiple Sclerosis
P3	Female	Professor	Healthy
P4	Male	Entrepreneur	Healthy
P5	Male	Computing teacher	Depression
P6	Female	Accountant	Healthy
P7	Female	Nurse	Healthy
P8	Male	Electrical engineer	Eye condition
P9	Female	Homemaker	Diabetic
P10	Female	Nurse	Healthy
P11	Male	Mechanical engineer	Healthy
P12	Male	IT technician	Healthy

5.1 Participants

A total of 12 participants were involved in this study. The interviews were audio recorded with the participants' consent. 6 men and 6 women participated in this phase, all of which are between 63 to 85 years of age. The socio demographics of the participants are presented in Table 1 below. All participants were living independently at home.

5.2 Procedure

The interview started with an introduction to the motivation behind the study and an overview of the study content. The interview started with collecting background information on how concerned the participants were with health matters. Participants were then asked to comment on their sharing behavior with their caregiver circle as well as information acquisition methods. Participants were encouraged to use material and technologies at home to demonstrate a walk-through process of researching a health topic of their choice. The researchers noted down all responses and observed the participants as they searched online for information.

In the second stage of the study, participants were about their relationship with doctors and factors that affect adherence to health information. Similarly, the third set of questions asked about support group and caregiving circle. This helped us understand the relationship OAs have with these two groups. It also revealed the factors that affect their information sharing and acquisition behaviors with the two social groups.

To better understand the social context of our participants, we have administered three relevant scales: the Duke Social Support Scale [26], the Three Item Loneliness Scale [36], and the Interpersonal Trust in a Physician scale [13].

The data was fully transcribed and anonymized before being coded (verbatim principle). Transcripts of interviews and researchers' field notes were analyzed using individual profiling and thematic analysis. This helped us contextualize participants' narratives [16], and to reveal OA's approaches to seeking answers to their health questions.

5.3   Results

The Phase 1 thematic maps are presented in Figs. 1, 2, 3 and 4.

Relationship Between Older Adults and Their Caregiver Circle. According to the results of the Duke and the Three Item social isolation scales, our participants had medium-strong family ties and connections, although several reported feelings of loneliness (in line with expected averages). Despite OAs' high levels of social connectedness, most are reluctant to share information with their family members as to not worry them or burden them with their health matters, as P2 mentions: "I like to appear healthy". This supports previous research on the importance of autonomy and privacy to older adults like [4, 8]. Participants commented that they feel empowered when they can make decisions on their own. Furthermore, they appreciate this level of independence which makes them appear in good health and hence lessens the dependence on and burden on caregivers.

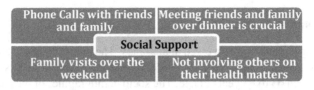

Fig. 1. Thematic Map 1, Social Support

Access and Validation of Health Information. All participants without any exception tend to be very concerned with health matters and are always looking for answers to any concern they have. There was no difference based on medical condition. They all tend to research on health matters that relate to their age group. As P4 mentions, "Because I want to live, I need to keep searching and reading". Interestingly, older adults are aware that if they must research for information online, they need to watch out for unreliable and fraudulent resources.

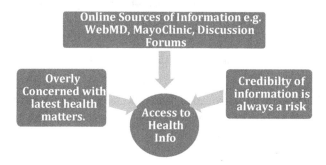

Fig. 2. Thematic Map 2, Health Information Access

8 participants identified a list of websites which they access when wanting to understand health information or read about health matters. These include the following reputable sources: Mayo Clinic, WebMD, University Health Network, healthy lifestyle books such as the spectrum, Goodtime Magazine Heath section, John Hopkins, Health Canada, and NIH (National Institute of Health). They are aware that those medical websites are trustworthy and present true reliable information that they can depend on. Credibility and reliability are crucial aspects when judging information online. Choi et al. [7] discusses how certain cues in an online website plays a role in credibility assessment of health-related websites. The study revealed most participants assess certain websites to be reliable when data provided is unbiased and when they are not presented with advertisements that promote a certain treatment. Others search on specific websites because they heard from relatives of a medical background about them or have seen their doctors searching information on such websites during visits.

Older adults tend to seek information online due to the lack of physicians' availability. They complain that doctors do not have enough time for addressing their lists of concerns. P12 mentioned: *"I look online without hoping to make an appointment"*. Furthermore, other participants lack mobility due to health condition, as P2 mentions *"I do anything to not have to move"*. Such a comment emphasizes the need to have a centralized, easy to access web tool to allow older adults to access information from the comfort of their home. Other participants noted that they receive further answers to health concerns from asking family members who are close to the participant, from those who have a medical background or from friends who shared the same experience.

Relationship with Physicians. We assumed that older adults suffer from bad relationships with practitioners which could be a leading reason for seeking information from online or other sources. On average, most older adults feel that the physicians' care is not of the best interest and most convenient to them. This is evident from those older adults who described situation where a doctor provided only one treatment plan and "you must follow it without any further questions, it is the best for you" as P6 mentioned. However,

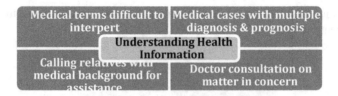

Fig. 3. Thematic Map 3, Understanding Health Info

others do trust the treatments provided to them especially when the practitioners lay out multiple treatments and engages the older adult in the decision-making process.

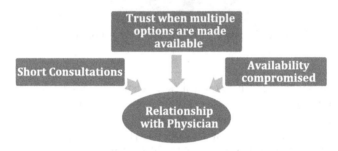

Fig. 4. Thematic Map 4, Relationship with Physicians

Contradicting our assumptions, most older adults do have a good relationship with their doctors. They emphasized that factors which lead to that is the long-term contact with the doctor, the good experiences they have witnessed together and the engagement in the decision-making process when it comes to different treatment plans. Only 4 participants out of the 12 suffered problems with their doctors because of a mistake in diagnosis or attitude towards questions they ask.

Key Findings Highlighted from Phase 1

1. Social Connectedness is a crucial aspect in older adults' lives. (Confirming prior work, e.g. [23], although we have found this to be much more prominent).
2. Bi-directional communication and the role feedback plays with information management has several advantages in the wellbeing of older adults.
3. Empowering older adults sense of independence comes from receiving adequate and sufficient information in an understandable format either from practitioners or caregivers. This is a novel finding, which is justifiable as prior work showed the importance of education (knowledge) in increasing autonomy [44]
4. Older adults are aware of reliable sources of information and have own criteria for judging trustworthiness of a source, yet lack understanding terminology and hence tend to have multiple interpretations which results in poor judgement. This slightly contrasts prior work that showed OAs struggle with assessing trustworthiness, but

concurs with same prior work in the relation between health literacy and reliability of interpreting sources [22]

5. Conceptual knowledge of health conditions provided by both practitioners' explanations and understandable health resources encourage proper decision making and promotes older adults' sense of autonomy and adherence to treatments. While we consider this a novel finding, it aligns with prior work showing how health literacy is a predictor of positive engagement with info seeking [33]

6. Understanding and outlining the above issues allowed us to design two mock-ups of tools for managing health information online. Both mock-ups provide the ability for older adults to search and share online health information with their circle of care. Phase 2 engages OAs as stakeholders by allowing them to comment and help draft functionalities they believe info seeking tools should have.

6 Phase 2: User Engagement Workshops

Upon successful completion and analysis of contextual interviews held in phase 1, phase 2 aimed to bringing design into action and context of use. This phase used information gathered in phase 1 to define and refine design requirements elicited from users during the contextual inquiry interviews. The session lasted 90 min and was held with no more than 4 participants per group. Each group has an equal gender split and as varied ages as scheduling permitted. Participants were the same as in phase 1.

6.1 Procedure

A use case scenario was created with workflow of the use of several prototypes developed by the research team. Older adults were asked about the likelihood of using the system and the workflow that would better mimic their way of seeking health information and the conceptual ease of use. Each use case was carefully designed to tackle a subset of the requirements elicited by participants. This gave insight on how the application may be used, design considerations and the perceptions and behavior related to the use of the app to understand health information.

Fig. 5. Mockup 1: Social Networking Platform

Participants were presented with the two mock-ups as shown in Fig. 5 and 6. They were asked to express their thought process out loud given the below use case scenario using the two mock-ups: *John woke up with terrible knee pain and would like to know causes and treatments for this pain. He searches knee pain and found many articles that*

*are of interest and would like to share it with his circle of care. Use the given mock-ups
and comment on how such tools support John's information seeking goal.*

The second part of this phase asked the participants to envision their won design
requirements and functionalities they believe would better assist their information practices. Drawing from participatory design (although more open-ended in terms of not
aiming for a formal design as output), the mockups and scenarios were used as a starting
point, and participants could annotate, draw new features, or simply orally formulate
suggestions. It is very important that older adults are involved in the design of the tool
to promote its usefulness. As proposed in [11] and [35] and discussed earlier above,
co-design is crucial in application development. Involving users in the design iterations
is essential for a usable and accessible technology.

Fig. 6. Mockup 2: Annotation and highlighting features

6.2 Results and Discussion

Participants articulated some key points during the workshops that helped shape our
understanding of what is required (and what is to be avoided) from an information
sharing and acquisition support tool. Older adults are afraid of loneliness, the exposure
from the loss of privacy due to their health information being accessible online and
being taken advantage of. Therefore, a design mock-up as in Fig. 5 was discouraged.
Older adults commented on feeling that their privacy and privacy of others are invaded
by having a newsfeed of all discussions and no control on what to share and what to
hide. Older adults also are challenged by new technology because they believe they lack
digital literacy, as mentioned by P9, "We *are not that tech savvy like you, at least I know
how to find internet explorer to open a website* ". They also suffer from not understanding
medical jargon and having to ask others for meanings which elicit a discussion on "*Are
you suffering from that? Is that why you are asking? I get furious from such questions*"
(P6).

Participants appreciated a tool that follows features presented in Fig. 6. All participants noted that such a tool provides them with ways of emphasizing areas of concern
using many features that are easy for them to use. They enjoyed highlighting and using
sticky notes as it mimics what they do when they print out articles to read. They requested
that commenting done on articles not be made available except to those they allow. This
emphasizes the importance of privacy control features.

The key requirements and functionalities elicited by participants as evident from the
thematic map in Fig. 7 are:

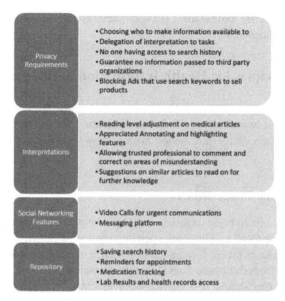

Fig. 7. Thematic Map [User Engagement Workshop]

1. Understating medical terms and lab results with sufficient interpretations adjustable at an appropriate reading level.
2. Instructions on how to be a healthy person.
3. Reminder systems for medicine tracking and appointments must be included.
4. Communication platform to allow them to contact health professional when they are spatially separated.
5. Centralized access to medical records and history with sufficient explanations for better understanding.
6. 24-h access to their health repository no matter where they are located.
7. Control over whom to share information with and at what level of granularity they are provided.
8. Privacy of information remains intact and is not outsourced to third parties or taken advantage of.

Research by Neves et al. [31] has shown that multi-modal tablet based applications can be designed specifically for older adults to improve communication and collaboration with their family members and caregivers. A typical use case for the proposed application is the older adult's ability to seek advice on a medical jargon from a specific family member. However, this interaction and collaboration should be facilitated without raising the concern of their family as to why the older adult is inquiring about this as suggested by participants during the workshops.

Therefore, Phase 3 was designed to assess the design recommendations and validate them through the creation of a web based interface named MyCare. This tool enables older adults to increase their control with respect to information-centric tasks. Using sharing features, discussion boards and natural language processing tools as elicited by the phase 2 findings, MyCare tool balances between social connectedness and collaboration, privacy and independence.

7   Design Principles for Health Information Seeking Support Tools

Two user-centred concepts, drawn from the literature but also from the analysis of data collected in the first two phases, provide the foundation for the proposed design recommendations for successful information management tools that satisfies older adults' needs.

7.1   Concept: Social Connectedness

Collaborative tools aim to bring targeted users together even when spatially separated to enrich social communication. However, spending time on socializing and collaborating using such tools reduces face to face interactions hence making older adults less socially involved as noted from our phase 1 and 2 results as well as literature review [32]. The aim of such platforms should be to enrich engagement by complementing traditional social interactions such as those conducted over phone or in person.

7.2   Concept: Health Information Literacy

Understanding health terminology is crucial for empowering older adults', improving decision making and enhances a better quality of life in terms of health care. Health literacy is the capability to search, proves and understand basic health information to make appropriate decisions [13, 14, 32]. This represents many aspects such as reading ability, health terminology knowledge, technology ease of use and fluency and information seeking skills.

Design Principles. To better design for the above elements, we propose the following principles to be followed. These are synthesized from the themes that emerged in the first two phases.

- **D1**: Inclusion of intuitive interactions to facilitate sharing and understanding of information.
- **D2**: Use of proper affordances and metaphors to display information in a way older adult easily reflect on.
- **D3**: Instant Communication to promote feedback cycles and enhance bidirectional communication.
- **D4**: Communication pathway allowing easy access to support network.
- **D5**: Adjustable Reading Levels as users find relevant to them.
- **D6**: Visualization tools to facilitate the understanding and connection between different health conditions.

8 Phase 3: Evaluation of MyCare Tool

Upon successful completion of Phase 1 and 2, the deployment of the MyCare tool started. The tool has been designed to validate the above design recommendations, by providing a collaborative tool for accessing and understanding health information privately and independently. In the next section we discuss the functionalities that MyCare provides.

8.1 MyCare: A Web Based Collaborative Tool

The MyCare prototype operates as a web-based tool that provides multiple functionalities. Annotations are supported by the prototype in the form of highlighting and sticky notes/pins. Highlights and notes can be created, deleted, and shared. This feature complements principles D1 and D2 (Figs. 8, 9, 10 and 11).

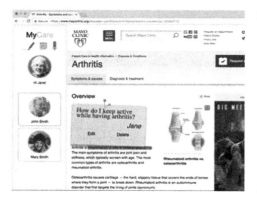

Fig. 8. MyCare Annotating Feature (Sticky Notes)

Fig. 9. Highlighting and Annotation

Fig. 10. Activity Log.

Fig. 11. Chat Log.

Annotations for a webpage can be shared with other contacts. This is done by clicking on the image of the desired target contact to enable sharing in the MyCare toolbar for the corresponding page. When sharing is enabled with another person, their image in the toolbar will have a border around it that has a colour corresponding with that user's highlight colour and pin colour (on a sticky note). When a webpage's annotations are shared with another user, they will immediately appear on their screen. Annotations support "concurrent" editing to provide a feeling for an online communication tool. Hence providing such a feature implements principles D1, D2 and D3. In addition to that, profiles and activity logs are created for each user. The Options/My Profile page allows users to adjust their settings and access profile-specific features. It also provides access to activity and chat logs which can be privately shared.

A contacts book is provided, which allows users to control whom they would like to share their annotations, activity log, and chat log. The profile info is carried over and displayed across other parts of MyCare. Chat logs, Activity Logs and a contacts list implement principles D2, D3 and D4.

8.2 Participants

Same participants attended this phase, in groups of 4 – shuffled to allow for fresh discussions and further insights.

8.3 Exploratory Methodology

The session lasted for 120 min where first, participants could freely play around with the tool. Second, they were given a set of tasks to understand how they can navigate the tool and explore if it reflects their thought process. The tasks provided were as follows:

Task 1: Search about Types II Diabetes
Task 2: Highlight and annotate the article you find with questions you have or important lessons you have learned.
Task 3: Send a message to one of your contacts asking them to check the article you found.
Task 4: Allow the annotations on this article to be shared with only two contacts.

Lastly, participants commented on what they liked and disliked about the tool, and were encouraged to express all concerns they had with using such a tool and areas of improvement for future versions. Transcripts from these activities were coded and interpreted with thematic analysis.

8.4 Results and Discussion

Through inductive thematic analysis and coding of the interviews as in Fig. 12 and 13, the results of this phase helped propose future work paths as well as improvements to the current state of the research tool.

The results of this phase proved which design requirements were appreciated by users. Additionally, it elicited further guidelines to better develop information management tool. The established requirements arise from the major themes (Fig. 12). Each theme consisted of concepts that older adults appreciated and their concerns.

1. *Collaboration*: Older adults appreciated the Skype like functionality in the form of chat logs and annotations. They felt that this tool provides a discussion board platform that allows older adults to communicate with others on matters they have in mind. The instant collaboration aspect of the tool is what they appreciate the most, as P3 mentions, *"I feel like I am working on one of those Mayo Clinic Discussion boards, posting a question and waiting for an answer."*

2. *Natural Language Tools*: The ability to write notes on articles and highlight important areas of concern or areas that require further researching. P7 mentions,*" I appreciate doing this easily on a computer rather than printing and highlighting, lets save paper better".*

3. *Forgetfulness:* Older adults are worried about forgetting what they wanted to ask their doctor or of important notes discussed during doctor visits. P12 mentions, "I always forget the paper with all questions I had, this is a life saver". This issue has been solved by allowing users to easily take notes and save them through activity log memos and notes. They could also easily send it to their caregiver circle if they want them to be aware of a specific detail or to promote a discussion later. Addition, the history of saved articles in the activity log was remarked to help access previous searches.

4. *Personalization and Control Over Sharing:* Older adults appreciate a personalized system for managing health information. Having a tool that allows immediate access *"Always on the Go"* as mentioned by P7 is an advantage.

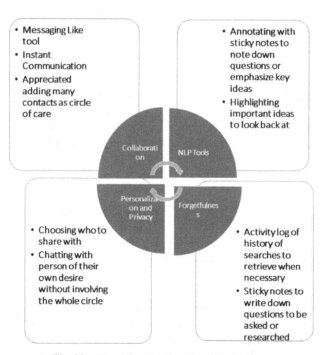

Fig. 12. Thematic Map for Phase 3 Interviews

Older adults suggested a few future work paths and improvements to the existing system which strengthened on our design recommendations proposed in the previous section but was not implemented due to time constraints. Participants emphasized that great work is needed in the form of natural language processing tools to make MyCare more powerful. They suggested the use of visualization tools in terms of graphs that show trends in health conditions such as thyroid hormone levels or for diabetic users, as P1 mentions, *"I like to see graphs, makes it better to understand trends and changes especially when you add lab results access to your tool"*. Second, the ability to undergo a smart search by the tool offering them a list of suggestions of similar conditions when they search for a specific matter. P7 mentions, *"Having a list of suggestions or like a repo of similar conditions that branch from one's search, more of a dictionary of conditions"*. Participants further asked for an online nurse navigator who would assist with research when needed just like in hospitals. Finally, they suggested the feature of a consultation video call with available health professionals, as a way of getting instant replies with a face to face aspect added to it. OAs understand the importance of face to face interactions in all aspects of their daily activities.

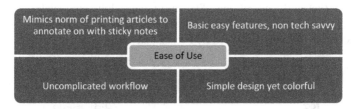

Fig. 13. User Evaluation Notes

The participants elicited concerns over how the medical professionals would react to such a tool. This concern has been noted by all participants in phase 3. As P8, P9 and P4 mention respectively, *"Will doctors be willing to be a part of MyCare?*, *"I am extremely worried about how practitioners would find such a tool"*, *"I fear that they find it disruptive and won't use it at all"*.

Finally, users emphasized the privacy concern matters. They worry about cyber safety and who would have access to such databases. They emphasized not wanting to be a target for pharma ads and calls due to their searches, just like what happens with ads on Google searches and Facebook pages.

9   Takeaways and Conclusion

Our contextual inquiry revealed several aspects about older adults in the context of health information seeking, some of which extend previous literature or contribute new knowledge. We found that OAs are information seekers who tend to read extensively from many sources and do not rely on one source of information or one method of information gathering. They have developed strategies leading to relying only on trustworthy sources; yet still struggle to fully process health information due to low health literacy. Their need for independence and autonomy is satisfied through searching for information online, asking professionals in the field and learning from stories told by those (peers) who have gone through similar situations. At the same time, they want prompt answers to health-related questions or concerns, which may pose a (perceived) conflict with practitioners and caregivers, who want to be aware of OA's concerns and to better assist them. OAs demand full privacy and control over their health information, primarily from third party (commercial) entities but also from their social circle (e.g. family members, as to not burden or worry them). OAs consider that practitioners' limited time and availability hampers their ability to patiently answer all their questions. Thus, OAs tend to search for information on their own to avoid creating a burden and to maintain their independence.

Through a contextual inquiry (Phase 1), engagement and co-design workshops (Phase 2), and a quasi usability evaluation of the MyCare test platform (Phase 3), we have iteratively developed, refined, and validated a set of design requirements. These are grounded in an understanding of user needs as synthesized from the literature surveyed (and refined through the contextual inquiry in Phase 1). Tables 2 and 3 detail the final set of design requirements for interactive tools that support older adults in their health information seeking. These requirements span several overarching categories: collaborative info seeking, user-controllable privacy and sharing, management of acquired information, and help understanding the information.

These recommendations, well received by our participants, emphasize the importance of digital independence and health literacy for older adults, while preserving privacy and social engagement. Observing these recommendations may help designers of interactive health info apps, doctor–patient portals, and in general, of e-health systems develop health information technologies and services geared toward older adults that better match their needs and expectations, and provide them the level of support that help them overcome current barriers to health information access.

Table 2. Functional Requirements

Functional Requirement	Definition	Design Feature
Personalization	Capability to Customize system to manage health information Centralized access to all medical records	Medication Tracking Reminders for Appointments Contact List of circle of care Lab Results, Health Records, Articles of Interest
Information Acquisition	Capability to comply with older adults' traditional ways of information acquisition but in a web-based tool	Visualization and tree networks for similar conditions Minimal Windows to reach goal
Autonomy	Capability to control with whom to share information with and at what level of detail	Choosing who to share notes and records with Color Coding
Collaboration	Capability to instantly communicate and collaborate with circle of care on matter of concern or interest while preserving privacy	Chat Logs Concurrent Editing and annotating with different contacts Instant communication

Table 3. Non-Functional Requirements

Non -Functional Requirement	Concept	Design Feature
Usability	Easy to use, matching metaphors with info presented, affordances, visualizations, user friendly	Graphs Sticky notes and highlighting
Privacy	Encrypted Communication, preserving personal information through controlled sharing	Secure login Controlled sharing and viewing
Performance	Immediate access to information	
Understanding (Interpretations)	Understating medical terms and lab results with sufficient interpretations adjustable at an appropriate reading level	Highlighting Sticky notes Voice annotations Video consults Nurse navigators
Recoverability	Capability to retrieve data already stored easily as well as tracking down notes for older adults to refer back to	Activity Logs Search History Notes

Acknowledgments. This work was supported by AGE-WELL, a member of the Government of Canada's Networks of Centres of Excellence program.

Disclosure of Interests. The authors have no competing interests to declare that are relevant to the content of this article.

References

1. Aly, Y., Munteanu, C.: An information-centric framework for mobile collaboration between seniors and caregivers that balances independence, privacy, and social connectedness. In: Stephanidis, C. (eds.) HCI 2016. CCIS, vol. 617, pp. 395–400. Springer, Cham (2016). https://doi.org/10.1007/978-3-319-40548-3_66
2. Bassuk, S.S., Glass, T.A., Berkman, L.F.: Social disengagement and incident cognitive decline in community-dwelling elderly persons. Ann. Internal Med. **131**(3), 165–173 (1999)
3. Birnholtz, J., Jones-Rounds, M.: Independence and interaction: understanding older adults' privacy and awareness needs for aging in place. In: Proceedings of the SIGCHI Conference on Human Factors in Computing Systems, pp. 143–152. ACM (2010)
4. Carmien, S.P., Fischer, G.: Design, adoption, and assessment of a socio-technical environment supporting independence for persons with cognitive disabilities. In: Proceedings of the SIGCHI Conference on Human Factors in Computing Systems, pp. 597–606. ACM (2008)
5. Chen, Y., Ngo, V., Park, S.Y.: Caring for caregivers: designing for integrality. In: Proceedings of the 2013 Conference on Computer Supported Cooperative Work, pp. 91–102. ACM (2013)
6. Chilana, P.K., Wobbrock, J.O., Ko, A.J.: Understanding usability practices in complex domains. In: Proceedings of the SIGCHI Conference on Human Factors in Computing Systems, pp. 2337–2346. ACM, April 2010

7. Choi, W.:. Senior citizens' credibility assessment of online health information: a proposal of a mixed methods study. In: Proceedings of the 2012 iConference, pp. 620–622. ACM, February 2012

8. Consolvo, S., Roessler, P., Shelton, B.E., LaMarca, A., Schilit, B., Bly, S.: Technology for care networks of elders. Pervasive Comput. IEEE **3**(2), 22–29 (2004)

9. Cornejo, R, Tentori, M., Favela, J.: Enriching in-person encounters through social media: a study on family connectedness for the elderly. Int. J. Hum. Comput. Stud. **71**(9), 889–899 (2013)

10. Crooks, V.C., Lubben, J., Petitti, D.B., Little, D., Chiu, V.: Social network, cognitive function, and dementia incidence among elderly women. Am. J. Public Health **98**(7), 1221 (2008)

11. Cortes, U., et al.: Assistive technologies for the new generation of senior citizens: the SHARE-it approach. Int. J. Comput. Healthc. **1**(1), 35–65 (2010)

12. Davidoff, S., Lee, M.K., Dey, A.K., Zimmerman, J.: Rapidly exploring application design through speed dating. In: Proceedings of the 9th International Conference on Ubiquitous Computing (UbiComp 2007), pp. 429–446 (2007)

13. Dugan, E., Hall, M., Trachtenberg, F.: Development of abbreviated measures to assess patient trust in a physician, a health insurer, and the medical profession. BMC Health Serv. Res. **5**, 64 (2005)

14. de Leon, C.F.M., Glass, T.A., Berkman, L.F.: Social engagement and disability in a community population of older adults the new haven EPESE. Am. J. Epidemiol. **157**(7), 633–642 (2003)

15. Glass, T.A., de Leon, C.M., Marottoli, R.A., Berkman, L.F., et al.: Population based study of social and productive activities as predictors of survival among elderly Americans. Bmj **319**(7208), 478–483 (1999)

16. Fereday, J., Muir-Cochrane, E.: Demonstrating rigor using thematic analysis: a hybrid approach of inductive and deductive coding and theme development. Int. J. Qual. Methods **5**(1), 80–92 (2006)

17. Fischer, S.H., David, D., Crotty, B.H., Dierks, M., Safran, C.: Acceptance and use of health information technology by community-dwelling elders. Int. J. Med. Inform. **83**(9), 624–635 (2014)

18. Flynn, K.E., Smith, M.A., Freese, J.: When do older adults turn to the internet for health information? Findings from the Wisconsin Longitudinal Study. J. Gen. Intern. Med. **21**(12), 1295–1301 (2006)

19. Detmer, D., Bloomrosen, M., Raymond, B., Tang, P.: Integrated personal health records: transformative tools for consumer-centric care. BMC Med. Inform. Decis. Mak. **8**(1), 45 (2008)

20. Gray, L.C., et al.: Sharing clinical information across care settings: the birth of an integrated assessment system. BMC Health Serv. Res. **9**(1), 71 (2009)

21. Huang, L.C., Liu, W.C., Chou, S.C.T.: Howcare: a personal health cloud archive and care-partners' community. In: 2013 IEEE/ACM International Conference on Advances in Social Networks Analysis and Mining (ASONAM), pp. 1237–1241. IEEE, August 2013

22. Huang, M., Hansen, D., Xie, B.: Older adults' online health information seeking behavior. In: Proceedings of the 2012 iConference, pp. 338–345. ACM, February 2012

23. Hurst, G., Wilson, P., Dickinson, A.: Older people: how do they find out about their health? A pilot study. Br. J. Community Nurs. **18**(1), 34–39 (2013)

24. Keselman, R., Logan, C.A., Smith, G.L., Zeng-Treitler, Q.: Developing informatics tools and strategies for consumer centered health communication. J. Am. Med. Inform. Assoc. **15**(4), 473–483 (2008)

25. Krueger, K.R., Wilson, R.S., Kamenetsky, J.M., Barnes, L.L., Bienias, J.L., Bennett, D.A.: Social engagement and cognitive function in old age. Exp. Aging Res. **35**(1), 45–60 (2009)

26. Koenig, H.G., Westlund, R.E., George, L.K., Hughes, D.C., Blazer, D.G., Hybels, C.: Abbreviating the Duke Social Support Index for use in chronically ill elderly individuals. Psychosomatics **34**(1), 61–69 (1993)

27. Kurniawan, S., Zaphiris, P.: Research-derived web design guidelines for older people. In: Proceedings of the 7th International ACM SIGACCESS Conference on Computers and Accessibility, pp. 129–135. ACM (2005)

28. Manafo, E., Wong, S.: Exploring older adults' health information seeking behaviors. J. Nutr. Educ. Behav. **44**(1), 85–89 (2012)

29. Modig, S., Kristensson, J., Troein, M., Brorsson, A., Midlöv, P.: Frail elderly patients' experiences of information on medication. A qualitative study. BMC Geriatr. **12**(1), 46 (2012)

30. Munteanu, C., Axtell, B., Rafih, H., Liaqat, A., Aly, Y.: Designing for Older Adults: Overcoming Barriers to a Supportive, Safe, and Healthy Retirement. Wharton Pension Research Council Working Papers. University of Pennsylvania Press (2018)

31. Neves, B., Rachel, L.: My hand doesn't listen to me! Adoption and evaluation of a communication technology for the oldest old. In: Proceedings of the 33rd Annual ACM Conference on Human Factors in Computing Systems, pp. 1593–1602. ACM (2015)

32. Pang, C.E., Neustaedter, C., Riecke, B.E., Oduor, E., Hillman, S.: Technology preferences and routines for sharing health information during the treatment of a chronic illness. In: Proceedings of the SIGCHI Conference on Human Factors in Computing Systems, pp. 1759–1768. ACM (2013)

33. Paek, H.J., Choi, M., Hove, T.: Intention to view health TV programs in South Korea: an application of the comprehensive model of information seeking. Journal. Mass Commun. Q. **94**(2), 526–551 (2017)

34. Prasad, A., Sorber, J., Stablein, T., Anthony, D., Kotz, D.: Understanding sharing preferences and behavior for mHealth devices. In: Proceedings of the 2012 ACM Workshop on Privacy in the Electronic Society, pp. 117–128. ACM (2012)

35. Reblin, M., Uchino, B.N.: Social and emotional support and its implication for health. Curr. Opin. Psychiatry **21**(2), 201 (2008)

36. Russel, D., Peplau, L.A., Cutrona, C.E.: The revised UCLA loneliness scale: concurrent and discriminant validity evidence. J. Pers. Soc. Psychol. **39**(3), 472–480 (1980)

37. Stewart, C.D., Hanson, V.L., Nind, T.J.: Assisting older adults in assessing the reliability of health-related websites. In: CHI 2014 Extended Abstracts on Human Factors in Computing Systems, pp. 2611–2616. ACM, April 2014

38. Stine-Morrow, E.A.L., et al.: Training versus engagement as paths to cognitive enrichment with aging (2014)

39. Sundar, S.S., Oeldorf-Hirsch, A., Nussbaum, J., Behr, R.: Retirees on Facebook: can online social networking enhance their health and wellness? In: CHI 2011 Extended Abstracts on Human Factors in Computing Systems, pp. 2287–2292. ACM, May 2011

40. Tixier, M., Gaglio, G., Lewkowicz, M.: Translating social support practices into online services for family caregivers. In: Proceedings of the ACM 2009 International Conference on Supporting Group Work, pp. 71–80. ACM (2009)

41. Tixier, M., Lewkowicz, M.: Looking for respite and support: technological opportunities for spousal caregivers. In: Proceedings of the 33rd Annual ACM Conference on Human Factors in Computing Systems, pp. 1155–1158. ACM (2015)

42. O'Leary, K., Wobbrock, J.O., Riskin, E.A.: Q-methodology as a research and design tool for HCI. In: Proceedings of the SIGCHI Conference on Human Factors in Computing Systems, pp. 1941–1950. ACM, April 2013

43. Silver, M.P.: Patient perspectives on online health information and communication with doctors: a qualitative study of patients 50 years old and over. J. Med. Internet Res. **17**(1), e19 (2015)

44. Tse, M.M., Choi, K.C., Leung, R.S.: E-health for older people: the use of technology in health promotion. Cyberpsychol. Behav. **11**(4), 475–479 (2008)
45. VanBiervliet, A., Edwards-Schafer, P.: Consumer health information on the Web: trends, issues, and strategies. Medsurg Nurs. **13**(2), 91 (2004)
46. Verdezoto, N.X., Wolff Olsen, J.: Personalized medication management: towards a design of individualized support for elderly citizens at home. In: Proceedings of the 2nd ACM SIGHIT International Health Informatics Symposium, pp. 813–818. ACM, January 2012
47. Vines, J., et al.: Making family care work: dependence, privacy and remote home monitoring telecare systems. In: Proceedings of the 2013 ACM International Joint Conference on Pervasive and Ubiquitous Computing, pp. 607–616. ACM (2013)

With or Without U(sers): A Journey to Integrate UX Activities in Cybersecurity

Daniela Azevedo[1]($\boxtimes$) iD, Justine Ramelot[1] iD, Axel Legay[2] iD, and Suzanne Kieffer[1] iD

[1] Université Catholique de Louvain, Institute for Language and Communication, Louvain-la-Neuve, Belgium
{daniela.azevedo,justine.ramelot,suzanne.kieffer}@uclouvain.be
[2] Université Catholique de Louvain, Institute of Information and Communication Technologies, Electronics and Applied Mathematics, Louvain-la-Neuve, Belgium
axel.legay@uclouvain.be

Abstract. Integrating human factors into cybersecurity system development is crucial if users are to make these technologies their own. This case study reports our introduction of UX activities in a cybersecurity project focused on creating cyber range scenarios. Research objectives include assessing non-UX stakeholders' UX literacy, examining the impact of user involvement on non-UX stakeholders' UX literacy, and identifying barriers and opportunities for UX integration. Data was collected at three key points, using a mixed method approach of survey, interview and observation. The findings reveal that although introducing UX methods progressively did not uniformly improve UX literacy, it reduced barriers to UX integration and increased confidence in conducting UX activities. Further, it facilitated effective communication within a multidisciplinary team, fostering consensus on development priorities.

Keywords: user experience · cybersecurity · UX literacy · UX integration

1 Introduction

As contemporary users are prone to reject systems that offer an inadequate UX, organizations must adopt human-centered design (HCD) to design technologies capable of competing successfully in a saturated global market [14]. Despite an abundance of related literature [18], the integration of software development and user experience (UX) remains challenging to practitioners and organizations attempting it [11,12,39]. There are several barriers to UX integration [4,6]: lack of understanding of UX return on investment (ROI); mistaken belief that performing UX requires no UX expertise or that UX can be performed informally; contentious attitudes toward users, UX practitioners and UX activities; and mistaking UX for aesthetics or user interface. Moreover, low UX literacy manifests

A. Moallem (Ed.): HCII 2024, LNCS 14728, pp. 212–231, 2024.
https://doi.org/10.1007/978-3-031-61379-1_14

itself in insufficient understanding of HCD and UX, insufficient awareness of UX return on investment (ROI), and contentious attitude toward users [4]. In turn, low UX maturity is characterized by a lack of resources for UX and difficulty in fully committing to UX design from the onset of the project [9].

Integrating human factors into cybersecurity systems and infrastructure development is crucial if users are to make these technologies their own. Further, creating CRS tailored to users is key for effective learning. Failure to meet user needs may result in disengagement from the system [8, 24], reduced relevance and practical application [16, 34], inability or disinterest in completing the training when tasks do not match trainees' capabilities (too easy or too difficult) [42].

This case study reports how we introduced and conducted UX activities in a cybersecurity project (2022-2025) aiming at supporting the creation of cyber range scenarios (CRS). The system is intended for CRS designers, trainers and trainees [37]. Trainers need a usable graphical user interface (GUI) to create CRS and monitor trainees' progress during the execution of the CRS, whereas trainees need the GUI to follow the CRS and complete their training. The project involves three stakeholders: a university (UNI), a center of excellence (COE), and an industrial partner (IND). The mission of UNI is to implement the HCD process as software development model, design a GUI, model, and implement an approach to generate and guide CRS; COE implements and integrates the GUI of the CR; and IND provides the cyber range (CR). We opted for UX methods without users to execute understanding, specifying, and producing HCD processes, as recommended by [19] when resources such as budget and time are limited. Moreover, we opted for a strategy without users due to their involvement being a pain point for technology-driven stakeholders, unlike stakeholders with a human-centered mindset [4]. Thus, we first conducted an expert review to improve the GUI of CR, which allowed us to get familiar with the existing system and domain. We then conducted prototyping workshops to design a GUI for CRS creation.

This case study objective is to explore the progressive integration of UX activities, first without, then with users, to promote an HCD-oriented mindset within a cybersecurity project. In particular, we aim to answer the following research questions (RQs):

- What are project stakeholders' perceptions of UX, specifically their UX literacy? (RQ1)
- How does involvement or lack of involvement of users in UX activities affect project stakeholders UX literacy? (RQ2)
- What are the barriers and opportunities to UX integration? (RQ3)

The contribution of this paper is to uncover and discuss ways to facilitate UX integration in a cybersecurity project. This case study presents a preliminary account of the gradual involvement of users into project development lifecycle to reduce the amount of friction between project stakeholders and UX staff. We believe that UX methods without users have increased stakeholders' UX literacy, which paved the way to further improve stakeholders' attitude toward users.

2   Background

2.1   UX and Cybersecurity

Integrating UX into cyber range development enhances the effectiveness of cyber-security training by prioritizing software usability and improving user acceptance. The UX design process, rooted in HCD, is guided by user needs and requirements to create systems that are not only functional but also provide user satisfaction and performance [33]. By focusing on understanding the context of use and specifying user requirements from the outset [20], UX helps aligning training content with trainees' competences, responsibilities and real-world environment. Integrating UX could help address the challenges related to cyber range scenario relevance and effectiveness highlighted in [8,16,34], ensuring a more seamless and engaging learning experience for trainees.

Conversely, lack of UX considerations engenders a disregard for user needs and poses challenges to the goal of improving trainees' competences. This oversight results in potential misalignments between cyber range's training content and the actual responsibilities of trainees. Moreover, the failure to incorporate context-driven and relatable scenarios may induce disengagement, as trainees struggle to bridge the gap between theoretical knowledge and practical application [8,16]. Engagement is also affected by misaligning trainees' abilities and the difficulty level of training scenarios [41,42], which diminishes training relevance and restricts the application of acquired knowledge in the real-world [16,34].

2.2   UX Integration

Organizations and project stakeholders struggle with UX integration and prioritization during software development [17]. To integrate UX activities, UX practitioners must build trust with project stakeholders, who are more inclined to trust UX practitioners before trusting the field of UX [35]. However, gaining trust and support from colleagues remains a challenge [32]. Ingrained beliefs tend to prevail in the face of uncertainty, such as individual-level risk aversion [4,35].

The inherent disparities between software development and UX stakeholders' rationales, priorities, and practices present considerable challenges to UX integration and create multiple friction points [30]. Developers' inability or unwillingness to adopt a user-centric mindset together with developers' focus and interest in the functionality and efficiency of the code rather than on usability [2,5] constitute one such challenge. Lack of mutual understanding between UX designers and developers leads to ineffective communication [3,21], further exacerbating the issue [23]. Moreover, senior managers' focus on safeguarding developers' time contributes to the prioritization of coding over UX, reinforcing the notion UX holds lower value, as it is dispensable unless insights are gained and thus lowers the expectations for UX quality [35].

Another challenge arises from insufficient prioritization and resources for UX. The neglect in UX implementation and resource allocation manifests through disorganized and erratic UX management, resulting in a product vision deficit and introducing uncertainty: e.g. lack of UX leadership, lack of UX representation at strategic levels, and lack of consistency in implementing UX activities across projects [35]. Lack of resources leads to in high workloads for UX designers [22], imposing limitations on productivity and creating bottlenecks [32].

2.3   UX Literacy

We contend that a lack of or limited UX literacy leads to numerous challenges to UX integration described in scientific literature. For instance, developers' tendency to expedite UX activities or resist accommodating UX outcomes, rooted in prior internal decisions or perceived lateness in the process, culminating in a hurried approach [35]. Another challenge is the misconception that UX is resource-intensive, indicating a limited knowledge about existing UX methods [5] and discount alternatives [38]. Additional challenges include conflating UX with aesthetics or visual design [4,15] and believing users are unable to express their needs and provide insights during evaluation [2]. Further, the absence of colleagues with UX literacy poses a challenge, as a certain level of UX literacy is necessary to effectively execute UX activities [28], which leaves UX practitioners feeling isolated and struggling to make their voices heard [32].

Yet, UX literacy is valuable when integrating UX into software development, where comprehension of UX ROI correlates with frequent UX evaluations and higher UX maturity [40]. Barriers also stem from a lack of UX literacy among the system commissioners, leading to the absence of UX requirements [2,37], as they undervalue UX and resist investing in UX [4,5]. This resistance in investing in UX is also prevalent in organisations' senior management [38].

2.4   UX Methods

There are two classes of UX methods [25,26]: knowledge elicitation methods and artifact-mediated communication methods, also referred to as UX design methods (Fig. 1). Knowledge elicitation methods include those not involving users and those involving users. Methods without users (e.g. expert review or heuristic evaluation) aim to predict the use of a system based on the opinion or expertise of an expert, without involving user data collection. Conversely, methods with users collect user data to incorporate the user's perspective into software development. There are three types of methods with users: (1) attitudinal methods focused on collecting self-reported data about users' feelings (e.g. interview); (2) behavioral methods focused on collecting and measuring data about actions of users and/or their physiologic state (e.g. observation); (3) the combination of both attitudinal and behavioral methods (e.g. contextual inquiry). Artifact-mediated communication methods rely on UX artifacts as means of communication means for helping/improving/organizing communication and collaboration for both internal and external parties, and should be available throughout the project for involved stakeholders [7]. There are two types of artifacts: those concerning stakeholders needs (e.g. UX goals) and those concerning communicating designs (e.g. wireframes).

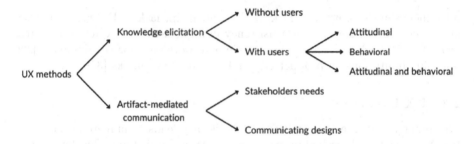

Fig. 1. Description of UX methods (variation of [26]).

3 Conducting UX Activities

The project involved UX methods with and without users (Figure 2). First, we used UX methods without users (i.e., expert review, prototyping workshops, and UX goals); detailed descriptions of expert reviews and prototyping workshops conducted until June 2023 can be found in [37]. The literature recommends using UX methods without users when resources (e.g., budget, time) are limited [19] and in case non-UX stakeholders exhibit contentious attitudes toward users and misunderstand the UX ROI [4,6]. Further, offering a venue for stakeholders to share their ideas and opinions helps minimize the risk of non-UX stakeholders acting independently in sessions with users that they themselves moderate [35].

Then, we interviewed a stakeholder from IND with over ten years' experience as a trainer and CRS designer. This experience makes them both an expert in teaching and a user of the intended system. Therefore, we consider this interview to straddle both classes of UX methods (Figure 2). The interview allowed us to gather information regarding the context of use of the intended system from both a trainer and trainee's perspective.

Finally, we used UX methods with users by conducting user testing. System evaluation generates the most enthusiasm from non-UX stakeholders [9], making user testing the most opportune UX activity to introduce methods with users.

3.1 UX Activities Without Users

Expert Review. A UX researcher (UNI) and a CR expert (IND) conducted an expert review of the GUI of a CRS creation tool, evaluating it against usability guidelines proposed by [31]. Initially, each reviewer independently assessed the relevance of every guideline for the review, evaluated the GUI's compliance with each relevant guideline, and assigned a confidence rating to their assessments. Subsequently, the two experts convened online to consolidate their evaluations of the 209 guidelines, suggesting redesign solutions in cases where they agreed on noncompliance with a given guideline. Disagreements on three guidelines prompted the collection of user feedback through a survey. As a result, 132 guidelines were deemed relevant, with 102 fully satisfied, 14 partially satisfied, and 16 not satisfied.

Prototyping Workshops. Two UX researchers (UNI) conducted 16 prototyping workshops with project stakeholders in total, five until June 2023 [37] and 11 until December 2023. The design team involved two information and communication technology (ICT) experts from UNI, two from COE, and the two UX researchers. The goal was twofold: (1) to design a GUI that would enhance trainees' learning experiences and offer valuable insights to trainers, and (2) to involve project stakeholders in HCD processes. Utilizing lo-fi prototyping facilitated rapid iterative design [19], triggering discussions on user requirements [25], and GUI layouts [27]. The team broke down the system into design chunks, hosting in-person or hybrid workshops for sketching and real-time visualization, and online sessions to refine data models. This multidisciplinary approach successfully addressed UX and functional requirements, identifying essential features for optimal CRS creation.

Definition of UX Goals. Two UX researchers (UNI) and the prototyping team defined the UX goals for trainees and trainers after consolidating the GUI design during prototyping workshops. The prototyping team defined the UX goals using the list of design sprints proposed in [29]. Setting UX goals helps establish clear expectations, prevent misunderstandings [6,23], ease decision-making, and prioritize fixes [39].

3.2 UX Activities with Users

User Tests. Two UX researchers (UNI) conducted and recorded online user tests for two me-fi prototypes, engaging with two distinct types of users. ICT and CR experts from COE and UNI observed one session for each prototype, either synchronously (in online sessions) or asynchronously (via recordings), and documented their observations using an analysis grid provided by the UX researchers.

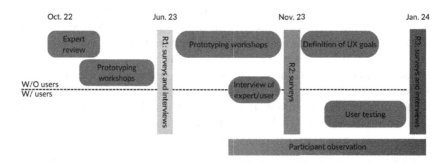

Fig. 2. Timeline of UX activities (blue rectangles) and data collection (grey rectangles) in the project. R1 refers to round 1, R2 to round 2, R3 to round 3. (Color figure online)

4 Methodology

4.1 Objectives and Approach

This case study aims to enhance the integration of UX activities in a cyber-security project, first through UX methods without users and then with users. The specific objectives of the research include assessing stakeholders' UX literacy (RQ1), examining the impact of user involvement on stakeholders' UX literacy (RQ2), and identifying barriers and opportunities for UX integration (RQ3). We conducted an exploratory case study since data on perception of UX is scarce and contextual conditions relevant to the RQs cannot be controlled [36]. The case study is not intended for generalizing findings but rather to provide insights into strategies for improving UX integration in cybersecurity projects, as well as a set of methods for repeating the case study in other projects. Earlier findings [37] suggest that even without direct user involvement, UX methods improve stake-holders' UX literacy and collaboration, and advocate phased user inclusion.

4.2 Data Collection Methods

To answer the RQs, we carried out three rounds of data collection (Figure 2): round 1 (R1) took place after conducting exclusively UX methods without users, while round 2 (R2) and round 3 (R3) took place after the introduction of UX methods with users. In each round, we used the survey presented in [4] to measure project stakeholders' UX literacy, specifically the UX dimensions: understanding of HCD (HCD), understanding of UX (UUX), attitude toward users (ATU), awareness of UX ROI (ROI), perceived opportunities (OPP) for and barriers (BAR) to UX integration. To operate the survey, project stakehold-ers indicated their level of agreement with statements on a 5-point Likert scale. In R1 and R3, we conducted a follow-up interview to collect additional insights into stakeholders' current beliefs regarding UX based on the set of questions pre-sented in [37] addressing UX integration into the software development model, impact on their roles, considerations for future projects, and desired UX-related information for decision-making. As can be seen from Fig. 2, we also used partic-ipant observation to collect observational data on non-UX stakeholders behav-iors during UX activities (i.e. interview, prototyping workshops, definition of UX goals, and user testing).

The combination of survey, interview and participant observation data enables us to answer the RQs by cross-analyzing data and cross-checking find-ings:

- Collecting survey data on UX dimensions allows us to measure the UX literacy of each participant (RQ1)
- Collecting survey and interview data at each rounds allows us to compare participants' UX literacy before and after using methods with users (RQ2)
- Collecting interview and participant observation data allows us to identify barriers and opportunities to UX integration and analyze the demand for implementation of UX activities (RQ3).

All parties entered into a memorandum of understanding, authorizing observation data collection between parties. Prior to survey and interview, non-UX stakeholders were required to read and sign a consent form. We recorded interviews via an online video conference tool.

4.3 Participants

In R1, a total of 11 participants took part in the survey, and 6 participants in interviews [37]. As this case study focuses on UX activities using UX methods with and without users, we sampled participants from project stakeholders who took part in UX activities without and with users: two participants from UNI and two participants from COE. Participants are all males aged between 30 and 49, with a solid experience in ICT, cybersecurity, or both. Table 1 presents the involvement of each participant in rounds of data collection.

Table 1. Participant sampling. Experience expressed in years. x indicates participation in rounds of data collection (S: survey; I: interview).

Participant	Stakeholder	Experience	R1-S	R1-I	R2-S	R3-S	R3-I
P1	UNI	8	x		x	x	x
P2	UNI	7	x	x	x	x	x
P3	COE	18	x	x	x	x	x
P4	COE	13	x		x	x	x

5 Results

This section is dedicated to presenting raw results per method for data collection, namely first survey, then interview, and finally participant observation. Data cross-analysis and findings cross-checking are discussed in Sect. 6.

5.1 Survey

Table 2 displays survey mean scores assessing UX literacy per round of data collection on a normalized scale ranging from 1 (poor answer) to 5 (good answer). We reversed scores for survey statements using a negative form. Table 3 displays the UX literacy scores (median and standard deviation) per survey statement.

Overall Tendencies. Participants perceive UX differently between rounds, both positively and negatively (Table 2). All participants scored better in BAR, meaning they beliefs present a reduced barriers to UX integration. In contrast, all participants scores decreased in OPP and to a lesser extend in ATU, meaning respectively they perceive fewer opportunities to UX integration and display a negative attitude toward users.

Table 2. Participants' mean scores per round of data collection. Green depicts an increase in score between R1 and R3, red depicts a decrease between R1 and R3.

Participant	Round	HCD	UUX	ATU	ROI	BAR	OPP
P1	R1	4.25	3.67	3.75	3.75	3.75	3.75
	R2	4.50	4.17	4.50	4.00	4.75	2.75
	R3	4.75	3.67	3.75	4.00	4.25	2.50
P2	R1	4.75	3.67	4.00	3.00	4.50	4.50
	R2	5.00	4.17	4.75	4.00	4.50	2.50
	R3	5.00	4.50	3.75	3.00	5.00	1.75
P3	R1	5.00	4.50	3.00	4.00	2.50	4.25
	R2	5.00	3.00	3.00	3.50	3.75	2.75
	R3	4.00	4.00	3.00	4.00	3.75	2.50
P4	R1	4.50	3.83	3.75	3.75	2.50	3.25
	R2	4.25	3.67	3.25	3.50	3.50	3.00
	R3	4.00	3.67	3.50	3.50	3.75	2.75

Table 3. Survey statement median for each round. * indicates the scale was reversed due to negative statement.

Survey statement	R1	R2	R3
Understanding of human-centered design (HCD)			
Grounded in-depth understanding of users, tasks and environments should be a focus at the start of development	4.50	5.00	4.00
UX research is a "blocker" to the real development work*	4.00	5.00	4.50
UX research is an optional add-on*	5.00	4.50	4.50
Design should be driven by user tasks, goals and evaluation	5.00	5.00	4.50
Understanding of user experience (UUX)			
Graphic design and UX design are the same and therefore are performed by the same person*	4.00	4.00	4.00
UX is subjective and therefore cannot be measured*	4.50	3.50	4.00
UX awareness is all you need to design good user interfaces or good user experience*	3.50	3.50	4.00
Non-utilitarian concepts (e.g., joy, stimulation, aesthetics) are part of UX	3.50	4.00	4.00
Utilitarian concepts (e.g., efficiency, effectiveness, satisfaction) are part of UX	4.50	4.50	4.00
UX is essential for acceptance, adoption and trust in a product	4.00	4.50	4.00
Attitude toward users (ATU)			
Users do not need a good UX, they just need training*	5.00	4.50	4.50
Users are able to express what they want	2.50	3.50	3.00
User expectations are difficult to manage*	2.50	3.50	2.00
Users should be at the centre of product development, not just have a supporting role	4.50	4.00	4.50
Awareness of UX return on investment (ROI)			
UX activities increase product attractiveness	4.00	4.00	4.00
UX activities reduce sales and revenues*	4.00	4.50	4.00
UX activities help reduce users' need for training and technical support	4.50	4.00	4.00
UX activities increase development costs and time*	2.50	2.50	3.00
Barriers to UX integration (BAR)			
We have enough resources (time, budget, staff) for UX	3.00	3.00	4.50
We have enough skills to conduct UX activities	2.00	4.50	4.00
UX conflicts with our current software development model*	2.00	4.00	4.00
Our projects are too small to incorporate UX into our software development model*	2.00	4.50	4.00
Opportunities for UX integration (OPP)			
Some of our projects or products fail because of poor UX design*	4.00	3.50	3.00
User needs for training and technical support are important*	4.00	2.00	2.00
The overall net loss in user productivity from UX issues is insignificant	4.00	3.00	1.50
The overall net loss in late design changes from UX issues is insignificant	3.50	3.00	3.00

HCD. Overall, P1 and P2 improved their scores, whereas P3 and P4 experienced a decline. In R1, both P1 and P2 recognized that UX research does not hinder development efforts. In contrast, in R2, P4 showed an improved understanding of HCD by emphasizing the importance of understanding users, tasks, and environments at the project's outset. However, P4 exhibited reduced conviction in the indispensability of UX research and the significance of user tasks, goals, and evaluation in guiding design. In R3, P1 strongly agreed that UX research is essential, while P3's scores declined across all statements.

UUX. Following R1, P1 and P2 recognized the inadequacy of relying solely on UX awareness for designing effective UI. Initially, P4 scored poorly for the statement "UX as subjective and therefore cannot be measured", but improved by R3. In R2, P3's scores declined regarding the inclusion of non-utilitarian (e.g. stimulation, aesthetics) and utilitarian (e.g. efficiency, effectiveness) concepts in UX, and the significance of UX for product acceptance. In R3, P1 and P3 demonstrated a reduced understanding of UX by misconstruing graphic design and UX as synonymous. P4's comprehension of non-utilitarian elements in UX decreased in R3, contrasting with an improved understanding of the importance of utilitarian elements after R1.

ATU. Participants displayed a negative attitude toward users. In particular, they perceived user expectations as challenging to manage. During R2, both P1 and P2's scores improved, but declined during R3. Between R1 and R3, both P1 and P3 scores regarding users' ability to express what they want improved, while P2's score declined. Despite an improvement, this statement still received a low score from participants. Moreover, although participants generally believed that training does not substitute for the need for good UX, P4's perception on this matter declined. Overall, participants believed users should be at the center of development. During R2, P3 and P4's scores decreased to a neutral stance on this statement, and in R3, P4's scores increased.

ROI. P2's awareness of UX ROI underwent an overall improvement in R2, but this positive trajectory reversed significantly in R3. In R2, P2's score improved concerning the recognition of UX activities in reducing users' need for training and technical support. Concurrently, P3 and P4's score declined for this particular statement. However, in R3, P2's score declined for the mentioned statement, while P4's score increased. In R2, P4's score for the statement "UX activities increase development costs and time" decreased, whereas P1's score increased. In R3, P3 score for this statement increased.

BAR. P1, P2 and P3 consistently perceived fewer barriers to UX integration between R1 and R3. Only P4's scores indicated a diminished view of sufficient UX resources, contrasting with the increased belief among all other participants in the availability of adequate resources for UX. Following R1, all participants gained confidence in the design team's skills for UX activities and expressed a decreased conflict between UX and their current software development model.

Furthermore, except for P3, who already held a high score, all participants increasingly believed that their projects are not too small for UX integration.

OPP. Across rounds, participants' scores declined, reflecting diminished opportunities for UX integration within the project. Participants' scores suggest a diminishing perception of the substantial nature of user needs for training and technical support. A shared perspective emerged, except for P4, indicating a consensus that projects are not at high risk of failure due to poor UX design, and the overall decrease in user productivity from UX issues is considered minor. Additionally, P2 and P3 expressed heightened confidence in the insignificance of the overall net loss in late design changes resulting from UX issues.

5.2   Interview

Participants consistently stressed that HCD is key to understanding user needs and ensuring a positive user experience. They highlighted the importance of prototyping workshops and user testing for identifying and preventing potential usability issues. In R1, P2 and P3 emphasized initiating UX activities early to prevent the development of non-usable systems. In R2, participants advocated for the early engagement of UX experts to design features aligned with user needs, emphasizing the ongoing necessity of UX activities throughout development to build successful and user-friendly systems.

Understanding HCD and UX value led participants to desire UX integration in other projects. P1 highlighted the proximity of UX experts to users as crucial for effective design, while P4 stressed their role in bridging the gap between users and developers. P3 and P4 found UX has value when the project's technology readiness level reaches a stage involving a GUI and users. Further, P2 emphasized the contribution of UX in building relevant systems and reducing both time and development costs.

Despite stating that UX activities are time-consuming, participants, particularly P2, stressed their indispensable role in understanding user needs, thus preventing "building features that do not align with user expectations". On the other hand, P1 noted that developers might become less engaged during the design phase due to a lack of clear features to code. P3 found conducting UX and functional activities in parallel challenging, as UX and system architecture influence each other. To address time constraints, P1 suggested parallelizing activities, and P2 proposed reducing iteration size to gather frequent user feedback and commence development based on validated insights.

Conducting UX activities prompted participants to prioritize understanding users and designing for their needs over coding features. Introducing UX activities triggered a shift in perspective within software development since users "view efficiency from a different perspective" that diverges from the developers' focus on code (P1). P3 perceived translating user needs into specifications as part of their job. Meanwhile, P4 viewed UX activities as an additional task within an already diverse portfolio, considering it without negativity.

Participants derived crucial insights from UX activities to guide decision-making. Wireframes aid in understanding and meeting user requirements (P2, R1), designing workflows (P1), and ensuring a streamlined and user-friendly system (P4). Visual representations help developers better understand what needs to be implemented and should be done "before starting development" (P3, R1). Moreover, P3 articulated a desire for UX guidelines, best practices, and style guides to facilitate development. Both P3 and P4 explicitly expressed the need for ongoing user feedback to enhance and refine the system.

Ultimately, active participation in a project integrating UX has provided P1 and P2 with firsthand experiences, reinforcing their conviction regarding the value of UX. P1 noted that "I already knew that UX would be useful for the development, but during the testing phase, I was mind blown". On the other hand, P3 and P4 maintained that their perspectives on UX have remained consistent. However, during R1, P3 specifically highlighted that UX activities, particularly wireframe prototyping, aided in effectively communicating the design solution to developers. This minimizes iterations and ensures unanimous agreement on project objectives (P3, R1).

5.3   Observation

UX activities not only facilitated the design of a system aligned with user needs and requirements but also contributed to facilitated communication among team members and elevated morale. In contrast with other development activities, UX activities established an environment conducive to consensus-building among team members following the exchange of opinions (Table 4). User testing was delayed as the design team was uncertain about what aspects to test and had reservations about collecting user feedback before implementing features closely resembling the final system. Further, toward the conclusion of the prototyping workshops, participants experienced growing frustration with the substantial time invested in designing the system, attributing blame to diverging objectives.

Table 4. Summary of UX activities (Sept.-Dec. 2023) with related goals and observation of non-UX stakeholders. UX activities displayed in chronological order for methods with and without users.

UX activity	Goal(s)	Observation(s)
Interview (2x)	Gather contextual information on CRS design and execution	Team displayed high level of interest, posed insightful questions, and patiently awaited their turn during the interview
Methods without users		
Prototyping workshop	Validate design solution proposed by UX team	UNI and COE sought active participation in the design process, expressing discontent over exclusion. COE consistently opposed proposed design solutions
Prototyping workshop	Redesign solutions proposed by UX team	Team collectively shaped proposed solution. COE showed significant support and friendliness, compared to previous meeting
Prototyping workshop	Consolidation of wireframes and discussion over design chunk	Sketches hanged on whiteboard, promoting visibility and fostering discussions on common themes. Session started with major and tense discussion between UNI and COE, consuming almost all allocated time and heightening formality in conversations
Prototyping workshop	Brainstorm ideas and design a solution for a design chunk	Discussion and sketching, COE absent initially, joining later. Initial half progressed smoothly with collaborative discussions on solutions. COE's arrival prompted revisiting and clarifying the methodology, causing frustration among engaged participants
Prototyping workshop	Brainstorm ideas and design a solution for a design chunk	Presenting individual design sketches sparked discussions, creating a respectful environment that valued each team member's input.
UX goals	Agree on workflow and UI design, select UX goals and measures for user testing	Shift from one key user to another, due to disagreement within team. Tension arose from past UNI and COE frictions over project technicalities
UX goals	Agree on workflow and UI design, select UX goals and measures for user testing	Team showed signs of disengagement, needing prompts for active involvement. Some individuals seemed preoccupied with unrelated matters. Observable tension emerged between UNI and COE, stemming from past disputes initiated in meetings without UX team, later affecting UX-driven sessions
Methods with users		
User testing	Test design solutions with users	Team actively took notes and demonstrated a keen interest in user feedback, recognizing its value and significance

6   Discussion

6.1   UX Literacy

Introducing UX methods without users and then UX methods with users did not consistently improve UX literacy. The design team's perception of UX activities was influenced by factors like the need to start development and meet project milestones. P3 and P4, both responsible for software development, experienced a decline in their HCD scores. Statements emphasizing the importance of understanding user tasks and the environment at the project's onset declined, with both individuals believing that UX research hindered actual development work. During interviews, participants recognized the importance of understanding user needs. However, they also raised the challenges related to conducting UX activities concurrently with development. Participants stressed the importance of allocating enough time for software development and running UX activities in parallel. However, the absence of a clear link between UX activities and developers' responsibilities, such as coding features, presented a challenge and reduced engagement in UX activities. For instance, the lack of a clear connection between defining UX goals and subsequent development phases resulted in decreased engagement, requiring interventions to prompt active participation. Conversely, UX activities with a clear link to feature building (e.g. interviews) or issue identification (e.g. user testing) led to heightened participant engagement.

The non-linear nature of learning also hindered consistent UX literacy improvement. For instance, in R2, P1 and P2 scored high for the statement indicating that managing user expectations is easy (ATU), after participating in a UX activity in which a user from IND effectively conveyed the challenges of their job and suggested potential improvements. However, during R3, user testing uncovered unexpected design flaws and, during a follow-up interview, users occasionally made statements that contradicted their actions during user testing. This experience might have reinforced the widespread belief among developers that involving users is time-consuming because users are unable to express their needs or provide valuable insights during evaluations, as documented in [2] and aligns with the results of the survey statements. Our findings suggest that these experiences may have prompted P1 and P2 to recognize that designing good systems entails more than just thinking about users during the design phase and asking them direct questions. Consequently, managing user expectations became challenging, as indicated by the decline in P1 and P2's scores for that statement. The same experience might have led P4 to conclude in R3 that good design alone may not be sufficient, and users may require training (ATU).

The prevailing negative attitude towards users is concerning, considering users' role in shaping effective interactive systems [30]. Further, the challenges encountered in systematically testing and validating requirements with users, as evidenced by our extended timeline (Figure 2), align with observations in [13]. The extended period of upfront design becomes a collaboration challenge [21], leading non-UX stakeholders to perceive UX as challenging due to its resource demands [35] and leading to tensions within the team regarding the amount of time dedicated to UX activities. Yet, participants demonstrated a pronounced enthusiasm for user feedback to improve the system. Survey findings underscore participants' strong belief that users should be a primary focus in the development process and that users need good UX, not just training. During interviews, participants mentioned wanting user feedback to inform decision-making, refine system design, and validate ideas in real-world settings. The design team's active engagement during the user testing phase underscores their commitment to valuing and incorporating user feedback throughout the development lifecycle.

6.2   UX Integration

Although integrating UX methods without and then with users did not uniformly improve UX literacy, it contributed to reduced barriers and increased confidence in the team's ability to conduct UX activities. Prototyping workshops encouraging discussions with developers helped participants to see the value of UX [2]. During the interview, P4 expressed appreciation for the prototyping workshops' methodology, highlighting how sharing ideas and consolidating design solutions collaboratively helped achieve consensus and ensured consideration of all ICT and UX requirements and constraints. Our findings, similar to [35], highlight the importance of fostering a safe environment for non-UX stakeholders. This environment encourages experimentation with UX methods with minimal barriers, gradually incorporating user-centric approaches. Observation notes indicate a more harmonious and cooperative atmosphere during UX activities, positively contributing to results and project progression when compared to activities without UX involvement. The engagement of developers during prototyping workshops facilitated the transition toward a human-centered mindset.

Participants' growing confidence in their ability to leverage UX within the current development framework reflects a positive attitude toward UX integration, which is further supported by the diminishing opportunities for UX Integration (OPP) scores observed across rounds. The perceived significance of user needs for training and technical support diminished, alongside apprehension about project failure or substantial decreases in user productivity due to UX issues. The decrease in OPP scores appears to be linked to the project's robust UX integration and suggests a plateau in the incidence of potential UX integration opportunities. Prototyping workshops played a pivotal role in gradually introducing UX practices and principles. However, the efficacy of conducting such UX activities hinges on participants' sufficient UX literacy, as observed in [28]. During the interviews, participants noted the project's immediate integration of UX activities deviates from their usual practices, expressing appreciation for this approach. Despite acknowledging potential cost and time implications (ROI), participants deemed UX activities key to project success. The presence of UX practitioners as intermediaries fostered confidence in system development alignment with user needs. In interviews, both P1 and P2 expressed pre-existing belief in the potential of UX. However, the project served as a practical demonstration, highlighting the feasibility and desirability of seamlessly integrating UX into the development process.

From R1, participants recognized the importance of understanding user needs and creating relevant systems. In interviews, participants explicitly stated that UX activities are indispensable; without them, there would be a lack of clarity on what constitutes user requirements and therefore on what needs to be developed. Additionally, participants acknowledged that developers often prioritize technical aspects, neglecting user concerns. This aligns with previous research [2], which notes that developers, even when recognizing the importance of usability, may maintain a "developer mindset", prioritizing programming aspects, technical challenges, and product functionality over UX considerations. The continual involvement of UX experts throughout development was crucial in steering the design team away from this mindset, which is supported by HCD high scores, particularly for statements emphasizing the vital role of UX research and advocating for development guided by user tasks, goals, and evaluation.

Conducting UX activities facilitated effective communication within a multidisciplinary team with diverse objectives, fostering consensus on development priorities. In line with [1], our research underscores the necessity of open, inclusive, and reflective discussions with developers to integrate UX successfully. UX cannot operate in isolation but must be collaboratively built with developers [1]. Our study aligns with [39], indicating that involving developers in design solutions, integrating them into user requirements, and sharing UX artifacts contribute to a shared understanding of the design vision. This collaborative approach helps address the common challenge outlined in [21], where a lack of regular communication between developers and UX designers results in a perceived misalignment between development and UX work. Contrastingly, participants emphasized the importance of understanding user needs and requirements in building and supporting design solutions. The interviews underscored the importance of user feedback, particularly through user testing. In R1, participants primarily highlighted the significance of gathering user feedback to inform the design process, whereas in R3, they further emphasized the crucial role of user testing in identifying design flaws, understanding overlooked aspects, and providing a reality check.

6.3   Limitations and Strengths

The study exhibited characteristics inherent to exploratory case studies and qualitative research, including a lack of control over the setting, a limited sample size, a reliance on narrative data, and a lack of intent to statistically generalize findings or demonstrate cause-and-effect relationships [36]. Moreover, the authors' active involvement in all study aspects, coupled with a year-long engagement with participants, may introduce bias. Potential biases were mitigated by employing the same survey and interview guide throughout the study [10]. Further, the authors maintained their role as UX practitioners throughout the mission.

This study's strength lies in its practical mixed-method approach, blending observational data with surveys and interviews to reduce bias. Cross-checking findings, maintaining a longitudinal approach, and focusing on a single group enables a thorough exploration of phenomena and identification of evolving patterns. The presence of all participants in all rounds ensures a representative sample and facilitates tracking perception changes and attitudes toward UX.

7   Conclusion

This exploratory case study focused on integration of UX methods with and without users into a cybersecurity project aimed at creating a graphical user interface for cyber range scenarios. We studied how non-UX stakeholders perceive UX after using UX methods without users and then UX methods with users. We tracked the changes in their perception of UX by collecting data through surveys, interviews, and observations at three key points: after using UX methods without users, after an interview with an expert, and after introducing UX methods with users. Our findings indicate participants perceived the added value of UX integration, as it helped understanding user needs, reducing development costs and time, facilitating decision-making, and improving communication of design decisions. Additionally, UX contributed to improved team communication and morale, as evidenced by [19]. Introducing UX at the project outset, first through methods without users and then through methods with users, aids non-UX stakeholders to progress toward a human-centered mindset, also observed in [1,35].

Future work in the project includes collecting data using the same methods at different intervals to track the changes in UX perception among non-UX stakeholders within and throughout the same project. Additionally, data collection efforts will extend to non-UX stakeholders who have limited involvement in UX activities. Other future work includes the replication of our protocol across multiple projects and teams. The aims are to (1) validate the data collection methods and (2) determine if introducing UX methods first without users and then with users helps non-UX stakeholders adopt a more human-centered mindset. A similar multiple case study approach will enable identification and pattern analysis from both similar and contradictory results, providing insights for the development of a theory for seamless UX integration.

Acknowledgments. The authors acknowledge the support provided by the CRS2 project (grant number 2110064) and CYBEREXCELLENCE project (grant number 2110186), both funded by Service Public de Wallonie, Belgium. They also acknowledge the support provided by the Institute for Language and Communication, UCLouvain. Appreciation is also extended to the anonymous reviewers for their insightful feedback on an earlier iteration of this work.

Disclosure of Interests. The authors have no competing interests to declare that are relevant to the content of this article.

References

1. Ananjeva, A., Persson, J.S., Bruun, A.: Integrating UX work with agile development through user stories: an action research study in a small software company. J. Syst. Softw. **170**, 110785 (2020)
2. Ardito, C., Buono, P., Caivano, D., Costabile, M.F., Lanzilotti, R.: Investigating and promoting UX practice in industry: an experimental study. Int. J. Hum Comput Stud. **72**(6), 542–551 (2014)
3. Argumanis, D., Moquillaza, A., Paz, F.: Challenges in integrating SCRUM and the user-centered design framework: a systematic review. In: Agredo-Delgado, V., Ruiz, P.H., Villalba-Condori, K.O. (eds.) Human-Computer Interaction: 6th Iberomarican Workshop, HCI-Collab 2020, Arequipa, Peru, September 16–18, 2020, Proceedings, pp. 52–62. Springer International Publishing, Cham (2020). https://doi.org/10.1007/978-3-030-66919-5_6
4. Azevedo, D., Rukonić, L., Kieffer, S.: The gap between UX literacy and UX practices in agile-UX settings: a case study. In: Abdelnour Nocera, J., Kristín Lárusdóttir, M., Petrie, H., Piccinno, A., Winckler, M. (eds.) Human-Computer Interaction - INTERACT 2023, pp. 436–457. Springer Nature Switzerland, Cham (2023)
5. Bak, J.O., Nguyen, K., Risgaard, P., Stage, J.: Obstacles to usability evaluation in practice: a survey of software development organizations. In: Proceedings of the 5th Nordic conference on Human-computer interaction: building bridges, pp. 23–32 (2008)
6. Bias, R., Mayhew, D.: Cost-Justifying Usability (Second Edition). Morgan Kaufmann, San Francisco, second edn (2005)
7. Brhel, M., Meth, H., Maedche, A., Werder, K.: Exploring principles of user-centered agile software development: a literature review. Inf. Softw. Technol. **61**, 163–181 (2015). https://doi.org/10.1016/j.infsof.2015.01.004
8. Brilingaitė, A., Bukauskas, L., Juozapavičius, A.: A framework for competence development and assessment in hybrid cybersecurity exercises. Comput. Secur. **88**, 101607 (2020). https://doi.org/10.1016/j.cose.2019.101607
9. Buis, E., Ashby, S.S., Kouwenberg, K.K.: Increasing the UX maturity level of clients: a study of best practices in an agile environment. Inf. Softw. Technol. **154**, 107086 (2023)
10. Campbell, D.T., Stanley, J.C.: Experimental and quasi-experimental designs for research. Ravenio books (2015)
11. Chamberlain, S., Sharp, H., Maiden, N.: Towards a framework for integrating agile development and user-centred design. In: Abrahamsson, P., Marchesi, M., Succi, G. (eds.) Extreme Programming and Agile Processes in Software Engineering: 7th International Conference, XP 2006, Oulu, Finland, June 17-22, 2006. Proceedings, pp. 143–153. Springer Berlin Heidelberg, Berlin, Heidelberg (2006). https://doi.org/10.1007/11774129_15

12. Choma, J., Guerra, E.M., da Silva, T.S., Zaina, L.M.: An approach to explore sequential interactions in cognitive activities of software engineering. Inf. Softw. Technol. **141**, 106730 (2022). https://doi.org/10.1016/j.infsof.2021.106730
13. Convertino, G., Frishberg, N.: Why agile teams fail without UX research. Commun. ACM **60**(9), 35–37 (Aug 2017). https://doi.org/10.1145/3126156
14. Djamasbi, S., Strong, D.: User experience-driven innovation in smart and connected worlds. AIS Trans. Human-Comput. Interact. **11**(4), 215–231 (2019). https://doi.org/10.17705/1thci.00121
15. Fraser, J., Plewes, S.: Applications of a UX maturity model to influencing HF best practices in technology centric companies-Lessons from Edison. Proc. Manufact. **3**, 626–631 (2015)
16. Ghosh, T., Francia, G.: Assessing competencies using scenario-based learning in cybersecurity. J. Cybersecur. Privacy **1**(4), 539–552 (2021). https://doi.org/10.3390/jcp1040027
17. Gray, C.M., Toombs, A.L., Gross, S.: Flow of competence in UX design practice. In: Proceedings of the 33rd Annual ACM Conference on Human Factors in Computing Systems, pp. 3285–3294 (2015)
18. Hinderks, A., Mayo, F.J.D., Thomaschewski, J., Escalona, M.J.: Approaches to manage the user experience process in agile software development: a systematic literature review. Inform. Softw. Technol. **150** 106957 (2022)
19. Hussain, Z., et al.: Agile user-centered design applied to a mobile multimedia streaming application. In: Holzinger, A. (ed.) USAB 2008. LNCS, vol. 5298, pp. 313–330. Springer, Heidelberg (2008). https://doi.org/10.1007/978-3-540-89350-9_22
20. ISO: Ergonomics of human-system interaction - part 210: Human-centred design for interactive systems (2019)
21. Jones, A., Thoma, V.: Determinants for successful agile collaboration between ux designers and software developers in a complex organisation. Int. J. Human-Comput. Interact. **35**(20), 1914–1935 (2019). https://doi.org/10.1080/10447318.2019.1587856
22. Jurca, G., Hellmann, T.D., Maurer, F.: Integrating agile and user-centered design: a systematic mapping and review of evaluation and validation studies of agile-UX. In: Proceedings - 2014 Agile Conference, AGILE 2014, pp. 24–32 (2014). https://doi.org/10.1109/AGILE.2014.17
23. Kashfi, P., Nilsson, A., Feldt, R.: Integrating user experience practices into software development processes: implications of the UX characteristics. PeerJ Comput. Sci. **3**, e130 (2017)
24. Katsantonis, N.M., Kotini, I., Fouliras, P., Mavridis, I.: Conceptual framework for developing cyber security serious games. In: 2019 IEEE Global Engineering Education Conference (EDUCON), pp. 872–881. IEEE (2019). https://doi.org/10.1109/EDUCON.2019.8725061
25. Kieffer, S., Rukonić, L., Kervyn de Meerendré, V., Vanderdonckt, J.: A process reference model for UX. In: Cláudio, A.P., et al. (eds.) Computer Vision, Imaging and Computer Graphics Theory and Applications: 14th International Joint Conference, VISIGRAPP 2019, Prague, Czech Republic, February 25–27, 2019, Revised Selected Papers, pp. 128–152. Springer International Publishing, Cham (2020). https://doi.org/10.1007/978-3-030-41590-7_6
26. Kieffer, S., Rukonic, L., de Meerendré, V.K., Vanderdonckt, J.: Specification of a ux process reference model towards the strategic planning of ux activities. In: VISIGRAPP (2: HUCAPP), pp. 74–85 (2019)

27. Kieffer, S., Vanderdonckt, J.: A comparison of paper sketch and interactive wireframe by eye movements analysis, survey, and interview. In: HICSS-56 (2023)
28. Kuusinen, K.: Task allocation between UX specialists and developers in agile software development projects. In: Abascal, J., Barbosa, S., Fetter, M., Gross, T., Palanque, P., Winckler, M. (eds.) Human-Computer Interaction – INTERACT 2015: 15th IFIP TC 13 International Conference, Bamberg, Germany, September 14-18, 2015, Proceedings, Part III, pp. 27–44. Springer International Publishing, Cham (2015). https://doi.org/10.1007/978-3-319-22698-9_3
29. Larusdottir, M.K., Lanzilotti, R., Piccinno, A., Visescu, I., Costabile, M.F.: Ucd sprint: A fast process to involve users in the design practices of software companies. Int. J. Human–Comput. Interact. 1–18 (2023)
30. Law, E.L.C., Lárusdóttir, M.K.: Whose experience do we care about? analysis of the fitness of scrum and kanban to user experience. Int. J. Human-Comput. Interact. **31**(9), 584–602 (2015). https://doi.org/10.1080/10447318.2015.1065693
31. Leavitt, M.O., Shneiderman, B.: Research-Based web design and usability guidelines. US DHHS (2006)
32. MacDonald, C.M.: "It takes a village": On UX librarianship and building UX capacity in libraries. J. Libr. Adm. **57**(2), 194–214 (2017). https://doi.org/10.1080/01930826.2016.1232942
33. Maguire, M.: Methods to support human-centred design. IJHCS **55**(4), 587–634 (2001)
34. Mases, S., Maennel, K., Toussaint, M., Rosa, V.: Success factors for designing a cybersecurity exercise on the example of incident response. In: IEEE EuroS&PW Conference, pp. 259–268. IEEE (2021)
35. Nielsen, S., Ordoñez, R., Skov, M.B., Jochum, E.: Strategies for strengthening ux competencies and cultivating corporate UX in a large organisation developing robots. Behav. Inform. Technol. 1–29 (2023)
36. Quintão, C., Andrade, P., Almeida, F.: How to improve the validity and reliability of a case study approach? J. Interdisc. Stud. Educ. **9**(2), 264–275 (2020)
37. Ramelot, J., Azevedo, D., Legay, A., Kieffer, S.: Toward interdisciplinary practice and increased social roi: a case study on downstream effects of integrating UX in cyber system design. In: Proceedings of the Annual Hawaii International Conference on System Sciences (2024)
38. Rosenbaum, S., et al.: What makes strategic usability fail? lessons learned from the field. In: CHI'99 Extended Abstracts on Human Factors in Computing Systems, pp. 93–94 (1999)
39. Salah, D., Paige, R.F., Cairns, P.: A systematic literature review for agile development processes and user centred design integration. In: Proceedings of the 18th International Conference on Evaluation and Assessment in Software Engineering - EASE '14 (October 2016), 1–10 (2014). https://doi.org/10.1145/2601248.2601276
40. Sauro, J., Johnson, K., Meenan, C.: From snake-oil to science: measuring UX maturity. In: Proceedings of the 2017 CHI Conference Extended Abstracts on Human Factors in Computing Systems, pp. 1084–1091 (2017)
41. Vykopal, J., Barták, M.: On the design of security games: From frustrating to engaging learning. In: ASE @ USENIX Security Symposium (2016)
42. Vykopal, J., Vizvary, M., Oslejsek, R., Celeda, P., Tovarnak, D.: Lessons learned from complex hands-on defence exercises in a cyber range. In: 2017 IEEE Frontiers in Education Conference (FIE). pp. 1–8. IEEE (2017). https://doi.org/10.1109/FIE.2017.8190713

Using a Digital Transformation to Improve Enterprise Security—A Case Study

David Brookshire Conner$^{(\boxtimes)}$ (iD)

University of Hawai'i at Mānoa, Honolulu, HI, USA
dbconner@hawaii.edu
http://www.hawaii.edu/

Abstract. In this case study, I review a specific digital transformation of the Hawai'i State Department of Education (HIDOE), over the time period from September 2017 to July 2021. While security was not a specific focus of the transformation, the transformation enabled the move to a single-sign-on authentication mechanism, which had substantial cybersecurity benefits. It facilitated investigations and substantially simplified both granting and revoking entitlements to sensitive systems. These systems had, among other concerns, major fiscal impact, and Federally mandated privacy requirements. These improvements occurred across the largest state agency in Hawai'i, serving more than 40,000 employees and approximately 175,000 students, with 257 schools, with at least one school on every island in the state with a permanent human population.

Keywords: Digital transformation · Enterprise architecture · Identity Management · Enterprise security

1 Introduction

In this case study, I review a major technology modernization effort undertaken at the Hawai'i State Department of Education (HIDOE), over the time period from September 2017 to July 2021. This effort was led by myself and implemented by a team of technologists reporting into me, as well as numerous other stakeholders across HIDOE. This case study thus represents first-person data, but is validated by both public records[1], public reporting, and independent peer-reviewed publications.

Technology modernization efforts, especially at large organizations, are often called a digital transformation, or a digital business transformation [9]. As with this transformation, most digital transformations focus on user functionality. The intent is to improve the organization's work by improving the tools, which in turn affects the processes used by the people in the organization. Better tools and better processes are intended to lead to more productive people, and hence a more capable organization.

---

[1] As a state agency, HIDOE is subject to "sunshine" laws, requiring key documents to be publicly available.

A. Moallem (Ed.): HCII 2024, LNCS 14728, pp. 232–244, 2024.
https://doi.org/10.1007/978-3-031-61379-1_15

The organization known locally as HIDOE is in fact the largest state government agency in Hawaii[2]. It employs more than 40,000 people. It educates approximately 175,000 students at 257 schools. If an island in the Hawaiian archipelago has a permanent population, it has at least one public school. Obviously, islands like Oʻahu with a substantial population have many schools, including multiple high schools. With an annual budget exceeding two billion dollars, HIDOE is large enough that, were it a for-profit corporation, it would compare in size to many Fortune 500 organizations. Hence, its overall technology environment very much fits into the realm of enterprise-scale technology.

Like many government agencies, HIDOE has had to work with limited budgets. Limited budgets would rightly be prioritized directly to the mission of the agency, which in this case is educating children. Given a choice between investing tens of thousands of dollars in new technology, and hiring another teacher, the choice is often straightforward. The teacher directly contributes to the mission. New technology often does not appear to, especially technology at the enterprise scale.

Prior to the digital transformation described here, staff would keep passwords for the numerous systems required to perform their jobs in physical notebooks, typically with a URL, login name, and full password. Every single school had separately implemented "shadow IT" solutions for email, using Google for Education to supplement the Lotus Notes[3] solution provided to some employees on an enterprise basis. Key systems, such as the core system-wide accounting system handling a multi-billion-dollar budget, were legacy systems (in the case of accounting, a thirty-year-old custom Cobol solution running on a mainframe). The Superintendent[4] determined that the technology for HIDOE needed to be modernized.

2   Choosing to Modernize

Accordingly, the Superintendent hired a new Chief Information Officer (CIO), this author [4]. Upon hiring, the Superintendent charged the CIO to present a five-year technology plan to the Board of Education for approval. This plan was to be presented within six months, or the soonest time thereafter that the Board agreed to place the subject on its agenda.

---

[2] For more on HIDOE, its official website is https://hawaiipublicschools.org/ and contains many documents on the current size, organization and more.

[3] For those unfamiliar, Lotus Notes was a database product providing email and custom application support. It was sold to IBM, and then to HCL. Lotus Notes requires a key file to be resident on a computer dedicated to a specific individual, making it impractical to use it for all employees at an enterprise like HIDOE. For instance, cafeteria and janitorial staff had no personally dedicated computer, and thus could not receive email using Lotus Notes.

[4] In a school district like HIDOE, the Superintendent is the senior-most executive, fulfilling a role equivalent to a Secretary in a Federal agency or a Chief Executive Officer in a corporation.

2.1   Developing the Plan

The interview process had identified multiple legacy technology systems, including the aforementioned Lotus Notes. For instance, interviewers asked the then-prospective CIO some carefully couched questions:

Interviewer: You may have noticed we use Lotus Notes...

The author: Yes, I noticed.[5]

Interviewer (with a suffering tone): Can you do anything about that?

The author (with a now enthusiastic tone): Absolutely! Let me tell you about how I helped transform the email at Estée Lauder Companies from an old Exchange system to Office 365.[6]

Having been part of prior digital transformations at other organizations, the author understood some of the work that would be necessary coming into a legacy-technology-rich environment [8]. Additional interview discussions identified several other areas. These included (but were not limited to) the following:

- A legacy accounting system running custom code on a mainframe.
- A legacy payroll system running on a VAX.[7]
- Custom systems for human resources support.
- Custom systems for student services support.
- Custom systems for bus scheduling.

Accordingly, the first day on the job consisted of starting the prioritization process of an already substantial list of individual modernization projects.

Two days later, one of a monthly series of leadership meetings was held, including all direct reports of the Superintendent (i.e., peers of the author) as well as all Complex Area Superintendents (or CASs). This leadership meeting included a "listening" session, where all members of the leadership team provided information on pain points in HIDOE's technology landscape.

CASs report to the Deputy Superintendent, a peer of Assistant Superintendents. Each CAS is responsible for two to four complexes. A complex consists of a high school and all the middle schools and elementary schools whose students would be zoned for that high school. The principal of each school in the complex reports to the CAS.

2.2   The Reporting Structure of HIDOE

Most digital transformations require engagement with stakeholders, [7] to ensure stakeholders buy in to the transformation by feeling that their concerns are being

---

[5] Not knowing yet whether HIDOE considered Lotus Notes a feature or a bug, the author was noncommittal in this initial answer.

[6] Now understanding that Lotus Notes was something that HIDOE wanted to move off of, the author could give a more direct answer.

[7] For those unfamiliar, the VAX is a server that was first introduced in 1977 and ended production in the early 1990s. One was preserved in a computer museum at the author's undergraduate university.

met. The engagement process with HIDOE bears some explanation, as HIDOE's organizational structure is unique in K12 education in the USA.

Most American states divide their K12 education system into a state-wide education agency (SEA) and several local education agencies (LEAs). LEAs are usually called "school districts" and a given state may have dozens or hundreds of districts. Each district usually has statutory authority to fund the district through property taxes. SEAs and LEAs both have to comply with Federal laws and regulations. The SEA must comply with state laws as well, and may set state regulations in addition. Aside from mandatory Federal reporting of educational data, and compliance with laws and regulations, the LEA is broadly independent of the SEA.

HIDOE is unusual in that it is both an SEA and an LEA. It does not have authority to fund itself through property taxes. Instead, it is funded primarily through general taxes in the state,[8] with funding specified by the state legislature. As a further consequence, every HIDOE employee ultimately reports into the Superintendent.

For example, a teacher at a school typically reports to that school's principal. The principal reports to the CAS for the complex in which their school is placed. The CAS reports to the Deputy Superintendent, who reports to the Superintendent. However, within their school, a principal has broad authority to make hiring decisions and determine reporting structure. A principal may have all teachers of a certain grade level report to a common person below the principal, or perhaps a similar organization by subject area.

This leads to a detail of HIDOE's structure that impacted stakeholder engagement. A principal has authority not only over hiring but also over most of their budget. A CAS may oversee the performance of the school, in terms of student outcomes. But if those outcomes meet or exceed expectations, the principal can take whatever approach they wish. Similarly, union agreements between the teachers' union and the principals' union provide teachers with substantial authority in how they teach and with substantial limits on principals' actions within a teacher's classroom. Thus, stakeholder engagement must occur at all levels of the organization.

2.3   Presenting the Plan

After a process of stakeholder engagement over six months, the plan for the transformation had been finalized. It was presented to the Education for discussion [6] on March 13, 2018. As a public agenda item, it was posted a week in advance, allowing anyone opportunity to review the material as preparation for possibly coming to provide public testimony. Since the plan did not require any policy changes, it was presented as a discussion item, not an item requiring formal motions, seconding, and voting. [11] The presentation [5] proceeded

---

[8] HIDOE also receives limited Federal funding, as most SEAs and LEAs do.

smoothly. It was apparent that it was an ambitious plan, but with opportunities to return to the Board for further input and oversight.[9]

As the principal of each school has substantial independent authority, the digital transformation plan was presented, less as a "digital transformation" (and therefore a massive change) but as an enterprise architecture encompassing the as-is state that would serve as a framework for discussing measured and incremental improvement.

It was felt that such an approach would be less likely to raise concerns. Readers of the minutes or the presentation will recognize that an enterprise architecture calling out what needs to change is in fact a roadmap for a digital transformation. By carefully phrasing of the presentation to allow for continued stakeholder input, the varied and autonomous stakeholders could feel that the change was something they could continue to steer. This was not simply wordplay. The intention was continued engagement, and that intention was in fact put into action as the plan was implemented.

It was also felt that, while enterprise architecture is well understood as a discipline and had been put into effect in government projects even a decade before, [1] the Board of Education did not have members experienced in the practice. Thus the plan was presented in largely non-technical terms. Further it was organized in a manner that would make it easy for someone familiar with HIDOE to map components to aspects of HIDOE the organization.

This enterprise architecture was thus presented in three tiers focused on organizational functional capabilities, to make it accessible to the non-technical Board as well as non-technical stakeholders such as the public. Under the acronym PIE, short for the "Playground for the Instructional Enterprise", capabilities were aligned with the organizational authority boundaries:

1. The Playground was the realm of the teachers, activities actually occurring in classrooms, such as attendance, instruction, and grading.
2. The Instructional layer was the school administration needs, such as enrollment, standardized test results, report cards, and school operation.
3. The Enterprise corresponded to state-wide shared functions, like hiring, financial operations, and shared technology.

Within this presentation, identity is called out as a foundational capability for large enterprises. Thus, while creating a single-sign-on was not identified as a key part of changes coming, it was identified as a necessary step, consistent with widely held best practices. [13] Given the existing practices, while a single-sign-on mechanism was thought to be something that would be appreciated, it was not highlighted because it did not have the perception of delivering as much organizational value as other areas.

Instead, consistent with the recommendations of many sources on digital transformations, [7,12] the focus was on improving products perceived by the

---

[9] In addition to the cited agenda and presentation materials, minutes of the meeting where the plan was presented are available from http://boe.hawaii.gov/ or directly from the Board of Education as an official document.

stakeholders as central to the organization's mission. Does this help us teach kids? If yes, then proceed. If no, maybe spend the time, money, and effort elsewhere.

3   The Transformation Timeline

This stakeholder focus thus helped define the timeline. There was clearly substantial concern about the technology team's ability to deliver improvements—the interview questions the author experienced about Lotus Notes demonstrated this. The leadership meeting also included robust feedback about responsiveness of the technology team. But specific products were identified too, including student information, and the core accounting system. The stakeholders also identified that all schools used Google for Education, but it had no central support from the technology team.

3.1   The Help Desk

Given the feedback about responsiveness from the technology team, it was apparent that changing that perception was paramount. Therefore, the first transformation in the plan was improved help desk support, through the implementation of ServiceNow. Implementing ServiceNow provided a unified experience where all end users could track the status of their request. As updates occurred, they were emailed to the requestor. Requestors could ask for help via phone, email, or logging into the system directly. The result was an early signifier that change, that improvement to technology was underway.

But ServiceNow's implementation was not just a public relations event. It was the first step in an enterprise architecture centered around an authentication approach able to become an enterprise-wide single-sign-on. The ServiceNow implementation included deployment of Azure ActiveDirectory as the authenticator for ServiceNow. Azure ActiveDirectory is an enterprise-scale product, as is ServiceNow itself.

But in order to serve as a foundation for single-sign-on, Azure ActiveDirectory needed to be provisioned for every possible user of ServiceNow, for every employee of HIDOE. There was only one data source for every employee, HIDOE's proprietary human resources system called eHR.[10] It included identifying information for everyone who received a paycheck, even part-time employees. A custom connector between Azure ActiveDirectory and eHR provided authentication for every single employee of HIDOE. Custodial staff, substitute teachers, part-time assistants, teachers hired but not yet started, all were supported.

The first step was made available within a few months of the Board of Education presentation.

---

[10] This legacy system was actively maintained by a local technology provider and less mission-focused than, say, student information. Thus, replacing it was lower priority than other systems.

3.2   Integrating the Student Information System

HIDOE makes use of a commercial product called Infinite Campus, produced by the company of the same name, as its student information system. Infinite Campus had been deployed a few years earlier, as the last major technology upgrade undertaken by the Department as a whole. As implemented at HIDOE at the start of the digital transformation, Infinite Campus was responsible for enrollment, attendance, and report cards,[11] or student information records.

For a K12 district, though, there is much more. Student support services, such as support for discipline tracking,[12] special education,[13] English learners,[14] and more. At HIDOE, student support services were tracked in a custom system at a cost to the Department of two million dollars per year. However, Infinite Campus provided comparable capabilities that were already licensed.[15]

Accordingly, a multi-year plan begun to move support services, one component at a time, into Infinite Campus. The first phase was enhance support for Infinite Campus to the end users by moving Infinite Campus's authentication to use the same Azure ActiveDirectory instance used by ServiceNow. Infinite Campus separately managed entitlements, ensuring that student information would not be shared inappropriately.

Single-sign-on for Infinite Campus deployed just prior to the start of the 2018–2019 school year, six months after the Board presentation.[16]

3.3   Implementing Google for Education

The next major modernization effort was replacing Lotus Notes. On the whiteboard list of technology projects the author created on his first day, one of them was replacing Lotus Notes with either Microsoft Office 265 or Google for Education. The assumption was that a "bake-off" would determine objectively which product was best suited.

The leadership meeting two days later made it clear what solution was correct, and the author erased Office 365 from the whiteboard. Other HIDOE leaders had explained that every single school in the state, all of them, had independently implemented Google for Education. Each school had gone to the trouble of implementing their own tenant. Each school had set up accounts for their own staff, and in some cases their own students. Clearly, the field wanted Google for Education, not Office 365.

---

[11] In educational environments, this is commonly known as "student information" and so Infinite Campus was referred to as a Student Information System (SIS), replacing the prior, custom solution called eSIS.

[12] Required for Federal reporting.

[13] Also required for Federal reporting.

[14] Again, mandatory reporting.

[15] Infinite Campus the company bundled the additional capabilities as part of other functionality that HIDOE was actively using.

[16] Operationally, school systems tend not to implement major technology changes during a time school is actively in session, as technology interruptions during instructional time could interfere with the core mission of instruction.

Accordingly, plans began to implement a single Google for Education tenant supporting all staff. Engineering meetings with Google showed that Azure ActiveDirectory not only could serve as the authenticator but could also be used to provision accounts. Given the existing Azure ActiveDirectory instance was already connected to eHR, this meant that HIDOE could automatically create a Google for Education account for every single person receiving a paycheck. This was a much more comprehensive provisioning of email, calendaring, and collaboration than possible with Lotus Notes, as Notes requires a dedicated computer per authorized user.[17]

In early 2019, this implementation was tested on a relatively small group of users, the approximately 175 people working on the HIDOE technology team. The thinking was that if it doesn't work for the technologists it will never work for anyone else. It did in fact work for the technologies. The implementation also tested activating Webex accounts for the same users. While Google supports Google Meet, HIDOE's network infrastructure is largely Cisco, and using a Cisco product was thought to be more manageable at scale.[18]

Shortly thereafter, testing was conducted on the same set of users, migrating existing Lotus Notes data into Google for Education. This also worked.[19]

During spring, announcements were made that Google for Education was coming, and that training was available. It was also announced that Lotus Notes was not being de-activated, to assuage the concerns of legacy Notes users uncomfortable with the change. Technology-savvy teachers leaned in and offered additional support and training.

In June, Google for Education accounts were created for every single employee.

During the month of July, every single day, the Lotus Notes data for approximately a thousand users was copied into Google for Education. By the end of the month, about 23,000 users' data had been copied, totaling several terabytes. The migration was complete. The Superintendent started using Google for Education as her primary email, and the rest of HIDOE quickly followed suit. The next phase was complete.

3.4   Modernizing the Accounting Section

HIDOE's core accounting system, named FMS (for Financial Management System), was based on custom COBOL code from the 1990's. It ran on a mainframe managed by another government agency, Enterprise Technology Services

---

[17] Which, in addition to being impractical for some users, came with a per-user licensing cost. At the time, Google for Education was free for LEAs, which the reader may recall is what HIDOE is.

[18] This turned out to be a prescient concern a year later when the demand for video conferencing multiplied by several orders of magnitude in a week.

[19] This led to the author's amusement at reading his earliest email in his Google for Education account, which started "Welcome to Lotus Notes!".

(ETS).[20] Mandatory security updates from IBM needed to be deployed to this mainframe.

In October of 2018, HIDOE's core accounting system underwent the mandated update, which did not successfully complete. FMS was completely online, and HIDOE's chief financial officer hand-wrote checks to major suppliers while FMS was offline. During a period of approximately three weeks, the State and HIDOE teams worked together to bring the legacy system back online. That was ultimately successful, but it was clear that replacing the system was now mandatory. A risk of outage had become an incident. The likelihood of another outage was deemed both likely and unacceptable. Accordingly, the planned schedule presented to the Board of Education early in 2018 was updated and presented for approval in 2019 [2]. This update also included the plans to implement Google for Education that summer.

During the summer of 2019, bids for replacement were submitted by vendors. The selection process continued into the fall, and a contract was signed in January 2020 for a vendor to implement Oracle Financials in the Cloud as quickly as possible. Implementation was completed in time for the new financial system to be used at the start of the following fiscal new year, July 1, 2021. In eighteen months, a multi-billion dollar organization had replaced its core accounting system. The cutover to the new system proceeded smoothly, and a month after the start of the new year, the legacy accounting system was de-activated and the substantial mainframe capacity was returned to ETS.[21]

Now, financial transactions were under single-sign-on as well. Most strategic systems had made the move behind a unified single-sign-on mechanism.

4   Security Improvements

Thus, over several years, strategic modernizations all implemented single-sign-on, including modernization of HIDOE's financial system to Oracle Financials in the Cloud, modernization of email and collaboration to an enterprise-wide Google for Education, implementation of universal video conferencing through Google Meet and Webex, and build out of the student information system based on Infinite Campus. This provided single-sign-on across major parts of HIDOE's technology, automatically provisioned.

The overall security benefits may be grouped into four areas:

1. Improved resilience, especially noted during the COVID-19 Pandemic

---

[20] ETS's mandate is to provide shared technology services across Hawai'i state agencies. The two largest agencies, HIDOE and the University of Hawai'i System are each larger than the rest of the state government and thus make limited use of ETS's services. The mainframe was one.

[21] This had a significant benefit to ETS, as the state's unemployment system was running and at the time of this writing was still running on the same mainframe. Due to the COVID-19 Pandemic, Hawai'i had very high unemployment, since the biggest industry in the state is tourism.

2. Easier and faster investigations
3. Cleaner revocation of access upon change of employment status
4. More effective incident response

4.1   COVID-19 and Resilience

The astute reader will have noticed that the dates of the migrations described above span the start of the COVID-19 Pandemic and the resulting lockdowns.

Organizations world-wide experienced substantial strain during this time. But in part because of the transformations that had occurred, HIDOE fared fairly well. This is not to say there were not impacts. The challenges for students learning remotely, the teachers teaching remotely, and the impact to learning were substantial. But HIDOE did it. We collectively continued to support children across the state.

The fact that Google for Education and Webex were widely available prior to the start of the lockdown was both fortuitous and an example of why such transformations are important. During the month of March, video conferences went from a few dozen **per week**[22] to tens of thousands **per day**.

As the pandemic continued, the unified environment provided a platform for providing access to students who had no tor insufficient technology at home. Even a family with a computer at home was challenged when parents and several children all need to video conference at the same time. Various COVID relief funding sources provided for mass delivery of ChromeBooks and iPads to students without sufficient access to devices at home. But onboarding and managing those devices would not be possible without the unified platform. It should be noted that the unified enterprise platform (aside from the financial system) was implemented entirely within budget—Federal funding bought devices for kids, but did not pay for the platform.

The Federal support was critical as HIDOE's funding comes from Hawaiʻi state tax revenue, which is derived largely from general taxes, including sales taxes. The COVID Pandemic prevented tourism and dramatically reduced the financial outlook across the state, which almost resulted in wide-spread furloughs. [3]

The unified environment also provided support to schools by reducing their need to configure technology for themselves. The unified Google for Education environment was connected to the student information system, Infinite Campus. This provided sufficient information to create accounts for every single student automatically. It also provided sufficient information to provide a Google Classroom for every class and automatically provision that Classroom with all appropriate students and teachers. Schools thus had the ability to focus on a new way of teaching, rather than on the technological logistics of making it possible to teach remotely at all.

---

[22] Hawaiʻi, being spread across several islands, found several valuable use cases for video conferences over plane flights.

In the end, the single-sign-on solution provided through the digital transformation of HIDOE was a critical provider of resilience in the face of a global catastrophe.

4.2   Benefits to Investigations

Moving to single-sign-on made investigations easier to undertake. Both as a public agency and simply as a large agency, investigations of possible misbehavior occurred frequently. Of course, not all investigations turned out to confirm misbehavior. But whatever the outcome of the investigation, it was easier to execute the electronic aspects knowing that most systems used the same identity for the same individual. Skilled digital investigators are familiar with this (it is literally textbook [10]) but it was a substantial benefit to the human resources team of HIDOE (who were skilled investigators, but not skilled in digital or forensic techniques).

In the event of lawsuits, the Office of the Attorney General may request data from HIDOE. Again, single-sign-on facilitated these requests. It made it simpler and more straight-forward to comply with discovery requests in a timely fashion, and to demonstrate the accuracy of the search results.[23] This eased the workload both on HIDOE's technology team and on the Attorney General's litigation team.

4.3   Benefits to Access Control

In some cases, an investigation would lead to some sort of human resources action. An employee may be suspended with pay during the investigation. An employee's employment may end because of the discoveries of the investigation. Having a single-sign-on mechanism covering the most strategic information systems both sped up this process and assured its accuracy. De-activate the single-sign-on identity of the person involved, and that person immediately loses all access.[24]

4.4   Benefits to Incident Response

Investigations due to lawsuits or alleged misbehavior are not the only place where single-sign-on provides substantial improvements in speed and effectiveness. Malware, cyberattacks, and unauthorized access attempts are all security incidents where having a stronger and cleaner sense of identity will be beneficial:

– If an identity is compromised, searching for what that compromised identity may have done is much simpler.

---

[23] Again, this is a textbook improvement, so this simply confirms that the benefit in fact occurred.

[24] This is another textbook improvement.

- Similarly, a compromised identity can be contained quickly by de-activation. The widespread locally created identities used in the legacy environment could not be quickly contained.
- Reseting a possibly compromised identity is similarly facilitated. One password can be reset, rather than dozens.

One could argue that single-sign-on can also facilitate things for attackers. After all, they only have one password to crack under a single-sign-on mechanism. However, password managers are widespread tools, meaning even with multiple logins and IDs, compromising one identity locally may be sufficient to compromise many systems, but without the ability to quickly revoke that access. Comprehensive single-sign-on is widely accepted as an overall improvement in incident response. [10,13]

5   Conclusions

By deploying value-added capabilities within an existing enterprise architecture grounded by single-sign-on, the digital transformation of HIDOE provided improved enterprise security. This included incident response, investigation, access control, and resilience. While resilience effects were most visible during the COVID-19 Pandemic, all areas of improvement proved valuable for the organization as a whole.

The transformation was undertaken in an extremely cost-effective manner, resulting in an successful and economical solution. [14] With additional costs incurred only by bringing on a major new financial system[25] and by the sudden and unanticipated need for at-home devices and network access driven by the COVID-19 lockdown, the entire transformation was undertaken within existing budget.

Many will opine that you can have any two of good, fast, or cheap, but not all three. But by rethinking your approach, it can be possible upend that platitude. You can have all three. No added budget (cheap). Less than five years (extremely fast for an enterprise of this scale). And current products set on a continuous upgrade path (good).

HIDOE's transformation, documented in this case study, demonstrates the effectiveness of well-considered change. Good, fast, cheap. And secure.

Acknowledgments. The author greatly appreciated the opportunity to serve the students of the great State of Hawai'i. Anywhere I went in the state, I would see one of our schools and realize my work was making things better. I would especially like to thank then-Superintendent Dr. Christina Kishimoto for her leadership, then-Assistant Superintendent of the Office of Human Resources, Barbara Krieg for the process of bringing me in, and every member of the Board of Education for their unpaid dedication to overseeing the work of the Department.

---

[25] Again, a not-unreasonable cost for a multi-billion-dollar budget.

Disclosure of Interests. The authors have no competing interests to declare that are relevant to the content of this article. While this work was performed as an employee of HIDOE, the author no longer has any association with HIDOE and receives no compensation or other recognition from the Department.

References

1. https://obamawhitehouse.archives.gov/node/18007
2. 18 April 2019. https://alala1.k12.hi.us/-STATE/-BOE/-Minutes.-nsf/-a15fa9df1-1029f-d70a2565-cb0065b-6b7/1aa04467e9-faab760a2-583f6007bc46b?-OpenDocument
3. 17 December 2020. https://alala1.k12.hi.us/-STATE/-BOE/-Minutes.nsf/-a15fa9df11029fd-70a2565cb0065b6b7/-ce605942f7ca-48820a25866a0-00dcd04?-OpenDocument
4. Hawaii DOE | Department announces appointments for top leadership positions. https://www.hawaiipublicschools.org/ConnectWithUs/MediaRoom/PressReleases/Pages/HIDOE-announces-appointments-for-top-leadership-positions.aspx
5. HI BOE Minutes, 13 March 2018. https://alala1.k12.hi.us/-STATE/-BOE/-Minutes.nsf/-a15fa9df-11029fd7-0a2565c-b0065b6b-7/9585c01-31538bd520a-25829-20000710e?-OpenDocument
6. FIC Presentation on Five-Year Technology Plan, March 2018 (March 2018). https://boe.hawaii.gov/Meetings/Notices/Meeting%20Material%20Library/FIC_03132018_4F%20Presentation%20on%20Overview%20of%20DOE%20OITS%20Five%20Year%20Technology%20Plan%20(rev).pdf
7. Hanna, N.K.: Mastering Digital Transformation: Towards a Smarter Society, Economy, City and Nation. Innovation, Technology and Education for Growth, 1st edn. Emerald Publishing Limited, Bingley (2016)
8. HCLTech: HCL takes Relationship Beyond the Contract with Estée Lauder Companies, September 2017. https://www.youtube.com/watch?v=J4HyDy1fyoA
9. Sacolick, I.: Driving Digital. AMACOM (2017)
10. Nelson, B., Phillips, A., Steuart, C.: Guide to Computer Forensics and Investigations, 6th edn. Cengage, Boston, MA (2019). oCLC: on1039396078
11. Robert, H.M., et al.: Robert's Rules of Order Newly Revised, 12th edn. Public Affairs, New York (2020). A new and enlarged edition edn
12. Satell, G., Kates, A., McLees, T.: 4 Principles to Guide Your Digital Transformation. Harvard Business Review (Nov 2021), https://hbr.org/2021/11/4-principles-to-guide-your-digital-transformation, section: Digital transformation
13. Sherwood, J.: Enterprise Security Architecture: A Business-Driven Approach, 1st edn. CRC Press, Boca Raton (2005). https://doi.org/10.1201/b17776
14. Shostack, A., Stewart, A.: The New School of Information Security. Addison-Wesley, Upper Saddle River (2008). oCLC: ocn181142577

Japanese Users' (Mis)understandings of Technical Terms Used in Privacy Policies and the Privacy Protection Law

Sachiko Kanamori[1]([✉]) [iD], Miho Ikeda[2] [iD], Kumiko Kameishi[2] [iD], and Ayako A. Hasegawa[1] [iD]

[1] National Institute of Information and Communications Technology, Tokyo, Japan
kanamori@nict.go.jp
[2] NTT Social Informatics Laboratories, Tokyo, Japan

Abstract. "Notice and Consent" has been a major practice used by service providers to make users give informed consent for their personal data to be processed; however, there are some barriers that prevent users from giving "true" consent. The most serious barrier is users' misunderstanding of the data processing procedures described in privacy policies. Tang et al. investigated the U.S. users' misunderstandings of technical terms used in privacy policies. In this paper, we conducted a replication study adapted to Japanese users. In addition, we investigated Japanese users' expectations of the Japanese privacy protection law. By conducting an online survey of 362 Japanese users, we found that less than half of the participants were able to correctly define 15 of the 20 technical terms in our main study. We also found that the technical terms of privacy policies significantly affect the user acceptance rate of policies. Furthermore, we identified that the participants have incorrect expectations of the law; they expect the law to provide more stringent data protection than the protection it actually provides. Based on our findings, we recommend that researchers and service providers should make substantial improvements in the documentation of privacy policies to prevent users' misunderstandings.

Keywords: Privacy policies · Technical terms · Privacy protection law

1 Introduction

Several research efforts have been made to give insight into user perceptions and reactions to privacy policies[1] and to emphasize the importance of usable privacy policies. However, users have still difficulties understanding privacy policies provided by actual services due to the length and complexity of such policies [4,18,19]. As a result, most users do not read privacy policies [16,21].

---

[1] In this paper, "privacy policy" refers to any document, such as privacy policy, personal information protection policy, or terms of service documents, that describes types of personal data processing by service providers.

A. Moallem (Ed.): HCII 2024, LNCS 14728, pp. 245–264, 2024.
https://doi.org/10.1007/978-3-031-61379-1_16

In 2021, Tang et al. [27] investigated the role of technical terms in policy transparency and found pervasive misconceptions among users in the U.S. Their results indicated that using technical terms in privacy policies is a barrier for users to give informed consent.

An important factor in user privacy-related misconceptions is user culture/na- tion. For instance, Herbert et al. [9] revealed that users' counties of residence are the most crucial factor affecting their misconceptions of privacy technologies such as virtual private networks (VPNs) and end-to-end encryption (E2EE). Furthermore, user privacy perceptions and expectations can also differ due to differences in culture [20, 28].

Based on these studies, we assume that the degree of user understanding of technical terms may differ between Western and Japanese users because the Japanese privacy perception and the laws and regulations in Japan are different from those in Western cultures [22]. Additionally, the representation of technical terms in Japanese has different characteristics from that in English. In this study, based on the study conducted by Tang et al. [27] on U.S. user (mis)understandings of technical terms, we conduct a similar investigation for Japanese users. Furthermore, inspired by the findings reported in [27] that many U.S. users misunderstand the term "privacy policy" as a document that guarantees protection and confidentiality of data, we assume that users may have incorrect expectations about data processing described in privacy policies. Specifically, we are concerned that Japanese users may have incorrect expectations about data processing implemented by service providers under the Act on the Protection of Personal Information [14][2] (hereinafter, we refer to this Act as "the law"). We address the following research questions (RQs):

RQ1 To what extent do Japanese users misunderstand the technical terms used in privacy policies, and how do they misunderstand them?

RQ2 To what extent and how do Japanese users misunderstand the privacy protection law?

We conducted an online survey of 362 Japanese participants. In this survey, we asked the participants to define 16 technical terms and investigated their willingness to accept privacy policies written in technical terms; additionally, we investigated their expectations of the law. We found that less than half of the participants were able to understand each technical term correctly and that the accuracy rates were significantly lower in Japan than those in the U.S. for most technical terms. In addition, we found that the acceptance rates of the privacy policies written in technical terms were significantly different from those written in non-technical explanatory language for three out of six technical terms. Furthermore, we found that a certain number of participants expect the law to provide more stringent data protection than the protection it actually provides; for example, 27% of the participants incorrectly believed that their personal data

---

[2] Act No. 57 of 2003, which is abbreviated as Act on the Protection of Personal Information.

could not be transferred to foreign third parties, at least not to unauthorized foreign countries.

By conducting an online survey of 362 Japanese users, we found that less than half of the participants were able to understand each technical term correctly. We also found that the technical terms of privacy policies significantly affect the user acceptance rate of such policies. Based on our findings, we propose support for users to accurately understand the technical terms and data processing under the law. Specifically, we propose the unification of different Japanese representations of technical terms; additionally, we identify those descriptions that users often misunderstand. Based on our results, we recommend cross-cultural studies on user misconceptions to be conducted and carefully designed support to be provided to address the discrepancies between user expectations and actual data processing procedures in different countries.

2   Related Work and Background

2.1   User Understanding of Privacy Policies

Considering that many users do not read the privacy policies [16,21], the factors that prevent users from reading or understanding such policies were investigated and discussed. For example, in 2017, Fabian et al. [4] presented the first large-scale study of nearly 50,000 privacy policies and showed that over 1,700 words and 70 sentences (on average) contained in those policies. They also found that to understand privacy policies, users had to be high-school graduates or needed to have attended some college years. Karegar et al. [19] reported that users find difficult it to comprehend lengthy and jargon-filled texts and ignore them. Service providers employ privacy policies to demonstrate compliance with legal requirements. Additionally, Kacsmar et al. [18] indicated that ambiguous term representations, such as "third parties" and "partners", with whom personal data are shared, may lead to user difficulties in understanding privacy policies.

To address the above factors, a format for improving the readability of privacy policies and a system that helps users to understand them was proposed [5–7,25]. For example, Gluck et al. [5] showed that short-form privacy notices lead to increased participant awareness of privacy practices. They also found that further condensing privacy notices to succinctly include only those practices that users are not generally aware of leads to the opposite results. Reinhardt et al. [25] proposed a visual interactive privacy policy that displays types of collected data, their usage, and user data disclosure. By conducting an empirical evaluation, they showed that visual representations received higher attractiveness, stimulation, novelty, and transparency scores than those received from a standard long text.

2.2   User Misconceptions of Privacy-Enhancing Technologies

It has been reported that user misconceptions of privacy technologies may prevent them from adopting these technologies or using them correctly. For example,

Abu-Salma et al. [2] investigated user understanding of E2EE encryption and found that user misconceptions inhibit them from using it. In addition, Story et al. [26] conducted a survey on user understanding of five privacy-enhancing technologies, such as VPN and Tor, and found that users thought that these technologies provide privacy protection and protection from security threats. Wu et al. [29] demonstrated that users overestimate the private mode browsing protection by wrongly assuming that using this browsing mode prevents geolocation, ads, and viruses from being tracked by the websites visited and the network provider. Subsequently, based on the above studies, Herbert et al. [9] investigated and compared user (mis)conceptions of privacy-enhancing technologies in 12 countries. They found that the most important factor affecting user misconceptions is the user's country of residence and highlighted the importance of conducting cross-cultural research on user misconceptions.

2.3 Original Study

Here we review the original study conducted by Tang et al. [27] on which we conducted a replication study. Tang et al. [27] (hereinafter, referred to as the "the original study") examined the impact of using technical terms on the transparency of privacy policies for U.S. users. Initially, starting in June 2020, they manually analyzed Alexa's top 10 U.S. websites and selected apps from the Android Play Store to identify the technical terms appearing in privacy policies. Next, they conducted a pilot user study by showing sentences of privacy policies containing technical terms to participants and asking them to define these terms in their own words. In the main survey ($N = 800$), the participants were asked to select the correct definition of 20 technical terms among several options that included the common misconceptions identified in the pilot study. The results showed some pervasive misunderstandings among U.S. users; for 15 of the 20 technical terms, less than half of the participants could define the term correctly. They also showed that using technical terms in privacy policies affected the comfort level and acceptance rate of participants by comparing the participant responses to the policies with and without technical terms.

2.4 Representation of Technical Terms in Japan

Service providers provide privacy policies in different languages across the globe; therefore, language issues may arise in the communication between users and service providers.

For example, the Japanese language has different characteristics from the English language; this may prevent Japanese users from understanding the meaning of the technical terms. Japanese words are written using three types of characters: kanji (Japanese-Chinese characters), hiragana, and katakana [8,11]. Kanji is an ideogram, whereas hiragana and katakana are phonograms. In Japanese, words loaned from foreign languages, including technical terms related to computers and the Internet, are often written in katakana. For example, the technical term *"tracking"* can be written in two ways in Japanese, " " (kanji) and

" ' (katakana); however, in Japanese privacy policies, it is often written using katakana (" ") characters. In kanji, " " means "trace" and " " means "trail"; thus, people can easily infer that the meaning of " " is "trace the trail." On the other hand, katakana is a phonogram that only represents the sound of an English technical term; thus, it is difficult for users to infer the meaning of a term from katakana " " unless one knows the meaning.

3   Methodology

3.1   Survey Structure

We conducted an online survey to quantitatively measure the misunderstanding of technical terms and the laws among Japanese users. Our survey includes four parts: (I) comprehension of technical terms used in privacy policies, (II) acceptance of policies, (III) user expectations of the Japanese privacy protection law, and (IV) demographic data. Parts I and II are a replication study of the original study, whereas Part III is our study. Each part was included in a separate questionnaire page; the participants were not allowed to return to previous parts to review their questions or modify their answers.

Since the questionnaire in the original study was written in English, two authors of this paper translated it into Japanese. The meanings in the translated questionnaire were the same as those in the original questionnaire, and the sentences were in natural Japanese. We conducted a pilot study in two phases, as described in Sect. 3.3, and confirmed that the Japanese participants appropriately understood our questionnaire.

3.2   Questionnaire Design

Part I: Comprehension of Technical Terms. In part I, we asked the participants to select the best description for the definitions of 16 technical terms[3] These terms are shown in Fig. 1. To determine the corresponding Japanese definitions of each original English technical term, we initially examined 14 popular global services that publish privacy policies in both English and Japanese. These services are ranked in Alexa Japan's Top 100. We also examined the translation of GDPR [13].

As described in Sect. 2.3, the options provided for incorrect answers were obtained from the participant misconceptions of the pilot study included in the original study. For example, the options provided for the definition of "*privacy policy*" consisted of one correct answer "It is a legal document that says how users' data will be collected and used," three incorrect answers "It explains how your data will be protected," "It explains how the company keeps confidential the

---

[3] We excluded several terms, such as "*PII (Personally Identifiable Information)*", "*personal information*," and "*anonymized information*", for the Japanese participants because the definitions of these terms are different under the law, the general data protection regulation (GDPR), and California consumer privacy act (CCPA).

information it collects on users," "It says that the company will not share users' data with other sites or companies without permission," and "I don't know." The questions and options were presented in a random order. We asked the participants to select the best description for the definitions of terms without using an Internet search similar to the original study. We also asked the participants to select "I don't know" honestly in case they did not know the answer.

Part II: Acceptance of Policies. In part II, six policy sentences containing a technical term or its corresponding explanation were presented to the participants. Then, the participants were asked to rate the likelihood of acceptance of each policy on a 5-point Likert Scale (from "very unlikely" to "very likely"). The six terms used in the survey are presented in Table 4. We divided the participants into two groups: 1) participants presented with policies written in technical terms and 2) participants presented with policies written in non-technical explanatory language (i.e., a between-participant design[4]). The questions were presented in a random order. We inserted an attention check in the middle of Part II.

Part III: Expectations of the Privacy Protection Law. Part III consisted of two parts: 1) questions asking the participants to best describe data processing employed by online services under the Japanese privacy protection law and 2) questions asking the participants whether the personal information they were presented is defined as "sensitive personal information" according to the law. In the first group of questions, the participants were asked about four data processing; data provision of pseudonymized personal information, data provision of anonymized personal information, data transfer to foreign third parties, and data usage of users with no account. We will explain the correct answers to these questions in Sect. 4.3. All four authors of this paper, including two law experts, carefully discussed the design of the questionnaire in this part of the survey. The definitions of legal terms, such as pseudonymized personal information, were initially presented to the participants. Then, the participants were asked about their expectations of data processing. Similar to Part I, the participants were asked to provide their answers without using an Internet search and to select "I don't know" honestly in case they did not know the answer.

Part IV: Demographics Data. In the last part of the questionnaire, the participants were asked to provide their demographic data, i.e., age, gender, occupation, educational background, and experience in computer science (CS) education and/or jobs.

3.3 Recruitment and Ethical Considerations

Recruitment. Our survey was assessed and approved by the Institutional Review Board (IRB). We initially conducted a pilot study, which included seven members of our laboratory, to ensure that Japanese participants appropriately

---

[4] The original study employed a within-participant design; here, we employed a between-participant design to reduce the anchoring effect.

Table 1. Participants' Demographic Information.

		Original [27]	Ours	Japan Stat [15]
Age	18–24	5.5%	3.0%	8.0%
	25–34	44.4%	21.8%	12.0%
	35–44	27.9%	37.6%	14.4%
	45–59	17.1%	32.3%	25.0%
	60–74	5.0%	5.2%	23.2%
	75+	0.1%	0.0%	17.4%
Gender	Male	60.8%	62.7%	48.2%
	Female	38.8%	37.0%	51.8%
	Other/No	0.5%	0.3%	N/A

*The denominator is the total population aged 18+.

understood our questionnaire. Then, in April 2023, we recruited participants through Lancers [12], which is a widely used Japanese crowdsourcing service.

Our survey title was "Survey on the Use of Online Services." We did not use the term "privacy" in the survey title to avoid recruiting only the participants who were particularly interested in privacy. In the survey instructions, we explained the purpose of the survey, the data processing procedure, and the usage of the collected data. We also explained that the amount of compensation does not depend on the participant's performance in answering the questions. The participants agreed to voluntarily participate in the survey. Based on the above-mentioned pilot study, we estimated that the completion time of the survey would be 20 min and set the amount of compensation to 400 yen[5], which is sufficiently higher than the minimum wage in Japan.

Initially, we recruited 40 participants to verify that the assumed completion time and the compensation amount were sufficient. Additionally, we ensured that the questions or options were not difficult for participants to understand. Next, we recruited the remaining participants. Considering that the participant demographics could be biased, depending on the date and time of recruitment, we separated them into three groups of different days and times. Finally, we analyzed the valid responses obtained from 362 participants who passed the attention check. We stored the collected data confidentially by allowing access to only a limited number of people.

Participants' Demographics. The demographic data of the recruited participants ($N = 362$) are presented in Table 1. Our participants skewed male, similar to those in the original study, but our populations showed less of a younger skew. The percentage of the University graduate participants was 60.5%, and the percentage of the participants with experience in CS education and/or jobs

---

[5] Considering that Lancers deduct a commission from the workers' compensation, we carefully set the compensation amount so that a worker's actual compensation after deducting the commission would be 400 yen.

was 11.0%. In addition, we ensured no substantial differences in the distribution of age, gender, education, and CS experience between the two groups in our between-participant design.

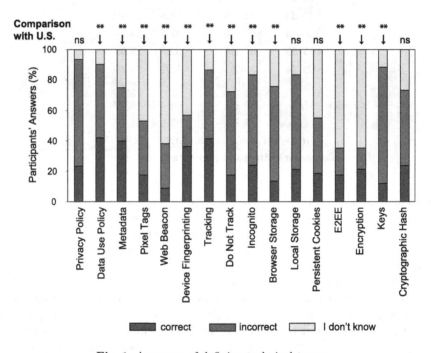

Fig. 1. Accuracy of defining technical terms.

For each term, we conducted a Chi-square test to compare the percentage of correct answers given by the Japanese and U.S. participants. Regarding significance levels, * indicates that the original p-value is under the 0.05 cutoff value but above the threshold value after applying the Benjamini-Hochberg multiple comparison correction. ** indicates the p-values under the threshold value, even after applying the multiple comparison correction.

4   Results

4.1   RQ1: Comprehension of Technical Terms

To address RQ1, we compared the percentage rate of the correct answers given to the definitions of the technical terms and the acceptance rate of the policies between the Japanese and U.S. participants. Then, we analyzed the characteristics specific to Japanese participants. The comparison was performed by obtaining detailed data, including the percentage rate of the given correct answers, coding rules, and contents of incorrect answers, from the authors of the original study.

Figure 1 shows the distributions of the Japanese participant responses to the definitions of the technical terms. Overall, the knowledge of the Japanese participants on technical terms was lower than that of the U.S. participants; for 12 of the 16 terms, the accuracy achieved by the Japanese participants was significantly lower than that of the U.S. participants. Of the 16 terms we studied, three terms were correctly defined by more than half of the U.S. participants; in contrast, no term was correctly defined by more than half of the Japanese participants. Specifically, the Japanese participants tended to select "I don't know."

Table 2 shows the percentage rates of the terms incorrectly defined by more than half of the Japanese participants; it also shows some common misconceptions. Specifically, they incorrectly believed that the term "*access key*" allows users to access their account without logging in every time; additionally, they believed that when using "*Do Not Track*", the websites they visit cannot track them. We found that the Japanese participants tended to expect that the technical terms were more secure than their actual definitions. For example, they incorrectly believed that the term "*privacy policy*" explains how a company keeps the information it collects from users confidential; additionally, they believed that when using "*private browsing/incognito mode*," the websites they visit cannot track them, and their browsing data are not saved. Such misconceptions may lead to user data being processed despite the user's will; therefore, the participants need support to clarify such misconceptions.

Next, we investigated whether there are common misconceptions between the Japanese and U.S. participants. For this purpose, we compared the responses given by the participants to 13 technical terms for which multiple incorrect options were provided. The results are presented in Table 3. We found almost identical misconceptions between the Japanese and U.S. participants; the most common misconceptions in each country were the same for 11 technical terms, excluding "*web beacon*" and "*persistent cookie*". Many Japanese participants incorrectly believed that a "*web beacon*" identifies data belonging to a specific user and that "*persistent cookie*" is deleted when users close the tab or navigate away from the website. For "*metadata*", "*pixel tags*", and "*local storage*", the most common misconceptions were the same between the Japanese and U.S. participants; however, the second most common misconceptions in each country differed. For example, the second most common misconception of the term "*local storage*" among the U.S. participants was that user data is stored on machines located locally; additionally, the percentage of the participants who incorrectly believed that the word "local" means a physical place was higher in the U.S. participants than in the Japanese participants.

For 12 terms, the percentage of the participants who answered correctly significantly differed between the Japanese and U.S. participants (Fig. 1). The biggest difference was found in the following terms: "*E2EE*" (U.S. participants: 44.5%, Japanese participants: 17.1%),"*private browsing/incognito mode*" (U.S. participants: 46.8%, Japanese participants: 24.0%), and "*device fingerprinting*" (U.S. participants: 56.5%, Japanese participants: 36.1%). Since it is difficult to

Table 2. Technical terms with higher incorrect answer rates.

Technical terms and incorrect answer rates	The most common incorrect answers and their rates
Key (76.5%)	Information that allows users to access their account without logging in every time. (61.3%)
Privacy policy (70.4%)	It explains how the company keeps confidential the information it collects on users. (37.3%)
Local storage (62.2%)	User data stored on machines or servers that are onsite to the company. (30.9%)
Browser web storage (61.9%)	Users' information can be stored on any machine or server. (26.5%)
Private browsing /Incognito mode (59.4%)	When using private browsing/incognito mode, data from their browsing session stored nowhere. (37.6%)
Do Not Track (55.0%)	If a user submits a Do Not Track request, the web- site cannot track the user. (55.0%)

identify why the percentage rates of the correct answers to these terms are particularly low in Japan based only on this survey, it is necessary to investigate the effect of dark patterns caused by the katakana representations [10], the appearance rate of each term in privacy policies, and the differences in security education between the Japanese and U.S. participants. For example, U.S. users may be able to infer the technical meaning of "end-to-end" and "fingerprinting", even if their knowledge of technical terms is low; however, the Japanese users may not be able to infer the meanings from the katakana representations as mentioned in Sect. 2.4. For the terms "end-to-end encryption," "encryption," and "web beacon," more than half of the Japanese participants selected "I don't know." This indicates that Japanese users are either unfamiliar with these terms or find them difficult to understand.

In the original study, 71% of the U.S. participants incorrectly believed that "privacy policies" guarantees data protection, confidentiality, or consent. On the other hand, when the participants were asked to provide the definition of "data use policy," only 39% of the participants selected incorrect answers. Considering these results, it was proposed that companies should adopt the alternative term "data use policy" instead of "data use policy." However, in Japan, less than half of the participants correctly answered the definition of "data use policy." Therefore, the alternative term is ineffective in Japan.

We also analyzed the relation between participant demographics and the accuracy of the definitions of the technical terms. Initially, we performed a t-test to determine the differences in the accuracy rates between the participants with and without a CS background. 33.8% (on average) of the participants with a CS background correctly defined the technical terms, whereas the percentage of the participants without a CS background who correctly defined the technical terms

Table 3. Technical terms for which the Japanese and the U.S. participants had different misconceptions.

Terms	Country	Common misconceptions and their rates*	
Web Beacon	U.S.	1st	A tool transports data between servers. (38.0%)
		2nd	A tool allows companies to access user's device. (34.7%)
	Japan	1st	Identifies data belongs to a specific user. (61.3%)
		2nd	A tool transports data between servers. (22.6%)
Persistent Cookies	U.S.	1st	Deleted when users close their browser. (40.3%)
		2nd	Deleted when users sign out of the website. (35.3%)
	Japan	1st	Not deleted until users close the tab or navigate away from the website. (44.4%)
		2nd	Deleted When users close their browser. (30.6%)
MetaData	U.S.	1st	A set of data or information. (35.4%)
		2nd	A large collection of data. (30.4%)
	Japan	1st	A set of data or information. (42.5%)
		2nd	Combined data from different sources. (32.3%)
Pixel Tag	U.S.	1st	A way to identify an image. (45.6%)
		2nd	A small piece of color in an image. (30.6%)
	Japan	1st	A way to identify an image. (52.7%)
		2nd	A way to identify which people are in an image. (36.4%)
Local Storage	U.S.	1st	User data stored on machines onsite to the company (30.9%)
		2nd	User data stored on machines in their local area. (33.1%)
	Japan	1st	User data stored on machines onsite to the company (65.9%)
		2nd	User data stored on any machine/server. (22.9%)

*Rate indicates the percentage of the participants who selected the option "out" of all participants who answered incorrectly (i.e., we excluded the participants who answered and correctly selected "I don't know").

was 23.1%; this difference is statistically significant ($p < .001$). Next, for each term, we performed a Chi-square test to determine a possible percentage difference between the participants with a CS background who correctly defined the technical terms with those without a CS background (the Benjamini-Hochberg multiple comparison correction was applied). We found significant differences for the terms "*browser web storage*," "*local storage*," "*device fingerprinting*," and "*web beacon*."

Regarding the age groups, 22.7% (on average) of the participants aged 18–24 correctly defined the terms; the corresponding percentages of the participants aged 25–34, 35–44, 44–59, and 60–74 were 24.5%, 23.6%, 24.3%, and 29.3%, respectively. The t-test results showed no significant differences among the age groups ($p = 0.289$). In general, it has been found that older people have limited knowledge of the security and privacy [1] terms; however, older people registered with crowdsourcing are exceptionally knowledgeable [24]. Our results are consistent with those reported in these studies, i.e., we did not find evidence that older Japanese people have significantly lower knowledge of the technical terms used in privacy policies than younger people.

4.2 RQ1: Acceptance Rate of Policies Written in Technical Terms

Table 4 shows the participants' average acceptance rate of the policies written in technical terms and the policies written in non-technical terms. Importantly,

Table 4. Average acceptance rate of policies (written in tech vs. non-tech language).

	Japan			U.S. [27]		
	Acceptance (Tech)	Acceptance (Non-tech)	p-value	Acceptance (Tech)	Acceptance (Non-tech)	p-value
Web beacon	**2.58**	1.91	<0.001*	2.66	2.43	0.069
Tracking	**2.62**	2.35	0.013*	2.82	2.64	0.105
Session cookie	3.30	3.25	0.608	3.17	3.17	1.000
Persistent cookie	3.05	3.07	0.862	2.91	2.81	0.416
E2EE	3.72	3.76	0.680	4.08	4.04	0.747
Encryption	3.18	**3.86**	<0.001*	2.94	**3.66**	<0.001*

We converted the participants' responses expressed on the Likert scale to a numerical scale, i.e., we set "very unlikely" to 1 and "very likely" to 5. We conducted a t-test to compare the participants' acceptance rates of privacy policy written with technical terms and written with the corresponding non-technical explanatory language. * indicates that the p-value is under 0.05. Note that in the original study, paired t-tests were performed because the within-participant design was adopted, whereas we performed unpaired t-tests because we adopted the between-participant design.

in Japan, significant differences in the acceptance rates between policies written in technical terms and policies written in non-technical terms were found for three out of the six terms. Thus, we demonstrated that using technical terms in privacy policies affects the acceptance rate of Japanese participants and becomes a barrier to "true" consent. As described in Sect. 4.1, the low correct answer rate of the Japanese participants for defining technical terms leads to significant differences in the acceptance rates.

In the original study, it was found that if common user misconceptions fail to appreciate the security and privacy policy provided by a company, users accept a policy written in non-technical explanatory language more easily than a policy written in technical terms. In other cases, if common user misconceptions fail to appreciate the full scope of data use practices, users are significantly less comfortable with a policy written in non-technical explanatory languages than a policy written in technical terms. We analyzed the participants' responses and acceptance rates and found the same tendency among the Japanese participants.

We conducted a further analysis for the participants who were provided with policies written in technical terms. Specifically, for each term, we performed t-tests to find the difference in the average acceptance rates between the participants who answered correctly and those who answered incorrectly. No significant difference was found in any of the terms. Combining the two results, i.e., (i) significant differences in the acceptance rates between policies written in technical terms and policies written in non-technical terms for three out of six terms and (ii) no significant difference in the acceptance rates between those who provided the correct definition of a term and those who provided an incorrect definition, it is possible that Japanese participants are more likely to think seriously about sharing their data, regardless of the accuracy of their understanding of the terms when they are provided with policies written in non-technical terms.

4.3   RQ2: Expectations of Data Processing Under the Law

Table 5. Expectations of data handling under the law.

Provision of pseudonymized personal information to other companies	
Prohibited.	**18.0%**
Allowed if with appropriate informed consent	42.5%
Allowed without informed consent	10.5%
I don't know.	29.0%
Provision of anonymized personal information to other companies	
Prohibited	16.6%
Allowed if with appropriate informed consent	36.5%
Allowed without informed consent.	**24.3%**
I don't know.	22.7%
Data transfer to foreign third parties	
Prohibited	13.5%
Not allowed to unauthorized countries	13.5%
Allowed if with appropriate informed consent	**49.2%**
Allowed without user consent	1.9%
I don't know	21.8%
Data usage of users with no accounts	
Cannot collect due to no consent to PP	9.4%
Can collect, but cannot utilize due to no consent to PP	40.6%
Can collect and utilize as described in PP	**34.3%**
I don't know	15.7%

The bold items show the best description of the Japanese privacy protection law (Act on Protection of Personal Information [14]). PPs: privacy policies.

Table 5 shows the options for data handling under the law and the participants responses.

Pseudonymized/Anonymized Personal Information. The Act on the Protection of Personal Information(APPI), which was promulgated in 2003, enforced in 2005, and last revised in 2023, lays down the scope of personal information and the duties of entities handling personal information in order to protect the rights and interests of individuals. In APPI, "Pseudonymized personal information" means information related to an individual can be prepared in a way that makes it impossible to identify the individual unless collated with other information. "Anonymized personal information" means information related to an individual can be prepared in a way that makes it impossible to identify the individual; it also makes it impossible to restore personal information. In 2019, the European Commission decided that Japan provides an adequate level of personal data protection for personal data to be transferred from the EU to a foreign country. Notably, no concept in the GDPR exactly matches either "pseudonymized personal information" or "anonymized personal information."

As shown in Table 5, for both pseudonymized personal information and anonymized personal information, less than a quarter of the participants correctly answered data handling under the law. Furthermore, the percentage of the participants who correctly answered was lower than the percentage of the participants who incorrectly believed that pseudonymized personal information could be transferred to other companies with their consent. It is also remarkable that although the provision of anonymized personal information to other companies without consent is permitted, some participants believed that it could not be conducted. This discrepancy between user expectations and the law may lead to the transfer of anonymized personal information against the user's will. Such unexpected data transfer can be problematic in terms of the user's right to control their own information and their right to privacy.

Data Transfer to Foreign Third Parties. Under the law, service providers can provide user personal data to a third party in a foreign country by obtaining user consent after providing information about the name of the foreign country and the personal data protection system of the country. Approximately half of the participants (49.2%) correctly answered this question. However, over a quarter (27%) incorrectly believed that service providers could not transfer user data to foreign countries (or at least to unauthorized countries). This result indicates that users may unintentionally consent to unexpected data handling if they do not carefully read privacy policies. In fact, some service providers use cloud services and social media provided by foreign companies or outsource their services to foreign countries to improve business efficiency and service quality.

Data Usage of Users with No Account. We asked participants how service providers process user information when users just browse websites without creating an account on the website. 34.3% of the participants correctly believed that service providers collect information about user devices and use the data as described in their privacy policies[6]. Half of the participants incorrectly believed that service providers do not collect or use user information. This misconception may lead to data processing against the user's will. Actually, we confirmed that some services in Japan collect and use the device information and browsing history of users with no account. Note that the best description for this question is that service providers cannot collect personal information due to no consent to a privacy policy under GDPR. Websites designed in accordance with GDPR display informed consent forms for the collection of personal information, including cookies, when users browse these websites for the first time. User experience of

---

[6] According to APPI, the data of a user who does not have an account are considered as "information related to personal information," meaning information related to a living individual which cannot be categorized as personal information, pseudonymized personal information, or anonymized personal information; however, the user past data are regarded as personal information after the user creates an account.

such an informed consent form may lead them to believe that Japanese service providers cannot collect or use the information of users with no account without their consent.

Table 5 shows that 41.3% (on average) of the participants with CS education and/or work experience correctly answered the questions, whereas 30.2% (on average) of the participants without CS experience correctly answered the questions. This difference is statistically significant ($p = 0.005$). On the other hand, there was no significant difference among age groups ($p = 0.958$).

4.4   RQ2: Expectations of "Sensitive Personal Information."

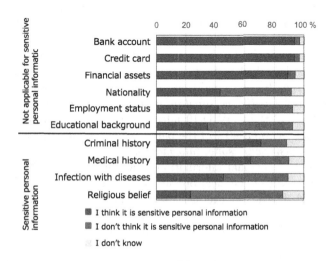

Fig. 2. Expectations of "Sensitive Personal Information."

APPI defines certain information as "Sensitive personal information" that requires special care so as not to cause unjust discrimination, prejudice, or other disadvantages to a person (Article 2, Paragraph 3 of the law) [14]. Figure 2 shows the participant responses to whether each factor of personal information is classified as "*sensitive personal information.*" Overall, we found discrepancies between participant expectations of "*sensitive personal information*" and the actual law.

Approximately 90% of the participants incorrectly believed that financial information (e.g., bank accounts, credit cards, and income) is "*sensitive personal information.*" On the other hand, even though religious beliefs are defined as "*sensitive personal information,*" only 14.4% of the participants correctly believed that they are classified as "*sensitive personal information.*" Our results indicate that the participants may assess personal information as "*sensitive personal information*", considering the economic loss if their personal data are leaked. The Japan Network Security Association (JNSA) [17] noted that the impact of personal data leakage can be quantified by two scales; economic loss and privacy. For example, bank account and credit card data are rated three out of three on the economic loss scale; financial asset data are rated two out of three points on the economic loss scale. Almost all participants regarded these data as "*sensitive personal information.*" On the other hand, religious beliefs and infection with diseases are rated one out of three points on the economic loss scale and three out of three points on the privacy scale[7]; nationality and educational background are rated one out of three points on the economic loss scale and two out of three points on the privacy scale. In our survey, not many participants regarded religious beliefs, infection with diseases, nationality, and educational background as "sensitive personal information."

These results indicate that two issues may arise due to user misconception of "*sensitive personal information.*" The first issue is that users may have an excessive expectation that service providers strictly protect finance-related data[8], as shown in our survey. This is because, according to our survey, a certain number of participants expected the law to provide stricter data protection than it actually does, as described in Sect. 4.3, and incorrectly regarded the financial information as "*sensitive personal information.*" The second issue is that users may disregard the "*sensitive personal information*" of others. For example, users may carelessly reveal the COVID-19 infection history of their colleagues without their consent, as about 40% of the participants regarded that infection with diseases is not "*sensitive personal information.*"

For each type of personal information shown in Fig. 2, 40.3% (on average) of the participants with CS education and/or work experience provided the correct answer, and 36.8% (on average) of the participants without CS experience provided the correct answer. This difference is not statistically significant ($p = 0.174$), contrary to the accuracy of defining technical terms (Sect. 4.1) and data handling under the law (Sect. 4.3). In fact, among the 10 types of personal information, no significant difference in the correct answers was observed between the participants with CS experience and those without CS experience (the Benjamini-Hochberg multiple comparison correction was applied). Additionally, no significant difference in the correct answers was observed among age groups ($p = 0.277$).

5   Discussion

5.1   Promoting Japanese User Understanding of Technical Terms

In this study, we found that Japanese participants have less knowledge of privacy-related technical terms than U.S. participants and that the use of technical terms

---

[7] In particular, almost all data items rated one out of three points on the economic loss scale; three out of three points on the privacy scale are defined as "*sensitive personal information*" under the law or sensitive personal information under a guideline [3].

[8] The guideline [3] restricts the handling of "*sensitive personal information*" under the law and sensitive information under the guideline. Note that it does not restrict the handling of another factor of information such as bank account data.

in privacy policies significantly affects their acceptance rate. However, we believe that these findings do not necessarily mean that the potential security and privacy skills of Japanese users are lower than those of U.S. users. We consider that the following two problems affect Japanese users' misunderstanding of technical terms. First, as mentioned in Sect. 2.4, in Japan, English technical terms are usually represented by katakana characters; such representations are difficult for Japanese users to predict their meaning. Recently, Hidaka et al. revealed that such a representation issue acts as a dark pattern to deceive users and that such representations are actually included in Japanese apps [10]. Second, in Japan, the same technical term is sometimes expressed in different representations by different services. We showed that different services use different Japanese representations in their privacy policies, e.g., " " and " " for the English term *"pixel tags."*

In the original study, it was proposed to add explanatory definitions to privacy policies, either in dedicated sections or in combination with interactive elements such as hover. This intervention is considered effective for the first issue mentioned above. However, in Japan, the second issue requires a different approach. We believe that an academic-industrial collaboration approach is needed; specifically, experts should standardize Japanese representations of technical terms and encourage service providers to use these representations.

5.2   Promoting Japanese Users' Understanding of the Law

This study revealed the Japanese participants' misunderstanding of both the definition of technical terms and the Japanese privacy protection law. Particularly problematic is the fact that a certain number of Japanese participants expect the law to provide stricter data protection than it actually does, which may lead to unexpected user data handling. In 2016, Rao et al. [23] showed that user expectations of data practices included in online services do not match the actual data practices of the services. For example, although users expect financial websites to collect only financial data and health websites to collect only health data, financial websites sometimes collect health information. Although the discrepancies between user expectations and actual data practices reported by Rao et al. are limited to certain categories of online services, our results indicate a more serious issue; users have a fundamental misconception of data practices, regardless of the service category. For example, 27% of the participants incorrectly believed that their data could not be transferred to foreign third parties, at least not to unauthorized foreign countries. As data sharing between companies has become more active due to AI-powered large-scale data analysis, legal but unexpected user data handling may increase. Users' misunderstanding of the data handling stipulated by the law can be a barrier to true informed consent when users agree to a privacy policy without reading it carefully.

To address such users' misunderstandings, service providers should not only clearly explain the purpose of data collection for each data item in their privacy policies but also highlight those data practices that many users misconceive, such as when service providers transfer a user's personal data to a third party in a foreign country, or when they collect and use information that users incorrectly regard as *"sensitive personal information"* (e.g., bank account information). Service providers can accomplish this by highlighting the data practice and independent confirmation buttons for each data practice. To motivate service providers to implement these interventions, Ministries and relevant industry associations need to establish appropriate guidelines. On the other hand, the above interventions do not address the Japanese user misunderstanding that user data cannot be collected and used while browsing without an account. A possible solution is to publish educational content for users to explain the law and, in particular, the type of data processing that service providers can do under the law. It is important to note that service providers need to tailor these measures to each country, as privacy laws and regulations and user expectations are likely to be different in different cultures/countries.

5.3 Limitations and Future Work

Although our survey provides much insight into users' misunderstandings of technical terms and the law, it has several limitations.

First, in our replication survey of the original study (RQ1), it is difficult to conduct a perfect comparison of the results between the Japanese and the U.S. participants because of the difference in the timing of the surveys and the demographics of the participants. However, as indicated in Table 1, the participants' demographics used in our study and those used in the original study are similar regarding the proportion of male participants, which is slightly higher than that of female participants and the proportion of the 18–24, 60–74, and 75+ age groups, which is lower than other age groups.

Second, we examined Japanese users' misunderstandings of the 16 technical terms that the original study showed to be commonly misconceived by U.S. users. There may be other technical terms apart from these 16 terms that many Japanese users misunderstand. In addition, although the participants were given a Japanese representation that is most commonly used in Japanese privacy policies for each term, different services sometimes use different Japanese representations, as mentioned in Sect. 5.1. Therefore, in a future study, we need to find all the technical terms misconceived by Japanese users, examine the different Japanese representations of the English technical terms used in different privacy policies that users misconceive, and identify the reasons for Japanese users' misunderstandings. Furthermore, we need to investigate what kind of data practices Japanese users want the service providers to implement for each type of personal information, including *"sensitive personal information."*

Third, in Part II of our questionnaire, we asked the participants about their acceptance of the policies. Because this question was asked after Part I (i.e., after the questions about the definitions of technical terms), the participants might have been well aware that they did not understand the technical terms. This may have caused participants to respond somewhat differently than they normally would to privacy policies.

6   Conclusion

Our study showed that the percentage of users who correctly understand the definition of technical terms was lower in Japan than that in the U.S. We also demonstrated that Japanese users have incorrect expectations of the data practices that online services employ under the Japanese privacy protection law. Based on our findings, we proposed interventions and measures to promote Japanese users' understanding of technical terms and the law. Our study suggests the need for service providers to implement interventions tailored to the users in each country.

Acknowledgement. We would like to thank Jenny Tang, Hannah Shoemaker, Ada Lerner, and Eleanor Birrell, the authors of the original study [27] for supporting our replication efforts. A part of this work was supported by JST, CREST Grant Number JPMJCR21M1, Japan.

References

1. Abrokwa, D., Das, S., Akgul, O., Mazurek, M.: Comparing security and privacy attitudes among US. Users of different smartphone and smart-speaker platforms. In: Proceedings of the of SOUPS'21 (2021)
2. Abu-Salma, R., Sasse, M., Bonneau, J., Danilova, A., Naiakshina, A., Smith, M.: Obstacles to the adoption of secure communication tools. In: Proceedings of the S&P'17 (2017)
3. Personal Information Protection Commission, Financial Services Agency: Guidelines for protection of personal information in the finance sector. https://www.japaneselawtranslation.go.jp/notices/view/99
4. Fabian, B., Ermakova, T., Lentz, T.: Large-scale readability analysis of privacy policies. In: Proceedings of the of WI'17 (2017)
5. Gluck, J., et al.: How short is too short? Implications of length and framing on the effectiveness of privacy notices. In: Proceedings of the SOUPS'16 (2016)
6. Habib, H., et al.: Toggles, dollar signs, and triangles: how to (in)effectively convey privacy choices with icons and link texts. In: Proceedings of the CHI'21 (2021)
7. Harkous, H., Fawaz, K., Shin, K.G., Aberer, K.: PriBots: conversational privacy with chatbots. In: Proceedings of the WSP@SOUPS'16 (2016)
8. Henshall, K.G., Takagaki, T.: Learning Japanese Hiragana and Katakana: Workbook and Practice Sheets (2013)
9. Herbert, F., et al.: A world full of privacy and security (mis)conceptions? Findings of a representative survey in 12 countries. In: Proceedings of the CHI'23 (2023)
10. Hidaka, S., Kobuki, S., Watanabe, M., Seaborn, K.: Linguistic dead-ends and alphabet soup: finding dark patterns in Japanese apps. In: Proceedings of the CHI'23 (2023)
11. Hiraide, Y., Yamada, M.: Impressions of Japanese character katakana strings. In: Human Systems Engineering and Design II (2020)
12. Lancers, Inc.: Lancers. https://www.lancers.jp/
13. Personal Information Protection Commission, Japan: GDPR (general data protection regulation) written in Japanese. https://www.ppc.go.jp/enforcement/infoprovision/EU/

14. Personal Information Protection Commission, Japan: Act on the protection of personal information (written in Japanese) (2023). https://www.ppc.go.jp/personalinfo/legal/

15. Statistics Bureau of Japan: Population estimates (2022). https://www.stat.go.jp/english/index.html

16. Jensen, C., Potts, C., Jensen, C.: Privacy practices of internet users: Self-reports versus observed behavior. Int. J. Hum Comput Stud. **63**, 203–227 (2005)

17. JNSA: Investigation report on information security incidents (attachment) written in Japanese. https://www.jnsa.org/result/incident/data/2017incident_survey_sokuhou_attachment_ver1.0.pdf

18. Kacsmar, B., Tilbury, K., Mazmudar, M., Kerschbaum, F.: Caring about sharing: user perceptions of multiparty data sharing. In: Proceedings of the USENIX Security'22 (2022)

19. Karegar, F., Pettersson, J.S., Fischer-Hübner, S.: The dilemma of user engagement in privacy notices: effects of interaction modes and habituation on user attention. ACM Trans. Priv. Secur. **23**, 1–38 (2020)

20. Li, Y., Kobsa, A., Knijnenburg, B.P., Nguyen, M.H.C., et al.: Cross-cultural privacy prediction. Proc. Priv. Enhancing Technol. **2017**, 113–132 (2017)

21. McDonald, A.M., Cranor, L.F.: The cost of reading privacy policies. I/S J. Law Policy Inf. Soc. (2008)

22. Mizutani, M., Dorsey, J., Moor, J.: The internet and Japanese conception of privacy. Ethics Inf. Technol. **6**, 121–128 (2004)

23. Rao, A., Schaub, F., Sadeh, N., Acquisti, A., Kang, R.: Expecting the unexpected: understanding mismatched privacy expectations online. In: Proceedings of the SOUPS 2016 (2016)

24. Redmiles, E., Kross, S., Mazurek, M.: How well do my results generalize? Comparing security and privacy survey results from MTurk, web, and telephone samples. In: Proceedings of the S&P'19 (2019)

25. Reinhardt, D., Borchard, J., Hurtienne, J.: Visual interactive privacy policy: the better choice? In: Proceedings of the CHI'21 (2021)

26. Story, P., et al.: Awareness, adoption, and misconceptions of web privacy tools. In: Proceedings of the PETS'21 (2021)

27. Tang, J., Shoemaker, H., Lerner, A., Birrell, E.: Defining privacy: how users interpret technical terms in privacy policies. In: Proceedings of the PETS'21 (2021)

28. Ur, B., Wang, Y.: A cross-cultural framework for protecting user privacy in online social media. In: Proceedings of the WWW'13 (2013)

29. Wu, Y., Gupta, P., Wei, M., Acar, Y., Fahl, S., Ur, B.: Your secrets are safe: how browsers' explanations impact misconceptions about private browsing mode. In: Proceedings of the WWW'18 (2018)

Alert Interaction Service Design for AI Face Swap Video Scams

Jing Luo, Xin Zhang, Fang Fu[(✉)], and Hanxiao Geng

College of Art and Design, Division of Art, Shenzhen University, Shenzhen, Guangdong, China
fu.fang@szu.edu.cn

Abstract. This study examines the design of an early warning service for artificial intelligence(AI)video face-swapping scams, aiming to increase users 'awareness of this new type of fraud. With the development of generative AI technologies, such as ChatGPT and Stable Diffusion, AI video face-swapping fraud is gradually becoming a new problem that threatens the security of personal property and privacy. The study adopts a quantitative research method to analyze the factors affecting the interaction willingness of users of AI video face-swapping fraud alert services through questionnaires, and constructs a model of influencing factors based on the technology acceptance model. The results of the study show that perceived usefulness, perceived ease of use and risk perception have a significant positive effect on user interaction willingness, which in turn significantly affects user interaction behavior. The study also suggests optimization directions for interface design, including simplifying the operation process and clearly presenting the information hierarchy. The results of the study are of great significance for designing more effective AI video face-swapping fraud alert services, which can help improve users' ability to recognize, alert and protect themselves against emerging fraudulent tactics.

Keywords: AI face swap · fraud alert system · UI design

1 Introduction

The new AI era has been introduced by generative AI, which is exemplified by ChatGPT and Stable Diffusion. It has accomplished exceptional success in quickly synthesizing and diversifying content creation across various sectors [1]. However, as AI technologies evolve, it also means that the governance and transparency rules for its safety, ethical and moral issues need to be reconfigured to accommodate its transformative momentum [2, 3]. The collection, storage, and sharing of large data sets raises ethical issues related to safety, standards, privacy, and data ownership [4], and one of the solutions to the related issues lies in the development of smart devices that can monitor and address AI violations to ensure that other AI systems do not violate ethical regulations and standards [5].

AI video face-swapping fraud developed on the basis of onomatopoeia and AI generation technology is gradually becoming a new type of fraud. With the help of this

© The Author(s), under exclusive license to Springer Nature Switzerland AG 2024
A. Moallem (Ed.): HCII 2024, LNCS 14728, pp. 265–280, 2024.
https://doi.org/10.1007/978-3-031-61379-1_17

technology, fraudsters can produce incredibly lifelike face-swapping videos, appear as mature individuals during real-time video chats, and dupe victims into sending money and disclosing personal information so they may profit illegally. It is also difficult to pursue responsibility in related cases, posing a serious threat to people's property and privacy security.

However, there are some restrictions on how AI face-swapping video fraud can be handled by the anti-fraud measures now in place. It is challenging to successfully identify and stop this kind of rising fraud using conventional security awareness training and technological methods. To address this issue, it is crucial to create an interactive early warning system that is tailored to the needs of users.

2 Method

This project adopts a quantitative research method to explore the interaction influencing factors affecting AI video face-swapping fraud service through questionnaire method. Based on the technology acceptance model, the actual situation and previous related studies, we put forward hypotheses and establish a model of the influencing factors, then publish the questionnaire to obtain scores by adapting the scale, and finally conduct data analysis through structural equation modeling to validate the model and optimize the interaction page based on the results. The study is mainly based on the video call interface of WeChat (the most commonly used chat application in China).

2.1 Research Hypothesis

Impact of Perceived Usefulness on User Interaction Intention of Early Warning Services. In-Chu Liao et al. found that perceived synchronization and perceived seamless migration are two important determinants in continuous interaction. The model showed that perceived seamless migration, perceived usefulness and user attitude were the strongest predictors of user decision to use multi-screen services [6]. A. Hussain et al. marked perceived usefulness as a key determinant of user acceptance of interactive mobile maps [7]. Based on the above studies, this paper proposes the following hypotheses:

H1: Perceived usefulness positively influences the willingness of users to interact with early warning services.

Impact of Perceived Ease of Use on Users' Willingness to Interact with Early Warning Services. A study on users' acceptance of interactive mobile maps found that perceived ease of use had a significant positive impact on users' acceptance of the technology, along with perceived usefulness and perceived enjoyment [7]. Ye P et al. conducted a questionnaire survey with 318 sharing economy users, and analysis through structural equation modeling (SEM) showed that the quality of the interaction had the Perceived Ease of Use (PEU) has the greatest impact, while security factors have a significant impact on Perceived Trust (PT), and Perceived Ease of Use (PEU) and Perceived Trust (PT) have a significant impact on users' adoption of the sharing economy [8]. Based on the above research, this paper proposes the following hypotheses:

H2: Perceived ease of use positively affects the willingness of users to interact with early warning services.

Impact of Risk Perceptions on the Interaction Intentions of Users of Early Warning Services. A study explored the impact of source credibility and risk attitudes on the risk perceptions, benefit perceptions, and purchase intentions of millennial young adults toward genetically modified (GM) foods. The study found that risk attitudes significantly influenced the purchase intention of genetically modified (GM) foods among millennial consumers in the United States and China [9]. Another study examined the relationship between risk perceptions and participation in prevention behaviors and testing during the early stages of the COVID-19 pandemic in China. It was found that risk perception had a significant effect on the intention to participate in self-protective behaviors [10]. Based on the above studies, the following hypotheses are proposed in this paper:

H3: Risk perception positively influences the intention to interact with users of early warning services.

Impact of the Willingness of Users of Early Warning Services to Interact on Users' Interaction Behavior. The willingness of users of early warning services to interact refers to the degree of activity and willingness of users to participate in and use early warning services. It reflects users' interest in, recognition and acceptance of the early warning service, as well as their tendency to actively participate and interact with the service. Early Warning Service User Interaction Behavior refers to the specific actions and operations related to the Early Warning Service that users actually participate in and perform. It includes the series of behaviors in which users receive, view, understand, and respond to early warning information, as well as their interactions with the service provider, such as providing feedback, asking questions, and seeking help. Understanding users' interaction willingness and behaviors is important for evaluating the effectiveness of early warning services, improving service quality, and increasing user satisfaction.

Studies by Voutsas C, Beldad A et al. have classified users' willingness to interact into factors such as their attitudes towards writing reviews, their perceptions of their behavioral competence, and the influence of the social environment, and have demonstrated that it is a key factor influencing whether or not they actually write reviews. These findings also help mobile app developers and marketers to better design strategies to encourage users to participate in reviews, which improves the visibility and user engagement of the apps [11]. Gu Z, Wei J et al. showed the influence of multiple factors on users' willingness to interact, and thus their willingness to interact with wearable commerce for interaction [12]. Based on the above research, this paper proposes the following hypotheses:

H4: User interaction willingness of early warning services positively affects user interaction behavior.

Theoretical Model. Based on the analysis of the previous research hypotheses, from the technical characteristics of AI video face-swapping fraud as well as the reference technology acceptance model selects perceived usefulness, perceived ease of use, and risk perception as the antecedent variables of the user's willingness to interact, and subsequently the user's willingness to interact further affects the user's interaction behavior. This project proposes AI video face-swapping scam interaction experience influencing factors and constructs an influence model, as shown in Fig. 1.

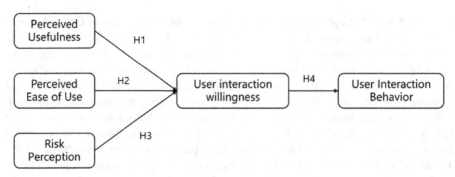

Fig. 1. Model of factors influencing user interaction behavior of AI face-swapping fraud alert service

2.2 Questionnaire

The questionnaire consists of questionnaire instructions, demographic information and scales. The questionnaire description section explains the basic definition of AI video face-swapping scam based on WeChat video calls. Gender, age, education level and occupation of respondents are collected in the demographic information section.

In the main part of the questionnaire refer to the measurement items in the existing studies, and adjust appropriately with the scenario of this study. The questionnaire was in the form of a seven-point Likert scale, with 1 representing «completely disagree «and 7 representing «completely agree». In order to ensure the reliability and validity of the variables, the metrics of each hypothetical variable proposed in this paper are based on the measurement questions of latent variables commonly used in foreign literature as the theoretical basis, and then refer to the measurement items of the relevant literature that have been revised to the theoretical basis, and finally modified and supplemented in combination with the actual use of anti-fraud products.

Perceived usefulness was referred to the scale developed by Ghazali N N [13], Addae J H [14], perceived ease of use was referred to the scale developed by Addae J H [14], and risk perception was referred to the scale developed by Ghazali N N [13]. The scale developed by Almaiah M A [15], Wang E S T [16], Addae J H [14] was referenced for the willingness to interact section and the scale developed by Ghazali N N was referenced for the user interaction behavior section. After the questionnaire design was completed, a small pre-survey was conducted, and the questionnaire was modified again according to the feedback from the respondents, and the final questionnaire contained 5 factors and 22 measurement items. The specific measures and literature sources for each variable are shown in Table 1.

Table 1. Variable construction and sources.

latent variable	Measurement problem items	Sources
Perceived Usefulness	Q1 Personal information security is more likely to be protected with the use of early warning services	Ghazali, Addae J H
	Q2 The security features of the Early Warning Service allow me to have better control over my video chat security and privacy	
	Q3 Turning on the alert service gives me more peace of mind when using video chats	
	Q4 Overall, I think the alert service helps protect my device from AI face-swap fraud	
Perceived Ease of Use	Q5 Learning to use an AI face-swapping fraud alert service was easy for me	Addae J H
	Q6 I don't need to spend a lot of effort when interacting with the alert interface	
	Q7 I can easily upgrade the security features of the alert service to the level I want	
	Q8 It takes very little effort on my part when it comes to early warning interface interactions	
Risk Perception	Q9 I could be facing a cyber fraud threat from AI face swapping scams	Almaiah M A, WangE S T, Addae J
	Q10 I am at risk of being victimized by cyber fraud attackers	
	Q11 I could be a victim of internet fraud	
User interaction willingness	Q12 I may be eligible for personalized alert service notification	

(*continued*)

Table 1. (*continued*)

latent variable	Measurement problem items	Sources
	Q13 I'm sure I'll be looking at alert services that are customized to my personal preferences	
	Q14 I should be able to adjust my alert service to improve my video chat security	
	Q15 I intend to continue to use early warning services in the future	
	Q16 I anticipate continuing to use the Early Warning service because of its innovative interactions	
User Interaction Behavior	Q17 I intend to protect myself from AI face-swapping fraud when using video calls	Ghazali
	Q18 I will learn about AI face swap scams and use video calling services safely	
	Q19 I'm willing to spend more money to protect myself from AI face-swapping fraud when using video calls	
	Q20 I will take precautions to protect my personal information from online fraud when using video calling	

Data Collection. The data collection process of this project adopts the online platform "Questionnaire Star" (a commonly used questionnaire research website in China) to collect data. At the beginning of the questionnaire, users were informed about the definition and occurrence of AI video face-swapping scam, and the questionnaire was released through social media. To ensure the validity of the questionnaire, the questionnaire setup inserted attention checking questions and trap questions in order to exclude unqualified questionnaires. A total of 253 questionnaires were distributed as of January 26, 2024, and 53 invalid questionnaires were excluded to obtain 200 valid questionnaires, and the descriptive statistics of the samples are shown in Table 2.

Table 2. Descriptive statistics of the survey sample.

Classification		Value	Percentage (%)
Sex	Male	98	49
	Female	102	51
Age	18–25	90	45
	26–30	23	11.5
	31–40	19	9.5
	41–50	22	11
	51–60	11	5.5
	>60	35	17.5
Educational background	High school and below	38	17
	Undergraduate/Specialized	128	64
	Masters and PhD	34	19
Total		200	100

3 Data Analysis

3.1 Reliability and Validity Testing

Firstly, the applicability test was conducted. The applicability test of the six dimensions describing the perceived risk was carried out by SPSS 25.0 in accordance with the principal components to reduce the dataset dimensional data, in which the value of the KMO test was 0.882, and the significance probability of the $\chi 2$ statistical value of the Bartlett's sphere test was 0.000, which indicates that the feasibility criteria of the principal component analysis are fully met, and it is suitable to carry out the factor analysis.

Next, the principal component analysis was performed, and the results shown in Table 4 were obtained. The cumulative variance contribution rate of the five principal components extracted in Table 4 reached 65.288%, indicating that it can reflect the original data more adequately.

Then the reliability test was conducted to test the consistency and reliability of the measurement results using Cronbach's alpha and combined reliability (CR). The combined reliability (CR) of each variable was greater than the recommended value of 0.7. Based on Cronbach's alpha to test the degree of consistency of each measurement questionnaire, the Cronbach's alpha coefficients of the study variables were all greater than the 0.7 recommended value, which indicates that the internal consistency reliability among the variables is good, and the results are shown in Table 3. In terms of validity, the standardized loadings of the questionnaires are greater than 0.6, which meets the criteria of factor loading. Meanwhile the Average variance extracted (AVE) values are greater than 0.5 suggested value, indicating that the convergent validity criterion is met.

The above indicates that the questionnaire data of this study has good discriminant validity and is suitable for subsequent structural equation modeling test and hypothesis testing data analysis (Table 5).

Table 3. KMO and Bartlett's test.

KMO Quantity of Sample Suitability		.882
Bartlett's Test of Sphericity	Approximate chi-square	1683.883
	Degrees of freedom	190
	Significance	.000

Table 4. Total Variance Explained.

Total	Initial eigenvalues			Extract load sum of squares			Rotate load sum of squares		
	Percentage of variance	Cumulative %	Total	Percentage of variance	Cumulative %	Total	Percentage of variance	Cumulative %	Total
1	6.977	34.883	34.883	6.977	34.883	34.883	3.179	15.897	15.897
2	1.877	9.387	44.271	1.877	9.387	44.271	2.615	13.073	28.970
3	1.520	7.601	51.871	1.520	7.601	51.871	2.544	12.720	41.690
4	1.424	7.120	58.991	1.424	7.120	58.991	2.418	12.092	53.782
5	1.259	6.297	65.288	1.259	6.297	65.288	2.301	11.506	65.288

Table 5. Validation factor analysis results.

Latent variable	Observed variable	Factor loading	C.R	AVE	Cronbach's alpha
Perceived Usefulness	Q1	0.707	0.831	0.552	0.805
	Q2	0.765			
	Q3	0.772			
	Q4	0.727			
Perceived Ease of Use	Q5	0.752	0.820	0.532	0.772
	Q6	0.731			
	Q7	0.710			
	Q8	0.723			
Risk Perception	Q9	0.761	0.855	0.664	0.828
	Q10	0.819			

(continued)

Table 5. (*continued*)

Latent variable	Observed variable	Factor loading	C.R	AVE	Cronbach's alpha
User interaction willingness	Q11	0.861	0.832	0.500	0.855
	Q12	0.730			
	Q13	0.686			
	Q14	0.728			
	Q15	0.668			
	Q16	0.720			
User Interaction Behavior	Q17	0.741	0.811	0.518	0.788
	Q18	0.763			
	Q19	0.652			
	Q20	0.718			

3.2 Structural Modeling and Hypothesis Testing

Evaluation of the Overall Fit of the Equation Model. The AMOS 26.0 software was used to carry out the structural equation test to validate the constructed theoretical model, and after comparing with the given recommended values of the fitness indexes, except for the NFI value which was very close to pushing 0.9, the fitted values of the other fitness indexes fell within the acceptable range, and the theoretical model had a better model fit, and the results are shown in Table 6.

Table 6. Fitness index values for structural equation modeling.

Adaptation index	Acceptable range	Fitted value
$\chi 2$		203.106
$\chi 2/df$	<3.0	1.246
GFI	>0.9	0.908
AGFI	>0.8	0.881
RMSEA	<0.08	0.035
NFI	>0.9	0.884
IFI	>0.9	0.975
CFI	>0.9	0.974
TLI	>0.9	0.970

Research hypothesis testing results. The structural relationship between the latent variables and their standardized path coefficients are shown in Table 7 as the estimated values, p-values and hypothesis testing results, etc. It can be seen that all hypothesized path coefficients are significant at the level of confidence $\alpha = 0.001$, and the hypotheses are all valid. The actual model and path coefficients obtained are shown in Fig. 2.

Table 7. Results of hypothesis testing.

Hypothesis	Path relationship	Standardized path coefficient	P-value	Test conclusion
H1	User interaction willingness ← Perceived Usefulness	0.392	***	Supported
H2	User interaction willingness ← Perceived Ease of Use	0.442	***	Supported
H3	User interaction willingness ← Risk Perception	0.177	0.004	Supported
H4	User Interaction Behavior ← User interaction willingness	0.655	***	Supported

Note: *** indicates significant correlation at the 0.001 level.

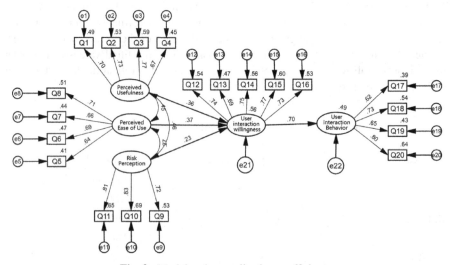

Fig. 2. Model and normalization coefficients.

This paper constructs AI video face-swapping scam interaction experience influence factor model based on technology acceptance model, covering perceived usability, perceived ease of use, risk perception, user interaction willingness and user interaction behavior potential variables. Combined with the above analysis, it can be obtained that the research hypotheses are all supported by the data, in which the most influential factor is perceived ease of use, in fact, it is perceived usefulness, and finally, it is risk perception. The details are discussed as follows:

Effect of Perceived Usefulness on User Interaction. Willingness. Perceived useful-ness has a significant positive impact on user interaction willingness in AI face-swapping fraud alert services, which can be derived from its standardized path coefficient of 0.392 and p-value of less than 0.001. It represents the ability of users to receive real-time protection, allowing the platform to accurately identify AI-generated content during real-time video calls and remind users of object identification, as well as forming a complete fraud prevention experience in conjunction with functions such as rapid case filing, legal assistance, psychological guidance and knowledge popularization after being defrauded. Compared with traditional fraud prevention platforms, it can meet the needs of users for safe calls and protection of personal rights and interests, and form an effec-tive identification, reminder and protection against emerging fraudulent means. This is consistent with the findings of Rebecca Schnall et al. In order to facilitate the use of mobile apps by people living with HIV (PLWH) for their healthcare needs, mHealth technologies need to be perceived as useful, easy to use, and accompanied by trust in the creator of the technology, as well as low perceived risk [17]. As the ecosystem of safety and protection products is built and improved, the services provided to users will be more effective and accompanied by an excellent sense of experience.

Effect of Perceived Ease of Use on User Interaction Intention. Perceived ease of use has the most significant effect on users' willingness to interact, with a standardized path coefficient of 0.442 and a p-value of less than 0.001. Perceived ease of use means that users can use and understand our services very easily, whether it's using a simple interface design to help users quickly find the functions and information they need, or using clear icons, labels and text descriptions, as well as reasonable interface layout to make users understand and operate easily. Whether it's the use of simple interface design to help users quickly find the functions and information they need, or the use of clear icons, labels and text descriptions, or the layout of the interface to make it easy for users to understand and operate, the service should be user-friendly and simple. Most importantly, users should be able to clearly understand the real-time situation, be able to know that the other party has used AI-generated content in the call when AI video face-swapping fraud occurs, be able to quickly and easily use the action and problem identification suggestions that we provide, and finally deal with all kinds of prognostic issues in a quick manner. Relevant studies have also demonstrated that the element of perceived ease of use affects the user's willingness to interact and the experience of using it, Wulandari et al. found that perceived ease of use and other factors positively affect interaction efficiency and affective willingness in chatGPT [18].

Effect of Risk Perception on User Interaction Intention. Risk perception exerts a positive influence on user interaction intention, with a standardized path coefficient of 0.177 and a p-value of 0.004, which is not as influential as perceived usefulness and perceived ease of use on user interaction intention. Risk perception represents users' awareness of AI face-swapping technology, their ability to recognize fraudulent behavior, their trust in fraud prevention services, and their awareness of the consequences of fraud. It is necessary to consider how to improve users' awareness and understanding of AI face-swapping technology, improve users' ability to recognize fraudulent behavior, enhance users' awareness of personal information protection, improve users' trust in fraud alert services, and let users fully understand the consequences of fraudulent behavior, so as to improve the effectiveness of the service and users' satisfaction. Adam Raihan Rianthomy and Su -Jung Nam et al. Related studies also confirm the idea that elements such as risk perception affect user satisfaction and willingness and trust [19].

The Effect of User Interaction Willingness on User Interaction Behavior. User interaction willingness has a significant positive effect on user interaction behavior, with a standardized path coefficient of 0.655 and a p-value of less than 0.001. User interaction willingness plays the role of a mediator variable between perceived usefulness, perceived ease of use, and perceived risk, and user interaction behavior. Tao et al.'s findings suggest that in economic interactions, risk preference determines the willingness to participate and affects the development of cooperation. The level of risk a person is prepared to accept when pursuing a goal leads to different levels of willingness to participate, which in turn affects the evolution of cooperation [20]. In the context of social commerce, a study investigating how personified communication affects consumer behavior found that perceived interactions positively influence consumers' attitudes and, consequently, their willingness to purchase [21]. There is consistency between these studies and the ideas in this paper.

The user interaction willingness of AI video face-swapping scams is affected by a variety of factors, and users will expand the scope of its application because of the quality of the service, or stop using the service because of the inconvenience of its interactions, so the platforms should consider them comprehensively and continuously optimize their own services and logics from the perspectives of perceived usefulness, perceived ease of use, and perceived risk, and then promote the user interaction behaviors.

4   Improved Interface Design

4.1   Optimization Direction

Combined with the above questionnaire data analysis and chart analysis, we can summarize the following 2 design optimization directions:

Simplification of Operation Flow. The operation flow of the service should be simple and intuitive, and users do not need to perform complex operations or think. For example, the system can provide one-click operation or guided flow to reduce the cognitive burden of users.

Information Hierarchy Presentation. The interface information design should be intuitive and simple so that users can quickly find the required functions and information. For example, the use of clear icons, labels, and text descriptions, as well as a reasonable interface layout, allow users to understand and operate easily.

4.2   Interface Redesign

Simplify the Interaction Logic of Core Functions. According to the conclusion of data analysis to strengthen the willingness of user interaction behavior, it can be optimized in two dimensions: perceived usability and perceived ease of use. Sort out the user requirements of core functions and simplify the interaction process. The simplified process follows the logic of "detection - prompting - identification", which can detect forged content in advance to avoid users being deceived by fraudsters, and provide users with multi-channel identity verification in a timely manner in the middle of the crime. Provide users with multi-channel identity verification shortcuts and visually more in line with the native style of the ios mobile terminal, users are not easy to produce a sense of strangeness.

Simplified Interaction Process for "detection of AI-generated content - identity verification pop-up window prompts - multi-channel identity verification/identification advice - identity verification/direct identification", the specific process shown in Fig. 3.

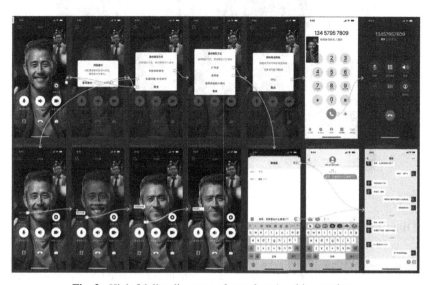

Fig. 3. High fidelity diagrams of core functional interactions.

Clear Information Hierarchy. The platform's interface layout adopts a card-type layout, which enables different functional modules to be distinguished from each other and is easy for users to understand and operate. The interface information design strictly follows the grid system and is categorized according to importance, with different weights corresponding to different icons, labels, font sizes and transparency. For difficult-to-understand and rarely seen conceptual information, additional explanatory text and icons are attached. The detailed design is shown in Fig. 4.

Fig. 4. Complex information page layout.

5   Discussion

In today's increasingly developing and changing artificial intelligence, this project discovers the protection gap of AI video face-swapping fraud based on the real situation. Secondly, this project takes WeChat (the most widely used chat software in China) as the main platform, and studies the characteristics and user needs of AI video face-swapping fraud protection during real-time video calls.

Pre-research hypotheses are proposed in combination with domestic and international literature, and the interaction influencing factor model is constructed. Then according to the five dimensions of the variables based on the authoritative scale adaptation, through the form of questionnaires to collect people's ratings on the five dimensions of perceived usability, perceived ease of use, risk perception, user interaction willingness and user interaction behavior, to summarize people's preferences and problems in the process of use.

After the questionnaire was collected, the reliability and validity of the questionnaire were analyzed, and it was found that both of them were at a good level, and then combined with the assumptions and models in the previous period, the structural equation model fit test was conducted, and it was found that the fit effect was good, and the assumptions of the previous period of the study were valid, and it was further analyzed and explored the significance of the influence of different paths for the subsequent design.

Finally, according to the conclusions of the data analysis to summarize the optimization direction of the interactive interface, and carry out specific design practice. AI video face-swapping fraud overcomes the shortcomings of traditional telecommunication fraud, which poses a serious threat to the safety of people's property, so it is very necessary to study the relevant design of fraud protection.

6 Conclusion and Future Work

According to the data analysis, it is summarized that perceived usefulness, perceived ease of use, and risk perception have a significant positive effect on user interaction willingness, and user interaction willingness has a significant effect on user interaction behavior. However, due to the condition limitations, the samples analyzed by the questionnaire are not many.

At the same time, we also know that there are some limitations in the design of the detection and interaction function module based on WeChat real-time video chat. In the future, we will design relevant experiments to specifically analyze the needs of different users in this situation, and carry out multiple rounds of iterative optimization of the prompting method, identification function and other module functions to continuously enhance the detection effect and identification effectiveness.

Today, the development speed of artificial intelligence has exceeded our imagination, and it has brought various conveniences and problems at the same time, so we need to be vigilant against the abuse of technology and let it serve human society better.

References

1. Zhang, C., et al.: A complete survey on generative AI (AIGC): is ChatGPT from GPT-4 to GPT-5 all you need?. arXiv preprint arXiv:2303.11717 (2023)
2. Dwivedi, Y.K., et al.: Artificial Intelligence (AI): Multidisciplinary perspectives on emerging challenges, opportunities, and agenda for research, practice and policy. Int. J. Inf. Manage. 57, 101994 (2021)
3. Zatarain, J.M.N.: The role of automated technology in the creation of copyright works: the challenges of artificial intelligence. Int. Rev. Law Comput. Technol. 31(1), 91–104 (2017)
4. Zandi, D., et al.: New ethical challenges of digital technologies, machine learning and artificial intelligence in public health: a call for papers. Bull. World Health Organ. 97(1), 2–2 (2019)
5. Etzioni, A., Etzioni, O.: AI assisted ethics. Ethics Inf. Technol. 18, 149–156 (2016)
6. Factors affecting user intention in continuous interaction: a structural model (2020)
7. Hussain, A., Mkpojiogu, E.O.C., Yusof, M.M.: Perceived usefulness, perceived ease of use, and perceived enjoyment as drivers for the user acceptance of interactive mobile maps. In: AIP Conference Proceedings, vol. 1761, no. 1. AIP Publishing (2016)
8. Ye, P., Liu, L., Tan, J.: The impact of information and communication technology factors on the user intention to participate in the sharing economy. Int. J. Technol. Hum. Interact. (IJTHI) 18(1), 1–24 (2022)
9. Sun, R., Meng, J.: Looking at young millennials' risk perception and purchase intention toward GM foods: exploring the role of source credibility and risk attitude. Health Mark. Q. 39(3), 263–279 (2022)

10. Xu, T., Wu, X.: Risk perception, media, and ordinary people's intention to engage in self-protective behaviors in the early stage of COVID-19 pandemic in China. Risk Manage. Healthc. Policy 1459–1471 (2022)

11. Voutsas, C., Beldad, A., Tempelman, M.: Because it's good for my feeling of self-worth: testing the expanded theory of planned behavior to predict Greek users' intention to review mobile apps. In: Meiselwitz, G. (ed.) SCSM 2018, Part II. LNCS, vol. 10914, pp. 126–136. Springer, Cham (2018). https://doi.org/10.1007/978-3-319-91485-5_9

12. Gu, Z., Wei, J., Xu, F.: An empirical study on factors influencing consumers' initial trust in wearable commerce. J. Comput. Inf. Syst. **56**(1), 79–85 (2016)

13. Ghazali, N.N., Hassan, S., Ahmad, R.: Fortifying against cyber fraud: instrument development with the protection motivation theory. Int. J. Adv. Comput. Sci. Appl. **14**(10) (2023)

14. Addae, J.H., et al.: Exploring user behavioral data for adaptive cybersecurity. User Model. User-Adapt. Interact. **29**, 701–750 (2019)

15. Almaiah, M.A., et al.: Examining the impact of artificial intelligence and social and computer anxiety in e-learning settings: students' perceptions at the university level. Electronics **11**(22), 3662 (2022)

16. Wang, E.S.-T.: Influences of innovation attributes on value perceptions and usage intentions of mobile payment. J. Electron. Commer. Res. **23**(1), 45–58 (2022)

17. Schnall, R., et al.: Trust, perceived risk, perceived ease of use and perceived usefulness as factors related to mHealth technology use. Stud. Health Technol. Inform. **216**, 467 (2015)

18. Wulandari, A.A., Nurhaipah, T., Ohorella, N.R.: Perceived ease of use, social influencers, facilitating conditions, user experience on the influence of human-machine interaction on interaction efficiency, emotional impact of using chat GPT. J. Digit. Media Commun. **2**(2), 61–75 (2024)

19. Rianthomy, A.R., et al.: Influence of risk perception and destination image mediated by satisfaction towards destination loyalty in Tanjung Lesung tourism. Inte. J. Appl. Bus. Int. Manage. (IJABIM) **8**(2), 127–141 (2023)

20. Tao, Y., Hu, K., Shi, L.: Risk-preference–driven participate willingness provides alternative routes to solve social dilemma. Europhys. Lett. **135**(2), 28001 (2021)

21. Zhao, J., Zhu, C.: Modeling and quantifying the impact of personified communication on purchase behavior in social commerce. Behav. Sci. (Basel Switz.) **13**(8), 627 (2023)

Human Factors and Security in Digital Twins: Challenges and Future Prospects

Sanjay Misra[1], Kousik Barik[2], Harald P.-J. Thunem[1],
and Sabarathinam Chockalingam[3(✉)]

[1] Department of Applied Data Science, Institute for Energy Technology, Halden, Norway
{Sanjay.Misra,harald.p-j.thunem}@ife.no
[2] Department of Computer Science, University of Alcala, Alcala, Spain
Kousik.Kousik@edu.uah.es
[3] Department of Risk and Security, Institute for Energy Technology, Halden, Norway
Sabarathinam.Chockalingam@ife.no

Abstract. The advent of the information technology industry has had a progressively beneficial influence on the value chain through the modernization and optimization of production and distribution processes. Digital Twins (DTs) are a combination of advanced technologies applied in several industrial areas like energy, health, and transportation. The objective of the *Human Digital Twin* is to digitally depict not only the external aspects of an individual, such as their physical and physiological attributes, but also their internal aspects, such as personality and thoughts. This study explores the values, acceptance factors, and models of human DT. Furthermore, this study examined the use of DT to address cybersecurity issues. Finally, this study is concluded with future research directions such as developing user trust, building standards, and enhancing the connection between security protection and human-centric considerations.

Keywords: Automation · Cybersecurity · DT · Human digital twin · Security

1 Introduction

Integrating information and operational technology has gradually enhanced the entire value chain through modernization and process optimization. The domains of Artificial Intelligence (AI), cloud computing, edge computing, Internet of Things (IoTs), and 5G and beyond are rapidly growing and hold great potential [1]. Digital Twin (DT) technology is a component of emerging digital technologies that facilitate digital transformation by offering the ability to help with unique business prototypes and decision-support approaches. Multiple institutions have already integrated data, information, and analytics capabilities into their usefulness offerings [2].

The concept of a human DT enables the extension of human activities beyond the physical realm into the virtual domain [3]. A person's DT serves as the only channel of interaction and communication between their real-life representation in the virtual world and themselves. Human DT enables immediate coordination of the physical and

A. Moallem (Ed.): HCII 2024, LNCS 14728, pp. 281–295, 2024.
https://doi.org/10.1007/978-3-031-61379-1_18

virtual worlds, leading to more accurate and thorough measurements of unexpected and unpredictable events [4]. The key benefits of DT technology include decreasing errors, uncertainties, inefficiencies, and costs in any system or process [5]. DT requires synchronizing and linking with corresponding physical asset to reflect the attributes and condition of that physical asset. Figure 1 demonstrates the usage of DT in different areas.

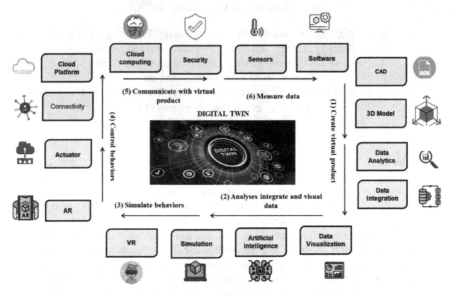

Fig. 1. Usage of DT Technology

The composition of a human DT extends beyond the mere inclusion of data about one's state and behaviour [6]. It encompasses a model articulating one's individuality and emotions, encompassing inclinations toward judgment and behaviour. It facilitates engaging in social interactions within a virtual community and independently. Human DTs can support addressing human factors issues related to cybersecurity, like social engineering attacks [7]. In contrast, human DTs can bring additional cybersecurity and privacy issues when handling various tasks in a virtual platform involving real-time data.

There are various human factors in DT, like user interface design, user experience, training and education, collaboration, communication, data privacy and security, adaptability, flexibility, accessibility, and feedback mechanisms [8]. Several essential concepts are included in user interface design, which as a combination, offer the best possible user experience. User-centered design, an approach that emphasizes creating with the end-user in mind, is a fundamental element [9]. In DT development, user experience strongly emphasizes usability by ensuring easy navigation and incorporating user feedback through usability testing. The significance of cybersecurity has grown because the world has grown more digitally linked and dependent [10].

This study identifies the factors for values, acceptance factors, and model acceptance of human DT and its advantages and prospects. The study discusses the usage of DT in addressing cybersecurity issues. This study addresses the two Research Questions (RQs):

- **RQ1.** What are the values, acceptance factors, and models of human-based DT?
- **RQ2.** How can DT be used to address cybersecurity issues?

The research protocol for this study was formulated using various search strategies, including source identification, study selection, and execution of the selection process. The search method was adopted and adjusted with the explicit purpose of this study [11]. The review commenced by conducting initial searches to identify preexisting systematic reviews and evaluate the quantity of potentially pertinent studies incorporated as sources. The identification of pertinent articles in this review was conducted using the following criteria: (1) Extract primary keywords from the research inquiries; (2) Identify alternative spellings and synonyms for the keywords; (3) Determine key terms in pertinent articles (4) Utilize the Boolean operators "OR" or "AND" to establish a connection between significant terms. The result of the search query used to find pertinent papers is as follows: (Human DT OR DT) AND (Cybersecurity OR DT) AND (Human DT OR values OR Acceptance factors OR model). The review process and selection of the PRISMA flow chart present suitable articles at different stages, as demonstrated in Fig. 2.

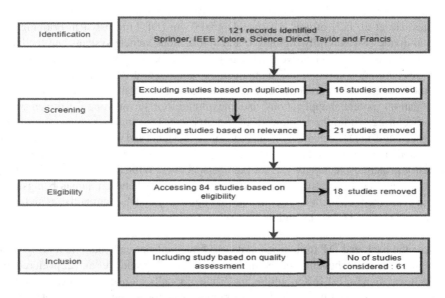

Fig. 2. PRISMA flow chart for review process

The remaining paper is formulated as follows: The related works are presented in Sect. 2. Section 3 demonstrates the value of human-based DT, acceptance factors, and model. The usage of DT for cybersecurity is demonstrated in Sect. 4. Section 5 presents the discussion. Finally, conclusions and future work directions are provided in Sect. 6.

2 Related Works

This section discusses the various aspects of DT and usage. Holmes et al. [12] studied the risks related to the cybersecurity of platforms employing DT technology, the possibilities for DT to reduce cybersecurity risks, and become an essential part of an in-depth security defense. Alcaraz et al. [13] examined the DT paradigm's current condition and categorized potential risks, incorporating its operational specifications and functional layers to produce an improved and valuable classification. Additionally, the authors presented an initial set of security rules and strategies that can guarantee the proper and reliable application of a DT. Diego et al. [14] proposed a runtime-verifiable DT-based security dissociation technique for IoT device interactions. The suggested method is predicated on the IoT server's ability to deploy a local agent, or security module, to the IoT device. Eckhart et al. [15] illustrated DT as improving cyber-physical security by maintaining their physical counterparts in every aspect of their existence. Their paper's findings suggest that DTs can create safety in Cyber-Physical Systems. However, the resources needed for implementing this concept on a large scale impede DTs' efficient development, upkeep, and operation, posing a substantial technological challenge.

Mihai et al. [16] presented a model to identify the dual-direction context connections among harmful code phrases. The outcomes demonstrated that, for vulnerability detection, the proposed strategy is more effective than most advanced DL-based techniques. Hu et al. [17] offered a Driver Digital Twin (DDT) to assist in bridging the digital divide between fully digitalized and autonomous vehicle systems and facilitate the creation of a comprehensive driving human cyber-physical system. Understanding requires building a harmonious, human-centric, intelligent driving system that considers the human driver's proactive and sensitive nature. Lu et al. [18] demonstrated the implications, potential applications, and unexplored RQs surrounding DT-driven smart manufacturing within the framework of Industry 4.0. This study examined the recent advancements in DT technology in manufacturing systems and processes. Liu et al. [19] presented an extensive and thorough literature assessment to examine DT from various industry principles, technology, and usage perspectives. Wilhelm et al. [20] offered an overview and analyses of the combination and interaction between human beings and DT in automated production systems. The findings illustrated the common uses and situations of DT-based HMI and outlined the existing labour-sharing arrangements between humans and DT. Lehtola et al. [21] examined how AI technologies could automatically update the back-end DT from sensor data and how the front-end could be leveraged to generate significant benefits for the urban ecosystem. Pylianidis et al. [22] offered an operational map for DT in agriculture, including gradually more complicated scenarios. The authors described the distinctive attributes of DT for agriculture. Berti et al. [23] focused on the present state-of-the-art regarding DT and how it can be used to assess and incorporate ergonomics or other human factors into ML systems. Semeraro et al. [24] presented a broad overview of the current state of research and the technical challenges involved in designing and developing DTs about various application areas and related technologies. The common applications of DT are presented in Fig. 3.

Based on the studies, recognizing and dealing with the complexities of decision-making, user interactions, and human behavior in the DT presents a challenge, as would maintaining strong security measures to safeguard confidential information and thwart

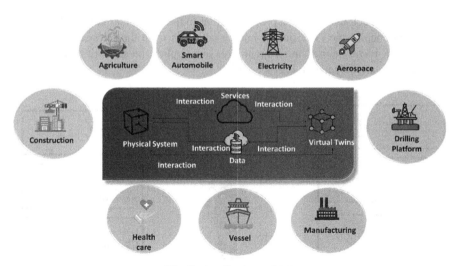

Fig. 3. Applications of DT

illegal access. This problem statement explores difficulties balancing security consider-ations with human factors in DT technology. It endeavors to inquire about the possible consequences of ignoring these elements and to suggest future directions and approaches that can improve the balance between rigorous security standards and human-centric concerns in the developing field of DT technology. Realizing the full potential of DT applications across industries while preserving the integrity, availability, privacy, and ethical aspects of human interaction in these virtual environments requires addressing these issues. This study explored the key aspects of a user-centered approach to system design, data privacy, and security in DT.

3   Values of Human-Based DT and Acceptance Factors

This section discusses the values, acceptance factors and models of human DT, address-ing RQ1. A human digital twin comprises data representing its shape and behavior and a model encapsulating its individuality and emotions, including inclinations toward judg-ment and behavior [25]. Extending the scope of human activity from the actual world to cyberspace is attainable using a Human DT [26]. Human DT is the mechanism by which individuals interact with each other and themselves in cyberspace and with their inner selves, such as their thoughts and personalities. The behavior of a DT is defined by a Human DT model replicating humans' uniqueness and qualities, such as a personality model that predicts behavioral tendency, personality, and values or an ability model that suggests vision, skills, language proficiency, and physical capacity [27]. Human analysts use the DT to analyze, develop action plans, and implement those strategies in real life. The action plans pinpoint potentially beneficial modifications to the real-world twin's composition or characteristics. The analyst in these systems subsequently changes the real-world twin, which can improve this entity's performance. Particularly, the exchange of information between the virtual and physical twins allows the virtual twin to perceive, understand, and act, resulting in a process similar to the perceptual loop [28]. A human digital twin enables the extension of human activities from the physical world to the virtual world. It can be used in different roles and application areas [29]. The benefits of human DTs are depicted in Fig. 4.

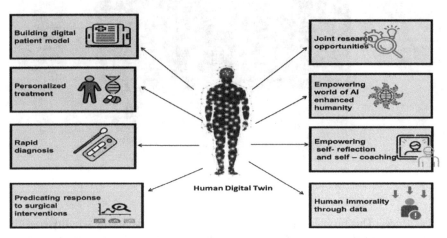

Fig. 4. Benefits of Human DTs

A human DT consists of data that reflects the state and behavior of a human, as well as a model that represents their distinct individuality and emotions, including their tendencies towards decisions and techniques. Consequently, it allows one to engage with others in a digital community and independently perform tasks as if humans were physically present. The first is being utilized for many tasks that surpass our physical limitations. In cyberspace, many computational tasks can be executed rapidly, surpassing real-time constraints [30]. The processing occurs during interpersonal communication. An additional benefit is that employing a model capable of expressing emotions enables the direct transmission of a wide range of emotions. Within this virtual society, one can express subtle distinctions, constructing a realm where one's thoughts are devoid of inconsistencies. The third benefit lies in the capacity to engage with individuals based on social factors and diversity. This capability enables us to (i) meticulously examine these interactions while considering the unique characteristics of individuals and (ii) forecast future outcomes. It is a versatile advantage that can be utilized in multiple ways, including consultations targeting and modifying an individual's behaviour [29]. The advantages stem from the incorporation of human personality and the development of emotional models.

The Human DT is an online replica of an authentic individual in the world [31]. Figure 5 depicts the Human DT model. The digitized profile is stored in digital format on a cloud server. Any updates made to the data about them are reflected in the databases. Information synchronization requires connecting a physical person and cyberspace via services like the Internet, 4G, 5G, Wi-Fi, and others [32]. The use of technologies like cloud computing and deep learning is to examine current, historical, and inherited data to extract meaningful insights. It offers feedback information, including predictions, diagnoses, and other recommendations [33].

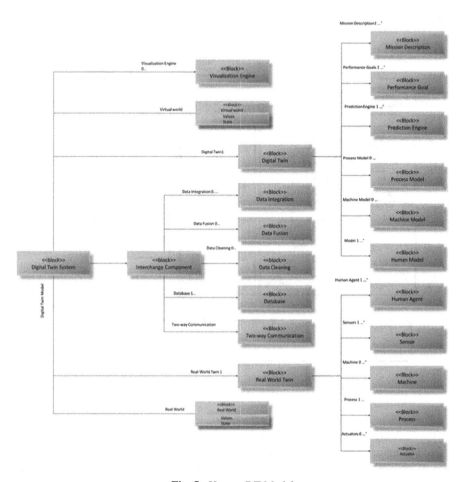

Fig. 5. Human DT Model

A human DT comprises a model representing the unique personality and emotions, including inclinations towards perception and action, and data representing the condition and behavior [34]. This relation has several benefits, such as its versatility, which extends beyond the physical limitations. A significant quantity of processing goes into online communication, which can process information at a rate of speed that is faster than the real-time communication between actual individuals can achieve. It is feasible to communicate different emotions exactly as they are when utilizing a model that conveys emotions [35]. Figure 6 represents the values and empathy of Human DT [36, 37]. A user-centric approach is provided by providing user desires and preferences when designing the DT. Interactions can be made more user-friendly and connective by being tailored to the values and expectations of the user [38]. Continuous improvement is facilitated

DT receives and responds to user feedback. The DT adapts to the user's changing needs through constant iteration, improving user experience by fine-tuning its behaviour.

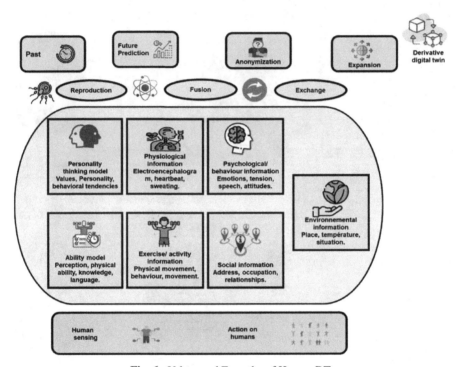

Fig. 6. Values and Empathy of Human DT

Concerns about privacy ethics, legal compliance, and commercial needs are all part of data security and include a major factor while creating and utilizing Human DT. From a technical standpoint, security and privacy research in general and Human DT data security share similar ideas and implementations [39]. Human DT is expected to increase individual abilities and yield positive outcomes. But for people to profit from these advantages, the social acceptance of a perspective by Human DT must be considered completely. Raising people's awareness and acceptance of certain issues, such as (i) psychological resistance to the development of DTs that are exact replicas of themselves and (ii) privacy concerns about the collection and use of personal data, is crucial. A human DT can engage in similar economic endeavors as the humans it simulates, which could lead to the development of new legal and social structures [40]. A significant paradigm change can result from the social and economic impacts of Human DT, which can double human knowledge and capacities and multiply human activities many times. It is necessary to search for the ideal form of Human DT while discussing the various effects its creation and popularization will have on actual life with experts from fields like law, sociology, and the humanities [41]. DT can give rise to various hazards and threats when it is supposed that Human DT and elements of DT reflect every detail in the real world. A user-friendly interface with basic controls heavily influences acceptance.

Further, a key factor that improves acceptability is the correct and consistent portrayal of user attributes [42]. Robust privacy and security safeguards are closely related to trust in the technologies [43]. Following moral principles becomes essential to gaining the trust of users. Additionally, more individualized experiences result from actively involving consumers in the design and customization process, which promotes acceptance [44]. Integrity, openness, and a commitment to moral conduct are the foundations of ethical conduct.

4 DT for Cybersecurity

This section demonstrates the usage of DT in cybersecurity issues, addressing RQ2. Using DT, security teams could overcome adversaries and lower the dangers connected to cyber-physical systems and IoT in critical infrastructures. The use cases in Cybersecurity only scratch the surface of what DTs may accomplish [45]. Security experts can use DT to mimic various cyber-attacks on physical systems and observe the system's response [46]. Before these devices leave the manufacturing floor, their design can be improved with the help of these simulated attacks. Analyzing the system's response to cyber-attacks is essential for designing more resilient systems with higher fault tolerance. Furthermore, by lowering the attack surface, DT improves the security of a system's architecture [6]. In addition to attack simulations, thoroughly examining the system's architecture, traffic patterns, and communications protocols during normal operations can reveal potential vulnerabilities that malevolent external parties could try to exploit. Extra services must be removed from the design to lower the system's attack surface [47]. Table 1 depicts the interaction of DT and Cybersecurity.

The challenges that DTs tackle are data security and efficiency, data integrity enhancement, delay, modeling and gathering in real-time, smart data analysis, assessment, capacity prediction, responsibility, and broadening of technologies across various application domains [4]. The existence of ideas closely related to DT, such as modeling, IoT, and cyber-physical systems (CPS), could be a source of misconceptions. Given the substantial technological parallels, there can undoubtedly be much overlap between DTs and Industrial IoT (IIoT). The misconception between DT and CPS is fundamental since many physical elements from which a DT can be produced are also CPS [48]. Human DT is vital for strengthening Cybersecurity defenses, especially social engineering threats. Their importance stems from their capacity to conduct in-depth behavioral evaluations and create baselines of typical user behavior. This capacity becomes extremely beneficial when abnormalities in behavior representative of social engineering attempts are identified early, adding an extra layer of protection.

Human DT presents a unique chance for simulation and training. Users can experience realistic training environments by simulating social engineering attacks using the behavior of their artificial counterparts. This method increases awareness and responsiveness by strengthening their capacity to identify and resist social engineering actions [49]. An additional layer of behavioral biometrics is introduced to user identification systems by integrating Human DT. By analyzing behavior patterns, such as mouse clicks

Table 1. Interaction of DT and Cybersecurity

Factor	DT	Cybersecurity
Data privacy	Sharing, access, and preservation of personal data	Encryption, access controls, data anonymization
Authentication	Biometric data, behavioural patterns	Multi-factor authentication, secure login procedures
Behavior Monitoring	Analyzing real-time actions, decisions	Anomaly detection, behaviour analytics
Vulnerability Analysis	Identifying weaknesses in DT infrastructure	Regular security audits, penetration testing
Communication Security	Interactions with other DTs, systems	Secure communication protocols, encryption
Access Controls	Managing permissions and privileges	Role-based access control, least privilege principles
Incident Response	Reacting to security breaches or anomalies	Automated response systems, incident response plans
Compliance	Adherence to regulatory requirements	Compliance monitoring, legal frameworks
Training and Awareness	Human DT education and awareness	Cybersecurity training programs, awareness campaigns
Patch Management	Updating software and security patches	Timely application of patches, vulnerability management
Identity Management	Managing DT identity	Identity and access management systems
Network Security	Protecting data during transmission	Firewalls, intrusion detection/prevention systems
Cloud Security	Security of data stored in the cloud	Encryption, secure access controls, cloud security best practices

and keystrokes, user authentication is strengthened and becomes more resistant to social engineering attempts. Access controls can also be dynamically altered in real-time in response to user behavior due to Human DT. This proactive strategy effectively prevents the loss of confidential data through social engineering strategies by implementing temporary limits or increasing inspection in response to suspicious behavior [50]. The extensive log of user interactions generated by Human DT is extremely beneficial in incident response and forensics. Customization is a significant advantage when dealing with security training programs led by Human DT. Security awareness programs are more effective when they are customized depending on the behavior and vulnerabilities of the DT that have been identified. Human DTs are inherently capable of alerting and monitoring continuously [51]. Enabling real-time user behavior monitoring makes it possible to identify suspicious activity quickly, set off alarms, and respond quickly to social engineering threats. This approach emphasizes the significance of comprehending and reacting to human behavior in the digital sphere, which aligns with the rapidly changing cybersecurity scenario [52].

DT is susceptible to cyber-attacks, which can jeopardize digital systems, exchanges, physical hardware and sensors, and the necessity to update the condition of physical objects by network connections constantly. A data integrity attack could involve an adversary directly attacking a device used as a source of information, forcing it to upload false or erroneous data [53]. Besides, a malicious party can infiltrate the gateway by which IoT devices upload and receive data, combining false or inaccurate information with the data the devices have gathered. Furthermore, the adversary could feed erroneous data into the DT directly. Any attack can negatively impact the entire system integrity on the DT because of its close relationship to physical items. DT programs contain personal information like medical records, data from autonomous vehicles, and real-time smart grid operations [48]. A method for verifying digital communications, machine-to-machine transfers, and cyber-physical entities is required. A DT program builds a digital model of the physical structure using data from sensors from the object layer. Attackers may use malware propagation or denial-of-service (DoS) attacks to target sensors or gateways [54].

5   Discussion

This study addressed the two RQs. The first question highlights human DT's values, acceptance factors, and model. It indicates that user acceptability is correlated with efficient engagement and interaction, highlighting the benefits of the DT experience. For the widespread adoption process, compatibility with current systems is essential. Users interacting with the DT should have their privacy and security concerns addressed to promote acceptance and confidence. The usage of DT in agriculture, automobile, aerospace, manufacturing, healthcare, and contribution is depicted in Fig. 3. The benefits of human DT in healthcare, research areas, empowering self-education, human immortality through data, and rapid diagnostics are depicted in Fig. 4. Figure 5 summarizes the human DT model, which consists of interchange components, data integration, data cleaning, database, two-way communication, and real-world twins. The values and empathy of human DT are illustrated in Fig. 6. The second research question focused on using DT to address cybersecurity-related issues, like social engineering. DTs are critical to cybersecurity because they facilitate constant user behavior monitoring and real-time analysis, which helps to spot abnormalities that could be signs of social engineering attempts, as demonstrated in Table 1. Table 1 also depicts the interaction of DT and cybersecurity. Further, predictive models are developed using historical information from DT, which helps organizations predict possible social engineering risks and take preventative action.

Security of the networks, servers, and virtualization systems that comprise the DT itself is especially important. The defense in depth is the basis of the DT system protection strategies, necessitating security measures to prevent access to digital assets, including

Automation ML requirements [55]. Security operations center (SOC) can analyze events created by DTs, such as virtualization systems and protocols, to determine each DT area's vulnerabilities, attack points, and other dangers, such as APTs, including the digital thread. Therefore, specialized systems are SOCs under the supervision of cyber security specialists who manage incident responses, maintain security-related events, and organize forensics tasks [13]. DTs can comprehend security concerns inside their organization using security information and event management (SIEM) systems. The ability of these monitoring strategies and analytics to quickly gather, analyze, and display reliable data and their reaction systems to handle incidents and forensic evidence are other factors that determine effectiveness [56].

6   Conclusions and Future Work Directions

Significant barriers and promising future possibilities are present at the intersection of security concerns and human aspects in DT technology. The challenge is to integrate strong security measures to protect private information with human-centric components like behavior and decision-making. Acquiring informed consent, protecting privacy, and addressing ethical issues are significant problems that need thorough review. But there are a lot of potential advantages. This study addressed two research questions, values of human DT while creating models, acceptance factors, and how DTs can be used to address cybersecurity issues. The uses of human DT are considerable, ranging from improved training scenarios and remote surveillance abilities to personalized healthcare and behavioral analysis-based predictive modeling. The opportunities for future studies include developing user trust, building standards, and enhancing the connection between security protection and human-centric considerations.

References

1. Walia, G.K., Kumar, M., Gill, S.S.: AI-empowered fog/edge resource management for IoT applications: a comprehensive review, research challenges and future perspectives. IEEE Commun. Surv. Tutorials (2023)
2. VanDerHorn, E., Mahadevan, S.: Digital Twin: generalization, characterization and implementation. Decis. Support. Syst. **145**, 113524 (2021)
3. Wang, S., Zhang, J., Wang, P., Law, J., Calinescu, R., Mihaylova, L.: A deep learning-enhanced Digital Twin framework for improving safety and reliability in human–robot collaborative manufacturing. Robot. Comput.-Integr. Manuf. **85**, 102608 (2024)
4. Yin, Y., Zheng, P., Li, C., Wang, L.: A state-of-the-art survey on Augmented Reality-assisted Digital Twin for futuristic human-centric industry transformation. Robot. Comput.-Integrat. Manuf. **81**, 102515 (2023)
5. van Dyck, M., Lüttgens, D., Piller, F.T., Brenk, S.: Interconnected digital twins and the future of digital manufacturing: Insights from a Delphi study. J. Product Innov. Manage. (2023)
6. Lampropoulos, G., Siakas, K.: Enhancing and securing cyber-physical systems and Industry 4.0 through digital twins: a critical review. J. Softw. Evol. Process **35**(7), e2494 (2023)
7. El-Kady, A.H., Halim, S., El-Halwagi, M.M., Khan, F.: Analysis of safety and security challenges and opportunities related to cyber-physical systems. Process Safety and Environmental Protection (2023)

8. Kamdjou, H. M., Baudry, D., Havard, V., Ouchani, S.: Resource-Constrained eXtended reality operated with digital twin in industrial Internet of Things. IEEE Open J. Commun. Soc. (2024)

9. Ystgaard, K.F., et al.: Review of the theory, principles, and design requirements of human-centric Internet of Things (IoT). J. Ambient. Intell. Humaniz. Comput. **14**(3), 2827–2859 (2023)

10. Barik, K., Misra, S., Konar, K., Fernandez-Sanz, L., Koyuncu, M.: Cybersecurity deep: approaches, attacks dataset, and comparative study. Appl. Artif. Intell. **36**(1), 2055399 (2022)

11. Abayomi-Alli, O., Misra, S., Abayomi-Alli, A., Odusami, M.: A review of soft techniques for SMS spam classification: methods, approaches and applications. Eng. Appl. Artif. Intell. **86**, 197–212 (2019)

12. Holmes, D., Papathanasaki, M., Maglaras, L., Ferrag, M.A., Nepal, S., Janicke, H.: Digital Twins and Cyber Security–solution or challenge? In: 2021 6th South-East Europe Design Automation, Computer Engineering, Computer Networks and Social Media Conference (SEEDA-CECNSM), pp. 1–8. IEEE, September 2021

13. Alcaraz, C., Lopez, J.: Digital twin: a comprehensive survey of security threats. IEEE Commun. Surv. Tutorials **24**(3), 1475–1503 (2022)

14. de Hoz Diego, J.D., Temperekidis, A., Katsaros, P., Konstantinou, C.: An iot digital twin for cyber-security defence based on runtime verification. In International Symposium on Leveraging Applications of Formal Methods, pp. 556–574. Springer, Cham (2022)

15. Eckhart, M., Ekelhart, A.: Digital twins for cyber-physical systems security: State of the art and outlook. Security and Quality in Cyber-Physical Systems Engineering: With Forewords by Robert M. Lee and Tom Gilb, pp. 383–412 (2019)

16. Mihai, S., et al.: Digital twins: a survey on enabling technologies, challenges, trends and future prospects. IEEE Communications Surveys & Tutorials (2022)

17. Hu, Z., Lou, S., Xing, Y., Wang, X., Cao, D., Lv, C.: Review and perspectives on driver digital twin and its enabling technologies for intelligent vehicles. IEEE Trans. Intell. Vehicles (2022)

18. Lu, Y., Liu, C., Kevin, I., Wang, K., Huang, H., Xu, X.: Digital Twin-driven smart manufacturing: connotation, reference model, applications and research issues. Robot. Comput.-Integr. Manuf. **61**, 101837 (2020)

19. Liu, M., Fang, S., Dong, H., Xu, C.: Review of digital twin about concepts, technologies, and industrial applications. J. Manuf. Syst. **58**, 346–361 (2021)

20. Wilhelm, J., Petzoldt, C., Beinke, T., Freitag, M.: Review of digital twin-based interaction in smart manufacturing: enabling cyber-physical systems for human-machine interaction. Int. J. Comput. Integr. Manuf. **34**(10), 1031–1048 (2021)

21. Lehtola, V.V., et al.: Digital twin of a city: Review of technology serving city needs. Int. J. Appl. Earth Observ. Geoinform., 102915 (2022)

22. Pylianidis, C., Osinga, S., Athanasiadis, I.N.: Introducing digital twins to agriculture. Comput. Electron. Agric. **184**, 105942 (2021)

23. Berti, N., Finco, S.: Digital twin and human factors in manufacturing and logistics systems: state of the art and future research directions. IFAC-PapersOnLine **55**(10), 1893–1898 (2022)

24. Semeraro, C., Lezoche, M., Panetto, H., Dassisti, M.: Digital twin paradigm: a systematic literature review. Comput. Ind. **130**, 103469 (2021)

25. Wang, L., Gao, R., Váncza, J., Krüger, J., Wang, X.V., Makris, S., Chryssolouris, G.: Symbiotic human-robot collaborative assembly. CIRP Annals **68**(2), 701–726 (2019)

26. Chen, M., et al.: Artificial intelligence and visual analytics in geographical space and cyberspace: Research opportunities and challenges. Earth-Science Reviews, 104438 (2023)

27. Salvi, A., Spagnoletti, P., Noori, N.S.: Cyber-resilience of critical cyber infrastructures: integrating digital twins in the electric power ecosystem. Comput. Secur. **112**, 102507 (2022)

28. Zeb, S., Mahmood, A., Khowaja, S.A., Dev, K., Hassan, S.A., Gidlund, M., Bellavista, P.: Towards defining industry 5.0 vision with intelligent and softwarized wireless network architectures and services: a survey. J. Network Comput. Appl., 103796 (2023)

29. Agrawal, A., Thiel, R., Jain, P., Singh, V., Fischer, M.: Digital Twin: where do humans fit in? Autom. Constr. **148**, 104749 (2023)
30. Iwaki, T., Satoshi, K., Hajime, N., Takao, K., Keiichi, H., Shiro, O.: Challenges facing human digital twin computing and its future prospects. NTT Techn. Rev. **18**(9), 19–24 (2020)
31. Barricelli, B.R., Fogli, D.: Digital twins in human-computer interaction: a systematic review. Int. J. Human-Comput. Interact. **40**(2), 79–97 (2024)
32. Pahlavan, K., Krishnamurthy, P.: Evolution and impact of Wi-Fi technology and applications: a historical perspective. Int. J. Wireless Inf. Networks **28**, 3–19 (2021)
33. Aminizadeh, S., et al.: The applications of machine learning techniques in medical data processing based on distributed computing and the Internet of Things. Comput. Methods Programs Biomed., 107745 (2023)
34. Chen, Z.S., Chen, K.D., Xu, Y.Q., Pedrycz, W., Skibniewski, M.J.: Multiobjective optimization-based decision support for building digital twin maturity measurement. Adv. Eng. Inform. **59**, 102245 (2024)
35. Li, Y., et al.: DTBVis: An interactive visual comparison system for digital twin brain and human brain. Visual Informatics (2023)
36. Mazumder, A., et al.: Towards next generation digital twin in robotics: Trends, scopes, challenges, and future. Heliyon (2023)
37. Amara, K., Kerdjidj, O., Ramzan, N.: Emotion Recognition for Affective human digital twin by means of virtual reality enabling technologies. IEEE Access (2023)
38. Mao, C., Chang, D.: Review of cross-device interaction for facilitating digital transformation in smart home context: a user-centric perspective. Adv. Eng. Inform. **57**, 102087 (2023)
39. Seegrün, A., et al.: Sustainable product lifecycle management with Digital Twins: a systematic literature review. Procedia CIRP **119**, 776–781 (2023)
40. Riedelsheimer, T., Dorfhuber, L., Stark, R.: User centered development of a Digital Twin concept with focus on sustainability in the clothing industry. Procedia CIRP **90**, 660–665 (2020)
41. D'Mello, S.K., Graesser, A.: Intelligent tutoring systems: How computers achieve learning gains that rival human tutors. In: Handbook of Educational Psychology, pp. 603–629. Routledge (2023)
42. Minghui, H., Ya, H., Xinzhi, L., Ziyuan, L., Jiang, Z., Bo, M.A.: Digital twin model of gas turbine and its application in warning of performance fault. Chin. J. Aeronaut. **36**(3), 449–470 (2023)
43. Thakur, G., Kumar, P., Jangirala, S., Das, A.K., Park, Y.: An effective privacy-preserving blockchain-assisted security protocol for cloud-based digital twin environment. IEEE Access **11**, 26877–26892 (2023)
44. Boje, C., Guerriero, A., Kubicki, S., Rezgui, Y.: Towards a semantic Construction Digital Twin: Directions for future research. Autom. Constr. **114**, 103179 (2020)
45. Babu, S.S., Mourad, A.H.I., Harib, K.H., Vijayavenkataraman, S.: Recent developments in the application of machine-leaning towards accelerated predictive multiscale design and additive manufacturing. Virtual Phys. Prototyping **18**(1), e2141653 (2023)
46. Balta, E.C., Pease, M., Moyne, J., Barton, K., Tilbury, D.M.: Digital twin-based cyber-attack detection framework for cyber-physical manufacturing systems. IEEE Trans. Automation Sci. Eng. (2023)
47. Suhail, S., Iqbal, M., Hussain, R., Jurdak, R.: ENIGMA: An explainable digital twin security solution for cyber–physical systems. Comput. Ind. **151**, 103961 (2023)
48. Manickam, S., Yarlagadda, L., Gopalan, S.P., Chowdhary, C.L.: Unlocking the potential of digital twins: a comprehensive review of concepts, frameworks, and industrial applications. IEEE Access **11**, 135147–135158 (2023)

49. De Benedictis, A., Flammini, F., Mazzocca, N., Somma, A., Vitale, F.: Digital twins for anomaly detection in the industrial internet of things: conceptual architecture and proof-of-concept. IEEE Trans. Ind. Inf. (2023)

50. Khan, S., Alzaabi, A., Ratnarajah, T., Arslan, T.: Novel statistical time series data augmentation and machine learning based classification of unobtrusive respiration data for respiration Digital Twin model. Comput. Biol. Med. **168**, 107825 (2024)

51. Böttjer, T., et al.: A review of unit level digital twin applications in the manufacturing industry. CIRP J. Manuf. Sci. Technol. **45**, 162–189 (2023)

52. Jia, J.,et al.: Digital twin technology and ergonomics for comprehensive improvement of safety in the petrochemical industry. Process Safety Progress (2024)

53. Sam, D.D.: The Impact of System Outages on National Critical Infrastructure Sectors: Cybersecurity Practitioners' Perspective (Doctoral dissertation, Marymount University) (2023)

54. Ma, X., Qi, Q., Tao, F.: An ontology-based data-model coupling approach for digital twin. Robot. Comput.-Integr. Manuf. **86**, 102649 (2024)

55. Shankar, D.D., Azhakath, A.S., Khalil, N., Sajeev, J., Mahalakshmi, T., Sheeba, K.: Data Mining for Cyber Biosecurity Risk Management–a comprehensive review. Comput. Secur., 103627 (2023)

56. Repetto, M.: Adaptive monitoring, detection, and response for agile digital service chains. Comput. Secur., 103343 (2023)

Visualizing Cybersecurity Diagrams: An Empirical Analysis of Common Weakness Enumeration Images

Benjamin Schooley[✉], Derek Hansen, Ethan James Richmond,
Malaya Jordan Canite, and Nimrod Max Huaira Reyna

Brigham Young University, Provo, UT 84602, USA
Ben_schooley@byu.edu

Abstract. Visualizations of cybersecurity diagrams can play an important role in understanding security weaknesses, vulnerabilities, and attacks. Unlike other computing and engineering domains, cybersecurity does not have a standardized visual modeling language that characterizes its core components. This empirical study analyzes 500 public images found via Google Image Search for the 2023 Common Weakness Enumeration (CWE) Top 25 Most Dangerous Software Weaknesses. We find all CWEs include at least some diagrams. Most (52%) diagrams show weaknesses, some (16%) show solutions, and very few (6%) show both. Code is found in at least some diagrams for all but one CWE and is positively correlated with the number of elements and words. Images showing a malicious attack typically (72%) include a representation of a hacker, nearly always (93%) include a payload, and typically (79%) include a target (i.e., an asset that is attacked or more rarely a victim represented). Diagrams vary widely in how they use visual elements, even within the same CWE. Implications of these findings on the development of new cybersecurity-specific visual modeling languages are discussed.

Keywords: Visualization · Common Weakness Enumeration · CWE · Modeling Language · Modeling Notation · Education · Communication · Security Awareness Training

1 Introduction

Cybersecurity is increasingly important for the protection of individuals, organizations, and their valuable resources. For example, the global costs of cybercrime have been estimated to amount to over US$10.5 trillion per year by 2025 [1]. As security threats continue to grow in number and magnitude, it is likewise essential to improve defensive capabilities. One of the most important defensive strategies to overcome adversarial attacks is to build individual and organizational capabilities to communicate and educate about different types of security weaknesses, vulnerabilities, and threats [2]. This explains the community efforts to classify and document cybersecurity weaknesses, vulnerabilities, and threats, which are funded by the U.S. government and operated by The MITRE Corporation. For example, the Common Weakness Enumeration (CWE) provides a list of

© The Author(s), under exclusive license to Springer Nature Switzerland AG 2024
A. Moallem (Ed.): HCII 2024, LNCS 14728, pp. 296–317, 2024.
https://doi.org/10.1007/978-3-031-61379-1_19

over 1,300 different hardware and software weaknesses (e.g., SQL Injection, Modification of Assumed-Immutable Data) [3]. While these efforts to comprehensively describe, classify, and enumerate security weaknesses are useful for cybersecurity experts, the highly technical text-based descriptions are not accessible to students, developers, engineers, and managers who are more peripherally involved in cybersecurity, yet need to understand these concepts.

Individual comprehension and learning can be effectively facilitated using modeling and visualization tools to communicate cybersecurity threats [4]. Although cliché, sometimes a picture is worth a thousand words, when trying to convey a difficult concept with multiple moving parts, such as a Cross-Site Scripting attack. While textbooks, blogs, and cybersecurity company websites often include diagrams to help explain cybersecurity weaknesses and attacks, there is no agreed-upon visual language to aid in this effort. Developing visual language standards for specific purposes has proven useful for developers (e.g., Unified Modeling Language diagrams) and engineers (e.g. Piping and Instrumentation diagrams). It is time to consider the development of such a visual language for cybersecurity weaknesses and attacks.

In this research, we take a first step toward the development of such a visual language by examining existing diagrams of cybersecurity weaknesses. Specifically, we examine public images found on the Internet for the "2023 CWE Top 25 Most Dangerous Software Weaknesses". By analyzing the current state of visual diagramming for cybersecurity, we aim to help identify commonly used visualization patterns, as well as weaknesses in how they are portrayed. Understanding these patterns will ultimately aid us in developing new visual modeling languages specifically designed to represent cybersecurity weaknesses, vulnerabilities, and attacks to further enable comprehension and learning across a wide range of users – from lay individuals, to computing professionals and organizational decision makers.

2 Background and Literature Review

2.1 Common Weakness Enumerations

Identifying, documenting, and communicating computing weaknesses, vulnerabilities, and threats is a core responsibility for cybersecurity professionals [5] involved in security planning, design and operations [6]. Common Weakness Enumerations (CWEs) are standardized text-based explanations and definitions created to help IT and cybersecurity professionals identify, communicate, and protect against common system weaknesses and vulnerabilities [7]. They contain relevant information for software developers to avoid the most common types of security flaws [8]. Effective communication about security weaknesses is a precursor to designing effective solutions and thus CWEs play a key role to standardize language and concepts relative to security weaknesses [9, 10]. Although CWEs are descriptive, they are often not well understood, communicated, nor applied in the professional cybersecurity and software development community [11]. CWEs can be complex in terms of their definitions, their relationships to other CWEs (and sub-domains), and application to industry software and architectural solutions.

An important strategy for overcoming this challenge and more fully comprehending technical and complex attacks, threats, and defensive strategies is to apply visual-based sense-making and reasoning [12]. This can be effectively facilitated using modeling and visualization tools. Cybersecurity visualization research applies visual-based sense-making and reasoning concepts to support better and faster comprehension of attacks, threats, and defensive strategies [12]. Visual models are valuable for a wide range of cybersecurity activities, including real-time cybersecurity operations, monitoring events, predicting future attacks, and for education, training, and communication. In this paper, we aim to understand how common weaknesses are communicated using visual diagrams to aid in security design efforts.

2.2 Cybersecurity Event Visualization

Data visualization is the graphical representation of information and data. Visual representations are often in the form of charts, graphs, diagrams, and maps, providing an accessible way to see and understand patterns in data. Some research efforts focus on visualization of large datasets to improve cybersecurity operations [6]. For example, CVExplorer allows users to visualize the relationships of various factors existing across a large number of vulnerability reports, such as types and levels of vulnerability, vendors, and products [13]. Others have created data analytic visualizations to aid in hands-on cybersecurity training exercises – such as presenting status, monitoring, and outcomes for capture-the-flag (CTF) competitions [12].

Visual modeling has also been applied for correlation and prediction of potentially large and complex attacks using attack graphs. Attack graphs are designed to show all paths of vulnerability across a network in order to assess attack likelihoods and thus demonstrate overall security of a networked system [4]. Significant prior work has applied graph models to visualize threats, monitor attacks, assess overall cybersecurity risks for organizations, and predict potential vulnerabilities for cyber operations [14]. There are many possible ways to conceptualize or create a meaningful graph drawing. Attack graphs of large datasets are complex, even for assessing a small number of networked assets, and thus are intended for the seasoned cybersecurity expert [4]. In this context, the goal of visualization of large datasets and graphs is to defend technical systems during operations. In contrast, our goal for visualizing CWEs is to help viewers understand cybersecurity weaknesses, which is critical to effectively implement security design – which aims to help create understanding and readiness to react dynamically during operations [6].

2.3 Visual Modeling for Cyber Physical Systems

Some research efforts have focused on modeling cybersecurity for computing infrastructure that controls and interacts with critical infrastructure. These cyber physical systems (CPS) include the power grid [15], smart cities and smart homes [15–17], nuclear power plants [18], intelligent transportation systems [19], autonomous vehicles [20] and others. These research efforts have proposed frameworks for identifying and monitoring CPS assets, assessing resource consumption and performance [21], communicating security requirements, and for large-scale threat modeling [16, 17]. For example, one study proposed conceptual representations of cybersecurity costs associated with the attacker and defender from a game-theoretic standpoint. Cost metrics included vulnerabilities such as loss of load indices, flow violations, or voltage violations for an electrical grid [15].

Cybersecurity visual modeling for CPS has been goal-oriented and focused on engineering design for a very specific type of cyber-physical context. In contrast, our aim is more generalized: to understand how common system weaknesses can be illustrated to better educate a wide range of technical and non-technical cybersecurity stakeholders, as well as foster more effective communication between them. Stakeholders include students, researchers, cybersecurity and business professionals and their associated teams who seek to plan, design, and assess common cybersecurity weaknesses, attack patterns, and techniques.

2.4 Cybersecurity Modeling Languages

A well-defined, standardized, and widely used modeling language, or notation, is lacking for cybersecurity engineering [22]. Some prior research has contributed understanding in this regard. One study sought to modify the existing systems engineering modeling language known as SysML to facilitate modeling in cybersecurity [22]. The resulting Security Modeling Language (SecML) can be used to model cyber-attacks and related defensive scenarios [22]. Like SysML, the SecML diagramming concept is largely derived from the Unified Modeling Language (UML) to be used for architectural design and requirements gathering and communication across software engineering teams. UML requires significant amounts of education and practice to be used and understood effectively [23].

Another modeling language, Cyber Security Modeling Language (CySeMoL), was developed for estimating the level of cybersecurity within an enterprise architecture [24]. The purpose is to assess attack probabilities based on an enterprise system architecture. The architecture must be modeled according to a defined standard and then assessed using CySeMoL. CySeMoL is designed to work with large enterprise systems from a systems design and engineering perspective. It is not intended as a general modeling tool for a wide range of cybersecurity applications to visualize and demonstrate specific weaknesses, attack types, nor techniques [22].

Some progress has been made with visual modeling for systems design and requirements documentation. For example, one effort proposed a general template to describe security threats that can be used in the early stages of software development [5]. In another study, researchers presents progress towards visual iconography (elements) and a grammar for Internet of Things (IoT) system representations and their cybersecurity requirements [25]. These efforts contribute to a range of concepts that, taken together, could provide valuable input into a comprehensive visual language.

In another more recent effort, [26] created and tested a web-based modeling tool for mapping cybersecurity related user journeys. The tool, called HORM Diagramming Tool (HORMDT), was developed based on the Customer Journey Modeling Language (CJML) and the Human and Organizational Risk Modeling (HORM) framework. Similar to UML activity diagrams and business process modeling notation (BPMN), this tool facilitates diagramming from a user-centered business process perspective. Essentially, the tool can be used to diagram a user experience with an attack and/or defense scenario. As the tool is centered on users, it is limited in its capability to model a wide range of system centered weaknesses and solutions.

The above tools and methods provide a useful foundation for building upon. The goal of this research is to understand the existing approaches, gaps, and needs related to a general use diagramming and visualization tool designed to represent common weaknesses and vulnerabilities. Such a tool could be used for a broad range of cybersecurity modeling activities, such as learning and communicating common cybersecurity weaknesses, attack patterns, or techniques as found in systems or employed by adversaries. The aim of the research reported here is to assess the quality and viability of publicly accessible diagrams that communicate CWE's, and analyze how existing visual diagrams are designed and structured to communicate common cybersecurity weaknesses.

3   Methods

To understand how CWE's are communicated within diagrams, we performed an empirical examination of existing images found via Google Images. Our analysis examined their relationship to CWE descriptions, their format, structure, and content as described below.

3.1   Image Selection

On November 15, 2023, we searched for images related to the 2023 CWE Top 25 Most Dangerous Software Weaknesses (Top 25 CWEs) as indicated and described by MITRE Corporation [7]. We constructed search terms from each CWE and downloaded the top 20 image results from Google Images resulting in a data set of 500 images using the GoogleImageScraper python library tool. Specifically, we defined the search keys of the scraper to conduct a Boolean search on Google Images using the following pattern:

[("CWE_NAME") OR ("ALT_NAME") OR ("ALT_NAME") ...] AND security AND diagram

CWE_NAME is the name of the CWE (e.g., "Improper Neutralization of Input During Web Page Generation ('Cross-site Scripting')". ALT_NAME is any Alternative Terms specified on the detailed CWE description page and were strung together using the OR operator: E.g., ("XSS") OR ("HTML Injection") OR ("CSS"). The phrase "AND security AND diagram" is used to state that we are searching for security related diagrams.

3.2 Analysis

The goal of our analysis was to gain insights into current practices related to visualizing cybersecurity weaknesses and vulnerabilities. Thus, we focused on classifying the 500 images into categories that described the focus of the image (e.g., if it showed a weakness or a solution), as well as salient features of the visualization (e.g., number of diagram elements; number of words).

Categories were determined and refined through an iterative process requiring consensus across the group of four researchers. To facilitate this process, the group created a code book with the name and description of each category. After the initial version of the code book was created, two raters independently rated a subset of images and met to discuss discrepancies. This led to refinement of the code book, which typically entailed adding more details to the descriptions that were previously ambiguous. The two raters discussed changes to the code book with the larger research group, which reviewed images of edge cases and further refined the categories. This process continued through multiple iterations until the group felt the code book was sufficiently detailed.

Once the code book was finalized, two researchers analyzed all the images independently. The inter-rater reliability was calculated using the Cohen's Kappa statistic [27, 28]. Scores ranged from 0.61 to 1.00, which we felt was high enough to proceed. In cases where there was a discrepancy, the two raters viewed the image in question, considered arguments for each rating, and jointly agreed on the best fit category. The final data results are available by request. The final categories are described in Table 1 along with Cohen's Kappa results.

In addition to the quantitative ratings, we performed a qualitative assessment of images from each category. For example, the Hacker category identified all images that represented a hacker. We reviewed these images as a group to identify the qualitative ways that hackers were represented. A basic visual thematic analysis approach was used for this analysis to identify common themes.

Descriptive statistics were calculated and are reported throughout the findings section. Additionally, the significance of correlations between categories of interest was calculated based on a two-tailed test evaluating if the correlation was significantly different than 0 [29]. Diagrams displayed in this article are not copies of the originals due to copyright considerations. Most diagrams herein have been recreated by the authors as similar representations of the original concepts.

Table 1. Code Book Schema

Label	Description	n =	Cohen's Kappa
Relevant (or Irrelevant)	Related to Computer Science or Information Technology or Cybersecurity	500	1.00
Diagram (or Not-Diagram)	Is the image a diagram? Diagrams include a depiction containing multiple components and their relation to each other. This does not include Slideshows, Web Article Pictures, or Charts (Pie, Bar, Line, Scatter, etc.)	489	0.94
Weakness (or Not Weakness)	Is the image depicting this specific weakness (i.e. CWE)?	399	0.88
Solution (or Problem)	Is the image depicting a solution to a weakness?	399	0.61
Contains Code (or No Code)	Is there computer code in the image (e.g., C++, Java, SQL, HTML, OOP Object, Binary, file extension)?	250	0.80
Number of Elements	How many elements are depicted in the image? Elements include: Shapes and arrows that convey meaning, structure, or show flow; named regions containing boxes and associated text (internal components will each be their own element); multiple components that have the same color that are not isolated; ignore diagram's legend	250	N/A
Number of Words	How many words are in the image? The following counts as one word: hyphenated words; words inside of parentheses; a formula counts; a block of code; a block of symbols/characters that imparts meaning. If the diagram is illegible, estimate the number of words	250	N/A
Malicious (Not Malicious)	Represents hacking in any capacity, depicting the presence of something malicious or fraudulent being attempted	500	0.86

(continued)

Table 1. (*continued*)

Label	Description	n =	Cohen's Kappa
Hacker (or no Hacker)	Does the image explicitly depict or refer to a person as a hacker?	197	0.96
Payload (or no Payload)	Does the image explicitly depict or refer to a payload being sent to or having already influenced a person or asset?	197	0.84
Affected (or no Affected)	Represents who or what was affected by the actions of a hacker/payload	197	0.92
Victim (or no Victim)	Does the image explicitly depict or refer to a person affected by a hacker or payload?	156	0.77
Asset (or no Asset)	Does the image explicitly depict or refer to a non-person affected by a hacker or payload? Examples of assets include: Computers; networks; systems	156	0.91

4   Findings

4.1   CWE Image Results, Relevance, and Diagrams

A total of 500 images (20 from each of the Top 25 CWEs) were collected from Google Images and analyzed (see Table 2). Most images (98%) were related to computing (i.e., were Relevant). And of those, the majority (82%) were Diagrams as opposed to charts or pictures from web articles or slideshows as depicted in Fig. 1. However, the percentage of Relevant images that were Diagrams varied based on the CWE, ranging from 50% ("Missing Authentication for Critical Function") to 100% (e.g., "Cross-site Scripting", "Server-side Request Forgery", and "Cross-Site Request Forgery"). This suggests that some CWEs are likely more difficult to visualize using a diagram than others, but that all CWEs are possible to visualize using diagrams. The Pearson's correlation between Rank and number of Diagram elements is positive, but not significant ($r(23) = -0.285$, $p = 0.167$). This suggests that the CWE rank position is not more or less likely to include images that are diagrams.

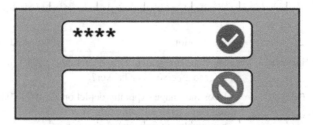

Fig. 1. Example image from a web article that is not a diagram for CWE 20 – Improper Input Validation

4.2 CWE Diagram Analysis

Each Diagram was analyzed to determine if it included a representation of the Weakness (i.e., the CWE in question), a Solution to the CWE, or both (see Table 3). Just over half (52%) of the diagrams represented the Weakness, with far fewer images (19%) representing a Solution. Only 6% of images include both a Weakness and Solution, suggesting the challenge of showing both in a single diagram. The presence of a Weakness in a diagram was found to be negatively correlated with the presence of a Solution (r(397) = −0.15, p = 0.003). Figure 2 illustrates a diagram representing both a weakness and solution for CWE 20 – Invalid Input Validation – because the reader could reasonably infer that both a problem exists if input validation does not occur and the appropriate system response (solution) when proper input validation does occur for a web form.

Fig. 2. Example diagram showing a weakness and a solution for CWE 20 – Improper input validation.

The percentage of Weaknesses and Solutions varied dramatically by CWE. Many showed primarily Weaknesses, with few or no Solutions (e.g., CWE 79, 89, 352, 119, 918, 362). Others showed primarily Solutions with few or no Weaknesses (e.g., CWE 862, 798, 269, 276). And a subset showed comparable numbers of each (e.g., CWE 94, 190, 287, 125, 20). This suggests that the topic of a CWE lends itself to showing either a Weakness or Solution, but typically not both. Figure 3 illustrates an example diagram that includes a solution only for CWE 798 – Use of Hard Coded Credentials. In this diagram, a specific solution is described using a commercial cloud service and it's prescribed authentication and authorization process. Iconography, directional arrows, a linear set of actions, and text descriptions are illustrated. Though the specific weakness may be inferred, it is not easily understood except by the IT professional familiar with the reasoning behind the authentication solution.

Table 2. CWE Image Relevance and Diagrams

Rank	CWE	CWE - Name	Relevant	Diagram
1	787	Out-of-bounds Write	20 (100%)	16 (80%)
2	79	Improper Neutralization of Input During Web Page Generation ('Cross-site Scripting')	20 (100%)	20 (100%)
3	89	Improper Neutralization of Special Elements used in an SQL Command ('SQL Injection')	20 (100%)	18 (90%)
4	416	Use After Free	20 (100%)	18 (90%)
5	78	Improper Neutralization of Special Elements used in an OS Command ('OS Command Injection')	19 (95%)	11 (58%)
6	20	Improper Input Validation	20 (100%)	18 (90%)
7	125	Out-of-bounds Read	20 (100%)	14 (70%)
8	22	Improper Limitation of a Pathname to a Restricted Directory ('Path Traversal')	20 (100%)	17 (85%)
9	352	Cross-Site Request Forgery (CSRF)	20 (100%)	20 (100%)
10	434	Unrestricted Upload of File with Dangerous Type	20 (100%)	19 (95%)
11	862	Missing Authorization	20 (100%)	19 (95%)
12	476	NULL Pointer Dereference	18 (90%)	15 (83%)
13	287	Improper Authentication	20 (100%)	18 (90%)
14	190	Integer Overflow or Wraparound	18 (90%)	12 (67%)
15	502	Deserialization of Untrusted Data	16 (80%)	14 (88%)
16	77	Improper Neutralization of Special Elements used in a Command ('Command Injection')	20 (100%)	11 (55%)
17	119	Improper Restriction of Operations within the Bounds of a Memory Buffer	20 (100%)	19 (95%)
18	798	Use of Hard-coded Credentials	18 (90%)	12 (67%)
19	918	Server-Side Request Forgery (SSRF)	20 (100%)	20 (100%)
20	306	Missing Authentication for Critical Function	20 (100%)	10 (50%)
21	362	Concurrent Execution using Shared Resource with Improper Synchronization ('Race Condition')	20 (100%)	18 (90%)
22	269	Improper Privilege Management	20 (100%)	15 (75%)
23	94	Improper Control of Generation of Code ('Code Injection')	20 (100%)	16 (80%)
24	863	Incorrect Authorization	20 (100%)	16 (80%)
25	276	Incorrect Default Permissions	20 (100%)	13 (65%)
Total		All CWEs	489 (98%)	399 (82%)

Table 3. CWE Diagram Analysis

CWE	Diagram	Weakness	Solution	Weakness or Solution			
				Total (W or S)	Contains Code	Elements AVG	Words AVG
787	16	11 (69%)	1 (6%)	11 (69%)	2 (18%)	19	69
79	20	20 (100%)	0 (0%)	20 (100%)	4 (20%)	9	38
89	18	18 (100%)	0 (0%)	18 (100%)	9 (50%)	11	23
416	18	13 (72%)	3 (17%)	13 (72%)	5 (38%)	11	21
78	11	8 (73%)	0 (0%)	8 (73%)	5 (63%)	12	31
20	18	12 (67%)	9 (50%)	14 (77%)	5 (36%)	16	42
125	14	2 (14%)	1 (7%)	2 (14%)	2 (100%)	9	19
22	17	11 (65%)	0 (0%)	11 (65%)	6 (55%)	14	41
352	20	17 (85%)	2 (10%)	17 (85%)	4 (24%)	9	36
434	19	16 (84%)	2 (11%)	16 (84%)	12 (75%)	14	21
862	19	1 (5%)	15 (79%)	16 (84%)	9 (56%)	24	40
476	15	2 (13%)	0 (0%)	2 (13%)	2 (100%)	18	65
287	18	2 (11%)	3 (17%)	4 (22%)	3 (75%)	16	41
190	12	4 (33%)	2 (17%)	5 (42%)	2 (40%)	19	27
502	14	4 (29%)	0 (0%)	4 (29%)	3 (75%)	22	53
77	11	7 (64%)	0 (0%)	7 (64%)	2 (29%)	12	33
119	19	17 (89%)	0 (0%)	17 (89%)	9 (53%)	16	37
798	12	2 (17%)	7 (58%)	7 (89%)	3 (38%)	21	53
918	20	19 (95%)	0 (0%)	19 (95%)	4 (21%)	10	18
306	10	0 (0%)	0 (0%)	0 (0%)	–	–	–
362	18	13 (72%)	0 (0%)	13 (72%)	3 (25%)	14	36
269	15	2 (13%)	9 (60%)	10 (67%)	0 (0%)	28	44
94	16	3 (19%)	3 (19%)	5 (31%)	3 (60%)	12	33
863	16	4 (25%)	11 (69%)	12 (75%)	5 (42%)	18	43
276	13	1 (8%)	9 (69%)	9 (69%)	3 (33%)	27	35
Total	399	209 (52%)	77 (19%)	260 (65%)	105 (40%)	15	36

A further analysis of diagrams that showed either a Weakness or Solution (or both) is shown in the rightmost columns of Table 3. About 40% include some code within the diagram, with an average of 15 elements and 36 words per diagram. Nearly all CWEs included at least one diagram with code, and most had multiple diagrams (CWE 269 was an exception). Similarly, words were a critical component to most diagrams in

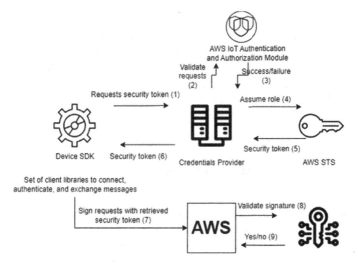

Fig. 3. Example diagram depicting a solution to CWE-798

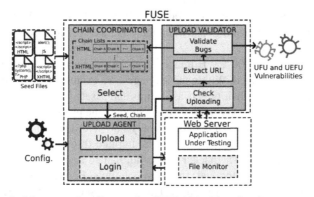

Fig. 4. More complex diagram for CWE-434 with code, elements, words

all CWEs. While the average number of diagram elements differed across CWEs, all were within a relatively narrow range from 9 to 28. In summary, existing diagrams rely heavily upon computer code and words, while including a relatively modest number of diagram elements that appear similar to other diagramming languages [22]. As an example, Fig. 4 illustrates some common diagramming elements for CWE-434 that includes code, word labels, and box elements connected by directional arrows to convey the CWE – Unrestricted upload of file with dangerous type.

Correlations between the number of elements, words, and existence of code were calculated. The number of elements in a diagram was positively correlated with the number of words present in the diagram (r(258) = 0.47, p < .001). This makes sense since many diagrams included text as element labels or content inside of elements. The presence of Code was positively correlated with the number of elements (r(258) = 0.14, p = .022), and number of words present in a diagram (r(258) = 0.14, p = .134), though the last was not significant. This suggests that code is typically included in more complex diagrams.

4.3 Analysis of Malicious Attack Diagrams

We performed a separate analysis of all images that depicted hacking in any capacity (e.g., included a clear malicious or fraudulent act being attempted). In total, 39.4% of all 500 images included a Malicious Attack. These were further analyzed to identify if the images included a representation of a Hacker, Payload, and/or Target (see Table 4).

The majority (72%) of Malicious Attack images portray a hacker explicitly in the diagram. Even more (93%) include a payload, such as malicious code being sent. And most (79%) show a target who is being attacked. The only significant correlation between the three categories was Hacker and Target (r(195) = 0.65, p < 0.001), which were positively correlated, suggesting that when there is a Hacker represented there is often also a Target represented.

While analyzing the 500 CWE images, we observed how the presence of attacks were visually communicated. Within these images, we examined the various depictions of hackers, payloads, and their targets as victims and assets. These images fluctuated in abstraction and differed greatly in how they displayed the process of an attack. Hackers were represented in various ways both visually and with text. The hacker was often referred to as attacker, perpetrator, and can be implied through words like "malicious entity" and "attacker site". The hacker is also not named in many cases, being inferred through icons of masked individuals or hazard symbols. Figure 5, a diagram depicting CWE-78, does not name the hacker, but visually conveys such with the widely understood Guy Fawkes mask symbol. In the image, red code is used to represent a payload, which points to an internet and server icon. In contrast, Fig. 6 names the hacker as a "Malicious User".

Fig. 5. Attacker represented as Guy Fawkes for CWE-78

Table 4. Analysis of Malicious Attack Diagrams

CWE	Total Images	Hacker	Payload	Target		
				Total	*Victim*	*Asset*
787	7	0 (0%)	7 (100%)	3 (43%)	0 (0%)	3 (100%)
79	20	20 (100%)	20 (100%)	20 (100%)	19 (95%)	20 (100%)
89	20	12 (60%)	20 (100%)	15 (75%)	5 (33%)	15 (100%)
416	1	1 (100%)	1 (100%)	1 (100%)	0 (0%)	0 (0%)
78	13	11 (85%)	13 (100%)	13 (100%)	5 (38%)	13 (100%)
20	9	7 (78%)	7 (78%)	5 (56%)	1 (20%)	5 (100%)
125	1	0 (0%)	0 (0%)	0 (0%)	0 (0%)	0 (0%)
22	11	9 (81%)	11 (100%)	11 (100%)	0 (0%)	11 (100%)
352	19	16 (84%)	18 (95%)	17 (90%)	17 (100%)	17 (100%)
434	15	11 (73%)	15 (100%)	13 (87%)	3 (23%)	13 (100%)
862	0	0 (0%)	0 (0%)	0 (0%)	0 (0%)	0 (0%)
476	0	0 (0%)	0 (0%)	0 (0%)	0 (0%)	0 (0%)
287	2	2 (100%)	2 (100%)	2 (100%)	0 (0%)	2 (100%)
190	2	0 (0%)	2 (100%)	2 (100%)	0 (0%)	2 (100%)
502	5	5 (100%)	5 (100%)	5 (100%)	1 (20%)	4 (80%)
77	13	11 (85%)	13 (100%)	12 (92%)	2 (17%)	12 (100%)
119	8	0 (0%)	8 (100%)	0 (0%)	0 (0%)	0 (0%)
798	1	0 (0%)	1 (100%)	0 (0%)	0 (0%)	0 (0%)
918	20	19 (95%)	17 (85%)	19 (95%)	2 (11%)	19 (100%)
306	3	1 (33%)	2 (67%)	1 (33%)	0 (0%)	1 (100%)
362	5	3 (60%)	3 (60%)	5 (100%)	1 (20%)	5 (100%)
269	1	1 (100%)	1 (100%)	1 (100%)	0 (0%)	1 (100%)
94	15	7 (47%)	15 (100%)	7 (47%)	0 (0%)	7 (100%)
863	5	4 (80%)	2 (40%)	3 (60%)	2 (67%)	3 (100%)
276	1	1 (100%)	1 (100%)	1 (100%)	1 (100%)	1 (100%)
Total	197	141 (72%)	186 (93%)	156 (79%)	59 (37%)	154 (99%)

Analysis of attacker images demonstrated a wide range of possible utility, from being undecipherable to informative. Some diagrams provided relatively few existing elements, often not displaying malicious action steps, and referring simply to "hacker action" or "bad result". Other diagrams provided informative descriptions about the hacker-victim relationship, showing action steps or results for the hacker. Still others provided elements and icons, including the use of some code and accompanying descriptive text explanations requiring deeper knowledge from the audience to decipher.

Fig. 6. Example visual representation of hacker described as "Malicious User"

Figure 7 displays a more informative diagram for CWE-863, describing how a malicious user can connect to a vulnerable server and obtain access tokens with a good amount of detail and explanation. Arrows and labels are used to depict a flow of activities while representing an unknown target user, a variety of assets (servers, devices), and entity and process descriptions necessary to understand the attack pattern.

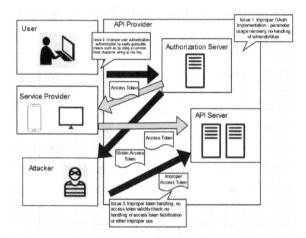

Fig. 7. CWE-863 – Incorrect Authorization – extensively diagrams the exploitation of servers by an attacker, utilizing multiple arrows and textboxes to detail each step.

4.4   Lack of Visualization Standards

During the examination of the 500 images, we were struck by the overall lack of standardization in how the CWEs were displayed. We found a wide range of visual expressions across and within CWEs. For example, Fig. 8 and 9 both depict CWE 862 "Missing Authorization". Notice how different they are in the components they choose to show, the use of color, arrows, lines, whether or not the hacker is shown, the use of code, and icons. This level of difference is common among images we analyzed. For Fig. 8, the general concept of an authorized user may be derived from the diagram, yet additional details may be much more helpful for gaining an adequate understanding of the CWE. In contrast, Fig. 9 illustrates a more complex diagram. Arrows, boxes, embedded boxes, labels, descriptions, iconography, and simple code representation are used to portray potentially dangerous file types to demonstrate the weakness and a solution.

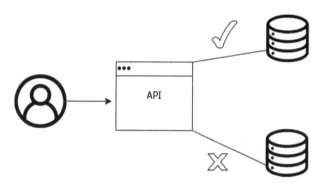

Fig. 8. Example simple diagram for CWE-862 – Missing Authorization

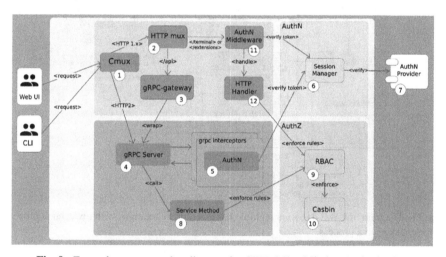

Fig. 9. Example more complex diagram for CWE-862 – Missing Authorization

Figures 10 and 11 provide another example of how different two diagrams can be. Both diagrams describe CWE 416 "Use After Free".

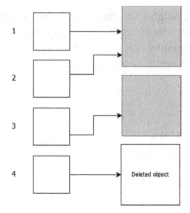

Fig. 10. Illustration of CWE-416 is a very abstract, high-level representation that uses arrows, boxes, colors, and minimal text to convey the core ideas.

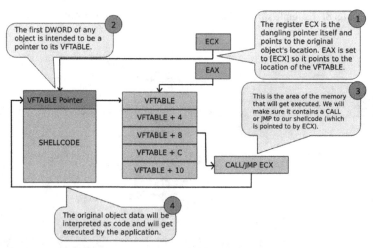

Fig. 11. Diagram of CWE-416 uses multiple boxes, color, annotations with text, and numbers to represent steps in a process.

Figures 12 and 13 serve as the final example of how two diagrams of the same CWE can vary dramatically. Both diagrams describe CWE 190 "Integer Overflow or Wraparound".

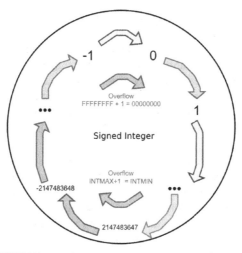

Fig. 12. Diagram for CWE 190 uses abstract curved arrows, code snippets, numbers, and minimal text.

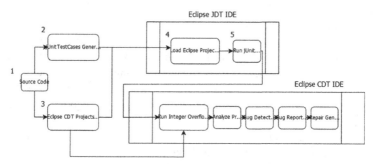

Fig. 13. Diagram for CWE 190 uses boxes, numbered process steps, arrows, dotted lines, and significant amounts of text.

While it makes sense that diagrams from different websites would use different stylistic choices, these examples show the wide range of meanings attributed to diagram elements such as boxes, lines, arrows, and numbers, as well as varied use of colors, icons, and amount of text. Differences across CWEs are even more stark as can be deduced from the examples provided in this section.

5 Discussion and Conclusion

This paper provides a glimpse into the current state of visualizing cybersecurity weaknesses by analyzing the top 500 Google Image results related to the "2023 CWE Top 25 Most Dangerous Software Weaknesses". Analyzing these public images helps us understand what typical users are confronted with when learning about these cybersecurity weaknesses. The analysis can also help inform the design of visual modeling languages specifically designed to represent cybersecurity weaknesses, vulnerabilities, and attacks. Below are some implications based on the key findings.

Although some CWEs seem to be harder to visualize using diagrams than others, all of the 25 CWEs included diagrams. Thus, internet searchers are likely to find examples of diagrams for CWEs, though they may need to add "diagram" to the search term (as we did) to find them. This finding also suggests that a single common visual modeling language for cybersecurity weaknesses may be feasible for many, if not all, CWEs. Further work will need to determine if this holds up for the large number of other CWEs that exist.

Few diagrams (6%) included both a Weakness and a Solution to the weakness and there was a negative correlation between having a Weakness and having a Solution. Those searching the Internet for CWEs are more likely to find diagrams of the weakness (52%) than solutions to the weakness (19%). Those creating a visual modeling language should consider having complementary weakness and solution diagrams, rather than trying to pack them all into a single diagram.

The use of code and text (i.e., words) were used in nearly all CWEs. This suggests that visual modeling languages for CWEs should have standards that allow for the use of code and text, though perhaps in more standard ways than they are currently used (see later discussion).

Diagrams that showed weaknesses and solutions typically included less than 30 elements (avg range of 9 to 28 for each CWE). Positive correlations between the number of elements, words, and code, suggests that some diagrams are more complex than others in many ways. Those designing CWE visual modeling languages for novices will need to find ways to limit a tendency to add unnecessary elements and text into a single diagram. While this may be challenging for some CWEs, we believe it is possible based on our analysis.

Approximately 40% of images represented an actual malicious attack. Most of these (72%) showed some representation of a hacker, using similar imagery and sometimes labels. Showing a victim was less common but did occur at times. CWE visual modeling languages should standardize how hackers and victims are represented, as well as when to include them. We found that showing a malicious payload was extremely common (93% of malicious diagrams), as was showing a targeted asset. Despite their common use, the ways in which malicious payloads and targeted assets were represented varied dramatically, with many of them implied rather than showing explicit indicators. We recommend that CWE visual modeling languages should create specific markers that indicate malicious payloads and targeted assets for clarity.

Perhaps the most noteworthy finding of all was the huge variation in the types of visualizations that were used to describe the CWEs. Differences across different CWEs were to be expected. Some are best represented as network diagrams, while others are better represented as stack diagrams. However, we were struck by the significant variety of visual elements used within the same CWEs. The patterns that do exist seem to be borrowed from other well-known diagramming notations that are intended for other purposes and not directly focused on communicating cybersecurity issues. This lack of standardization means that those learning about CWEs through diagrams are not likely to transfer understanding of visual norms across CWEs. It also means that cybersecurity-specific representations are often lacking. We believe these findings justify the need for a common visual language to describe CWEs, which is designed to be accessible to novices, yet rich enough to convey the wide variety of cybersecurity weaknesses found in CWEs.

This research includes several limitations. We were limited by the number of diagrams and CWE's that were assessed (i.e., 20 images per each of the most dangerous 25 CWE's) via a Google Image search. Assessing more diagrams related to additional CWE's from other sources, or related to other cybersecurity concepts such as common attack patterns (CAPEC), or the MITRE ATT&CK (i.e., adversarial tactics and techniques) framework may produce additional insights. There are also additional ways that the data could be analyzed, such as analyzing the exact ways that hackers are represented to create a "universal" hacker icon. To allow for the further analysis of our dataset, we will provide all images and classifications (e.g., images with a "hacker") upon request.

The research team implemented its own diagram assessment methodology that we believe demonstrates rigor towards identifying an important gap in the cybersecurity visualization literature. We believe it can help inform the development of a visual diagramming language, or notation, standard for communicating common computing weaknesses for a quickly growing field of research and professional activity.

References

1. Morgan: Cybercrime to cost the world $10.5 trillion... - Google Scholar. https://scholar.google.com/scholar_lookup?title=Cybercrime%20to%20Cost%20the%20World%2010.5%20Trillion%20Annually%20By%202025&publication_year=2020&author=S.%20Morgan. Accessed 06 Dec 2023

2. Shillair, R., Esteve-González, P., Dutton, W.H., Creese, S., Nagyfejeo, E., von Solms, B.: Cybersecurity education, awareness raising, and training initiatives: national level evidence-based results, challenges, and promise. Comput. Secur. **119**, 102756 (2022). https://doi.org/10.1016/j.cose.2022.102756

3. Howard, M.: Improving software security by eliminating the CWE top 25 vulnerabilities. IEEE Secur. Priv. **7**, 68–71 (2009). https://doi.org/10.1109/MSP.2009.69

4. Jajodia, S., Noel, S.: Advanced cyber-attack modeling analysis and visualization. In: 14th USENIX Security Symposium, Technical report (2010)

5. Wirtz, R., Heisel, M.: A systematic method to describe and identify security threats based on functional requirements. In: Zemmari, A., Mosbah, M., Cuppens-Boulahia, N., Cuppens, F. (eds.) CRiSIS 2018. LNCS, vol. 11391, pp. 205–221. Springer, Cham (2019). https://doi.org/10.1007/978-3-030-12143-3_17

6. Fluchs, S., Drath, R., Fay, A.: Evaluation of visual notations as a basis for ics security design decisions. IEEE Access **11**, 9967–9994 (2023). https://doi.org/10.1109/ACCESS.2023.3238326

7. Christey, S., Kenderdine, J., Mazella, J., Miles, B.: Common weakness enumeration. Mitre Corp. (2013)

8. Honkaranta, A., Leppänen, T., Costin, A.: Towards practical cybersecurity mapping of STRIDE and CWE—a multi-perspective approach. In: 2021 29th Conference of Open Innovations Association (FRUCT), pp. 150–159 (2021). https://doi.org/10.23919/FRUCT52173.2021.9435453

9. Martin, B.: Common vulnerabilities enumeration (CVE), common weakness enumeration (CWE), and common quality enumeration (CQE): attempting to systematically catalog the safety and security challenges for modern, networked, software-intensive systems. ACM SIGAda Ada Lett. **38**, 9–42 (2019). https://doi.org/10.1145/3375408.3375410

10. Wu, Y., Bojanova, I., Yesha, Y.: They know your weaknesses–do you? Reintroducing common weakness enumeration. CrossTalk **45** (2015)

11. De Bruijn, H., Janssen, M.: Building cybersecurity awareness: the need for evidence-based framing strategies. Gov. Inf. Q. **34**, 1–7 (2017). https://doi.org/10.1016/j.giq.2017.02.007

12. Ošlejšek, R., Rusňák, V., Burská, K., Švábenský, V., Vykopal, J., Čegan, J.: Conceptual model of visual analytics for hands-on cybersecurity training. IEEE Trans. Vis. Comput. Graph. **27**, 3425–3437 (2021). https://doi.org/10.1109/TVCG.2020.2977336

13. Pham, V., Dang, T.: CVExplorer: multidimensional visualization for common vulnerabilities and exposures. In: 2018 IEEE International Conference on Big Data (Big Data), pp. 1296–1301 (2018). https://doi.org/10.1109/BigData.2018.8622092

14. Hideshima, Y., Koike, H.: STARMINE: a visualization system for cyber-attacks. In: Proceedings of the 2006 Asia-Pacific Symposium on Information Visualisation, vol. 60, pp. 131–138 (2006)

15. Ashok, A., Hahn, A., Govindarasu, M.: Cyber-physical security of wide-area monitoring, protection and control in a smart grid environment. J. Adv. Res. **5**, 481–489 (2014)

16. Wan, J., Canedo, A., Al Faruque, M.A.: Security-aware functional modeling of cyber-physical systems. In: 2015 IEEE 20th Conference on Emerging Technologies & Factory Automation (ETFA), pp. 1–4. IEEE (2015)

17. Peisert, S., Margulies, J., Nicol, D.M., Khurana, H., Sawall, C.: Designed-in security for cyber-physical systems. IEEE Secur. Priv. **12**, 9–12 (2014). https://doi.org/10.1109/MSP.2014.90

18. Unal, B., Brunt, R.: Cybersecurity by design in civil nuclear power plants (2019)

19. Chattopadhyay, A., Lam, K.-Y., Tavva, Y.: Autonomous vehicle: security by design. IEEE Trans. Intell. Transp. Syst. **22**, 7015–7029 (2021). https://doi.org/10.1109/TITS.2020.3003000797

20. Geismann, J., Gerking, C., Bodden, E.: Towards ensuring security by design in cyber-physical systems engineering processes. In: Proceedings of the 2018 International Conference on Software and System Process, pp. 123–127. Association for Computing Machinery, New York (2018). https://doi.org/10.1145/3202710.3203159

21. Aloseel, A., Al-Rubaye, S., Zolotas, A., He, H., Shaw, C.: A novel approach for detecting cyberattacks in embedded systems based on anomalous patterns of resource utilization-part I. IEEE Access **9**, 103204–103229 (2021). https://doi.org/10.1109/ACCESS.2021.3088395

22. Easttom, C.: SecML: a proposed modeling language for cybersecurity. In: 2019 IEEE 10th Annual Ubiquitous Computing, Electronics & Mobile Communication Conference (UEMCON), pp. 1015–1021 (2019). https://doi.org/10.1109/UEMCON47517.2019.8993105

23. Reuter, R., Stark, T., Sedelmaier, Y., Landes, D., Mottok, J., Wolff, C.: Insights in students' problems during UML modeling. In: 2020 IEEE Global Engineering Education Conference (EDUCON), pp. 592–600. IEEE (2020)

24. Buschle, M., Holm, H., Sommestad, T., Ekstedt, M., Shahzad, K.: A tool for automatic enterprise architecture modeling. In: Bayro-Corrochano, E., Hancock, E. (eds.) CAiSE 2011. LNBIP, vol. 107, pp. 1–15. Springer, Cham (2012). https://doi.org/10.1007/978-3-642-29749-6_1

25. Gómez-Cabrera, A., Escamilla-Ambrosio, P.J., Rodríguez-Mota, A., Happa, J.: Towards a visual grammar for IoT systems representation and their cybersecurity requirements. In: 2020 IEEE Colombian Conference on Communications and Computing (COLCOM), pp. 1–6 (2020). https://doi.org/10.1109/COLCOM50121.2020.9219771

26. Orni, S.N.: Development and usability evaluation of a domain-specific modeling tool for cybersecurity-related user journeys (2022). https://www.duo.uio.no/handle/10852/100305

27. Gisev, N., Bell, J.S., Chen, T.F.: Interrater agreement and interrater reliability: key concepts, approaches, and applications. Res. Soc. Adm. Pharm. **9**, 330–338 (2013)

28. Hsu, L.M., Field, R.: Interrater agreement measures: comments on Kappa n, Cohen's Kappa, Scott's π, and Aickin's α. Underst. Stat. **2**, 205–219 (2003). https://doi.org/10.1207/S15328031US0203_03

29. Thirteen Ways to Look at the Correlation Coefficient. https://www.tandfonline.com/doi/epdf/10.1080/00031305.1988.10475524?needAccess=true. Accessed 06 Dec 2023

Author Index

Printed in the United States
by Baker & Taylor Publisher Services